THE PHILOSOPHY OF
SPORT

THE PHILOSOPHY OF SPORT

(A Collection of
Original Essays)

Edited by

ROBERT G. OSTERHOUDT, PH. D.
Assistant Professor of Physical Education
University of Minnesota
Minneapolis, Minnesota

CHARLES C THOMAS · PUBLISHER
Springfield · Illinois · U.S.A.

Published and Distributed Throughout the World by
CHARLES C THOMAS · PUBLISHER
BANNERSTONE HOUSE
301-327 East Lawrence Avenue, Springfield, Illinois, U.S.A.

With THOMAS BOOKS *careful attention is given to all details of manufacturing and design. It is the Publisher's desire to present books that are satisfactory as to their physical qualities and artistic possibilities and appropriate for their particular use.* THOMAS BOOKS *will be true to those laws of quality that assure a good name and good will.*

Printed in the United States of America
H-2

Library of Congress Cataloging in Publication Data

Osterhoudt, Robert G.   comp.
  The philosophy of sport.

  CONTENTS: The ontological status of sport: Weiss, P. Records and the man. Schacht, R. L. On Weiss on records, athletic activity, and the athlete. Fraleigh, W. P. On Weiss on records and on the significance of athletic records. Stone, R. E. Assumptions about the nature of human movement. Suits, B. The elements of sport. Kretchmar, S. Ontological possibilities: sport as play, [etc.]
  1. Sports—Philosophy—Addresses, essays, lectures.
I. Title.
GV706.O83   796'.01   73-5620
ISBN 0-398-02871-0

To my wife, Kerry,
and children: Kris, Nicole, and Kirk

CONTRIBUTORS

JAN BROEKHOFF, Ph.D.
Professor of Physical Education
University of Toledo
Toledo, Ohio

WARREN P. FRALEIGH, Ph. D.
Dean and Professor of Physical Education
State University College
Brockport, New York

P. J. GALASSO, Ph.D.
Dean and Professor of Physical Education
University of Windsor
Windsor, Ontario, Canada

JAMES W. KEATING, Ph.D.
Professor of Philosophy and Physical Education
George Williams College
Downers Grove, Illinois

FRANCIS W. KEENAN, Ph.D.
Assistant Professor of Physical Education
State University College
Brockport, New York

SCOTT KRETCHMAR, Ph.D.
Assistant Professor of Physical Education
State University College
Brockport, New York

PAUL G. KUNTZ, Ph.D.
Professor of Philosophy
Emory University
Atlanta, Georgia

WILLIAM MORGAN, M.S.
Graduate Assistant of Physical Education
University of Massachusetts
Amherst, Massachusetts

ROBERT G. OSTERHOUDT, Ph.D.
Assistant Professor of Physical Education
University of Minnesota
Minneapolis, Minnesota

TERENCE J. ROBERTS, B.P.H.E.
Graduate Assistant of Physical Education
University of Windsor
Windsor, Ontario, Canada

WILLIAM A. SADLER, JR., Ph.D.
Director of Interdisciplinary Studies
Professor of Sociology
Bloomfield College
Bloomfield, New Jersey

RICHARD L. SCHACHT, Ph.D.
Associate Professor of Philosophy
University of Illinois
Urbana, Illinois

ROSELYN E. STONE, Ph.D.
Assistant Professor of Physical Education
University of Toronto
Toronto, Ontario, Canada

BERNARD SUITS, Ph.D.
Chairman and Professor of Philosophy
University of Waterloo
Waterloo, Ontario, Canada

CAROLYN E. THOMAS, Ph.D.
Assistant Professor of Physical Education
State University College
Brockport, New York

PAUL WEISS, Ph.D.
Heffer Professor of Philosophy
Catholic University of America
Washington, D. C.

EARLE F. ZEIGLER, Ph.D.
Dean and Professor of Physical Education
University of Western Ontario
London, Ontario, Canada

PREFACE

Even though sport (broadly and variously conceived here to either exclude, include, or serve as the basis for distinguishing, what are commonly regarded as other major forms of human movement phenomena; such as, dance, exercise, game, physical education, play, and recreation) has become an enormously influential force in distinguishing the texture of contemporary culture, surprisingly little of a genuine and systematic philosophic character has been written of it. During the third, fourth, and fifth decades of the twentieth century philosophic reflections concerning sport were conducted principally by a small number of physical educationists and sport theoreticians with only a limited knowledge of, or appreciation for, the rigors of philosophy proper. That is, insufficient attention to the form and content of the purely philosophic endeavor was clearly in evidence during these embryonic periods in the development of the philosophy of sport. The result was a mosaic of largely dogmatic accounts of the most general nature of sport, and espousals as to its most significant use. Since that time, however, a greater number of genuinely philosophic treatments have been forthcoming; such that, at present we already have before us several very sophisticated works, and the prospect of many more. In recent years, then, the volume of literature concerning the philosophy of sport has steadily increased, and the quality of that literature improved commensurately. This phenomenon is in large measure attributable to the increasing accommodation of scholarly examinations of sport to the demands of true philosophy.

This more abiding consultation with the philosophic discipline itself has served to overcome the *truth by fiat* doctrines characteristic of an earlier era, and has, resultantly, allowed us a more informed, comprehensive, and systematic insight into the most general nature and significance of sport; as well as encouraged us to fashion a greater sensitivity for its true ideals. This process has been, and yet remains, essential to the construction of an identifiably coherent body of knowledge concerning the philosophy of sport. And this body of knowledge in turn must be employed so as to suggest a rationally defensible and appealing course of action, practice, and conduct with respect to man's involvement in sport. Indeed, if sport is to be preserved, even regarded as worthy of preservation in its present state of crisis, the light of philosophic reflection must be brought to bear upon it. For only by the intervention of this influence may we plausibly expect sport to be sufficiently well understood and thereby properly treated, engaged, and nourished.

The appearance of the present volume is largely attributable to the informed conviction that a more authentically philosophic treatment of sport than it has generally received is necessary to a fully satisfactory understanding and practice of it. In accord with the best expectations of philosophic inquiry, then, the twenty-two essays presented here attempt a reflective apprehension of the nature and significance of sport in its most general, accessible constitution. More specifically, these essays divide themselves into three major categories (from most to least synoptic): the ontology of sport, the ethics of sport, and the aesthetics of sport. And though the essays in some manner or measure similar to one another have been juxtaposed, they are otherwise presented in no particular order. The order of generality sought in each case exceeds that of the biological, psychological, sociological, and historical perspectives and thereby aspires to a different sort of understanding, albeit one taking account of these others and drawing them into a higher unity. In effect, the present tract is to be regarded as a collection of original, previously unpublished, essays concerning the philosophy of sport. And insofar as the editor has been been able to determine, these essays now represent the major unpublished, non-dissertation contributions to the literature concerning the philosophy of sport. Their scope, scholarly merit, and tenacious commitment to the rigors of both philosophy and sport qualify them uniquely well for inclusion.

Though several of the works were privately solicited (designated *a* in the *Contents*), the great majority have been first presented as symposium papers; either at the Symposium on the Philosophy of Sport (designated *b* in the *Contents*), State University College at Brockport, New York, February 10-12, 1972 (the first professional conference devoted exclusively to the philosophy of sport); at the First

Canadian Symposium on the Philosophy of Sport and Physical Activity (designated *c* in the *Contents*), University of Windsor, Ontario, Canada, May 3-4, 1972; or at the Symposium on Sport and Ethics (designated *d* in the *Contents*), State University College at Brockport, New York, October 26-28, 1972. Both Brockport symposia were conducted under the visionary guidance of Professor Warren P. Fraleigh, Dean of the Faculty of Physical Education and Recreation, State University College at Brockport, together with the astute assistance of his February Organizing Committee composed of Brockport Professors Joseph Gilbert of the Faculty of Philosophy, and Francis W. Keenan, Scott Kretchmar, Robert G. Osterhoudt, Ginny Studer, and Carol Susswein all of the Faculty of Physical Education; and his October Organizing Committee chaired by Professors Francis W. Keenan and Scott Kretchmar. Both symposia were also partially supported by the Center for Philosophic Exchange, State University College at Brockport, Professor Howard E. Kiefer, Center Director and Dean of the Faculty of the Humanities. The Windsor symposium owed its great success to its director, Professor P. J. Galasso, Dean of the Faculty of Physical and Health Education, University of Windsor, and to his outstanding faculty colleagues. My indebtedness extends equally to each of these persons and to the seventeen contributors, for the present volume is no more than a collection of their creative efforts. It is also appropriae at this time to acknowledge with gratitude the efficiency and kindness of the secretarial personnel who assisted so ably in the preparation of the manuscript: Mrs. Barbara Duffy of the State University College at Brockport and Mrs. Helen Schatzlein of the University of Minnesota.

Robert G. Osterhoudt

Minneapolis, Minnesota

CONTENTS

THE PHILOSOPHY OF
SPORT

(CHAPTER I)

THE ONTOLOGICAL STATUS
OF SPORT

INTRODUCTION

METAPHYSICS is the philosophic sub-discipline concerned with the general investigation of reality. It makes claims about the general form of reality, of its ultimate structure and the criteria for establishing that structure. It provides a contextual foundation (a framework, or perspective) from which reality may be apprehended and a general view of it constructed and refined. It is the most general of the philosophic endeavors; and, as such, tempers all other philosophic reflections. Ontology is that metaphysical sub-discipline which concerns the general nature of existence, or the general principles of being. It examines primarily the nature of man and his relation to the other two major metaphysical objects of inquiry, the cosmos (inanimate existence and nature) and God. It is more specifically devoted to an investigation of the nature of self, the relation of mind and body, and the problem of freedom. The essays here presented, then, address themselves to these ontological issues as they are located in the sport condition.

The anthology begins with a series of three essays. The first one of these (by Paul Weiss) presents a view to which the second and third (by Richard L. Schacht and Warren P. Fraleigh respectively) respond.

In "Records and the Man," Paul Weiss offers a general discussion of the nature and significance of athletic records. Such records, he contends, are most properly regarded as objective summaries of what man has done, as indications of that which he is capable, as a medium of comparison among men of differing times and places; more specifically, as symbols of the best that man has yet achieved under con-

[3]

trollable conditions through the agency of a well trained body. It is further observed that there are various sorts of records, that they are not obtainable in all sports (not a common attribute of sport generally), that they are neither entirely accurate (objective) measures of performance, and that they do not exhaustively chronicle the occurrences of a sporting event. With respect to this latter concern, Professor Weiss argues that records may be said to provide only partial evidence of what has been done. That is, all such facts fall short of an entirely accurate and complete description of what actually occurs in a sporting event. There are, by this view, aspects of every such event which invariably escape the grasp of measurement, for they occur in conditions which are concrete and unique (unrepeatable), subject to contingencies (every event could conceivably have occurred otherwise), involve novelties, are affected by luck, are beset by obstacles, and are benefitted by opportunities. Most important of those things which athletic records fail to indicate, it seems, are the qualities, or sources of abilities requisite to establishing them. They signify what the recordman has done, but not what he is. They have abstracted from the individual, and so say little of him. According to this account, then, in order to fully understand the sport phenomenon one must go beyond the records, toward the man.

In this essay, Professor Weiss also discusses his views concerning athletic activity and the engagement of the athlete in that activity. He contends that the athlete, through the rigorous and dedicated use of an excellent body, determines the articulation of past and future; that is, seeks a unification of a worthy past and a desirable end, so as to attain a maximal present result. By this view, the athlete attempts to realize an idealized conception of himself (a view of himself at his utmost) in an objectively judged and severe public test. Such that, a person engaged in a form of activity resembling sport in phenomenal appearance, but for the purpose of realizing pleasure or relaxation, is said to be inauthentically involved—playing at, and not in, sport.

It is precisely to this notion, and not specifically to that of athletic records that Richard L. Schacht's "On Weiss on Records, Athletic Activity, and the Athlete," objects most vigorously. Professor Schacht argues that it is Professor Weiss' emphasis upon the *results* of athletic activity, of which athletic records are an example, which leads him to his errant conception of it. According to this view, these results are quite incidental to the fundamental nature of athletic activity, and to the sort of intrinsic enjoyment and satisfaction available to participants in such activity who perform to the best of their ability. Professor Weiss' notion of an athlete is thereby regarded as an excessively limited and demonic one—one not dedicated to the attainment of a complete and fulfilled life. That is, its criteria for allowing one to be regarded as an athlete (or as being engaged in athletic activity) are much too strict and also give insufficient attention to the intellectual requirements of athletic involvement. In order to properly understand the nature and significance of athletic activity as a potentially important component of a truly human life, Professor Schacht contends, one must seek a thorough awareness of the nature and significance of man generally. One must not merely look beyond the record to the athlete, but look beyond the athlete to the man as well.

Professor Schacht concludes his examination of this matter by claiming that his view, unlike that of Professor Weiss, has the virtue of neither dehumanizing athletic activity nor placing the athletic goal beyond the reach of all but the very young and the very talented. This appeal comes to one of a largely existential dimension: it is an existential response to a predominantly idealistic thesis. And of athletic records themselves he suggests merely that the imprecision pointed to by Professor Weiss is generally the well known case for all historical records, and so says nothing peculiar, nor distinctly instructive, of their athletic form.

In "On Weiss on Records and on the Significance of Athletic Records," Warren P. Fraleigh holds that, like all such devices, athletic records are only capable of approximating that which actually occurs during an event. It is, therefore, not reasonable to expect complete insight from them. Professor Fraleigh then quickly turns his attentions from the nature of athletic records to an examination of that which an interest in keeping records tells us of humankind generally. He holds that they are of interest principally because they act as sources of symbolic meaning which are available and important to us. That is, they are significant in terms of which they satisfy a continuing human desire for knowledge of the human condition, of human status in the world, of self-identity. In effect, records (in various forms) offer a comparison between oneself, other selves, and certain standards of performance.

Professor Fraleigh also attempts to clarify Professor Weiss' notion of the distinction between the end sought by an athlete and that sought by musicians, scientists, philosophers, religious and ethical men. He suggests that more so like than dissimilar from involvement in these other endeavors, the athlete seeking the achievement of the so-termed well-played game uses his body in greater measure than these others, though not essentially unlike them; is able to articulate what a complete, fulfilled life is, though in somewhat different terms than these others; and is engaged in an essentially cooperative enterprise, also much like the others. That is, unlike Professor Weiss with respect to this issue, Professor Fraleigh argues that the difference here is primarily one of degree, and not one of a substantial order.

In "Assumptions About the Nature of Human Movement," Roselyn E. Stone examines the general theories of movement advanced by François Delsarte, Emile Jaques-Dalcroze, Rudolf Laban, and Rudolf Bode. In some measure, each of these theorists regarded movement as a medium for the expression of spirit/soul/self, the harmonization of body and mind, and the communication of the self with other and larger metaphysical entities.

To Delsarte is attributed the view that movement frees expressive impulses thereby bringing one into an unobstructed relationship with the Divine—that it effects an intimate fusion (unity) of Mind, Life, and Spirit, of art and science. To Dalcroze, Professor Stone attributes the view that movement harmonizes body and spirit in such a fashion as to create individuality, which is the basis of all the arts. By this view, then, movement may be further construed as an idealized form of musical rhythm through which the whole of man's spatio-temporal familiarity is established. Laban conceives of movement as a rhythmic relating and balancing of inner efforts to environmental (external) forces—as a medium of expression by which man's highest and most fundamental inspirations are cultivated and fulfilled. And to Bode is attributed the notion of movement as an individual, instinctive rhythm which manifests itself in terms of its freeing the individual toward his fuller expression. Professor Stone concludes that despite their general logical inadequacy, there is about each of these conceptions a certain intuitive attraction. And it is also apparent that each serves to draw our attention to the high ontological place enjoyed by movement and its various forms.

Through a rigorous analysis Bernard Suits in "The Elements of Sport" demonstrates that the elements of sport are essentially identical to those of game. Games are identified as attempts to achieve a particular state of affairs (prelusory end), using only means permitted by rules (lusory means), where the rules prohibit use of more efficient in favor of less efficient means (constitutive rules), and where such rules are accepted just because they make possible such activity (lusory attitude). And it is this lusory attitude which unifies the other elements into a cohesive view of game-playing. This sort of activity (game-playing), it is further argued, differs so signficantly from ordinary activities, that it allows one to realize that which is not otherwise readily realizable—a fact which serves to explain our engagement in it.

Also proposed is a conception of sport as any instance of game, which primarily involves skill (as opposed to chance) of a physical sort, and which enjoys a wide following that has achieved a certain measure of institutional stability. With an allegiance to the leisure (play) ethic, Professor Suits holds as well that sport is precisely like the other prominent leisure interests; that is, a type of intrinsic good (play) which gives work its derivative seriousness, and not, as the fashionable work ethic would have it, itself (as a form of play) metaphysically or axiologically derivative of work.

In the best traditions of phenomenologic treatments of sport, Scott Kretchmar's "Ontological Possibilities: Sport as Play" examines the possibilities of sport being play; that is, demonstrates the intelligibility of sport being played. Much in the form and spirit of the transcendental method of argument, the essay argues from an inchoate order of experience, or consciousness, which identifies sport as a form of play, and proceeds to an examination of the bases of this consciousness. Also in the best expectations of phenomenologic forms of inquiry, the essay seeks an apprehension of the absolute, or universal, cognitive bases of this consciousness, and is not content with a mere description of particular, external, biological, psychological, or socio-

logical reports of it. Professor Kretchmar's penchant analysis allows
him to reduce play and sport to their most fundamental levels and to
there determine the relationships among them. From this analysis
the essay attempts to offer a positive notion of the elusive nature of
play—to tell what it is—and to indicate what such a view says of
play (and subsequently of sport) as distinct from work.

The themes of freedom (from worldly concern), intrinsicality,
unique temporality and spatiality, and opposition are developed in an
effort to show that the play act, unlike that of work, is not a curtailed
thrust toward specific ends, but a spontaneous expression of self. The
analysis further leads Professor Kretchmar to a uniquely attractive
notion of competition as opposition. By this view, the phenomenon
of opposition as located in play is said to entail something distinct
from oneself, which fully cooperates in assisting one to express that
which he is. Such that, in play one expresses himself *with* the hindrance of so-termed opposing forces and not in spite of it. This motif
effects a sympathetic, self-constructive bond among players (and
sportsmen), which is not accessible to those who act in accord with
the spirit of work. In the work motif other men and the task at hand
are extrinsically valued and thereby regarded rather as empirical
objects to be vanquished or used in the achievement of a future goal.
The essay concludes with a denial of the notion that one's lived experience in any situation is defined by the pure content of either work
or play, but opts rather for the view that the phenomena of work
and play are most commonly admixed in the experience of all
activities.

In accord with its avowed existential and phenomenological
allegiances, William Morgan's "An Existential Phenomenological
Analysis of Sport as a Religious Experience" rejects conceiving of
the essence of sport in terms of its institutional forms. Such conceptions, he contends, merely report extraneous responses, or extrinsic
capabilities, and do not serve to distinguish the ontological status of
sport from that of play, recreation, physical education, and the like,
and thereby allow insufficient insight into its essential nature and
significance. Mr. Morgan proposes instead that, the quest for sport
is best regarded as an aspiration of being itself—being as disclosed
by conscious experience, and not as manifest in disparate social en-

counters. By this view, being is construed as the fundamental interpretive principle of reality, and, resultantly, as the source and end of all striving (to include that form common to sport). The essay further argues that the true stuff of sport is best revealed by cultivating the religious inclinations of being which are inherent in, and fundamental to, sport. The religious experience of sport, then, is defined as a self-surrender to the forces of being.

Discussions of such familiar existential themes as absurdity, anguish, anxiety, asociality, boundary situation, choice, despair, emptiness, faith, finitude-infinitude relation, revolt, struggle, and transcendence as they are located in sport as religiously experienced serve to further refine the general thesis of the essay. As a result of this analysis, Mr. Morgan comes to regard the other in sport not as a mere object of appropriation, but rather as one of love. In his examination of competition-in, competition-with, and competition-for, he holds that competitive success is most constructively regarded as an inward triumph, an integrating and liberating experience, an opportunity to be what one is most fundamentally.

It is the intent of Warren P. Fraleigh's "The Moving 'I' " to demonstrate in a phenomenologic-tending fashion, the terms in which self-knowledge, or self-identity, is available to participants in sport, dance, aquatics, and exercise; that is, to show the meaning of man as a moving being. Professor Fraleigh argues from a report of personal experience to an interpretation of the meanings, or significance, of that experience for man generally, as well as for his involvement in these human movement forms. He contends that through an experience of, and a reflection upon these forms one comes to an awareness of his own identity as an individual, and as a member of humanity (an awareness of being at once, though in discrete terms, different from other beings, yet alike them).

Further discussed in defense of this thesis are the ostensibly paradoxical lived-body experiences of freedom (the self as controlled only by the exercise of one's own free will) and necessity (the self as externally controlled, or determined), tenderness and violence, and cooperation and competition in these activities. By this view, the moving self may experience himself as a free agent, voluntarily choosing, or entering, a particular sport condition within which certain movements are necessitated. As such, he becomes aware of his identity as an objective I (represented by his action) and as a subjective I (represented by his intention), and realizes a unique conciliation of them. He may achieve here as well a direct bodily awareness of a personal capacity for both tenderness and violence, cooperation (which leads one to regard ones so-termed opponents as other subjects) and competition (which encourages the regarding of others as objects to be overcome). Professor Fraleigh is further convinced that participants in these activities are paradoxically enhanced by their association with these seemingly opposing experiences—that the positive and negative self-identity feelings accruing from such experiences are mutually reinforcing.

In his "Some Meanings of the Human Experience of Freedom and Necessity in Sport," Warren P. Fraleigh in a phenomenologic-tending fashion, further extends his analysis of the lived-body experience of freedom and necessity in sport. Once again, he proceeds from an experience to an interpretive treatment of its meaning in an attempt to show that sport provides an opportunity for the clarification of ones self-identity. Profesosr Fraleigh's insightful observations with respect to the differing senses in which men may experience freedom and necessity in sport suggest the conditional limitations of ones freedom therein.

The lived-body experience of necessity in sport is variously construed as: deterministic (the human body as an object subject to control by natural laws), a personal condition of motor inability (failure to perform motor acts effectively due to psychomotor insufficiency), a personal condition of physiological inability (failure to respond effectively to sport conditions due to physiological insufficiency), and a restriction upon the choice of movements performed (self-chosen rule restrictions). And the lived-body experience of freedom in sport is diversely conceived as: the freedom from deterministic necessity (the appearance of an ephemeral conquest of restrictive natural laws), the freedom for the realization of personal intentions (the ability to perform prescribed skills, to realize performance intentions), the freedom for creating new personal intentions (the ability to create new personal intentions by developing entirely new skill techniques), and the freedom to be unified (the unification with self and with not self—the acting in accord with all that which is both internal and external to self—the creation of a harmony of self and not self).

The first chapter concludes with Francis W. Keenan's "The Concept of Doing." In this essay, Professor Keenan examines the Deweyan concept of doing as a general educational activity, and suggests the implications of this view for physical education, sport, and physical activity. Though commonly overemphasized (under the guise of Deweyanism) in such endeavors as physical education and sport, doing is regarded by Dewey as only the initial stage, albeit a necessary one, of the learning process—as the foundation upon which all else is learned. Indeed, the doing stage of the curricular process provides only experiential data and a knowledge of *how to do* things, all of which acts as a mere prelude to achieving the sorts of understandings (cognitive forms of awareness) Dewey wished to cultivate foremost (in the information and science stages of curriculum). These understandings culminate, then, in the science stage, which seeks to create a better life for man by advancing an awareness of the continuity of socio-cultural values and thereby supporting a commitment to democracy.

According to Professor Keenan, consequently, physical education and sport are assigned a place in the curriculum for intellectual and social, rather than expedient, reasons. Like all other curricular inclusions, then, Professor Keenan concludes, physical education and sport must pursue an understanding (a refined, conscious experience) in this case of the fundamental nature and social significance of human movement phenomena, and not merely provide opportunities for a mindless doing of things. That is, physical education, like the whole of education, must promote an intelligence with respect to doing, and not merely engage in the performing of acts.

RECORDS AND THE MAN

Paul Weiss

I

Athletic records often have an attractive mathematical precision. They then allow one to measure with some accuracy just what is occurring. This can then be compared with what had been done previously, and both can be compared with similarly recorded achievements of others, near and far, present and past.

Athletic records purport to report what was accomplished. Often they signalize some outstanding occurrence, what is worth noting. Since men are most likely to extend themselves to the limit in extreme situations, the records frequently reflect the fact that the results have been achieved in crises or as the outcome of some crucial testing. Records of this desirable nature are most readily obtainable in those events where individual is pitted against individual, providing there is some agreement on how to determine what times and distances are involved, or a commonly accepted way of quantifying style—as is done in diving and gymnastics—and accuracy, as in fly casting and shooting.

Some records tell us mainly what one man achieved in comparison with others. This is the case with the shot put, pole vault, diving, running, swimming, golf. Other records tell how an individual stands in relation to a special group of competitors—those of the same sex, of such and such a weight or age, who have passed qualifying rounds or preliminary heats, and the like. Some records tell us about the achievements of individuals, but only within the frame of a team activity. Individual members of relay teams can be timed. The performance of every player in baseball is distinguished from every other; every play is accredited to some player. Here mistakes, errors, and failures, as well as successes and assists are noted, to be added up to make a profile of a career. The more extensive the records are, the more ready are we to accept them as objective summaries of what a man not only has done, but what he can do, and therefore what he truly is. But we then go much beyond where we should.

Similar programs are carried out to some extent in football, soccer, rugby, basketball, and tennis doubles. Though the final result is credited to a team, some of the things that some of the individuals do are also recorded. In these and in the other cases, clear, objective, useful, and pertinent material is sought, which will enable one to compare a number of athletes. This effort is carried out alongside or within a larger attempt to determine just what the team accomplished.

The ultimate object of all athletic records is to set down the best results that men have brought about, severally and together, in public matches under well-established conditions, governed by rules and competent judges. Ideally, one thereby learns what is the most men have been able so far to achieve through the agency of matured, trained bodies. The records in which we are most interested, tell us the limits beyond which no one has yet been able to go.

Records of individuals, even in well-judged contests, are not always obtainable. It is obviously hard to separate out the contributions of the members of a crew, of a tug of war, or perhaps even of a mountain climb. The most meticulous, detailed account of a baseball game fails to attend to all the helpful and hindering contributions of the individual players. The signals of the catcher, the move toward third by the shortstop, the jeer of a spectator, the demands of the coaches, racial slurs and a hundred other matters, making a difference to the motivation and effectiveness of a player, are not part of the record. The most complete account that we can obtain tells us much less than we want to know even about performances in contests where individuals compete against one another, or only against some established time or record.

Records are cherished because of their assumed impersonality, impartiality, exactitude, and objectivity. But they are achieved in situations which are qualified by—and therefore compromised by—the temper and judgment of officials, the alertness of umpires at vital junctures, by the prejudices and interpretations of those who decide and record. Watches, scales, and rulers are not absolutely accurate; they are affected by changes in climate and by wear and tear. If a number of them are used they will be found to be in some disaccord.

All records abstract from the nature of the track or field. They ignore the dullness or brightness, indoors or out; wind below a certain arbitrary velocity is neglected, yet its benefit when at the back and its hindrance when in the front can make a difference in the times of two equally speedy men, racing at different times. Advantages, if any, offered by playing on home grounds, by having the backing of enthusiastic supporters, by the number of spectators, though remarked upon by an occasional reporter, do not appear in the records.

At their best, records provide only partial evidence of what was done. Since they inevitably bundle together what the individual does and what circumstances, team mates, coaches, and opponents contribute to the final result, records can tell us only what men did in a number of incompletely described and inadequately understood situations. They report the accomplishments of outstanding contextualized individuals, and then only in certain sports, and in abstraction from various conditions which in fact made a difference to the result. Though still not entirely satisfactory, the records we have on race horses are superior in detail and perhaps in precision to those we have on men. The state of the track, the nature of the weather, previous performances, handicaps, the way they start off and the way they come to the end, and the times for parts of the entire distance are all noted. But even here we have only an abstract of what had been done, and far too little to tell us what in fact happened, and of course what will next occur.

The records we have yield only hints and rough indications of what might reasonably be expected of a player at some subsequent time. They can provide little help for one who would like to decide between those who have somewhat the same skills, experience, and reputations. Their different records could be due to any one of a number of unnoticed and unnoted factors.

Because the knowledge that records provide is necessarily inadequate, one must turn to reporters, coaches, and scouts to learn what in fact occurred, what was achieved by individual players, and what one might expect from them in other situations. These observers give weight to items not mentioned in the records, even though they contribute significantly to the final result. The weighing of these factors, the determination of their importance, role, and relevance is largely an individual matter. The assessments are subject to no controls, nor are they protected against caprice, prejudice, or poor judgment. Too much is unspecified and unquantified, and not subject to review. A more exact, objective procedure is desirable, and surely is possible. It is not enough, as is sometimes done today, to provide scouts with guide lines, a list of abilities which are scaled in importance in relation to one another. More attention should be paid to the speed of reflexes, to the kinds of experiences the men have had, the kind of coaching that has been received, the occasions on which one is making the observations, and above all to just what is being quantified and what is not, and why.

The reports of experienced observers, despite their inevitable limitations and faults, are invaluable. They provide irreplaceable means for enabling one to go beyond the records toward the man. Though the vagueness, arbitrariness, and subjectivity which spoils the accounts of seasoned students of sport cannot be altogether eliminated, their excesses are usually avoided because the judges know that they themselves will be judged. Their recommendations are noted and matched against the results attained by the athletes they endorse as well as those attained by the ones they reject. Every coach and scout has sometimes celebrated an athlete who fails dismally thereafter, and every once in a while the shrewdest of judges passes over one who later becomes outstanding.

The limitations which spoil the value of the records of individuals and teams operate, of course, to make the records we have of the reports and predictions of coaches and scouts not as reliable indices of their judgments as owners, administrators, and the public take them to be. Since those who are involved in sport and sport predictions are practical men, they rightly stop the regress at this point. They do not ask who is to assess the reports of the assessors, and on what basis. They are willing to accept as a sufficient testimony of excellence in judgment any record which shows a preponderance of endorsements of athletes who subsequently proved to be champions. But this, of course, is to leave the entire process in the intellectual limbo of mystery, hidden behind presumed *hunches, intsight, perceptiveness,* or *genius.*

II

There are aspects to every athletic performance which are forever beyond the reach of any recording, because they take place in situations which A. are concrete, B. are subject to contingencies, C. involve novelties, D. are affected by luck, E. are beset by obstacles, and F. are benefitted by opportunities.

A

A performance is a unique event, never to be repeated. It occurs just there and at just that time, inside a distinctive situation where it occupies an irreplaceable position. That is why one must go to an athletic event to know what occurs. Newspaper accounts provide only static generalizations and summaries of what in fact takes place. Movies and television, to be sure, let us see some of the action. But they necessarily provide only an abstract of the whole. Pauses, hesitations, preparations, rests, repetitions are ignored for the sake of dramatization. Even if they allowed us—as they now do not—always to take in the entire situation with its spectators, field, climate, and sky, they would, because of their need to attend to the dramatic, neglect, distort, and reorder what actually occurs. Athletic events are often dramatic, but they are only episodically so. The highs occur unexpectedly in the midst of a multitude of flat moments. But even if the whole were reproduced, it would fall short of what a spectator saw, if for no other reason than that the spectator affects and is affected by his neighbors, and these in turn affect and are affected by the players.

Predictions, like records, are abstract, general, confined to outlines, structures, forms. Every element in every situation is necessarily unpredictable in its full concreteness. Just as records fail and must fail to report what concretely occurs, so predictions fail and must fail to tell us what will actually occur, in all its concreteness.

B

Every element in a situation could conceivably have been different. Its presence there is contingent; something else could have happened instead. Even in a world ruled by necessitating causes, exhibiting implacable laws, there would be contingencies. Not only would there be intersections of different causal lines that need not have been, but there would be a working out of each causal line in only one of many alternative ways.

The particularity, the details of every occurrence are beyond all prediction, and outside the control of causes or laws. The fact is not remarked in our records. One reason is that it would complicate them unduly. But there is also the tacit supposition that the contingencies which lean in one direction will eventually be matched by others leaning in an opposite, thereby making unnecessary a remarking of either set. But there is nothing in fact or theory which shows that such matching must occur. An athlete who is persistently superior to others may be one who frequently but contingently is in accord with whatever contingencies there are.

C

In and of itself, every item is novel, no matter how similar it may be to that which had once or often occurred. That type of thing might reappear with tedious frequency, but in itself the item would be unpredictable. One might predict when it would take place and the kind of occurrence it was and perhaps even the natures of its effects. The prediction would refer, though, to what was summarizable, generalizable, repeatable, not to it as just that new occurrence.

Every athletic event has its element of novelty. The running of a race, the catch of a ball, the execution of a swing have structures which are filled out in novel ways. No matter how commonplace or familiar it seems, it is new. It could have been necessitated; it surely is contingent; it is inseparable from the concrete. But novelty is present too in thinking, with its abstractions and ideas.

D

A chance occurrence is one that takes place spontaneously, undetermined by law or will. It is not identifiable with the concrete, for though this is beyond control of law and will, it could conceivably have nothing spontaneous in it. It is also distinct from the contingent or novel, since these could be the outcome of the working out of previous conditions, whereas it is fresh, conditioned perhaps but never caused.

Chance events can be part of a series whose mathematical patterns can be stated with precision. The run of the cards, the roll of the dice do not provide ideal illustrations of such mathematically calculable distributions, since the different occurrences are far from random and are not necessarily of equal value. They are not even independent, due to the operation of human habits, the absence of perfect randomness in the operation, mechanical devices, and the presence of contingencies. Most important, the statistical results that are mathematically obtained need not be realized in any finite run—which is, of course, all that one can have in this world. Given a particular situation it is a matter of uncalculatable chance that it should occur just then.

In sport, chance refers to unpredictables which make a difference to the result. Luck is a special case. It refers to those chance events which make a significant difference to the likelihood of victory. Most often, luck adds a personal note to a supposed objective chance, and is called *good* or *bad* depending on whether or not ones success is promoted.

Chance and luck occur inside a game. But they can also intrude into a game. It is a matter of chance or luck that a needed wind suddenly comes up, that a dog runs in the way of a kick, that a spectator interferes with a swing. There may be nothing distinctively contingent or novel in these occurrences; they might have well understood causes. But they are chance occurrences in the game, entering it inexplicably in such a way as to change the outcome.

Favorable streaks of luck we think will eventually be balanced by unfavorable ones. But, once again, there is no reason for supposing this to be a true account of the course of the world. Appeals to laws of chance, to bell-shaped curves and the like relate to simple units in mathematical frames where they occur at random over an indefinite period. They are not pertinent to sport where we have complex human beings in concrete limited situations, confined by the rules of the game, and occupied with what occurs within short spans of space and time.

E

Where luck refers to what itself makes a difference, and the contingent refers to anything that could have been other than it is, obstacles refer to what demands that more than the usual effort be made to attain the usual result. One can credit to contingency or luck the obstacles that are produced by the responses of opponents, by the baffling juncture of a number of circumstances, by blunders and accidents. It makes little sense to say that one is unlucky to have a run of bad luck, but it makes good sense to say that one is unlucky to have to deal with such and such an obstacle. It makes little sense to say that it is contingent that there is contingency, or that it is novel that there is novelty, but it makes good sense to say that obstacles are among the contingencies, or that they are novel not only in their concreteness, but even in their kind.

F

An opportunity is an occasion in which appropriate action will increase the likelihood of success. It is not the simple negative of an obstacle. Obstacles in fact might provide opportunities for moves which one might otherwise not make, or which opponents might not expect. Lack of opportunity is not the same as facing an obstacle. A normal development provides neither undue opportunities or obstacles. Nor is overcoming an obstacle the same as producing an opportunity; it may merely bring one back to the normal position. Opportunities are unexpected openings; they may or may not be predictable, necessitated, or familiar. But, like obstacles, they are usually not noted in the records, despite the great role they sometimes play in the determination of an important result.

Concreteness, contingency, novelty, luck, obstacles, and opportunities all make a difference to what is achieved. Since records abstract from these, they tell us not what in fact did occur, but the outcome of a multitude of factors of which we take little or no note. When we credit the result to an athlete or a team, we isolate a fragment of a very complex, detailed, and unrepeatable whole.

III

The tendency today seems to be toward showing that intelligence is grounded in inheritance, despite the fact that early deprivation and pressing needs may prevent, hobble, or distort the exercise and proper use of the mind. There are those who would attribute crime to circumstance, though many a criminal act is willed and has its roots in attitudes and values which would make the crime reasonable or desirable. But there is little consensus as to just to whom or where one should credit the achievements in sport. The question, we have seen, gets little help from records. The records have no bearing on the question as to whether or not the athlete's actions are outcroppings of an inherited ability or disposition, are the fruits of training, or express something distinctive about a man as private, free, and self-determining. They not only abstract from the concreteness, the contingencies, the novelties, the luck, the obstacles, and the opportunities characteristic of a situation in which a record is set, but they abstract from the individual men, with their distinctive commitments, judgments, freedom, and dedications.

An athlete seeks to make maximal use of a trained body to attain an outstanding result in particular situations. He who does not try to make maximal use of his body is playing *at* and not *in* a sport. If his body is not trained, his mind, interests, and volition will not appreciably further his athletic activities, and he will, of course, lack the skills and readiness required by one who is to function as an athlete.

A man may exercise, enjoy himself and even engage in some sport for pleasure or relaxation. He will then not fully participate in the activity but will be idling to some degree. And if he does not make an outstanding effort in particular situations, publicly watched and judged, he will remain in a state of preparation, not yet engaged, even though he may be treated as a participant by himself and by others.

An athlete makes use of inherited bodily traits, an established cast of mind, and well-entrenched physical and mental dispositions. His upbringing and his experience make a difference. All are brought to bear on an end which he persistently seeks to realize. There is satisfaction for the athlete in a task well done here and now. He is satisfied because it embodies his end. If it did not it would be, at best, a detached grand stand play. His past gives him material to work upon; he makes best use of it if, while performing at his best, he also promotes the end to the maximum degrees that the situation permits.

IV

The athlete is more than a place where past and future meet. He determines the nature of that union. It is his task to bring about the best possible unification of a worthwhile past and a desirable end. This is done, not by simply allowing the end to control the act that his past now makes possible, but by so acting that a maximal result is attained. Did he not do this, his acts would be merely agencies for eventually attaining some remote objective. He would get no satisfaction now, he would achieve nothing today, but would instead merely be on his way, coming nearer perhaps but never arriving at his desirable goal.

That end is at once most desirable and efficacious which, when attached to an act, turns other occurrences into sufficient conditions for the repetition of that act. (Some such idea as this is at the root of Skinner's behaviorism. He attaches rewards to the particular moves which he wants to have repeated. The product of reward and movement then serves as a prospect that an organism acts to realize from the position of an antecedent. "Reinforcement," on his view, makes any antecedent a sufficient condition for the production of the result.)

An end to which a man is dedicated should be united by him to less remote, more limited prospects. The result will be an objective which he can seek to realize from any one of an indefinite number of positions. If he has dedicated himself properly, he will then be satisfied every moment on the way to a complete fulfillment. The end to which an athlete is dedicated is narrower than that appropriate to man at his best. It is an end which demands for its realization the use and preservation of an excellent body. To accept such an end is to be occupied with the realization of goals in which the body is used excellently.

It is not too difficult to entertain a worthwhile end. From child-hood on men are led to envisage ideal states of affairs. They see themselves to be central figures, enriched by and ennobling whatever environs them in an idealized world. Readily they imagine themselves idealized there. But it is not easy to hold on to such an end in sadness and in joy, in success and in failure, unless one had previously fully identified oneself with the idealized figure one had projected into the idealized world.

Each man idealizes himself. He also makes himself anew at every moment. We would like to know, particularly if we are engaged in putting together a successful team with a minimum waste of time and money, just which men will make themselves maximally, especially when subject to severe tests against others well-skilled. We cannot, of course, get to the center of anyone's privacy; we cannot tell in advance just what a man will make himself be at a given moment. But we can tell in advance what will be done by a man properly dedicated: he will do the best that he can possibly do then. He will charge the union of past and future with spontaneity, imagination, judgment, and a sense of what the responses of others might be. But though what he does then, neither he nor anyone else can fully know in advance, their nature and import can be anticipated on the basis of past performance.

Men are free, but they exercise their freedom more or less the way in which they had exercised it before. The most complete knowledge of their past, though it goes far beyond what any record can exhibit, falls short of telling us what men can or will do. It is necessary to know also whether or not they are dedicated. This can be surmised on the basis of what they do in other situations outside the game, in training sessions, in warm-ups, in the locker room, and far outside the arena of sport. If they move toward the self-same end in a multitude of diverse circumstances, some of which are trying and difficult, we have good grounds for supposing that they are dedicated, and therefore will come as close as conditions permit to doing what should be done.

The athlete chooses that fulfillment which requires and is affected by a perfected and operative body. He envisages himself in that body, with his basic needs and desires met. Usually his vision of this is dim; he may not know how to express it or to analyze it. But this need not affect what he does, for the efficacy of his dedicated end depends not on its details but on the value it promises, and the lure this provides.

Some men are able to perform in games better than most and yet do not seem to be dedicated at all. They are casual, irresponsible; they do not train or get ready. And there are men who seem to be dedicated but who are unable to become truly great. We sometimes speak of the one as *gifted* or as a *genius,* and say that the other has *insufficient courage* or *lacks sense,* or *has a failure of nerve.* But these are only devices for marking out exceptions from the general rule. By and large, those perform excellently who are not only well prepared but who persistently seek to be completed through the splendid use of their bodies in situations which test them to the limit.

Scientists, musicians, religious, and ethical men are also dedicated to the attainment of complete, fulfilled lives. They differ from the athlete in at least three ways. They do not seek, either now or later, to be fulfilled primarily by having an excellent body deployed excellently in severe, public tests, objectively judged. They have a somewhat clearer understanding than the athlete does of the nature of the end they seek to realize, and the import of the sacrifices that must be made to bring it about. Most important, the end that they envisage, though never freed from a reference to the self, is one in which their own completion is inseparable from the completion of others. When an athlete makes provision for the success of his team mates, it is usually because this is incidental to his own. If he puts team always above himself he may become popular, and be known as a prince among men; but he will not be the athlete he could have been. The excellence sought by the others, though not without its element of self-regard and self-seeking, is broad enough to be realized by many independently, but in such a way as to provide opportunities for the others.

The athletic goal rarely allows a man to work toward the achievement of anyone but himself, except incidentally and as a means. It provides a needed counterbalance to the radical idealism of youth with its willingness to sacrifice, and its devotion to what is noble and great. The young man is willing to punish himself, to subject himself to strain and pain because it is seen to be but a prepayment for the pleasure and glory, the satisfaction and completion that is part of the end which he has made his own.

Though, as we have seen, records are not credited only to the athlete, he deserves that credit more than his teachers or the circumstances do. Though they contributed, it was he who at crucial times served his dedicated end by giving it a maximum embodiment. It was he who made this time at bat, this tackle, this hurdle, this dive, this pass, be a unit act in a series of achievements all governed by the same demands and all promoting the same result.

Records tell us something about what a man has done. They do not tell us what he is. To know what he is, we must know what he would be. And to know this we must know what he now does. This requires the sifting out of the contributions made by his past, circumstance, contingency, chance, etc., and above all, by the end of being a man who is perfected by making excellent use of a perfected body, particularly in competition with others similarly dedicated and prepared.

ON WEISS ON RECORDS, ATHLETIC ACTIVITY AND THE ATHLETE

RICHARD L. SCHACHT

Professor Weiss would appear to think that what athletic activity is really all about is the achievement of certain noteworthy results through the deployment of an excellent body. Thus he says: "An athlete seeks to make maximal use of a trained body to attain an outstanding result in particular situations." (1:p.12) The specific kinds of results in question obviously differ from one sort of athletic activity to another; but they all are conceived by Professor Weiss to be a matter of achievements of a sort that may be "objectively judged" in "severe, public tests." It is for this reason that he devotes so much attention to "athletic records"; for, as he observes, "Athletic records purport to report what was accomplished." (1:p.1). The main thrust of the first half of his paper is that athletic records are not entirely satisfactory indicators of achievement or accomplishment in athletics; and I have no quarrel with him on this count—although I would observe that athletics is by no means unique in this respect, and that the reasons why athletic records fail to convey adequately "what was done" in athletic events are by and large simply the well-known reasons why historical records of any sort fail to convey adequately "what was done" in historical events generally.

I do find myself very much at odds with Professor Weiss, however, over the importance of achieving the kinds of results he has in mind in athletic activity; and it seems to me that the position he takes on this matter is closely connected with a number of things he says in the latter part of his paper, which I find very strange, and in some cases, rather disturbing. It seems to me to indicate that something is wrong with his analysis, when he reaches the conclusion that, ". . . the athletic goal rarely allows a man to work toward the achievement of anyone but himself, except incidentally and as means." A majority of the forms of athletic activity most commonly engaged in are team athletic activities; and teamwork (defined by Webster as "Work done by a number of associates, all subordinating personal prominence to the efficiency of the whole") is so central to every kind of team athletic activity, so vital to team athletic achievement, and so intimately connected with nearly everything each team member is supposed to do, that it cannot be as much at variance with anything which might properly be termed "the athletic goal" as Professor Weiss here suggests it to be. I cannot even make sense of this statement when I try to apply it, e.g., to an offensive guard or tackle on a football team, or to a basketball player whose forte is playmaking and defense. Have Wilt Chamberlin or Oscar Robertson abandoned "the athletic goal" and become lesser athletes, now that they have become team players? Did Bill Russell never really understand what "the athletic goal" required of him? If what Professor Weiss says here is true, both questions must be answered affirmatively. And I take this to show that what Professor Weiss says here is in need of modification.

Again: It seems to me to be a sign that something is wrong when Professor Weiss is led to say: "He who does not try to make maximal use of his body is playing *at* and not *in* a sport. . . . And if he does not make an outstanding effort in particular situations, publicly watched and judged, he will remain in a state or preparation, not yet engaged. . . ." (1:pp.12-13). Since by "making maximal use of his body" Professor Weiss means devoting oneself singlemindedly to some sport (1:p.14), it would follow from this that one for whom athletics is subordinate to other concerns, and who does not participate or no longer participates in organized athletic events, does not really engage in athletic activity at all, even though he might appear to play basketball or squash (or whatever) fairly frequently. Now, I am perfectly willing to allow that it would be inappropriate to term such a person "an athlete" if one were asked *what he is*. But I am quite certain that the question of whether a person may or may not truly and properly be said to engage in some form of athletic activity (e.g., to "play basketball") is to be settled by criteria which are much less strict than those which determine the answer to the question of whether a person may or may not truly and properly be said to *be* an "athelete" (e.g., "a basketball player"), in the sense in which other people may be said to *be* "scientists," "musicians," and so forth.

I believe that Professor Weiss is led to say such things because of the importance he assigns to the achievement of the kinds of results which athletic records are at least intended to capture and record— and more specifically, to the sorts of results with which athletic records *for individuals are concerned*. If what athletic activity is all about is the accomplishment of results which constitute (in Professor Weiss's terms) ". . . the most men have been able to achieve through the agency of matured, trained bodies" (1:p.2), then *of course* the team player, who takes no thought of achieving outstanding individual results, is not a true *athlete;* and *of course* the amateur squash player isn't either, even though he gives the game all he's worth three times a week at the gym. But is aspiring to equal or surpass "the most men have been able to achieve" in some sport really what athletic activity is all about? I do not think so.

Professor Weiss and I agree in denying that the "end" or "goal" of athletic activity can be adequately characterized in terms of setting records, or even compiling a respectable "record" over a period of time. But Professor Weiss's reason for denying this is simply that records are not an adequate measure of what he takes to be the truly important thing—namely, what he terms ". . . the results attained by the athlete." (1:p.6). Mine, on the other hand, is that I consider the achievement of the kinds of "results" he has in mind to be incidental to the fundamental nature of athletic activity—and moreover, incidental to the attainment of the sort of satisfaction which athletic activity as such is capable of affording to most people who engage in it.

At the risk of banality, I would suggest that athletic activity consists in engaging in some sport the rudiments of which one has mastered; and that the only "athletic goal" of which it makes any sense to speak, at least where all but the very finest athletes are concerned, is simply that intrinsic enjoyment which one may derive from engaging in the activity in question, through winning and/or playing to the best of one's ability and/or playing well. Professor Weiss may wish to respond that surely there is more to it than this where "the athlete" —as opposed to "the scientist," "the musician," or "the philosopher" who engages in athletic activity—is concerned. And I would agree. "The athlete" must possess considerable ability for the sport in question, must be highly trained in it, and must have a strong commitment to it, in order to merit the designation. But I can see no good reason to regard these traits as jointly necessary conditions of engaging in athletic activity at all. And I can see no good reason to add a fourth —a determination to equal or surpass "the most men have been able so far to achieve" in some sport—even in the case of "the athlete."

The title of Professor Weiss's paper is "Records and the Man"; and he contends that it is necessary to ". . . go beyond the records toward the man." (1:p.5). It seems to me, however, that a more appropriate title for his paper would have been "Records and the Athlete"; and that, in "going beyond the records" as he does, he at most moves "toward the athlete," while moving "toward the man" scarcely at all. This is suggested most clearly when he remarks that ". . . the end to which an athlete is dedicated is narrower than that appropriate to man at his best." (1:p.14). This remark is certainly true of "the athlete" as Professor Weiss characterizes him, since Professor Weiss's "athlete" strikes me as a kind of fanatic, who surely is a far cry from the sort of human being Professor Weiss seems to have in mind when he speaks of men ". . . dedicated to the attainment of complete, fulfilled lives." (1:p.17).

It is this which I find most disturbing in the latter part of his paper; and I would like to suggest that it is necessary to "go beyond the *athlete* toward the man," in order to achieve a proper understanding of the nature of athletic activity as a possible and potentially significant component of a truly human life. It would perhaps be well at this point to recall the classical ideal of *mens sana in corpore sano*— a sound mind in a sound body: an old horse, to be sure, but one with a good deal of life still in it. This ideal is one which, in Professor Weiss's terms, ". . . demands for its realization the use and preservation of an excellent body . . ." (p.1:14)—or at any rate, a well-developed body—but not only that. And it seems to me that if what Professor Weiss calls "the athletic goal" is cut lose from this balanced ideal, and is conceived both as narrowly as he conceives it and as the supreme goal in an athlete's life, the athlete becomes a rather demonic figure. It may be that ". . . a maximal result is attained . . ." (1:p.14) in athletic activity only by demonic figures of this sort; but that argues neither for the human desirability of the attainment of "maximal results," nor for the employment of dedication to the attainment of "maximal results" as a criterion for genuine engagement in athletic activity.

Human beings are creatures having the capacity to engage in both physical and mental activity, to acquit themselves more or less well in each, and to derive satisfaction from engaging in both. Further, their lives are incomplete if they engage exclusively in one, to the complete neglect of the other. Athletic activity is one sort of physical activity. And if we are to speak of "the goal of athletic activity," where this signifies the *proper end* of athletic activity, it seems to me that it ought not be conceived in such a way that it excludes activity along other lines, or requires that other men be treated only as means to one's own achievement, or makes the attainment of satisfaction depend upon excelling over everyone else. "The goal of athletic activity" cannot be winning a Gold Medal in the Olympics or being named Most Valuable Player of the Year or surpassing Babe Ruth or Wilt Chamberlin in the record books, even if that is what some of the very best athletes may do or aspire to do. Rather, it must be something like attaining satisfaction through the skillful deployment of a sound body under conditions in which such skillful deployment is required. This characterization may require modification or refinement; but I believe it to be a step in the right direction. And it has the virtue of neither dehumanizing athletic activity nor placing "the athletic goal" beyond the reach of all but the most exceptional of human beings.

Before concluding, I would make one further point. Up to now in my discussion, I have gone along with Professor Weiss's characterization of athletic activity as being primarily a matter of the skillful deployment of a sound body. It seems to me, however, that this constitutes something of a distortion of the nature of athletic activity. My football coach in high school used to tell us that football is 10 percent physical and 90 percent mental. This may be a bit of an exaggeration; but it brings out something that is importantly true, not only of football but of most forms of athletic activity. A good athlete uses his head as well as his body, and must do so if he is to play well. This is true not only of quarterbacks and pitchers, but also of linemen, hitters, basketball players, wrestlers and golfers, to cite only a few examples. And in saying that a good athlete uses his head, I have in mind more than the "cast in mind," "well-entrenched . . . mental dispositions," "upbringing," and "experience" to which Professor Weiss refers in passing. (1:p.13). I am thinking of *thinking*— sizing up situations, anticipating difficulties, weighing probabilities, choosing between alternate strategies, and so forth.

A very few athletes are so in tune with a given sport that they consistently do the best thing in particular situations by a kind of instinct; but most athletes must think in order even to approach doing so, and they cease to perform at all well when they revert to the level of mindless exertion. To be sure, Professor Weiss is correct in asserting that "If [an athlete] is not trained, his mind . . . will not appreciably further his athletic activities." (1:pp12-13). But there is another side of the coin: namely, that in most athletic activities the employment of one's mental powers is necessary to *enable* one to deploy the excellent, well-trained body of which Professor Weiss speaks even adequately.

This does not mean that the good athlete *per se* turns out to satisfy the ideal of *mens sana in corpore sano* after all; for the kind of mental activity under discussion here is much too narrow to satisfy the former condition at all adequately, at least by itself. But this does mean that an account of the nature of athletic activity is incomplete if it does not make reference to the fact that the skillful deployment of a sound body in an athletic activity commonly is inseparable from the exercise of considerable practical intelligence.

Professor Weiss has done philosophers (and perhaps also physical educationists) an important service by directing attention to athletic activity as an important sphere of human life, which demands philosophical investigation no less than any other—and is more in need of it than most, if only because it has been so long neglected. While he has opened the debate, however, I do not believe that he has also closed it; for as I have tried to suggest, the issues to which he has directed our attention in his paper require further discussion.

REFERENCES

1. Weiss, Paul: "Records and the Man." Essay presented at the Symposium on the Philosophy of Sport, Brockport, New York, February 10-12, 1972.

ON WEISS ON RECORDS AND ON THE SIGNIFICANCE OF ATHLETIC RECORDS

WARREN P. FRALEIGH

Men have expressed an interest in athletic records for centuries. A variety of references, allusions, and images pertaining to athletic

achievements have appeared in the *Odyssey,* Pindar's Odes, Paul in
the New Testament, minstrel songs of the medieval courts, and the
modern chronicles of athletic events with accompanying asterisks and
footnotes. In spite of this long history, little has been said in regard
to the meaning of athletic records for man. Professor Weiss has opened
this area of inquiry to our view in his paper "Records and the Man."

In his treatment of the topic Weiss clearly identifies several factors
which are associated with record keeping. He points out that "Athletic records purport to report what was accomplished." By such reporting, athletic records inform us of ". . . the best results that men
have brought about . . ." Additionally, "Records are cherished because of their assumed impersonality, impartiality, exactitude, and
objectivity." Because of assumed impartiality in addition to the effort
of reporting the best accomplishments, record keeping provides a basis
for the comparison of human achievements in the present and between
the present and the past.

Because of the factors noted above and their proper association with
record keeping, it seems logical to conclude that "The more extensive
the records are, the more ready we are to accept them as objective
summaries of what a man not only has done, but what he can do,
and therefore what he truly is." But with regard to this last phase
Weiss issued a warning that we ". . . go much beyond where we
should." For, Weiss warns us, upon closer examination of record
keeping we find many influences upon the actual achievement which
are not reflected in the record itself. To name a few unrecorded influences; the condition of the playing surface, the presence or absence
of wind, a friendly or hostile crowd, the decision of the officials, are all
things which help to determine what actually occurs in an athletic
event but are not a part of the record of the event. From these observations Weiss tells us, "At their best, records provide only partial evidence
of what was done."

As if these elements do not complicate enough the potential accuracy
of athletic records as an accurate reiteration of what actually occurs,
Weiss points out also that ". . . there are aspects to every athletic
performance which are forever beyond the reach of any recording. . . ."
These aspects, "Concreteness, contingency, novelty, luck, obstacles, and
opportunities all make a difference to what is achieved. Since records

abstract from these, they tell us not what in fact did occur, but the outcome of a multitude of factors of which we take little or no note." ". . . records provide only partial evidence of what was done."

To this point a summary of several points included in the first 2/3 of the Weiss paper has been made. This summary will provide a legitimate base for the following reaction since it is necessary to declare what is being reacted to in order for the reactions themselves to be clear.

Weiss has properly clarified many reasons supporting the contention that athletic records *cannot* provide complete insight into what really did happen during a particular athletic event. In so doing, he raises some problems for the athletic fraternity and its corps of record keepers. For example, the question, "If records do not describe what actually occurred and if the diverse modifying conditions present at differing athletic performances are never the same, how is a record (in the sense of the best all-time performance) a record at all?" To state the problem another way, "Given all the situational variables which are uncontrolled, how do we *know* what best performance is?" If we accept the points which Weiss has made we cannot state that we know, in any univocal sense, that any particular athletic record describes in a complete way what did occur at the time and place of any particular athletic performance. Perhaps the most we can say, in the words of Weiss, is ". . . records can tell us only what men did in a number of incompletely described and inadequately understood situations. They report the accomplishments of outstanding contextualized individuals, and then only in certain sports, and in abstraction from various conditions which in fact made a difference to the result."

Is it reasonable for us to believe that records should provide complete insight? In one sense, no, for it is the nature of a record to be capable only of approximation of some of what actually occurred during the event. The finest stereophonic recording is not the same as the experience of sensing the conductor, the orchestra, and the concert hall. The "instant" replays of televised sports are not the same as the original view on the screen while what is viewed on the screen is not the same as what is experienced by a spectator in the stands. To generalize, we should not expect more of a *re*port; *re*ply, or a *re*cord than it is capable of supplying.

But is this *approximation* of what happens during an athletic performance all that athletic records speak to us about? Perhaps another type of inquiry into what athletic records may tell us of humankind would be productive. As indicated, at the least, athletic records establish an *approximation* of the best contextualized performances so far achieved and, in so doing, provide a basis for comparison, present to present and present to past, of other so far achieved contextualized performances. Perhaps if we focus our inquiry upon the long standing, avid *interest* of humans in recording athletic performances, rather than upon the records themselves, we will find some promising directions.

To proceed from this point it is necessary to declare two corollary assumptions about human interest. First, humans do not persist in directing their interest to concerns which are insignificant to them as humans. Second, the positive corollary, humans persist in directing their interest to concerns from which important meaning is available to them as humans.

Now the question for exploration becomes, "Given the avid historic interest of humans in athletic records, what important meaning is available to humans through this interest?" The ancient Greeks said arete—excellence. The slogan of the modern Olympics says citius, altius, fortius—faster, higher, stronger. But excellence with respect to what standard? Faster, higher, stronger in regard to what comparative? The Greek concept of excellence was intimately interwoven with the anthropomorphic ideas of the gods as perfect men. Faster, higher, stronger at first glance means in comparison to other men, but if we look more deeply we may discern man's inexorable Sisyphus—like struggle with the space, the time, and the gravitational force of his world. Our lives and our language are filled with the symbols of Western man's continuing struggle to dominate his world. The first man on the moon said, "a long step for man." Alan Shepard executes a golf swing on the moon—an act which reiterates the symbolic acts of humans on earth to test their abilities to control themselves and the forces of their world to conform to their will. Humans are continually attending to the self-identity clues provided by feedback from athletic and dance performance, both human endeavors which use movement as the medium and the body as the instrument. In athletics, humans move their bodies to determine how fast, how high, and how much they compare. In dance, humans move their bodies to use space, time, and force to produce images of infinity, eternity and omnipotence as a symbolic means of overcoming their *earthliness*.

The significance of the interest of humans in athletic records may be explained as an expression of the continuing desire of humans to ascertain status in the world. The fact that the records themselves are but approximations of actual achievement is inconsequential in comparison to the continuing desire for knowledge of the human condition. Humanity seems not to be satisfied by the type of comparative of the dictum "man—the measure of all things." Man apparently demands comparatives other than himself. So, in history, he has compared himself with God, gods, angels, the devil, beings from other planets and his space-time-force world.

If status in the world is a comparative, athletic records provide opportunities for four kinds of comparisons. One of these is that of the individual non-record achiever to the best recorded performance in a particular athletic event. In effect, this is a comparison of the personally effective powers of the non-record achiever and the personally effective powers of the record achiever. Such a comparison responds to the implicit question, "How do I compare with him?"

A second is comparison of the present performance of an individual with his own best performance. This comparison is between the personally effective powers of the present "I" with the personally effective powers of the best past "I". The response is to "How do I compare with I?"

A third comparative is that of an individual record achiever to a presumed best possible performance. The comparison here is between the personally effective powers of the approximately best performer with the presumed limits on human performance imposed by an impersonal world. Years ago the four minute mile was a presumed best possible performance. The question to be responded to here is "How do I compare with it?"

The fourth comparative is between the current record achiever and the collective, historical record achievers in the same athletic event. This compares the personally effective powers of the current, approximately best performer with the historic *trend* established by the personally effective powers of many past, approximately best performers. The question here is "How do I compare with we?"

These four comparatives, born in athletic records, have two things in common. First, each is concerned with personal human effective powers, either individual, or collective, or historical. Second, personal human powers are measured by relative abilities to move a mass or masses in a spatial- temporal context governed by specified rules. Thus, the comparatives available in athletic records express symbolically the effective personal powers of humans to exert force in space and time. (2). Such symbolic expressions provide humans one source for their sense of personal status in a force-space-time world. Any single record, in and of itself, is not only incomplete as Weiss informs us but is also insignificant. However, any single athletic record as one point for a multitude of comparisons of personal, human effective power is a source for human symbolization regarding human status in the world.

Based on the assumption that humans persist in directing their interest to concerns from which significance is available to them as humans and the position that athletic records provide a source for human symbolization about human status in the world, it is appropriate to conclude that humans persist in their interest in athletic records because they are a source for symbolic meanings which are of importance to them.

In the last 1/3 of his paper Weiss makes several assertions which are very worthy of discussion. He speaks of such related matters as ". . . an end to which a man is dedicated. . . ." and ". . . the end to which an athlete is dedicated. . . ." also he mentions ". . . men . . . dedicated to the attainment of complete, fulfilled lives" and athletes who choose ". . . to be fulfilled primarily by having an excellent body deployed excellently in severe, public tests, objectively judged." Still further, Weiss states, "The athlete chooses that fulfillment which requires and is affected by a perfected and operative body" and ". . . the end to which an athlete is dedicated is narrower than that appropriate to man at his best."

This last statement apparently indicates that Weiss has something in mind as an end ". . . appropriate to man at his best." However, that end is not identified in "Records and the Man" and this would not be important except that Weiss has claimed "The end to which an athlete is dedicated is narrower than that appropriate to man at his best." Unfortunately, Weiss does not tell us to what end an athlete is dedicated and, since he also has not declared the end appropriate to man at his best, he provides no clear base for analysis of the consistency of his remarks, e.g., comparing the end of the athlete with the end appropriate to man at his best.

Perhaps a differentiation is needed in the use Weiss makes of the word "end." Whatever Weiss has intended as the end of the athlete, it may not be an end at all in the sense of that which is the mark of the fullest and most complete life. Maybe it is better termed an objective or, to be Deweyan, an "end in view." Such a term would be more accurate in describing those objectives which humans seek in the many *roles* they perform in life; for instance, the scientist as scientist or the musician as musician. The point is that no single role played by humans, be it musician, scientist, philosopher or athlete, has an objective which is, of itself, capable of providing a complete and fulfilled life. In this way, the roles of musician, scientist, philosopher or athlete do not entail a complete and fulfilled life but only the partial completion and fulfillment available from a partial role.

Although Weiss does not identify the end to which the athlete is dedicated or the end appropriate to man at his best he has declared that the end of the athlete is one ". . . which demands for its realization the use and preservation of an excellent body." This appears to identify the means for the undeclared end. However, Weiss states "Scientists, musicians, religious and ethical men are also dedicated to the attainment of complete, fulfilled lives." The "also" in this statement appears to imply that the end of the athlete is the attainment of a complete, fulfilled life. If this implication is correct it provides a base for comparing the end of the athlete to the end of the scientist, the musician, the religious and the ethical man. Both kinds of ends seem to be the same; namely, "the attainment of complete, fulfilled lives." Nonetheless, Weiss makes a distinction in this common end which is differentiated in three ways. Roughly, these are:

1. The instrument of a complete, fulfilled life—the body for the athlete, not the body for the scientist, the musician, and so on.
2. The clarity of understanding of the nature of the end of a complete, fulfilled life—clearer to the scientist, the musician and so on than to the athlete.
3. The "social" inclusiveness of the end-fulfillment for the scientist, the musician, and so on is inseparable from the completion of others while the "athletic goal rarely allows a man to work toward achievement of anyone but himself . . ."

Accordingly, the distinctions which make the athletic end "narrower than that appropriate to man at his best" are that the athlete uses his body for achievement, the athlete is less able to articulate clearly what a complete, fulfilled life is, and the athletic end is more "self-seeking."

The first distinction is obviously correct in at least a quantitative sense, that is, the athlete more totally uses his body for achievement. However, this distinction is a difference in degree and not in kind for scientists, musicians, and so on also use their bodies for achievement. Also, although detailed discussion cannot be entered into here, any implication that the athlete's use of his body is a "mindless" operation must be dispelled.

The second distinction regarding the athlete's inability to articulate the content of a complete, fulfilled life is partially correct in two ways. One, if verbal articulation is intended it is probably true but if non-verbal articulation of a complete, fulfilled life is included the distinction is less meaningful. Second, the distinction is correct in those cases where a particular athlete is dominated by the athletic role to the extent that other kinds of human roles are not contributing to fulfill-ment. There are *some* athletes like that but there are also many who do, in fact, engage in a variety of human roles. Some level of inability to articulate what a complete, fulfilled life is seems to characterize many persons whose day-to-day life is dominated by one kind of role, whether it is athlete, scientist or musician.

The second distinction is partially incorrect in that it ignores the possibility that the athletic experience provides a different kind of basis for articulation of what a complete, fulfilled life is and, thus, potentially enriches that articulation.

The third distinction is probably the most provocative and deserves to be fully repeated. Weiss says:

> Most important, the end that they [scientists, musicians, religious and ethical men] envisage, though never free from reference to the self, is one in which their own completion is inseparable from the completion of others. When an athlete makes provision for the success of his team mates, it is usually because this is incidental to his own . . . The excellence sought by the others, though not without its element of self-regard and self-seeking, is broad enough to be realized by many independently, but in such a way as to provide opportunities for the others.
>
> The athletic goal rarely allows a man to work toward the achievement of anyone but himself, except incidentally and as a means.

This distinction indicates a fundamental misunderstanding of athletic achievement as it is often experienced by athletes. Misunderstanding may come clearer if the nature of positive fulfillment in athletic achievement is revealed.

That kind of athletic achievement which is often most significant on a continuing basis for the athlete is a product of a certain kind of athletic engagement. It is the achievement of a well-contested and well-played game by all parties to the event. The ingredients of such a well-played and well-contested game are; (1) contestants who are well-matched in terms of performance skills and physical condition, (2) interesting and demanding strategic situations in conjunction with comparable strategic abilities among the participants and, (3) an outcome which is in doubt until the final moments of the event. (1). In combination, these elements show that a well-played, well-contested event is the product of the process of mutual facilitation by the participants. In their immediate pursuit of scoring in or winning of the event, the participants are actually engaging in the cooperative achievement of the well-played and well-contested event. Each point in the event is a mini-achievement to which all the participants contribute. The participants each utilize the very best of their abilities, conditioning and strategy. In so doing, they mutually aid each other in the cooperative achievement.

If one party in the athletic event increases the quality of his performance, his startegy, and his conditioning, he provides a basic condition for the completion and fulfillment of the other. That is, each qualitative increase is the condition whereby a corresponding qualitative increase is evoked in order for the participants to achieve the well-played, well-contested event. *Intrinsic in the structure of the well-played event is this back-and-forth facilitation of fulfillment.* Because of this intrinsic structure, the completion and fulfillment of one athlete is dependent upon and inseparable from that of the other athlete and not incidental, one to the other, as Weiss seems to propose. This explains why athletes who have contested often and well *with* each other have great respect and admiration for each other. The quality of their relationships is of mutual self-facilitation born structurally out of the achievement of many well-played events.

Some athletic records are produced from well-played, well-contested events. Inasmuch and insofar as such records are marks of achievement produced in a relationship of structured, mutual self-facilitation on the part of the athletes, it may be said that the excellence noted by the record results from the contributions of all the athletes involved. Though it is just and proper to *record* the approximately best achievement in the name of an individual athlete or team it is also necessary *to understand* that the particular, approximately best achievement often would not be so without the efforts of other athletes. This "indebtedness" of a record achiever to the facilitation provided by other contestants is, in fact, often verbalized by record achievers in such post-record remarks as "He pushed me to it." or "I couldn't have done it without his effort." When the athletic goal is fulfillment via the well-played, well-contested game, it may be stated that the structured mutual self-facilitation process *inherently* allows the athletes to work for mutual benefit simultaneously. This, of course, is directly contradictory to the Weiss proposition that "The athletic goal rarely allows a man to work towards the achievement of anyone but himself . . ." Thus, in the sense of the achievement of the well-played game which produces a record performance, it may be speculated that the record is indicative of the ceaseless effort of humankind to extend the boundaries of accomplishment.

In summary of this reaction the following points are appropriate. Athletic records do not tell us what man is. The avid historic *interest* of humans in athletic records tells us of the ongoing quest for symbolic self-understanding of human status in a world of time-space-force. Additionally, records produced from the well-played, well-contested game are the result of structured mutual self-facilitation. This inherent structure becomes a means by which humans extend the boundaries of achievement by thrusting a *superman* into history. This *superman* (the record achiever) is the best produced by many humans striving mutually for the fulfillment of the well-played game.

REFERENCES

1. Kaelin, Eugene: "The Well-Played Game: Notes Toward an Aesthetics of Sport," *Quest,* No. 10; 16-28 (May, 1968).
2. Metheny, Eleanor: *Connotations of Movement in Sport and Dance.* Dubuque, William C. Brown, 1965.
3. Weiss, Paul: "Records and the Man." Essay presented at the Symposium on the Philosophy of Sport, Brockport, New York, February 10-12, 1972.

ASSUMPTIONS ABOUT THE NATURE OF HUMAN MOVEMENT

Roselyn E. Stone

The title presupposes that human movement *has* a nature of its own —an inherent character or basic constitution—an assumption that may be fallacious. However, the issue of whether human movement has an essence or, in fact, has only a moment-to-moment existence dependent upon individual man's existence thus being susceptible to description but not definition, must be left to another time. Because the men whose theories are presented in this paper *did* accept the notion of a pre-defined essence the title is not incongruous.

Although the term "human movement" is ambiguous in its meaning, it is, perhaps, no worse in this regard than are other terms (such as sport, athletics, play, dance, activity) that we use to denote those phenomena coming under the scrutiny of the people gathered here. And it is a term gaining wider and wider usage because it does not delimit in the way that each of the aforementioned does. While I scarcely need remind this group that human movement does *not* refer to the migration of tribes over the earth's surface, nor to an effort after Free Speech, I must point out that sport and play (as I understand these terms) are *not* the subject matter of this paper. Dance is—but only tangentially in that the theories have affected dance technique. Exercise is too—and also only tangentially.

Each of François Delsarte, Emile Jaques-Dalcroze, Rudolf Laban, and Rudolf Bode postulated movement as a medium for the expression of the spirit/soul/self and as the means by which body and mind, or the self and Other, might be "harmonized." Delsarte centralized his thoughts around the trinity of Mind, Life, and Spirit; Dalcroze around the idealized form of musical rhythm; Laban around the concept of inner efforts; and Bode around the concept of individual, instinctive rhythm.

To pretend to deal fully with their movement theories in this paper would be unfair and, indeed, dishonest. While the theories are somewhat tenuously founded (indeed some of my hard-nosed scientific colleagues will give them *no* "head" room at all!) they nonetheless represent genuine attempts to understand a quicksilver phenomenon.

I will present synopses of their theories noting assumptions made pertaining to such primary principles as source, appearance, and effect.

FRANCOIS DELSARTE 1811-1871

Deploring the chaos into which, in his opinion, art (including music and elecution) had fallen because, he said,

> . . . all law rests upon the opinion of the master: thus all the science dwells in a confused mass of prescriptions and examples that no principle comes to support . . . (6:p.42).

he set out to find the science which he was sure existed to form the basis of art. He sought to disengage aesthetics from all conjecture and to constitute to under ". . . the severe forms of a positive science."

> The beautiful should be because of its consubstantiality with the True and the Good entirely disengaged from the capricious influences which attach to taste. (7:p.57).

Eventually his studies and observations led him to enunciate his Law of Correspondence with its dependent constructs and laws:

> To each spiritual function responds a function of the body. To each grand function of the body corresponds a spiritual act . . . thus from the concurrence of these two powers spirit and body in the same person results the intimate fusions of art and science. . . .(7:p.67).

Imagine a snowflake design bisected horizontally and separated at the bisection. At this area of separation stands man—the object of Art. Through man, he posits, is the celestial world of ideas, principles, and heavenly qualities made manifest. One arm of the upper triad denotes the state, and idea, of Mind; one, the state and idea of Spirit which includes Morality and Love; and one, the state and idea of life which includes Feeling and Vitality. Each of these has access, as it were, to three modes of manifestation—three "appearances," each of which, through its appropriate agent or apparatus, being modulated as a language. Accordingly, one arm of the lower triad denotes the language of Inflexion with its agents of lungs/larynx/pharnyx and its components of melody, rhythm, harmonic overtones; one, the language of Speech with its agents of tongue, lips, "voile du Palais," and its components of copula (verbs, conjunctions, prepositions), modifier, and the modified; and one arm, the language of Gesture with its agents of torso, head, and limbs, and its components of energy, spatiality and body locus.

Thus the universals of Idea, Morality, Love, Feeling make themselves manifest through gesture (or the other "languages") and their presence and proportion may be discovered therein, says Delsarte, according to the body parts used, direction, zone of personal space into which the action proceeds, amplitude, shape of action, its speed and force.

Delsarte enunciated nine laws of motion and an organizing Chart of the Ninefold Accord. As you will guess, the repeated occurrence of three, and its square, in his theory is no coincidence. Man's three-fold nature and his supposed three-fold causation (the Holy Trinity) reverberates throughout. Not to be left out, the body was divided into three zones: mental-intellectual—the head; spiritual/emotional—the upper torso; and vital/physical—the lower torso. And each of these was subdivided by threes. In passing it is interesting to note that the shoulder was named the Thermometer of Passion.

> When a man says to you in interjective form I love, I suffer, I am delighted, etc., do not believe him if his shoulder remains in a normal attitude. (6:p.40).

The elbow was the Thermometer of the Will coming close to the body in supplication and moving outward—as in arms akimbo—to express arrogance and assertion. And the wrist was the Thermometer of Vital Force—the limp wrist, for example, denoting weakness or a devitalized state. Additionally, hip action *measured* vulgarity and knee action, assertion.

The Ninefold Accord was based on the following categories of motion: eccentric (outward motion) expressive of the sensations of feeling which are of one's vital or physical nature; concentric (inward motion) expressive of the reason which is of one's mental nature; and normal ("poised" motion) expressive of the will or love which is of one's moral or volitional nature. Now, each of these contains the other two and the ninefold accord—normo-eccentric, con-eccentric, ex-eccentric, con-normal, ex-normal, et cetera,—emerges. And each of these finds within it elements of the vital or the mental or the spiritual accentuated according to the zone(s) of the body (which Delsarte assigned to each of these qualities) involved in the motion. Add the variables of velocity, apparent force, etc., and the mind begins to reel at the permutations of mental, vital, and spiritual raised to the nth power of three! From this grew the "aesthetic gymnastics" which had as their purpose the freeing of the "channels for expression."

EMILE JAQUES-DALCROZE 1865-1935

Dalcroze's involvement with the movement phenomenon stemmed from his musician's concern with rhythm. As Professor of Harmony at the Conservatoire de Geneva, he was concerned with his pupils' lack of "ear" for apprehending form in music. Specifically, they lacked perfect pitch, then deemed essential in musicians, and the inner sense of rhythmicity which would ensure a performance closer to the composer's intent than were the virtuoso, but artificial, performances characterising the music—and dance—of his day. Noting that students tended to move their bodies in various ways as they performed at the piano, he concluded that musical sensation of a rhythmic nature calls for the muscular and nervous response of the whole organism.

> Rhythm is the basis of all vital, scientific, and artistic phenomena. It produces alike the elements of order and measure in movement and the idiosyncracies of execution. (2:p.171).

Pursuing this notion of individuality he held that development of the arts required that an emphasis be placed on the creation of one's own style. He deplored the intellectualising of beauty with its enunciation of classic rules and formulae which, he said, ". . . are nothing until they are vitalised by artistic feeling." It was his observation that the tendency in his day of adhering too strictly to laws of design and meter was robbing the arts of the vitality which should have been their integral constituent. The breaking loose from rigid forms and the creation of one's own style depended, he said:

> . . . on a reunification of spiritual and corporal faculties, that can be achieved only by an assiduous training in movement in time and space, and a diligent cultivation of a muscular sense. (2:p.192).

The last was defined as:

> . . . the feeling for space and familiarity with its laws—as well as that for shades of time [which was developed by] the acquisition of aesthetic qualities and of the instinct for divining the results certain movements

will produce on others, and which enable the plastic artist to 'realise' with his limbs gestures and attitudes he has previously imagined. (2:pp.259-260).

This ". . . *inward* sense of decorative line and form, balance and dynamism" (2:p.260), he said, is ". . . complemented by what the scientists have called the kinaesthetic . . . sense . . . and what . . . [has been] aptly described as sense of gyration." (2:p.291). Not only did he see this "sense" having an important role in moving artistically (i.e., "moving plastic") but also in developing aesthetic judgement.

> . . . the receptive faculties of eye and ear will only develop an aesthetic activity when the muscular sense is sufficiently developed to convert the sensation so registered into movement. (2:p.260).
> As we have said elsewhere, and frequently, movement is the basis of all the arts, and no artistic culture is possible without a previous study of the forms of movement and a thorough training of our motor-tactile faculties. (2:p.260).

Turning his attention to movement as such, as distinct from movement as a prophylactic for ailing musical ears, he posited that "The music of movement, like the music of sound, aims at expressing the common emotions of humanity," (2:p.236), and body movements ". . . should be controlled by musical rhythms . . ." (2:p.237). Dalcroze likened pitch to position and direction of gestures in space, intensity of sound to muscular dynamics, melody to continuous succession of isolated movements, and form to the distribution of movements in space and time. (2:p.261).

> The eurhythmist [one whose movement has been musicalized] both creates (or re-creates) artistic emotion and experiences it. In him, sensation humanises the idea, and the idea spiritualises sensation. In the laboratory of his organism a transmutation is effected turning the creator into both actor and spectator of his own composition. (2:pp.257-258).

Expression in movement, he believed, was not inherent in *a* movement, but was to be found in a *succession* of movements. Temperament with its influence on nuances of dynamics, time shadings, manipulations of space and speed of gestures was ". . . obviously responsible for the motor form of corporal rhythmic phenomena . . ." (2:p.320). Movement, then, given the right conditions, materialised the ideal of Rhythm and in so doing harmonized body and spirit, thereby creating individuality.

RUDOLF LABAN 1879-1958

Laban was a fascinated student of human movement.

> Our own movements and those we perceive around us are basic experiences . . . Each movement has its form, and forms are simultaneously created with and through movement. (3:p.3).

While he shared with Delsarte and Dalcroze an interest in the deliberately expressive forms of the performing arts, he was also absorbed by the movement patterns of people as they moved through the regular events of their lives. And while, like them, he speaks of expression he differs from them in that he is not speaking of the corporal manifestation of the Eternal or the Ideal, but of the "effort rhythms" which speak of one's "inner efforts"—i.e., what one conceives of doing in one's attempt to relate to the people and things of one's environment. As a leading dancer-choreographer of his time and a consultant in industrial time-motion studies, he observed the movement patterns of a great many people of diverse movement background in diverse movement situations. He brought out of his study theories relative to individual effort and expression, a codification of movement and from that a system of movement notation. His propositions are still considered highly significant by many practitioners of movement today. However, they are coming, now, under sophisticated scrutiny.

The organizing concept of Laban movement theory is effort and effort rhythm, which Laban defined as ". . . sequences of efforts showing a definite form of flow with alternative stresses and relaxations . . ." (5:p.65). The word "effort" he defined as ". . . the inner impulses from which movement originates . . ." (4:p.11). These were held to signify the person within and as such were highly personal. Efforts (actions) could be diagrammed and identified by name according to their spatial, temporal, and dynamic content. Effort rhythms, growing out of the concatenations of efforts, were less susceptible to categorization. However, he decided there were effort rhythms which characterized men, women, temperament types, professional and industrial occupations, and cultural groups. Two additional observations are important here: because of the individualised rhythm inherent in them, effort rhythms were subtly expressive; and, individuals demonstrated a predilection for particular movement patterns which they used in spite of the nature of the task confronting them.

The significance of such intra-individual consistency was two-fold. It reflected a lack of "effort balance," thus severely limiting one's working efficiency because, lacking a vocabulary of action patterns and/or the habit of selecting from a variety of patterns, one would tend to move in a manner inappropriate for the task. Secondly, it reflected a temperament of limited development—a personality with few facets; hence a person with limited capacity to interact with people or react to the exigencies of life. "Movement," he said, "is itself a language in which man's highest and most fundamental inspirations are expressed, . . ." (5:p.65) and ". . . each phase of movement, every small transference of weight, every single gesture of any part of the body reveals some feature of our inner life." (4:p.21). He noted that ". . . sequences of movement are like sentences of speech, . . ." (4:p.98) because they flow and express an idea.

> Language [verbal] expressing feelings, emotions, sentiments or certain mental and spiritual states will but touch the fringe of the inner responses which the shapes and rhythms of mind evoke. Movement can say more, for all its shortness, than pages of verbal description. (4:p.98).

Mastery of Space was the other fundamental concept in his theory. It took pre-eminence in Laban's training for the mastery of movement. He placed the individual inside an icosahedron of space built of the four corners of each of the horizontal, frontal and sagittal planes and the points where each plane intersects with the other two. His "movement scales" of which the "table," "door," and "wheel" are examples, were designed to train the student in moving along specific paths to defined points in space. These scales had the further purpose of focusing the student's attention on the execution and feel of the basic efforts. He observed that people varied in the ease with which they consumed space—some reaching freely into space, others being much more tentative in their extensions. The amounts of space consumed varied not only in distance from the body but also in the nature of the path, direct or flexible, taken on the way to getting to the intended point.

Time does not permit a discussion of the relations posited by him to exist among mathematical forms, classical harmonies, movement patterns, and mastery of self (as the last-mentioned manifests itself in an enlarged movement vocabulary, a sensitivity to motion patterns, and an ability to select and do appropriate efforts). His belief in the mystical power of the crystalline form and the circle formed the theoretical basis for mastery of space. Through choreology (the science of circles) movement becomes, he said, ". . . penetrable, meaningful, understandable." (3:p.viii). By imposing circles, or circular paths, on mathematical polygons he arrived at his system of scales and exercises which, because they were derived from harmonics, would have the power of harmonising.

RUDOLF BODE 1881-

Like Dalcroze and Laban, Bode sought after the "freeing" of the individual toward his/her fuller expression. He assumed a rhythmical substrate for movement—both physical, in the sense of visceral, and cosmic.

> *Each individual movement* has a continuous and rhythmic character. [There are] . . . The almost imperceptible trembling of the arm which makes aiming impossible . . ., The larger rhythms . . . of the heart, . . . [and the] periodic cycles . . . [of] organic life, connecting the lives of individuals, of whole families, and of nations with the rhythmic movement of planets. (1:p.11).

Bode's concept of movement is one of an organic form which grows and pulses with a rhythmic life and has a highly individual nature which emerges as the restrictions imposed on it by the mind during volitional acts are removed. It is shaped according to the moment-to-moment relationship between its drive to continue in its natural mode and the will's attempt to alter its temporal pattern. He speaks of ". . . *the essential vitality of movement,* that secret combination of soul and body which follow the order of the spirit but immediately evolves its individuality, its organic unity." (1:p.53). It might be noted that where Delsarte, Dalcroze and Laban were carefully directing the limbs through space, Bode was allowing them to lift freely as the movement rippled from the trunk, thus, a control from inside out rather than outside in. This different viewpoint toward movement training stemmed from his observation that the centre of gravity was the crucial area to be displaced in order to bring about total body involvement. On his theory he based his Expression Gymnastics which are characterised by swings, leaps and runs, i.e., those acts which emphasize rhythm and displacing the centre of gravity.

TO SUMMARIZE UNDER SOURCE, APPEARANCE, AND EFFECT . . .

Delsarte, then, assumed human movement to have an insubstantial source, a triune causation located, to use his term, in the celestial world. Its material form comes into being through the medium of the body acting in concert with the Divine, and its spatial and dynamic constituents are directly related to the proportions of Intellect, Morality, and Vitality acting upon that medium. He posits a communicative content to the movement forms which is susceptible to reduction to common denominators of meaning. His disciples declare that he, like Dalcroze, Laban, and Bode, posited a desirable effect consequent upon following his system, i.e., "freeing the channels of communication." In Delsarte's case it brought one into an unobstructed relationship with the Divine.

Dalcroze does not speak of source, but does note a modulating agent in the kinaesthetic sense. Positing, as do the others, the teleological notion of Ideal Form, his ideal was the classical concept of Rhythm and he assumed that motoric form (locomotor and axial) could be transformed into the spatiodynamic form which is music. Movement concatenations, were they properly ordered and shaped, would so alter one's psychological status as to improve one's aesthetic sensitivity and one's ability to organise and execute self-designed forms congruent with one's inner feeling—"The ubiquitous self-expression!"

Laban identified the source of human movement as "inner efforts" (which he never really explained) and the modulating forces of personality structure and the harmonic laws which rule all the movements (e.g., of the celestial bodies) in space. He postulated a consistency of form according to the individual from task to task. While he did not reduce human movement on the basis of rectilinear attributes (in spite of his circle and polygons!), he did reduce it to eight basic efforts (e.g., gliding, slashing, dabbing, thrusting) sorted on the basis of topological attributes (viz., light/strong, flexible/direct, sustained/quick, fluent/bound. He also proposed that movement, properly formed, has a salubrious effect on the psyche, and that human movement has meaning content. More inclined than Delsarte to leave interpretation to the viewer, he did, nonetheless, equate upward action with exultation, downward with strength, or depression, across with exclusion, open with welcoming or inclusion, backward with alarm or anguish.

For Bode, the source of human movement lay in the visceral rhythm which was itself a result of the cosmic rhythm. "Mental aspects" (voluntary acts) disturb the original purity by channeling the natural flow but once the ego lets go (as it *must* be made to do!), the flow returns to its instinctual, rhythmic nature. This rhythm, in spite of its cosmic origin, he posited to be of the individual—but only when unimpeded by acts of the ego. (He does not resolve this contradiction.) The natural form of movement, he proposes, reflects one's inner (visceral) tempo and involves actively the centre of gravity.

Even granting their assumptions about the nature of man, these theories do not stand up to the scrutiny of logic. Experimental findings give them no support either. And yet . . . for those who have thought about their own experience of moving, these theories have about them a tantalising "rightness"—the impact of intuited knowledge.

REFERENCES

1. Bode, Rudolf: *Expression-Gymnastics*. New York, A.S. Barnes, 1931.
2. Jaques-Dalcroze, Emile: *Rhythm, Music and Education*. New York, Putnam, 1921.
3. Laban, Rudolf: *Choreutics*. London, Macdonald and Evans, 1966.
4. Laban, Rudolf: *The Mastery of Movement*. Second edition. London, Macdonald and Evans, 1966.
5. Laban, Rudolf and Lawrence, F.C.: *Effort*. London, Macdonald and Evans, 1947.
6. Shawn, Ted: *Every Little Movement*. New York, Dance Horizons, 1963.
7. Stebbins, Genevieve: *Delsarte System of Expression*. New York, Edgar S. Werner, 1902.

THE ELEMENTS OF SPORT*

Bernard Suits

I would like to advance the thesis that the elements of sport are essentially—although perhaps not totally—the same as the elements of game. I shall first propose an account of the elements of game-playing, then comment on the relation of game to sport, and finally suggest that the resulting view of sport has an important bearing on the question as to whether sport is or is not serious.

---

*An earlier version of this paper was presented at the Third International Symposium on the Sociology of Sport, University of Waterloo, August, 1971.

THE ELEMENTS OF GAME

Since games are goal-directed activities which involve choice, ends and means are two of the elements of games. But in addition to being means-end oriented activities, games are also rule-governed activities, so that rules are a third element. And since, as we shall see, the rules of games make up a rather special kind of rule, it will be necessary to take account of one more element, namely, the attitudes of game-players *qua* game-players. I add "*qua* game-players" because I do not mean what might happen to be the attitude of this or that game player under these or those conditions (e.g., the hope of winning a cash prize or the satisfaction of exhibiting physical prowess to an admiring audience), but the attitude without which it is not possible to play a game. Let us call this attitude, of which more presently, the *lusory* (from the Latin *ludus,* game) attitude.

My task will be to persuade you that what I have called the lusory attitude is the element which unifies the other elements into a single formula which successfully states the necessary and sufficient conditions for any activity to be an instance of game-playing. I propose, then, that the elements of game are (1) the goal, (2) means for achieving the goal, (3) rules, and (4) lusory attitude. I shall briefly discuss each of these in order.

The Goal

We should notice first of all that there are three distinguishable goals involved in game-playing. Thus, if we were to ask a long distance runner his purpose in entering a race, he might say any one or all of three things, each of which would be accurate, appropriate, and consistent with the other two. He might reply (1) that his purpose is to participate in a long distance race, or (2) that his purpose is to win the race, or (3) that his purpose is to cross the finish line ahead of the other contestants. It should be noted that these responses are not merely three different formulations of one and the same purpose. Thus, winning a race is not the same thing as crossing a finish line ahead of the other contestants, since it is possible to do the latter unfairly by, for example, cutting across the infield. Nor is participating in the race the same as either of these, since the contestant, while fully participating, may simply fail to cross the finish line first, either by fair means or foul. That there must be this triplet of goals in games

will be accounted for by the way in which lusory attitude is related
to rules and means. For the moment, however, it will be desirable
to select just one of the three kinds of goal for consideration, namely,
the kind illustrated in the present example by crossing the finish line
ahead of the other contestants. This goal is literally the *simplest* of the
three goals, since each of the other goals presupposes it, whereas it
does not presuppose either of the other two. This goal, therefore, has
the best claim to be regarded as an elementary component of game-
playing. The others, since they are compounded components, can
be defined only after the disclosure of additional elements.

The kind of goal at issue, then, is the kind illustrated by crossing
a finish line first (but not necessarily fairly), having x number of
tricks piled up before you on a bridge table (but not necessarily as a
consequence of playing bridge), or getting a golf ball into a cup (but
not necessarily by using a golf club). This kind of goal may be described generally as *a specific achievable state of affairs*. This description is, I believe, no more and no less than is required. By omitting to
say *how* the state of affairs in question is to be brought about, it avoids
confusion between this goal and the goal of winning. And because
any achievable state of affairs whatever could, with sufficient ingenuity, be made the goal of a game, the description does not include
too much. I suggest that this kind of goal be called the *pre-lusory*
goal of a game, because it can be described before, or independently
of, any game of which it may be, or come to be, a part. In contrast,
the goal of winning can be described only in terms of the game in
which it figures, and winning may accordingly be called the *lusory*
goal of a game. (It is tempting to call what I have called the pre-lusory
goal the goal *in* a game and the lusory goal the goal *of* a game, but
the practice of philosophers like J. L. Austin has, I believe, sufficiently
illustrated the hazards of trying to make prepositions carry a load of
meaning which can much better be borne by adjectives and nouns.)
Finally, the goal of participating in the game is not, strictly speaking,
a part of the game at all. It it simply one of the goals that people have,
such as wealth, glory, or security. As such it may be called a lusory
goal, but a lusory goal of life rather than of games.

Means

Just as we saw that reference to the goal of game-playing was susceptible of three different (but proper and consistent) interpretations, so we shall find that the means in games can refer to more than one kind of thing; two, in fact, depending upon whether we wish to refer to means for winning the game or for achieving the pre-lusory goal. Thus, an extremely effective way to achieve the pre-lusory goal in a boxing match—viz., the state of affairs consisting in your opponent being *down* for the count of ten—is to shoot him through the head, but this is obviously not a means to winning the match. In games, of course, we are interested only in means which are permitted for winning, and we are now in a position to define that class of means, which we may call *lusory* means. Lusory means are means which are permitted (are legal or legitimate) in the attempt to achieve pre-lusory goals. Thus a soccer player may use foot or head, but not hand, in his efforts to achieve that state of affairs wherein the ball is in the goal. And a player who does not confine himself to lusory means may not be said to win, even if he achieves the pre-lusory goal. But achievement of the lusory goal, winning, requires that the player confine himself to lusory means, so that confinement to lusory means is a necessary (but of course not a sufficient) condition for winning.

It should be noticed that we have been able to distinguish lusory from, if you will, illusory means only by assuming without analysis one of the elements necessary in making the distinction. We have defined lusory means as means which are *permitted* without examining the nature of that permission. This omission will be repaired directly by taking up the question of rules. But we may provisionally acknowledge the following definition: *lusory means,* means permitted in seeking pre-lusory goals.

Rules

As with goals and means, two kinds of rule figure in games, one kind associated with pre-lusory goals, the other with lusory goals. The rules of a game are, in effect, proscriptions of certain means useful in achieving pre-lusory goals. Thus, it is useful but proscribed to trip a competitor in a foot race. This kind of rule may be called constitutive of the game, since such rules together with specification of the pre-lusory goal set out all the conditions which must be met in playing the game (though not, of course, in playing the game skillfully). Let us call such rules *constitutive* rules. The other kind of rule operates, so to speak, *within* the area circumscribed by constitutive rules, and this kind of rule may be called a rule of skill. Examples are the familiar injunctions to keep your eye on the ball, to refrain from trumping your partner's ace, and the like. To break a rule of skill is usually to fail, at least to that extent, to play the game well, but to break a constitutive rule is to fail to play the game at all. (There is a third kind of rule in games which appears to be unlike either of these. This is the kind of rule for which there is a fixed penalty, such that violating the rule is neither to fail to play the game nor [necessarily] to fail to play the game well, since it is sometimes tactically correct to incur such a penalty [e.g., in hockey] for the sake of the advantage gained. But these rules and the lusory consequences of their violation are established by the constitutive rules, and are simply extensions of them.)

Having made the distinction between constitutive rules and rules of skill, I propose to ignore the latter, since my purpose is to define not well-played games, but games. It is, then, what I have called constitutive rules which determine the kind and range of means which will be permitted in seeking to achieve the pre-lusory goal.

What is the nature of the restrictions which constitutive rules impose on the means for reaching a pre-lusory goal? The effect of constitutive rules is to place obstacles in the path leading to a pre-lusory goal. I invite the reader to think of any game at random. Now identify the pre-lusory goal, being careful to remember that the pre-lusory goal is simply any specific achievable state of affairs. I think you will agree that the simplest, easiest, and most direct approach to achieving such a goal is always ruled out in favour of a more complex, more difficult, and more indirect approach. Thus it is not uncommon for players of a new and difficult game to agree among themselves to *ease up* on the rules, that is, to allow themselves a greater degree of latitude than the official rules permit. This means removing some of the obstacles or, in terms of means, permitting certain means which the rules do not really permit. But if no means whatever are ruled out, then the game ceases to exist. Thus, we may think of the gamewright, when he invents games, as attempting to draw a line between permitted and prohibited means to a given end. If he draws this line too loosely there is danger of the game becoming too easy, and if he draws it with utter laxity the game simply falls apart. On the other hand, he must not draw the line too tight or, instead of falling apart, the game will be squeezed out of existence. For example, imagine a game where the pre-lusory goal is to cross a finish line, with an attendant rule that the player must not leave the track in his attempt to do so. Then imagine that there is a second rule which requires that the finish line be located some distance from the track.

We may define constitutive rules as rules which prohibit use of the most efficient means for reaching a pre-lusory goal.

Lusory Attitude

The attitude of the game-player must be an element in game-playing because there has to be an explanation of that curious state of affairs wherein one adopts rules which require him to employ worse rather than better means for reaching an end. Normally the acceptance of prohibitory rules is justified on the grounds that the means ruled out, although they are more efficient than the permitted means, have further undesirable consequences from the viewpoint of the agent involved. Thus, although the use of nuclear weapons is more efficient than is the use of conventional weapons in winning battles, the view still happily persists among nations that the additional consequences of nuclear assault are sufficient to rule it out. This kind of thing, of course, happens all the time, from the realm of international strategy to the common events of everyday life; thus one decisive way to remove a toothache is to cut your head off, but most people find good reason to rule out such highly efficient means. But in games, although more efficient means are—and must be—ruled out, the reason for doing so is quite different from the reasons for avoiding nuclear weaponry and self-decapitation. Foot racers do not refrain from cutting across the infield because the infield holds dangers for them, as would be the case if, for example, infields were frequently sown with land mines. Cutting across the infield is shunned solely because there is a rule against it. But in ordinary life this is usually—and rightly—regarded as the worst possible kind of justification one could give for avoiding a course of action. The justification for a prohibited course of action that there is simply a rule against it may be called the *bureaucratic* justification; that is, no justification at all.

But aside from bureaucratic practice, in anything but a game the

gratuitous introduction of unnecessary obstacles to the achievement
of an end is regarded as a decidedly irrational thing to do, whereas
in games it appears to be an absolutely essential thing to do. This fact
about games has led some observers to conclude that there is something
inherently absurd about games, or that games must involve a fundamental paradox. (1). This kind of view seems to me to be mistaken.
(2). The mistake consists in applying the same standard to games that
is applied to means-end activities which are not games. If playing a
game is regarded as not essentially different from going to the office or
writing a cheque, then there is certainly something absurd, or
paradoxical, or simply stupid about game-playing.

But games are, I believe, essentially different from the ordinary
activities of life, as perhaps the following exchange between Smith
and Jones will illustrate. Smith knows nothing of games, but he does
know that he wants to travel from A to C, and he also knows that
making the trip by way of B is the most efficient means for getting
to his destination. He is then told authoritatively that he may *not* go
by way of B. "Why not," he asks, "are there dragons at B?" "No,"
is the reply. "B is perfectly safe in every respect. It is just that there
is a rule against going to B if you are on your way to C." "Very
well," grumbles Smith, "if you insist. But if I have to go from A to C
very often I shall certainly try very hard to get that rule revoked."
True to his word, Smith approaches Jones, who is also setting out for
C from A. He asks Jones to sign a petition requesting the revocation
of the rule which forbids travellers from A to C to go through B.
Jones replies that he is very much opposed to revoking the rule, which
very much puzzles Smith.

Smith.   But if you want to get to C, why on earth do you support a
         rule which prevents your taking the fastest and most convenient
         route?

Jones.   Ah, but you see I have no particular interest in being at C.
         That is not my goal, except in a subordinate way. My over-
         riding goal is more complex. It is "to get from A to C without
         going through B." And I can't very well achieve that goal if
         I go through B, can I?

Smith.   But why do you want to do that?

Jones.   I want to do it before Robinson does, you see?

Smith. No, I don't. That explains nothing. Why should Robinson, whoever he may be, want to do it? I presume you will tell me that he, like you, has only a subordinate interest in being at C at all.

Jones. That is so.

Smith. Well, if neither of you wants, really, to be at C, then what possible difference can it make which of you gets there first? And why, for God's sake, should you avoid B?

Jones. Let me ask you a question. Why do you want to get to C?

Smith. Because there is a good concert there, and I want to hear it.

Jones. Why?

Smith. Because I like concerts, of course. Isn't that a good reason?

Jones. It's one of the best there is. And I like, among other things, trying to get from A to C without going through B before Robinson does.

Smith. Well, *I* don't. So why should they tell me I can't go through B?

Jones. Oh, I see. They must have thought you were in the race.

Smith. The what?

I believe that we are now in a position to define *lusory attitude*: the knowing acceptance of constitutive rules just so the activity made possible by such acceptance can occur.

Summary

The elements may now be assembled into the following definition. To play a game is to attempt to achieve a specific state of affairs (*pre-lusory goal*), using only means permitted by rules (lusory means), where the rules prohibit use of more efficient in favor of less efficient means (*constitutive rules*), and where such rules are accepted just because they make possible such activity (*lusory attitude*). I also offer the following only approximately accurate, but more pithy, version of the above definition: Playing a game is the voluntary attempt to overcome unnecessary obstacles.

GAMES AND SPORT

As I indicated at the outset, I believe that sports are essentially games. What I mean by this is that the difference between sports and other games is much smaller than the difference between humans and other vertebrates. That is to say, sport is not a species within the genus *game*. The distinguishing characteristics of sport are more peripheral, more arbitrary, and more contingent than are the differences required to define a species.

I would like to submit for consideration four requirements which, if they are met by any given game, are sufficient to denominate that game a sport. They are: (1) that the game be a game of skill, (2) that the skill be physical, (3) that the game have a wide following, and (4) that the following achieve a certain level of stability. If I can persuade you that these features or something very much like them are at least the *kind* of differentiating marks we are seeking, I will be satisfied. I have no theory to support the list, except the theory that the features are more or less arbitrary, since they are simply facts about sport. Finally, I have little to say about them aside from presenting them, except as regards the question of skill, which I am interested in taking up on its own account.

Skill in Games

One may agree with my account of what it is to play a game and still find unanswered the rather pressing question why anyone would want to do such a thing (aside from professionals who do so for money and prestige). Smith was no doubt puzzled about this question even after Jones' explanation. Let me propose the following general answer. People play games so that they can realize in themselves capacities not realizable (or not readily so) in the pursuit of their ordinary activities. For example, some people enjoy running competitively, but the opportunities for this are severely limited in ordinary life. One can run for a bus, but even this small range of operations is further limited by the fact that one does not always have the good fortune to arrive tardily at a bus stop. One can, of course, intentionally allow less than enough time for getting punctually to the point of departure, in the hope that a race with the time table will then be necessary. But such a move is precisely to create a game where there was no game before, by virtue of the constitutive rule requiring you to leave your home or office late. Some kinds of game—such as racing games—have this rather obvious affinity with actions per-formed aside from games. But most games do not have such a clear counterpart in ordinary life. Ball games which are at all elaborate have affinities with ordinary life only piecemeal; in life, too, one throws and runs and strikes objects, but there is nothing in life which much resembles baseball or football or golf *in toto*. Board games pro-vide similar examples of the hiatus between games taken as wholes and the kinds of structured activities which characterize the rest of life. Thus, with the invention of games far removed from the pursuits of ordinary life, quite new capacities emerge, and hitherto unknown skills are developed. A good golf swing is simply useless in any other human pursuit. And despite the literary mythology which frequently represents superior military and political strategists as being (it is almost presumed to go without saying) master chess players as well, there is as much similarity between those two skills as there is between the skills of golf and wood chopping. Purely topological problems are just vastly different from political and military problems. So people play games not only because ordinary life does not provide enough opportunities for doing such and such, but also (and more interest-ingly) because ordinary life does not provide any opportunities at all for doing such and such.

Games are *new* things to do, and they are new things to do because they require the overcoming of (by ordinary standards) *unnecessary* obstacles, and in ordinary life an unnecessary obstacle is simply a contradiction in terms.

Although I believe, as I have said, that people play games in order to realize capacities not otherwise realizable (or not readily realizable), and although in most games these capacities are, or intimately in-volve, specific skills, there are certain activities called games which almost conform to my definition but which do not involve skill. I mean games of chance; that is, games of *pure* chance. Draw poker is not such a game, nor, perhaps, is standard roulette (perhaps a de-batable point), but show-down is, and so is Russian roulette. These games do not not involve the capacity to exercise a specific skill be-cause no skill is required to play them. Instead of skills, what is put into operation by such games is, I suggest, hope and fear. Bored people are deficient in these feelings, it seems safe to say, since if they

were not they would not be bored. But hope and fear can be arti-
ficially induced by games of pure chance. (They also appear in games
of skill, to be sure, but people to whom games of chance especially
appeal are too bored to learn new skills.) What games of chance
provide for their players may be described in almost the same words
that Jan Narveson has used to describe paranoia: a false sense of
insecurity. However, for games of chance the word *false* should be
replaced by the word *invented,* for there is nothing false about the
capacities which games bring forth, just something new.

All sports appear to be games of skill rather than games of chance.
I suggest that the reason for this is that a major requirement in sports,
for participants and spectators alike, is that what the participants do
must be admirable in some respect. The exercise of virtually any
skill—even the skills involved in goldfish swallowing or flag pole
sitting—will elicit *some* degree of admiration. But the spectacle
of a person sweating in hope and fear as the chamber slowly turns
in the revolver evokes not admiration but morbid fascination or
clinical interest.

Physical Skill

It is not difficult to draw a line between games which require
physical skill and games which do not. It is not necessary first to decide very grave metaphysical issues, such as the relation between mind
and body. It is a plain fact that how chess pieces are moved has
nothing whatever to do with manual dexterity or any other bodily
skill. One can play chess, bridge, and any number of other games
solely by issuing verbal commands, as is the case when chess is played
by mail. "Physical games" designates a quite definite class of objects,
and the term "sport" is confined to this class (though it is not necessarily coterminous with it). The issue is thus wholly terminological;
that is, the question "Why do sports have to involve physical skills?"
is not a well formulated question. The question should be, "What
kind of skill do we find in the class of activities we call sport?" And
the answer is "Physical skill." Thus, chess and bridge appear to have
all the features requisite for something to qualify as a sport, except
that they are not games of physical skill. They do involve skill, and
of a high order; they have a wide following and their popularity is

of sufficiently long standing so that each of them may be characterized as an institution rather than a mere craze. Each can boast international tournaments, a body of experts, teachers, coaches—all the attendant roles and institutions characteristic of the most well-established sports. It is just that physical skill is not involved. (The chess match between Boris Spassky and Bobby Fischer took place after the preparation of this manuscript. Since accounts of the match appeared regularly in the sports pages of the press I am happy, consistently with my view of the fairly arbitrary distinction between sport and other games, to retract, or at least substantially to qualify, my observations here about the relation of physical skills to sport.)

A Wide Following

I have prefected the following game originally created by Kierkegaard. A high ranking official of my university has the constitutional peculiarity that when angry his anger is manifested solely by the appearance of a bead of perspiration at the centre of his forehead which then rolls slowly down his nose, clings for an instant to its tip, and finally falls. If the official's ire continues or recurs, the same steps are repeated. Whenever I have a conference with him I adopt as a pre-lusory goal that state of affairs wherein three separate beads of perspiration shall have progressed through their appointed stages inside of fifteen minutes. And I adopt the constitutive rule that I will refrain from employing as a means to this goal either threats of violence against the person of the official or aspersions on his personal and professional reputation. Although this is, I flatter myself, a pretty good game, I readily admit that it is not a sport. It is too private and too personal to qualify for that status. Imagine my being asked by a colleague in the Faculty of Physical Education what sports I participate in, and my responding that I am very keen on Sweat-Bead.

Still, though Sweat-Bead is not now a sport, it could conceivably become one. If there were a great many people who shared the constitutional peculiarity of my official, and if there were a great many people equipped with the kind of sadism to which this game appeals, and if the rules were clearly laid out and published, and if there were to grow up a body of experts whose concern it was to improve the game and its players, then Sweat-Bead would become a sport. But short of these much to be hoped for developments I must accept the reality that it is simply a highly idiosyncratic game.

Stability

That a game is one of physical skill and that it is very popular is not quite enough to qualify it as a sport. Hula-Hoop, in its hey-day, met these requirements but it would be proper to call Hula-Hoop a craze rather than a sport. The popular following which attends sports must have a stability which is more than mere persistence through time. Even if Hula-Hoop had lasted for fifty years it would still be a craze, only a very tiresome craze.

What is required in addition to longevity is the birth and flowering of a number of attendant roles and institutions which serve a number of functions ancillary to a sufficiently popular game of physical skill. The most important of these functions appear to be the following: teaching and training, coaching, research and development (Can the sport be improved by making such and such changes?), criticism (sports pundits), and archivism (the compilation and preservation of individual performances and their statistical treatment). Not all sports, of course, require all of these ancillary functions in order to be accepted as sports, but at least some of them will be associated to some degree with every game worthy to be called a sport.

SPORT AND SERIOUSNESS

The conventional wisdom about fun and games which, with brief and infrequent counter-tendencies, has prevailed from classical antiquity to the very recent past is well expressed by the following observation of Aristotle: ". . . to exert oneself and work for the sake of playing seems silly and utterly childish. But to play in order that one may exert oneself seems right." Play, games, and sport are seen, on this view, as subordinate to other ends, so that they may be taken seriously only if the ends to which they are subordinate are taken seriously. Thus, sports are regarded as serious insofar as they promote, for example, health, which is accepted as a serious matter; but sport unjustified by some such serious purpose is just frivolity. In a "work" ethic, work is the serious pursuit which gives play (and indeed health) what derivative seriousness it possesses. But in a leisure ethic, of the kind which much of the world appears now to be assuming, these old priorities are rapidly changing. For a person in whom the protestant ethic is quite firmly established it is difficult, if not impossible, to ask the question, "To what further interests is work itself subordinate?" and in times and societies where human and material resources are exceedingly scarce it is perhaps as well for the survival of the human race that such questions are not asked. For under conditions where unremitting labor is necessary for the bare preservation of life, the answer to the question "What are we working for?" is "Just to live." And since the life whose preservation requires continuous toil is just that toil itself, the toiler might well wonder whether the game is worth the candle.

But in a leisure ethic we have not only the leisure to ask why we are working, but the fact of leisure itself provides us with an answer which is not too bleak to bear. The industrial unionist of today who makes a contract demand for shorter working hours is not prompted to do this by Aristotelian considerations. He does not want more time for fishing, bowling, the ball park, or television so that, renewed and refreshed, he can increase his output on the assembly line on Monday. (In any case, that output will also be fixed by the new contract, and cannot be increased.) The attitude of the contemporary worker about work may be expressed as the exact inversion of Aristotle's dictum: "To play so that one may work seems silly and utterly childish; but to work in order that one may play seems right."

I do not think it is too great an overstatement to say that whereas for the Puritan it was work which gave play (as, e.g., exercise) what derivative seriousness it was accorded, it is now play—or at least leisure activities— which gives work a derivative seriousness. Another way to put this is to acknowledge that work is good because it provides us with leisure as well as the means to enjoy leisure. Work is good chiefly because it is *good for* something much better. The things for which it is finally good are good in themselves. They are intrinsic goods. This is not, as a general view, at all novel. It, too, goes back to Aristotle. The only difference in Aristotle's view (and in the view of many others who are in this respect like him) is that for him just a very few things count as intrinsically good, things like virtue and metaphysics. Partisans of this kind have typically managed to get a kind of monopoly on the notion of intrinsic good and have tried, with some success, to persuade the rest of us that only such and such pursuits were worthy of the name. Sometimes it has been holiness, sometimes art, sometimes science, sometimes love. But it seems perfectly clear that any number of things can be intrinsic goods to someone, depending upon his interests, abilities, and other resources, from philately to philosophy (including work itself, if you happen to be Paul Goodman). This view has quite wide, even if tacit, acceptance, I believe, outside of churches and universities.

The new ethic, then, is not only one of greatly increased leisure, it is also one of pluralism with respect to the goods we are permitted to seek in the new time available. It has been some time since our sabbaths were confined to theological self-improvement with the aid of the family bible, of course, but recent changes in our views of leisure activity are just as striking as was our emergence from puritanism. Thus, the view no longer prevails (as it did in the quite recent past) that although leisure was a good thing it was wasted if one did not devote most of it to the pursuit of Culture with a capital C. Today people with the most impeccable cultural credentials may without impropriety savour jazz (even rock) and motor racing.

Although we recognize a class of things which are serious just because they are intrinsically worthwhile, there seems some reason to believe that sports (and games in general) cannot be among these things. It is as though there were something built into the very structure of games which rendered them non-serious. This view is conveyed by the expression, "Of course, such and such is just a game," as though there were something inherently trifling about games. And by the same token, if we find that someone takes a sport or some other game with extraordinary seriousness, we are inclined to say that the pursuit in question has ceased to be a game for him.

This view, though incorrect, may be made quite plausible, I believe, by the following example. Consider The Case of the Dedicated Driver. Mario Stewart (the dedicated driver in question) is a favoured entrant in the motor car race of the century at Malaise. And in the Malaise race there is a rule which forbids a vehicle to leave the track on pain of disqualification. At a dramatic point in the race a child crawls out upon the track directly in the path of Mario's car. The only way to avoid running over the child is to leave the track and suffer disqualification. Mario runs over the child and completes the race.

One is inclined to say that for Mario motor racing is not a sport at all (and certainly not a game!), but a kind of madness. Games (and sports) require a limitation on the means their players may employ, but Mario is obviously the kind of driver who would do anything to win the race. By his insane refusal to stay within proper limits he is no longer playing a game at all. He has destroyed the game.

I submit, however, that we now know what it takes to destroy a game, and that the behaviour of Mario is not what it takes. If Mario had cut across the infield in his efforts to get ahead of the other ,drivers, or if he had earlier violated a rule governing engine capacity in the construction of his vehicle, then his behavior would cease to be game-playing, for he would have broken a constitutive rule. It is thus true to say that there is a limitation imposed in games which is not imposed in other activities, and it is also true that the limitation has to do with the means one can legitimately employ. Hence the plausibility of concluding that Mario was not playing a game, since there appeared to be absolutely no means he would not adopt. But it will be recalled that we earlier discovered that more than one kind of goal is associated with games, and more than one kind of means. The plausibility of the claim that racing for Mario had ceased to be a game rests on a confusion between two of these goals. It is perfectly correct to say that not any means whatever may be used to achieve a *pre-lusory* goal, but this limitation in no way entails a quite different kind of limitation, namely, a limitation on the means for *playing* the game (i.e., attempting to achieve what I earlier called the lusory goal of life.)

The point of the story, of course, is not that Mario did a terrible thing, but that it is possible to make a game or a sport the over-riding concern of one's life without falling into some kind of paradox. That extreme dedication to a pursuit should somehow destroy the pursuit would be the real paradox. But that a person will do anything to continue playing a game does not destroy the game, even though it may destroy the person. So saying to Mario that motor racing is just a game is very much like saying to the Pope that Catholicism is just religion, to Beethoven that the quartets are just music, or to Muhammad Ali that boxing is just a sport.

I therefore conclude that sports are precisely like the other interests which occur prominently as leisure activities. They are a type of intrinsic good which, along with many others, make up the class of goals to which we ascribe that primary seriousness which provides such things as factories, armies, and governments with the derivative seriousness to which they are entitled.

Author's Note. The section of the paper titled *The Elements of Game* is a restatement of the substance of the thesis advanced in "What Is a Game?"[3] However, the language used here is different from the language of that version, and the definition of game-playing that I propose has been somewhat altered. The strategies of the two versions also differ. In "What Is a Game?" I attempted to produce an adequate definition by successively modifying a series of proposed definitions. Here, assuming the adequacy of that definition, I explain and illustrate the elements of game-playing which the definition designates. I should also note that some of the examples used in the present paper were originally used in "What Is a Game?"

REFERENCES

1. Kolnai, A.: "Games and Aims," *Proceedings of the Aristotelian Society* (1966).
2. Suits, Bernard: "Games and Paradox," *Philosophy of Science* (1969).
3. Suits, Bernard: "What Is a Game?" *Philosophy of Science* (1967).

ONTOLOGICAL POSSIBILITIES: SPORT AS PLAY

Scott Kretchmar

It is often thought that play and sport are highly, if not totally, incompatible. The competitive projects of sport stand at odds with the freedom, spontaneity and lack of seriousness thought to be characteristic of play. The extreme goal orientation of sport, including the drive to win, the quest for honor and the thirst for excellence, seems to beg a work, not a play, orientation. It is more correct to say, so the argument runs, that one *works* sport, not plays sport.

In this paper an opposing viewpoint is presented. It is maintained that the competitive fullness of sport and the play gesture are, in a most fundamental sense, wholly compatible but not coextensive. One can *play* sport without compromising elements essential to this highly polarized activity.

The starting point of this analysis is the identification of a given experience which has been lived in its fundamental aspects repeatedly. This phenomenon, including the two aspects of playing and that which is played (sport), is taken as the datum for subsequent scrutiny. Thus, the question suggested by the title— *Ontological Possibilities: Sport as Play*—is not one of sport as play or as something-other-than-play, but a question of the nature of sport as one mode of play. An attempt is made to reduce the play and agonistic elements to fundamental levels and reveal their relationship. The only "conclusions" drawn are descriptions of sport as play, namely—opposition as play and physically strategic opposition as play.

Some may wish to argue that taking a starting point with a given phenomenon is unwarranted. Each time that one steps onto a ball diamond, so the critique might run, he experiences many different phenomena. Sometimes he's happy, sometimes sad, sometimes highly competitive and sometimes noncompetitive. How can a given phenomenon be taken as sport in the play realm? But the phenomenon identified is a reality whether or not persons encounter it frequently or infrequently in certain social settings. One can identify a distinctive cognition and can be ". . . aware of the object as being the same as that which (he) may expect to be aware of in a future experience, as the same as that which, generally speaking, (he) may be aware of in an indefinite number of presentative acts." (10:p.119). Thus, the lack of concern for establishing the identity of sport as play on a majority report of lived experience in a given social setting indicates that the reality of the phenomenon to be described does not depend upon social observation. Agreement is found with Willard who stated that ". . . cognizance is just as cold and hard a fact, is just as much a phase of reality, as is the growth of a tree, the chemical composition of water, or the motion of a planet." (22:p.523).

But it could be argued at this point that if one identifies a phenomenon for analysis, the very identification thereof presupposes a knowledge of that datum. Any subsequent analysis would be nothing more than the gratuitous activity of describing that which was already known. However, an ability to *identify* a phenomenon is quite distinct from an ability to fully *describe* it. One can, as it were, pick many things out of a crowd without being able, in their absence, to describe them. This draws attention to two kinds of knowing (the traditional distinction between "knowing how" and "knowing that"). Thus the identification of a phenomenon does not preclude the possibility of describing the yet obscure or unknown.

An important aspect of the present procedure involves "bracketing" the phenomenon. An attempt is made to gain an access to the datum which is uncontaminated by social, psychological or biological bias. The phenomenon is "disconnected" from the context in which one lives it for the purpose of "seeing" it more clearly. A search is made for the very roots of its intelligibility. While one has no assurance that the "bracketed" phenomenon is ever fully described, the analysis is one which "transcends" the accidents of particular situations in favor of more general distinctions and connections.

A consideration of this stance in relationship to several others which have confronted the issues of sport, play and/or games may help to clarify the rationale for the aforementioned procedure. Neale, Caillois and Schiller produced descriptions of play which, while they may be compatible with one another, have not been reduced to their possible common bases. Neale, speaking from a psychological standpoint, stated that play is adventure which itself is composed of freedom, delight, illusion, and peace. (13). Caillois in surveying the relationship between play and other social forms of behavior indicated that play ". . . remains separate, inclosed, in principle devoid of important repercussion upon the solidarity and continuity of collective and institutional life." (3:p.99). Finally, Schiller, from an aesthetic standpoint, stated, "We must therefore do justice to those who pronounce the beautiful, and the disposition in which it places the mind, as entirely indifferent and unprofitable, in relation to knowledge and feeling." (15:p.266). The question must then be put: in terms of these three perspectives, is there an identifiable common base? While each description provides a broad foundation which itself would support numerous particular lived experiences or social interactions, the analyses still leave important questions unanswered. For example, on what basis is illusion, unimportance and indifference intelligible? One can reduce the experiences further and more fully describe them.

The procedure employed in this paper requires that one begin with his lived experience and as such diverges radically from a second approach to the issues surrounding sport as play, namely—the biological and biologically-based psychological theories. Schiller (15) and subsequently Spenser's (7) notion of play as a manifestation of excess energy, Lazarus' (7) view of play as recovery from work, Hall's (7) recapitulation theory and Groos' (9) teleological concept of play as preparation for adult life are representative of this standpoint. While this is not the place to critique each theory separately several possible problems relative to this general approach should be noted.

First, the biological criteria for play are "realities" which cannot be experienced or lived. One does not confront genetic operations or purposeful biological mechanisms but things such as colors, shapes, bats, balls, joy and anxiety. Curiously, play is defined as something which *has to be present* (e.g. recapitulation) but which cannot be experienced. As Groos stated, "Animals cannot be said to play because they are young and frolicsome, *but rather they have a period of youth in order to play* (emphasis his); for only by so doing can they supplement the insufficient hereditary endowment with individual experience, in view of the coming tasks of life." (9:p.75). Groos subsequently is forced to talk of the "conscious accompaniments" of play though they be fundamentally irrelevant to the question of what play is. That which is closest to man, his sensations and cognitions, are discounted in favor of that which is inaccessible to him but which, on scientific grounds, has to be present.

Second, it should be noted that those who identify play on biological bases must presuppose a given descriptive knowledge of that object. Otherwise, how could Groos, for example, claim that play is teleological necessity? How could he ever discover instances of play? How would he know play when he saw it? Clearly, a descriptive understanding is a prerequisite to a scientific hypothesis. Too often this prerequisite is ignored or only incompletely acknowledged.

Finally, but still very importantly, these theories characterize play in contrast to work or serious adult life. Particularly in the case of Lazarus' notion of play as recovery from work and Groos' play as preparation for adult life, play is seen as a partner to work. In essence, play, in these characterizations, is highly utilitarian. It marks the accomplishment of tasks as important as those of work itself. A possible conclusion to be drawn from this juxtaposition of work and play is that such "play" is indeed itself work. "Play" too stands as a major contributor ot the actualization of important human ends.

A non-biologically-based correlate of this utilitarian notion of play is Walsh's (21) description of play as that which is useful in returning man to a recognition of his "possibilities." Play is a means, a way of reinstating man in Being-in-the-World. (21:p.212). How ironic it is that he accuses the compulsive "worker" of an inability to view play as anything but purposeless when it is precisely the compulsive worker who cannot conceive of play in anything but terms of utility. Again, play is viewed as crucially functional in relationship to valued objectives.

Another approach is that taken by Wittgenstein (23) who claimed that a consideration of games produces understandings labeled "family resemblances." He entreats the reader to "look" at a variety of games and acknowledge the fact that he finds nothing common to all but only similarities and relationships.

Granted, with Wittgenstein's starting point given, one must, if he looks at a great enough variety of games, find exceptions to even the best prospective common elements. But the question remains as to how Wittgenstein can so readily describe the "presence" or "absence" of phenomena such as amusement, patience and competition. (23: p.32e). Are these "proceedings" themselves characterized by "family resemblances?" If so, his descriptions themselves rest upon uncertain, broad similarities. And even if this presents no difficulty, the fact that phenomena are discounted because they are not always "present" in certain culturally-defined social settings seems beside the point in terms of the reality of one's cognizance of amusement, competition or whatever. Patience, for example, is no less a reality by virtue of its *occasional* presence in given existential situations.

With this incomplete description of the method and expectations of this paper and an analysis of some previous alternate procedures, the more substantive portion of the paper must be started. Let us take, for purposes of analysis, participation in a basketball game. As a player I may first be struck by the fact that not as much seems to be "at stake" as there was while performing as, one might say, a beginning college professor. I experience a freedom of separation from worldly concerns. Most obviously, this recreational contest does not involve large sums of money, my financial well-being. But I may immediately sense that this is a rather provincial understanding of supposed distinctive realms of activity. Apart from the difficulty of distinguishing between that which is personally necessary and that which is not, it would seem that whatever the object desired, whether or not it can be shown to be biologically necessary, psychologically critical or socially important, I encounter a fundamentally identical motif. Here I stand, to put it graphically, and there "stands" the object of my desire, perhaps food this time, companionship the next or victory the next. In all cases a something "out there" as yet unsecured, as yet not part of myself hangs in the balance of my thrusts toward it. Despite the fact that I, as a player, can feel that the game has no impact on my "real" life, that it is being played "for itself," I may still stand in wanting relationship to a particular object—victory, glory, or happiness, to name a few. It would seem that the variously-defined "necessary-unnecessary" distinction characterizing work and play respectively is essentially one motif. Removing the biological, sociological and psychological bases for distinguishing the relative value of different projects, I am left with projects of an identical character, namely —gestures aimed at securing that which is not mine.

My unique cognizance of a freedom from as much being at stake must then be based upon something other than a separation from the various "real necessities" catalogued above. When I remove the bases for that bogus distinction I seem to be left with a plain lack of anything missing, or to put it in more positive terms, a fullness or plentitude. The foundation which gives my cognizance distinctiveness is not freedom from *certain* necessities (for that may still be essentially an orientation toward the missing) but simply freedom from absence. Fullness is incompatible with the missing. Fullness is incompatible with anything which will serve as a complement, "savior" or deliverer. Fullness is, however, intelligible in relationship to ex-pression, response or testimony.

One might come at this understanding obliquely from another common experience of his activity, that of a unique temporality. I see the game clock on the wall. The clock serves as an indication that my participation will terminate after forty minutes of play. This constitutes the highly arbitrary temporal boundaries to which I commit myself in the contest. Without needing to, why would I engage in the activity of basketball for forty minutes? Furthermore, during the game I will stop and start time by calling "time outs" and subsequently resume play. "Real time," it seems, is not lived in relationship to such arbitrary ventures, and it cannot be so readily manipulated through many "stops" and "starts." This may be taken by myself as a distinctive characteristic of play.

But again I can intuit a possible identity between this conception of play time and "ordinary" or work time. Time in either case can be considered as a construction or fabrication in response to an incompleteness which change is destined to remedy. In other words, I posit a "sometime" (either a continuity toward a future objective or an historical event) in recognition of my present relative destitution. This temporality can be constructed, in principle, as easily in response to the change required to gain a victory as it is to the change needed to gain happiness, financial security or prestige.

Time as continuity is invented when something is seen as "moving" toward a specific culmination. Fink (5:pp.95-100) spoke of this teleological phenomenon in terms of the striving of a fragmented being for, in his case, *Eudaimonia*. Man, according to Fink, emphasizes the future because it is that which will permit the realization of his objectives. (5:p.99). This time is irreversible. It is the flight forward to a not yet actualized status. As Berger described this alternative, "Having opted for time I would think that plenitude ought to be conquered within time." (1:p.199). The clock time of the game and the work time of futures of fruition are, in the sense mentioned here, essentially identical.

Thus, my distinctive cognition must be based upon a radically different conception of time, a time which is not, as has been shown, validly described in terms of artificiality, arbitrariness or "time-in-time-outs." This reduced awareness of time must acknowledge change (otherwise we have a congealed eternity) but change which is not constructed around a specific sometime. The temporality recognized from this standpoint is a "presence" (5) or a "thick present." (1). It it the catching of a fly ball as the catching of a fly ball, not as a temporal point in a constructed chain of events which leads to victory. It is the drive for a layup as a drive for a layup.

Time as a "thick present" includes acts which are more expressions than strivings. The present stands in relationship to no specific time of fruition. It does not serve as that construction which "carries" man to fulfillment. Thus, my implicit acknowledgement of presence in the act of playing basketball clarifies that act as an expression or, in the more religious terminology of Neale, a celebration. As Berger stated a similar idea, "Time is no longer a milieu in which I work and which encloses me but that of which I have something to make, and my acts are much less works than testimonies." (1:p.199).

To conclude, the artificial time of games can yet be the constructed time leading to a sometime of victory, glory or "total bliss." This time is identical to work time which likewise provides continuity toward a presently desired and presently lacking status. Play time is a simple "birth and death" which issues from fullness.

I can take a third common orientation toward my participation in basketball. I notice that the game includes artificial spatial boundaries. Black lines outline the court. Play space exists only within those lines. I might conclude that these boundaries partially or wholly constitute the uniqueness of play. In the "real" world I encounter no such lines, but only boundaries which signify utility. I do not, in my work world, place myself within artificial spaces which, for utilitarian ends, need not be there. But if I ignore the court lines, may I still maintain my unique cognition of space? It seems so.

To take the position of the antithesis first, one may intuit a possible identity between certain activity in artificially-bound space and work space. This space is dislocated. It is space forever related to an "over there" or a "somewhere." Whether it be a basketball player who feels "lost" in not occupying an appropriate location or a businessman who must trek to another city to close a deal, the actor stands dislocated, in relationship to another place. Thus, the ball-player and businessman may occupy identical spatiality; they both acknowledge a specific inappropriateness or incompleteness relative to their location.

The reduced phenomenon is one of man *with location* not dislocation. In distinction to the dichotomous spatiality without a locus, play space is full locatedness. It is space with a focal point or center. It is the full location of expression. It is the location under the basket as location under the basket, not a locale which is one point among many other points.

Play space is open space because it has a focal point. It is not "in debt" to other places. It does not "stand" as a place on a path of places. It cannot be understood, in short, in terms of number. It is the full and open "here-with-there" as opposed to a "here" in relationship to a specific number of "there's."

To this point play has been identified as resting upon a base of fullness or plenitude and has been described in two of its manifestations, temporality and spatiality. The fullness of play grounds acts of a different order from those based upon incompleteness. The play act, to expand upon one of Neale's points, might be called "adventuring" in the sense that it is not a curtailed thrust toward specific ends. It is abstaining from "writing the script" before the fact. It is facing the unexpected. It is surprise. It is testifying spontaneously to one's fullness *regardless* of the extenuating circumstances in a particular life situation (e.g. one might be taking a terrific beating in a basketball game). It is the courage to remain open to one's possibilities.

Analysis must now be turned more specifically to sport so that compatibility between playing and that which it intends (sport) can be described. My teammates and I face five opponents on the basketball court and attempt to keep them from scoring while we thwart their inhibitory thrusts toward us.

One's first reaction, in light of the previous analysis of play, might be that play in connection with the opposition of sport would force an emasculation of the latter phenomenon. Opposition seems to require the notion of an opponent who stands, as it were, between myself and the coveted victory. If I am successful in overcoming the opponent, the prize is mine. But the prize remains, during the contest, an object which I lack; it is won only in the sometime if I reach a sufficient number of strategic "somewhere's." Those who compete are, by definition, the unfullfilled, the fragmented individuals who contest with one another precisely to rectify this situation. In short, it may appear that opposition, to retain its competitive fullness, must fall into a work motif.

Judgment, however, must be suspended until a more careful examination of opposition is pursued. What is required to maintain the intelligibility of opposition? First, I recognize the importance of my opponents. But are those specific five people necessary? Certainly those five individuals could as easily be another group, and it seems that the actual presence of people themselves may not be required. I can compete as readily, in essence, against myself in striving to make a greater number of shots from a certain place than I did yesterday. I oppose, in a sense, a phantom adversary whose presence is implicit in the record (either actual or hypothetical) to which I attend. Thus, if the actual presence of other persons is not necessary, I must still recognize, at minimum, some variable other distinct from self. A fundamental dichotomy presents itself. I cannot, in short, think of opposition without considering *that* which is opposed.

It is most important to note that this other need not be that which I want to become or that which threatens my acquiring something else which I lack. This point needs to be argued. Beside the self-evident fact that the oppositional dichotomy must be a variable one (I must change in my attempts to oppose you, and you must change— either actually as I face you or virtually through your record to which I attend—to oppose me. I cannot oppose an inanimate object such as a mountain.), opposition seems to require the presence of *theme*. The polarities of the dichotomy require that which will assure intersection. Theme is often manifest in spatial, temporal and intentional phenomena. We share a given space; we share a given time; we share a certain kind of project. Quite clearly the other in this dichotomy must be seen as a cooperator, as Suits (19), Fraleigh (6), and others have indicated, before opposition becomes intelligible. A view of the other, at least in terms of this prerequisite of theme, as the embodiment of something which I want to become or as that which holds me in my possible incompleteness is not required.

But this intersecting, variable dichotomy betrays another characteristic, that of hindrance. It is here that the apparent incompatibility between full play and full opposition seems to shine through most brightly. When one considers hindrance he must think of *hindrance from* something. In basketball I am hindered from either scoring points or blocking other persons' attempts to do the same. In this sense opposition does include a recognition of the not-yet completed or negotiated. If this is the only way in which I can understand hindrance, then I am indeed blocked from that which will complete me, that which constitutes my fulfillment. If this is the only way in which I can understand hindrance, then I am condemned to perpetual *working* sport toward satisfaction.

Such a recognition of hindrance serves as a reminder that I may remain forever discordant, fragmentary or insufficient. Hindrance blocks the path to the sometime, somewhere or something of the work world. It threatens my urgent projects.

Paradoxically this hindrance is still necessary in the sense that it is required for the successful termination of the work-quest. Happiness cannot be gained unless one overcomes something, unless one prevails in spite of hindrance. Hindrance, therefore, is at once feared and needed.

Hindrance in this work ethos is a result of minimal sharing under the prerequisite of theme. Only those necessities which allow projecting polarities to intersect are in evidence. Cooperation is merely condoned as a means to an end. I cooperate with the other only in the extent to which it allows me to gain that which is lacking, that from which I am hindered.

But the question remains whether or not the made basket or successful block of another's shot need be only that which I lack, that which I am only *hindered from*. It seems that hindrance from is also a *hindrance for* and that under this notion the compatibility of play and opposition becomes more apparent. I may be hindered from making baskets, but such hindrance *allows* me to express my testimony. I express myself *with* hindrance, not through or in spite of hindrance. It is valued for itself.

Hindrance in this mode is not threatening, for it blocks nothing which is lacking. It is rather to be preserved because continued testimony depends upon its presence. This does not suggest that I do not try to convert baskets. It merely indicates that "victory" is a continuously unfolding experience. It *is* my expression, not a pre-existent object which I somehow secure for myself.

Such hindrance also has implications for the concept of theme. Theme is not a minimal agreement but rather a maximal cooperation. The recognition is one of mutual dependence. I need the hindrance you can offer for my expression, and you need the hindrance I provide for your testimony. We do not have the ambivalence of the worker on a quest who needs us only to surpass us in his conquest, who both searches us out and fears us, who wants our resistance only to ultimately "annihilate" that force.

Metheny's discussion on the etymology of "contest" (a derivation of *con* and *testare* meaning to testify with) is instructive. (12). When one testifies, he expresses or displays that which he has whether it be knowledge, physical prowess, faith or some other ability or trait. He "lays out" his particular or unique fullness. Thus, the physically contesting individual, in the true sense of the term, displays that which *is* his, his particular grace, his particular strength, his particular agility. In the contest, one is indeed hindered for.

Two motifs of opposition have been outlined, each one, in principle, equally intelligible in that dichotomy, variation, theme and hindrance are acknowledged. The work schema includes a characterization of the other (dichotomy) as minimally cooperative (variation-theme) and as that which stands between (hindrance) me and my objective. Victory or defeat is something distinct from my unfolding self which I, at a future time, gain. The other must be eliminated for my goal to be secured.

On the other hand the play impulse requires a characterization of the other (dichotomy) as fully and essentially cooperative (variation-theme) in the mode of inhibiting me (hindrance) for a certain expression. The hindering other needs to be preserved, for expression ends when a verdict is reached, when the other is "destroyed" or when the other "destroys" me.

The analysis needs to be carried further to include a discussion of physical contributions to oppositional projects. I intuit, on the court, a certain relevancy in terms of my movements or static positions. I am too early, on time, too far downcourt or positioned correctly. Self as body is lived as strategic for changes desired.

It seems evident that relevancy could retain its nature of strategic relationship in either the play or work motif. My body limitedness temporally and spatially could be conceived of as strategic in terms of my desire to exhibit my particular fullness. Or this limitedness could be relevant in terms of a future objective.

As indicated above, my body relevancy in expression would be a relevancy in the "now," a becoming which paradoxically requires no construction of futures in which something is to be gained. Likewise my relevancy with regard to location is a relevancy for the "here," the locale of my unfolding expression. In psychological terminology this total experience of body relevancy in play can be described as "grace." (13). Play relevancy is complete relevancy. This is no relationship to other changes needed.

My relevant temporal and spatial action in work, on the other hand, is relevancy related to the "not here" and the "not yet." Relevancy is understood as that which *can be* done as body, changes which can be provoked, conclusions which can be achieved. Relevancy is always incomplete relevancy. It stands in relationship to the unaccomplished.

In drawing these ideal distinctions between one's consciousness of play and work it is not being suggested that one's lived experience in any situation would include the pure content of one or the other phenomenon. In playing a ball game an individual's lived experience may be grounded in play one moment and in work the next. Likewise while "on the job" a person may alternate between playing and working and live the nuances of both.

In reflecting upon personal lived experiences in terms of the above analysis, we may have more difficulty discovering instances of full play than work. It seems that when we interact, even on the "play" field, we often stand in relationship to yet other things which are desired. We work at basketball to gain the victory; we work at jogging to feel better; we work at taking vacations to find relaxation.

The schema of opposition may be particularly vulnerable to the work motif because it provides an other which presents an image of hindrance. Our common response is to assume that hindrance stands in the way of something which we lack. We may encounter opposition at the office, for example, and respond to it in terms of self-preservation, self-advancement and self-gratification. Thus, many of us, even those in physical education and others who profess an allegiance to sport, have difficulty playing.

It may be significant that several theorists consider dance a more viable form for the manifestation of play. Huizinga stated this directly,

". . . dance. . . is always at all periods and with all peoples pure play, the purest and most perfect form of play that exists." (11:p.164). And Van der Leeuw wrote, "When something matters in life, one feels festive; the expression of life becomes stylized into a fixed, rhythmical form." (13:p.149). Or as Neale put it quite simply, "To *play* (emphasis mine) a game is to dance." (13:p.64).

Thus, it may be the rare performer who consistently *plays* sport, though on the basis of this analysis such an activity was found to be wholly intelligible. It is the playing sportsman whose cup "runneth over" and whose becoming is more an adventurous celebration than a determined quest.

REFERENCES

1. Berger, Gaston: "A Phenomenological Approach to the Problem of Time." *Readings in Existential Phenomenology,* Nathaniel Lawrence and Daniel O'Connor (eds.). Englewood Cliffs, Prentice-Hall, 1967.
2. Blumenfeld, Walter: "Observations Concerning the Phenomenon and Origin to Play," *Philosophy and Phenomenological Research,* Vol. 1, 470-478 (June, 1941).
3. Caillois, Roger: "Unity of Play: Diversity of Games," *Diogenes,* Vol. 19, 92-121 (Fall, 1957).
4. Dearden, R.F.: "The Concept of Play," *The Concept of Education,* R.S. Peters (ed.). London, Routledge & Kegan Paul, 1967.
5. Fink, Eugen: "The Ontology of Play." *Philosophy Today,* Vol. 4, 95-110 (Summer, 1960).
6. Fraleigh, Warren P.: "The Moving 'I'." Unpublished manuscript, San Jose State College, 1968.
7. Giddens, A.: "Notes on the Concepts of Play and Leisure," *Sociological Review,* Vol. 12, 72-89 (March, 1964).
8. Graves, H.: "A Philosophy of Sport." *Contemporary Review,* Vol. 78, 877-893 (Decmeber, 1910).
9. Groos, Karl: *The Play of Animals.* New York, D. Appleton, 1898.
10. Gurwitsch, Aron: "On the Intentionality of Consciousness," *Phenomenology,* Joseph J. Kockelmans (ed.). Garden City, Doubleday, 1967.
11. Huizinga, Johan: *Homo Ludens.* Boston, Beacon Press, 1950.
12. Metheny, Eleanor: *Connotations of Movement in Sport and Dance.* Dubuque, Wm. C. Brown, 1965.
13. Neale, Robert E.: *In Praise of Play.* New York, Harper & Row, 1969.
14. Riezler, Kurt: "Play and Seriousness," *The Journal of Philosophy,* Vol. 38, No. 19, 505-517 (September, 1941).
15. Schiller, J.C. Freidrich: "Letters upon the Aesthetic Education of Man,"

Harvard Classics—Literary and Philosophical Essays, Vol. XXXII, Charles W. Eliot (ed.). New York, P.F. Collier & Son, 1910.

16. Schmitz, Kenneth L.: "Sport and Play: Suspension of the Ordinary." Unpublished paper presented at the Annual Meeting of the American Association for the Advancement of Science, Dallas, Texas, December 28, 1968.
17. Seward, George: "Play as Art," *The Journal of Philosophy,* Vol. 41, 178-184 (March, 1944).
18. Sheets, Maxine: *The Phenomenology of Dance.* Madison, The University of Wisconsin, 1966.
19. Suits, Bernard: "What Is a Game?" *Philosophy of Science,* Vol. 34, 148-156 (June, 1967).
20. Vernes, Jean-Rene: "The Element of Time in Competitive Games," Victor A. Velen (trans.). *Diogenes,* Vol. 50, 25-42 (September, 1965).
21. Walsh, J.H.: *A Fundamental Ontology of Play and Leisure.* Ann Arbor, University Microfilms, 1969.
22. Willard, Dallas: "A Crucial Error in Epistemology," *Mind,* Vol. 76 (October, 1967).
23. Wittgenstein, Ludwig: *Philosophical Investigations.* G.E. Anscombe (trans). Oxford: Basil Blackwell, 1953.

AN EXISTENTIAL PHENOMENOLOGICAL ANALYSIS OF SPORT AS A RELIGIOUS EXPERIENCE

WILLIAM MORGAN

The encompassing nature of sport, its compelling, essential substantive quality is a thematic little attended to either in a systematic vein or as a philosophic fragment contained in essay form. Instead a myriad of observations, proffered in a passive superficial rendering, occasion the contemporary heightened interest in the study of sport. Clothed in the rubric of an extraneous lexicon, frequent allusions are made concerning sport and its instrumental propensities (i.e., as that which involves and assuages aggressive impulses, as that which offers an objectively garnered vision of man via its social, political manifestations). The logical implication inferred from this extrinsic perspective is the equation of the alleged profundity of sport to its affective regulated interest, to wit, its institutionalization as a collective social entity. Boyles' comments regarding sport discern this proclivity towards the mass appeal of sport:

Sport permeates any number of levels of contemporary society, and it touches upon and deeply influences such disparate elements as status, race relations, business life, automative design, clothing styles, the concept of the hero, language, and ethical values. (6:pp.3-4).

This appeal itself is often used as an exemplar case in identifying sport as a social institution.

Hence, the provocative elements of sport are attributed to its extraneous capacity to generate a varied sort of collective responses. So construed, the quintessence of sport is identified precisely in such overt terms. In a similar ontological supposition, in which essence is correlative to the generation of mass appeal, some suggest that any form of habitual regulated praise deserves subsequent classification as a form of the religious (a theme entertained by Seeley as found in James magnum opus *Varieties of Religious Experience*). The admittance of sport as a religious manifestation on the assumption advanced in this criteria is an obvious one, indeed, and one frequently made in a surreptitious manner. However, the analytical intent of this paper lies in an opposite affect, and therefore constitutes an antithetical alternative to those who espouse an identification of sport and religion to their extrinsic capabilities. Such a view denigrates the living substance of sport in favor of an appeal to its exploited forms, especially the inculcation of sport from a political and economic perspective. In a contrary manner, the primordial quest embodied in the athletic domain belies the ostensible, instrumental claims made upon it and coalesces in the heart of being, as a fundamental aspiration of being itself. Our concern then, remains with sport as it is, as it reveals itself to be in conscious experience, and not with its synthetic, provincial substitute, its inimical, displaced, extrinsic focus.

It is in terms of being that the essential structures of sport are rendered intelligible as incisive meaning forms. The ontological sphere of sport is unveiled in its cultural-artistic form and ultimately in its religious development. As a stirring cultural force, sport shares with the other forms of culture a transcendent pursuit. The forms of culture are primarily articulated (Hegel, Dilthey) in the fine arts, philosophy, religion, and may we add sport and athletics. The import of their respective forms is based in being, the life of the spirit. As Wilde notes:

The forms of culture are not mere forms of knowledge about the world of existence but are the forms in which man articulates, discovers, has and fulfills his being, or in which Being fulfills itself in man. (40:p.19).

These sublime forms of human actuality all converge in the encompassing forms of infinite existence as realized and encountered through the finite individual.

Thus, through the pursuits of philosophy, the fine arts, sport and athletics, and ultimately the religious consciousness we find a fundamental spiritual intent in terms of the ontological polar elements of finite and infinite existence. These transcendent forms, albeit differing in their phenomenological structures, aspire to absolute spirit, the reality of being. The philosophic encounter of the absolute takes the form of a reflective illumination and conceptualization of the life of the spirit, consciousness as embedded in human existence, through reason and the intuitive comprehension and understanding of meta-phenomenal reality. It arises out of our *being-in-the-world* in response to the primary datum of philosophy, wonder or astonishment. In Heideggerian terms it involves a tuning-in manner of correspondence with relational being. Consequently, the ontological stance remains as the primordial quest of the philosopher in which the "mystery of being" is not simply dispelled but affirmed in a reflective manner. Similarly, in the artistic sphere we witness a further illumination of reality and a concomitant transformation of reality in an integrative fashion. The object of the artistic consciousness, being, is mediated in and through the representative products of creative, expressive existence. Hence, the artistic sphere involves a sensual form embodying a spiritual content, a supra-conscious, ideal intention. Hegel comments on this quality of the artistic consciousness:

The task of art is to represent a spiritual idea to direct contemplation in sensuous form . . . The value and dignity of such representation lies in the correspondence and unity of the two sides, of the spiritual content and its sensuous embodiment. (24:pp.318-319).

The athletic realm involves the quest for being, realized through its fundamental mode of embodiment the human body and through the medium of human movement. As a cultural form it expresses an artistic pursuit mediated through the perfection of athletic performance whose constraint is an artistically-embodied athletic excellence. The athletic situation also aspires to a basic embodiment of the religious consciousness realized through the contingencies of bodily existence. This ultimate religious quest transcends the representative artistic sport performance in an affirmation of total strife in which the forces of spiritual existence unwind in the serious pursuit of meaning. Forrest articulates the thin tension and unity between the artistic and religious spheres which we have noted concerning the athletic situation:

> The aesthetic experience contains already within itself the intent of the religious experience, and it anticipates that which is of a purely religious nature. The aesthetic experience prepares the ground for something which transcends it and in this manner it announces within us the advent of a new order. (12:p.159).

In its most majestic form sport aspires to the evincement of pure spirit obtained only by the purely religious act. The athlete embodies the totality of his being in the projected performance, as the abiding concern of his involvement. Hence, sport as an existent form is predisposed, in a relational manner, to the import of the contest. Form and import conjoin as elements in the religiously inspired performance. Thus, the dimension of the religious, of the unconditioned substance of existence, as saturated within the athletic phenomena constitutes a fundamental nuance of sport, cognizant of the very basis of spirit to sport as a cultural form.

The relation of sport, as existent form, to its ultimate import is not one of annihilation in which sport becomes religion but contrarily, one of basic transcendence in which form and import are unified in meaningful actuality. Hence, this union is best formulated in linguistic terms in the following manner: sport as a religious, conscious experience, not sport in religion nor religion in sport. The athletic phenomenon attains religious dimensions as a fused identity and not as a merger of two discernible entities, such that one implies the other. Sport then, attends to being and arouses spirit in its ultimate form although spirit is never possessed but grasped, illuminated but neved definitively deciphered. Tillich's theological categories of form, content, and import, delineate the spiritual form of cultural creations in light of their religious import:

> Form and content reside on one polar element and at the other polar

element we find import—meaning . . . The form can lose its necessary relation to the content because the content may recede in significance before the predominant abundance of the import. In this way the form acquires the quality of being detached from the content; it may stand in immediate relation to the import. It becomes a form in a paradoxical sense . . . In the import, then, appears that ultimate reference which is called the religious. (1:p.78).

Hence, the religious aspiration constitutes the most grandiose quest of the sport and athletic phenomenon. This transcendent form persists as the primordial structure of sport, it formulates the very core of its intimate searching pursuit, and is not merely an ascribed accidental feature.

Finally, noting our previous considerations, all the various forms of culturally productive activity culminate in the heart of the religious consciousness. Thus, in one sense the religious reality is found in the abyss of these cultural manifestations as the ground of all activities of the spirit. Tillich speaks to this point:

Religion is the aspect of depth in the totality of the human spirit . . . The religious aspect points to that which is ultimate, infinite, unconditional in man's spiritual life. (37:p.7)

Hence, the religious reality is not only one separate entity among other entities but the *depth* of all cultural aspirations. The multifaceted ideals underlying the pursuit of the various cultural forms, beauty, truth, reality, and athletic excellence, achieve fruition through their import in the religious consciousness. Their particular endeavors belie apparent exclusiveness and merge in the desideratum of and for being.

Yet in another sense, from the standpoint of reason, the esoteric nature of the religious consciousness resists any reductionistic attempt to render the religious reality to a pre-determined mode. Its substance is the unconditional character of the absolute beyond mediation, pure spirituality. Hegel depicts the unmediated quality of the religious consciousness in noting this axial point as the basis of transition from the artistic to the religious consciousness. "When the mind perceives that no material embodiment is adequate to the expression of spirit, it passes from the sphere of art to that of religion." (9:p.279). The object of the religious is thus, pure spirituality and, hence, the religious consciousness constitutes the supreme form and expression of spirit. In sum, the heart of the religious is the absolute, which also assumes the substance of the culturally educed efforts and thus, the form of the religious is for the most part a cultural one.

Given the ontological foundation of sport as cultural-religious form and our brief discussion of the transcendental nature of the forms of culture, some pertinent considerations command our attention. Particularly, in this line, it is deemed necessary to more definitively decipher the major characteristics of sport before proceeding to the more compelling concerns of our major thesis, sport as a religious form. It is with the identification of spirit as the nexus of the sport and athletic situation that we may distinguish sport from its putative bedfellows; namely, play, recreation, and physical education. In terms of the latter activities, recreation and physical education are bent towards utilitarian considerations. That is, as decided modes of ongoing and undergoing activity they operate principally upon exoteric parameters. In the case of recreation the element of extrinsicality is the axiom of hedonism. Recreation is bound to the pursuit of gratuitous well-being as governed and interpreted by the hedonistic principle of gratification. The other element of utility underlying the recreative impulse is a form of pedagogy. In formal and practical locution recreation is further controlled by the mandate to propagate worthwhile leisure goals through the use of varied sorts of leisure activities whether they be predominantly physiological or cerebral in morphological type. The appeal is then, basically a sensual one inculcated further by fundamental instrumental concerns as construed from a pedagogical base.

Physical education, in a similiar vein, is an enterprise founded upon exclusively pedagogical goals. The utility invested is, then, a pedagogical one which focuses on the use of physical activity to perpetrate communally based goals from a pragmatic foundation. The outcomes it actively seeks are utilitarian, tangible goals such as health, social adaptation, developmental motor skills, mental health, etc. Such goals are solicited from a diverse and vast conglomerate of physically oriented activities to include sport, athletics, game situations, exercise, dance, etc. all under one label which makes their scope and perspective suspect. The justification here as in recreation lies separate from the activity itself. It proceeds then, on the instrumental claims made for it and not upon the activity itself.

Sport is thus, to be distinguished from recreation and physical education by virtue of its intrinsic, spiritual focus, as that which is utterly based in being, and by the latter group's disposition to the extrinsic, as that undertaken or participated in for reasons other than the medium itself. However, the relation and distinction of sport to and from play persists on different and somewhat consonant grounds. In its broadest sense, the play impulse encompasses a universal attitude, one which accompanies a broad spectrum of spiritual creations. Hence, it is a perspective of spirit in its ideal sense. "In play there is something at play which transcends the immediate needs of life and imparts meaning to the action . . . the very fact that play has a meaning implies a non-materialistic quality in the nature of the thing itself." (18:p.23). In this sense play is similar to sport, art, philosophy, and religion in terms of a non-utilitarian intentional base. As Cassirer argues noting the relationship of play to art:

> . . . play and art bear a close resemblance to each other. They are non-utilitarian and unrelated to any practical end. In play as in art we leave behind our immediate practical needs in order to give our world a new shape. (8:p.164).

In terms of a permeating attitude play embodies a spiritual character.

However, beyond noting the relationship of intention in play as similarly embraced in sport, we propose a fundamental distinction between the two entities. That is, play in its delimited sense lacks a substantive base, it fails to achieve a coherent form, and consequently its manifestations are dominated by a sentiment of diversion, an air of illusiveness pervades. Hence, the forms of culture, to include sport, although discharged in a basic play spirit, attend to a higher comprehension of spirit in a more definitive manner which belies any tint of diversion. They go beyond play in their serious, intensifying command of spirit. Osterhoudt's comments relating to the respective treatments of play by Santayana, Kant, and Schiller lend insight to this contention:

> In each instance the play element is a mere condition of interaction, a quality of activity and is not a specific form of activity, nor a conceptual entity. It is one manner in which man confronts his milieu, entertains and treats it. As such, it is somewhat non-descript, and deficient in terms of being a necessary condition for art, to include sport. (29:p.16).

Cassirer's remarks concerning the diversionary and illusive nature of play further elucidates our proposed distinction between play and sport, although it is expressed in terms of play and art:

> What we call aesthetic semblance is not the same phenomenon that we experience in games of illusion. Art gives us a new kind of truth—a truth not of empirical things but of pure forms . . . The enjoyment of art does not originate in a softening or relaxing process but in intensification of all our energies. The diversion which we find in play is the very opposite of that attitude which is a necessary prerequisite of aesthetic contemplation and aesthetic judgment. (8:pp.164-165).

It is the case, then, that sport, art, philosophy, and religion are occasioned by a basic play spirit. Yet the play sentiment is transformed in each of these forms in a new, more enriching apprehension of spirit. Thus, sport is not simply an extension of play for they subsist on different ontological levels. More concisely, sport promulgates the intent of the play spirit in the formation of a new transcendent nuance, one which goes beyond and is more than play:

> . . . sport is more than play. It includes devotion, care, respect, concern, and responsiveness toward the desired outcomes. It is serious. (36:p.6).

In sum, it is evident that sport is amenable to play, though no more so than the arts, philosophy, or religion, and yet it is equally true that it is much more than play, that it involves a more decisive form of human actuality.

In passing, it is noted that the primary disposition of sport, the intrinsic, conscious aspiration of being, is accompanied by other definitive characteristics which further distinguishes the realm of sport. Concisely, sport is viewed as an activity which demands assiduous exertion, the employment of complex and diffuse psychomotor skills, and is intensely competitive in nature. It is then, permeated by the demand for bodily displayed excellence, as realized in a total manner, incorporating the discursive medium of human movement in a defined pattern. It shares with play a free intention, specific space and time parameters, stands apart from the every-day world, involves a specific form of ritual, and manifests an intent participation.

In its purest form it is known as athletics which is specified by the athlete's unmediated constraint to being. The form of this athletic encounter involves: the direct confrontation of the athlete with his particular medium, the encounter of the athlete with the elemental forces of nature, and finally the encounter of the athlete with another bodily opponent. In this context, it is appropriate to regard the athletic situation, not as a game occurrence but rather as a basic contest. The universal category of games remains a legitimate label for the domain of sport which differs from athletics principally in its mediated, dependent form. In this case the athlete is subject to extenuating circumstances, albeit the focus retains a predominately individual intent. However, the quality of involvement lacks the categorical participation of the athlete in response to the ascetic, demanding nature of athletics. Thus, sport includes team sports and those individual sports exhibiting a dependent quality, for instance such sports as automobile racing display a resolve dependent, in a great measure, upon the performance of a mechanical object. This cursory definition of sport persists in consonance, for the most part, with those distinctions espoused respectively by Keating and Osterhoudt and in fact proceeds principally from their provocative investigations.

Our present exposition of sport has attempted to argue for its most compelling nature, its constitutive, enduring form. The primordial impetus of sport as an enterprise has been traced to its cultural-religious form, as that which enhances spirit in an artistically based excellence and most convincingly in its ultimate religious form. Spirit is, then, the summum bonum of sport. It accounts for its essential nature. In general, all activities of the spirit involve both the depth of being and its unfolding meaning, the logos, the dynamic opening quality of the spirit. Hence, spirit embraces an all encompassing spectrum, it transcends expressed dualisms and is monistic in a theistic manner. As Tillich remarks:

> Life as spirit transcends the duality of body and mind. It also transcends the triplicity of body, soul, and mind . . . Spirit is not a part nor is it a special function. It is the all embracing function in which all elements of the structure of being participate. Life as spirit can only be found by man and only in man, for only in him is the structure of being completely realized. (15:p.273).

In sum, sport demands consideration in terms of its fundamental spiritual intention such that it is rendered intelligible only in that constraint to being.

However, our remarks at this juncture have presupposed the dialectical lived forms of being unveiled in the actuality of the conscious experience of sport. Our ontological formulations, disclosed and bound to a metaphysics of being rather than to a metaphysics of pure categories, are adjudicated in terms of the existential elements from which they proceed. Hence, ensuing discussion will, in a cursory fashion, attempt to briefly sketch the major existential elements indigenous to the sport experience, focusing primarily on their transcendent qualities. It is in these immersed impressions of sport that the genuine unfolding of an ontology of sport may be consumated. Our reflections then, remain attuned to the essential manifestations of the sport experience as consciously structured. The necessity of this perspective is requisite to resisting the notion of sport as a dynamic form in a purely analytical or linguistic approach. For it is apparent that sport is only truly capable of being known as it is existentially lived.

The existential demand of being is basic to the athletic condition as a lived quest. Its appeal is manifested in a dialectical manner. The dialectic form evinced in sport revolves around the intensification of existence affected in sport and aroused in a vitiating fashion in the form of experiential antinomies. Slusher's analysis provides insight:

> . . . within the drama of the activity all of existence is revealed—joy and sorrow, excitement and boredom, hope and despair, victory and defeat, and ultimately life and death. When man is faced with situations of this magnitude the question of being is fundamental. (36:p.17).

The conflicting forms encountered in sport have as their object the negation of every object, non-being. The demonic force of non-being is found within the very aspiration of being embodied in the athlete's performance, as an element of that quest itself. It is included or self-contained in being in a negative sense, albeit, its presence presupposes the a priori form of its intended negation:

> Being has non-being within itself as that which is eternally present and eternally overcome in the process of the divine life . . . Non-being is dependent on the being it negates . . . It points first of all to the ontological priority of being over non-being. (37:pp.34-40).

Sport involves experiences which are tension-producing, reflecting the keen focusing of all the available energies of the athlete into his medium of expression. Hence, the destructive, vitiating tendencies of sport, as one polar element of its nature, leads the athlete to an existential awareness of his finitude as manifested in anxiety. Anxiety implicates the purge of being, non-being, which in turn inextricably brings out the finite character of the athlete's endeavor. The basic ontological element, non-being, as revealed in the form of anxiety, adheres steadfastly to the sport phenomenon as itself an element essential to its spiritual aspirations. Indeed, Tillich contends that an ontology of anxiety is basic to human existence: "The basic anxiety, the anxiety of a finite being about the threat of non-being, cannot be eliminated. It belongs to existence itself." (37:p.39).

The demonic, invested structures of sport comprise a basic encounter to existence spiritually through the loss of meaning, the despair of emptiness. This apprehension proceeds along a particular path but inevitably trickles back to a general estrangement from meaning. Hence, absurdity becomes an increasingly real element in the athletic encounter. An encounter characterized by its elusive potentiality in which the constraint to serious pursuit is subject to dissipation. The absurd datum manifests itself in the self-world encounter as intensified in the sport context: "The absurd is essentially a divorce. It lies in neither of the elements compared; it is born of their confrontation." (7:p.23). The absurd consciousness arises in the struggle to be, a struggle constantly discharged to the athlete. The spirit is of no consequence if its absurd possibility is not lived. Hence, elements of deep-seated struggle, emptiness, agony, despair, conscious restlessness, which Camus warns us not to mistake as immature unrest, are all found in the athlete's search for meaning. Most assuredly it is found as a sort of interlude in which one's self, in conscious form, encroaches upon one's serious pursuit, an awakening of the vestige of flesh, finiteness:

> When I am not my dance, I am self-conscious. I am naked and exposed . . . Every motion is an effort. I'm too acutely me. I am necessarily me. (13:p.67).

Human revolt, in Camus' sense—as an act precipitated for the sake of the act itself, devoid of meaning—is the enigma of actuality revealed in the absurd encounter. The revolt of the athlete, in a specific sense, takes on the absurd dimension in response to the antinomies confronted therein. Yet despair engenders its own destruction in the void of empty actuality: "To despair over oneself, in despair to be rid of oneself, is the formula for all despair." (22:p. 153).

The encompassing magnitude of sport is located in its concrete stratum, as a boundary situation of existence. The ground of existence, of the conditioned subject, is aroused in the full depth of the athlete's performance. As a boundary situation it cannot be glossed over but only encountered or disengaged. Jaspers elucidates the nature of situations which repose at the limits of thought and determinant action:

> . . . the questionableness of all existence means the impossibility of find-ing peace within existence as such. The way in which this latter, in all ultimate situations seems shattered through and through is its antinomical structure . . . those are antinomies that are insoluable, stand at the limit of knowing and thinking, and, when properly comprehended, prove incapable of being dismissed as errors, mistakes, misunderstandings, or as merely apparent. (39:p.159).

It is precisely within the compelling, concrete crisis of sport as lived struggle, in which all formulas fail to apply, beyond the limits of pure reason, that being or transcendence is encountered.

The synthesis culminating in being is then, a lived synthesis, affirmed in a total manner. This is not to adhere to a philosophy of paradox, for we wish to avoid things of this nature, but to admit a truth re-vealed by Kierkegaard: "The systematic Idea is the identity of subject and object, the unity of thought and being. Existence, on the other hand, is their separation." (40:p.65). The only genuine synthesis, from the standpoint of an actual religious comprehension, of the finite and the infinite is in existence, as a holistic conscious-experience. This unity however, is not an identity-in-difference but a recognition of a separating of the finite from the infinite, although not implying their absolute separation but contrarily their legitimate basis of union. Hence, synthesis is affected in a total manner, and in the grasp of faith for the transition to the religious is itself insecure and never possessed. The absurb cannot be simply dispelled con-ceptually despite the effervescent grandeur of the mind. For the synthesis can only arise in the athlete's affirmation of finite actuality in terms of infinite, absolute potentiality, the profound relation of self to being itself. Transcendence becomes the finite's grasp of infinite spirit as the ground of its being. It unfolds as the total relation to and awareness of the unconditioned power of being in that finiteness:

> The finite is posited as finite within the process of the divine life, but it is reunited with the infinite within the same process. It is distinguished from the infinite, but it is not separated . . . Man is aware of his finitude because he has the power of transcending it and of looking at it. (1:pp. 275-276).

The existential relationship of self to absolute spirit is presupposed in a purely conceptual transition of the finite to the infinite. The latter implies an abstract impersonal infinite being. For as Schelling notes concerning the distinction between positive and negative philosophy, prior to suggesting their legitimate re-unification, from ideas all one can deduce is ideas:

> Without an active God . . . there can be no religion, for religion presupposes an actual, real relationship of man to God . . . At the end of negative philosophy, I have only possible and not actual religion . . . It is with the transition to positive philosophy that we first enter the sphere of religion. (9:p.170).

The idea takes on meaning in its turn to existence and the embracing of a complete existential-ideal union, for religion is not merely feeling, nor is it purely theoretical, nor is it simply practical or concrete, but it is all of these things bound in and to being. Hence, the athlete embodies the total intentional structure indigenous to the religious sphere in response to the ultimate situations encountered in the athletic context. Bannister, premier four minute miler, and Maurice Herzog, mountain climber, provide incisive articulation:

> Sooner or later in sport we run into situations too big for us to master. In real life we dodge them . . . in sport we cannot. As a result, sport leads us to the most remarkable self discovery. (3:p.218).

> In overstepping our limitations, in touching the extreme boundaries of man's world, we have come to know something of its true splendor. In my worst moments of anguish, I seemed to discover the deep significance of existence which till then I had been unaware. (17:p.12).

These situations are not incidental to sport but rather they are attributable to the dynamic nature of sport itself, as basic to its most enduring form.

The lucidity of being in sport is precisely realized in the athlete's turn from the mundaneness of mere existence to the meaningfulness of enriching conscious existence. The ego then, retains its necessary self-centered character, of course devoid of the egocentricity of the child, but is led beyond itself not by lauding the ego but by challenging the self such that superficiality is disparaged in the wake of sincere and earnest commitment. "Athletes do not retreat from life during sports performance, they immerse themselves completely and authentically." (14:p.43). Sport in one sense is an exercise of the ego but in this case ego is compelled in a far greater and more arduous manner than in the case of mere egoism. For sport unveils a maddening quality of power based in being, in the form of incessant commitment. Sport, then, becomes a genuinely ultimate concern, apart from its false, idolatrous and manufactured benefactor. The unconditioned life of spirit is liberated in magnificent performances attesting to the spirit that we embrace as ours, to the spirit which embraces all that we are and yet more. In sport, the athlete does not derive actuality from potentiality nor potentiality from actuality but unites both polar elements as equally true and equally significant in striving performance.

The madness of sport, heretofore, examined from a narrow psychological perspective, to wit Beisser's *Madness in Sport,* delineates the ultimacy of the athletic pursuit. It is not a psychological aberrant form that we allude to here but, contrarily, the intent resolve of the athlete to usurp the ordinary in search of the extraordinary, the constraint to being as evidenced in the athlete's performance: "Running becomes almost an inescapable way of life, and certainly the focus of life." (10:p.63). In this sense perhaps the athlete is a fanatic but no less than the philosopher, the artist, and the religious man. For those grasped by spirit in which the grandeur of being fulfilled itself in man are all in one manner of speaking mad, in that they depart from the common, the ordinary, the pragmatic, in terms of spirit. In this departure true fulfillment arises in the confrontation and overcoming of self, not in fantasy but through pain and agony and the realization of life at a far greater and deeper level. Laing incisively remarks:

> The ego is the instrument for living in this world. If the ego is broken up or destroyed then the person may be exposed to other worlds, real

in different ways from the more familiar territory of dreams, imagination, perception or fantasy . . . True sanity entails in one way or another the dissolution of the normal ego, that false self competently adjusted to our alienated social reality: the emergence of the inner archetypal mediators of divine power, and the eventual re-establishment of a new kind of ego functioning, the ego now being the servant of the divine, no longer its betrayer. (23:pp.139,644).

Madness, from our perspective, indicates a breakthrough accomplished through significant human actuality.

The resolve to being as experienced in the athletic structure is predicated, not on a claim of knowledge concerning the phenomenal world, but on a fundamental act of faith. An act emanating from the core of the self in response to that which engulfs self. The dialectical affirmation of being, its very basis, is founded on faith, on an act impregnated in the midst of the demonic yet leading beyond in total affirmation. There is then, as we have alluded to before, no apparent rational continuity from the finite to the infinite, as in Hegel. Rather, faith acknowledges the cleavage present between man and absolute spirit which can only be conjoined in the tension of complete struggle. Thus, faith is not commensurate to knowledge or belief, the latter implying an element of probability which is dependent on knowledge, but rather its appeal escapes the realm of phenomenal reality. Profoundly, it is that act which affirms the unconditioned elements of our lives. Hence, the certitude of faith remains on an existential level, "to be or not to be," on a dimension devoid of epistemic certitude.

The faith of the athlete, then, is the basic affirmation of his being in sport as one undergone and actualized in a totally committed response in which the elements of doubt and risk continually linger within. Logical necessity finds no empirical root in the confines of sport, except for its superficial ramifications, and meaning can indeed be obscure and subject to instant devastation: "We run, not because we think it is doing us good, but because we enjoy it and cannot help ourselves." (3:p.222). Faith lifts the embargo of meaningfulness, not blindly but in response to "ultimate concern" and thereby grasps being beyond the aesthetic illumination of the performance and transports it into the compelling depths of the religious, the absoluteness of being itself. But it is an act which must be continuously renewed and forged in the quest of and for spirit.

Thus, being lies at the heart of the sport conscious-experience located within the streaming flux of the concrete situation. The distinguishing character of sport, then, is to be found in its transcendental locus, being, in which spirit is unfolded in the primacy of the lived situation. "Sport is more than a link with life, it is a vital aspect of existence, one which opens the self to the mystery of being." (36:p.8). However, the mystery of the unclarified, being, prevails as a formless existential presence, as that which literally permeates human existence yet retains its finite, insatiable claims: "For an athlete the mystery of this simple situation always remains. He cannot explain it further, or if he could he probably would not run well anymore." (4:p.65). Yet, the consciousness of the presence endures as a reality which stirs the roots of being beyond mere perception. As James relates concerning the posited ideal object of the religious experience:

> . . . it is as if there were in the human consciousness a sense of reality, a feeling of objective presence, a perception of what we may call something there, more deep and general than any of the special and particular senses by which the current psychology supposes existent realities to be originally revealed. (21:p.62).

The conscious awareness of the ontological presence of being, invoked in the sport and athletic context, constitutes the ideal object of the religious consciousness itself. As such, it is with this conscious presence that absolute spirit, being itself, or if you will, God, as a meta-phenomenal dimension is realized. Hence, this awareness of spirit as an extra-human element belies the formulation of an anthropomorphic view of spirit which equates absolute being to an illusion, whose presence is explained by the mere projection of human consciousness. For the intended ideal object, which is neither object nor subject itself but the unity of all things, involves a supra-conscious presence available to man yet above and beyond man. Moreover, it is that being, used here symbolically for the absolute spirit, which is not a mere being but being itself, that intrudes upon the finite consciousness in its supreme moments of human actuality, to wit, its cultural-religious aspirations to include sport. Its very presence is necessarily accompanied by an intrinsic disposition, as embodied in the forms of culture, by which a genuine apprehension of absolute spirit may be realized. Scheler's provocative discussion of love in its artistic and religious, non-cosmic form, as directed against the anthropomorphic proclivities of Feuerbach and Comte, provides penetrating insight:

> . . . in genuine love of art on the other hand we are concerned through-
> out with an extra-human element, with something which elevates man
> in his human capacity above himself and his experience. The same is
> most eminently true of the love of God; for this is devoted, not to man's
> own shadow in the universe, but to the intrinsically Holy, Infinite and
> Good, which is by nature transcendent of man and all finite things.
> (34:p.156).

Slusher speaks to this point specifically in reference to the spirit of sport:

> It is the quality the athlete knows is present yet he can't touch or
> explain it . . . Words only serve to hide the feeling. Apparents only
> distort what is real. But each man who has really been involved in sport
> knows the spirit well. It is too much like religion not to be associated
> with the mystic. Something of faith, something of peace, a touch of
> power, a feeling of right, a sense of the precarious—all of these and
> more is what the real spirit of sport is. (36:p.140).

Any discussion of the primordial spirit of sport inevitably faces the task of explicating the agonistic elements indigenous to sport in the light of this compelling fundamental force of sport. If not undertaken for purposes of systematic exposition, it at least begs consideration in any genuine ontology of sport which seeks to unveil and extract the essential from the less essential, the sincere from the frivolous. There appears to be two predominant views of sport and athletic competition supported in an antithetical manner; on the one hand sustained by an overt ontology and on the other, unwound in an unassumed metaphysical manner. In the first case, we witness a decided distaste for competition, whatever its apparent form, and an attempt to phase out the competitive elements of sport. Sadler's remarks are particularly representative of this view:

> If sports are to have a future in a more humane society, then those of
> us who are virtually interested in both sports and human values will
> have to demonstrate different meanings and values in sport than those
> associated with competition. This will mean, of course, that we shall
> simply have to de-emphasize the competitive element of sports. (33:p.23).

The ontological equivocation here is that between being and the identification of sport as a mere extension of play; such that, metaphysically play controls and discharges the proper perspective of extended sport, in this case competition. This argument usually offered in response to the begotten ills of sport, and in one delimited sense rightly so, logically infers that the perturbative elements of modern competitive sport are to be located precisely in the suppression of the play spirit. Huizinga comments:

> In the case of sport we have an activity nominally known as play but raised to such a pitch of technical organization and scientific thoroughness that the real play spirit is threatened with extinction. (18:p.225).

The conclusion begged then, is that ". . . sport is a distorted frame of play." (19:p.43).

The antithetical constituent of this bifurcation, contrarily, extols the intrinsic value of athletic competition as a decisive way of proving one's superiority. However, the ontological guise in which this view is rendered construes this quest for superiority not as a movement of the spirit, but as a form of appropriation in which the subjugation of someone or something becomes the explicit raison d'etre of athletics. The intention to be is submerged into the intention to have, manufactured as a mode of achievement, of delineating tangible success. It is then, a view infatuated exclusively with winning, construed synonymously as the "will to power" in a transcribed Nietzschean sense. Winning becomes the token and autocratic objectification of the sublime. This leads to the pronouncements of such sacred aphorisms as "Winning isn't everything, it is the only thing." In succinct terms, the sport and athletic sphere is reduced to, in covert metaphysical fashion, a basic work structure. Hence, athletic activity returns to the everyday world in the form of a glorified work structure. Sadler concisely remarks,

> I think it erroneous to suppose that the rise in sports is to be explained by a shift in existential objectives and goals associated with the supposedly new era of leisure. On the contrary, sport occupies so significant a position in American society precisely because it reinforces our work ethic. (33:p.13).

It is the expressed contention of this paper that both of the above notions of competition, and in turn their competing ontologies, constitute an effort distorted by mindless, reductionist thinking. Concisely, there appears to be no attempt to adequately, in a sympathetic man-

ner, take up the agonistic structures of sport as they reveal themselves
to be phenomenologically. Divorced from the essentials of lived
experience such conceptualizations appeal to a synthetically conceived
form of sport obscured by a fixation on the objective avarice of the
superficial.

Prior to our analysis, then, it is contrarily suggested that the generic
force of the spirit of sport is tangentially woven in the fabric of the
agonistic struggle. Hence, it is partially amenable to Scott's conception of the radical ethic as applicable to competition:

> The radical ethic says there is nothing wrong with the essence of com-
> petitive sport. It says that the agonistic struggle in sport of team with
> team, man with man, man with himself or man with nature is a healthy,
> valuable human activity. (35:p.50).

The prosecution of our analysis will thus attempt to extract the essential elements of the competitive strife. Hence, it is posited that the
core of the competitive strife is revealed in a tripartite fashion:
competition-in, competition-with, and competition-for. Our analysis
will proceed around these three structures of competition which are
themselves further grounded in an artistic-religious ideal.

Competition-in, as our first structure, consists of an inward act which
embraces the pre-competitive moment with the actuality of the contest
in a unified movement response. In the pre-competitive phase this
inward turn resembles the similar contemplative turn of the artist
and mystic. The contemplative intent of this act is the detachment
from the sensible aspects of reality so as to achieve a state of acute
conscious awareness. Parry O'Brien, former world class shotputter,
provides ample description: "When I'm ready for a toss, I'm all
wrapped up in myself. I'm in a different world." (10:p.343).
O'Brien characterizes this pre-competitive state as his competitive
trance. In more succinct terms, it involves an active summoning of a
serene presence of mind: "Before all doing and creating, before he
ever begins to devote and adjust himself to his task, the artist sum-
mons forth this presence of mind and makes sure of it through practice." (16:p.60). This aroused presence of mind is achieved through
a disinterested and enamored response initiated in a self-liberating
leap of concentration upon the essential, compelling necessities of the
contest. As a phenomenological structure it is akin to the creative

dimension of the artistically and religiously inspired attunement to reality.

These virgin competitive acts are evinced within and around the gnawing pangs of intense anxiety amidst the anticipatory gap between ensuing actuality and present awaiting. Frank Shorter, long distance runner, speaks to this remark in terms of an important track competition:

> This is the kind of nervousness you only go through two or three times a year. It's something you can't control. It sort of creeps up on you. You know you've oriented your life towards this kind of moment. (31:p.20).

Such moments reveal the solemnity of the athletic contest and the commensurately assiduous quest of the inspired athlete. Pasorell's description of the pre-competitive practices of tennis player Pancho Gonzalez further testifies to the validity of this assertion:

> He goes off into a place where he's by himself . . . and in there he pictures himself playing every variety of shot there is. Chasing an overhead. Trying to serve out the game. He transfixes himself in there. I mean he sees himself making these shots so clearly that he begins to feel it, so that when he comes out his hands are actually sweating. He's ready. (30:p.60).

The propensity of such actions attach themselves to decisive forms of ritual which reinforce, in a symbolic manner, the actualized substantiality of the sport context. The functional significance of ritual in this situation is the symbolic demarcation of the serious and ultimate nature of the realm of sport as opposed to its frivolous and destructive exploited form in which a spectacle-like atmosphere predominates.

Thus, the pre-competitive moment is linked directly to the actual competition in which the consciousness previously engendered flows delicately into the actuality of its proposed potentiality. In effect, the pre-competitive intent is decisively maintained in its detached, sensible stance and its correlative inward entreaty. Yet, the competition demands that such an act is paradoxically related to another more enriched perceptual movement such that one does not get stuck in a kind of static conscious state. It dynamically leads one from a contemplative, mind-intuited union to a further union enhanced in a totally affirmed manner through decisive human actuality. Thus, the onslaught of competition requires a further immersion dialectically emanating from the pre-competitive conscious level. This competitive thrust is effected in response to the agonistic struggle productively garnered in the contextual situation. As Bannister relates during the pitch of the competitive response, ". . . his boldness forced me to abandon my time schedule and loose myself completely in the struggle itself." (3:p.216). The nature of this competitive rejoinder seeks to dissolve into a non-positional consciousness in response to the situation. It is, then, an active promulgation of the mind-probing, pre-competitive state propelled into the heart of the contesting effort. This is not an assertion of the primacy of a physiological, instinctive, subconscious level, but in a contrary manner it involves a form of mystical, intuitive penetration, a celebration of a higher form of actuality and recognition.

The disposition of this maddening quality of absorption characterizes the intentional referrents of the structure competition—in as directed into a communion of the athlete with his provocative medium, athletic competition. It is not fundamentally a rational process but rather unwinds as an intuitive response which goes beyond the dictates of reason. The progression arises out of reason but flows into the non-rational forms of human actuality. The resultant response is an integrative one which does not seek to devastate reason but bring reason to its necessary fruition with the non-rational, creative dimensions of human existence: "In the creative act we witness neither disassociation or biassociation—but integration and synthesis. The whole self creates." (5:p.85).

The creative disposability to being aroused in the competitive retort seeks to go beyond the finite horizons of human experience. The intentional referrent of its actual response assumes the form of a self-surrender to the encompassing forces of existence. Starbuck alludes to this movement of self-surrender in terms of a discussion concerning religious conversion, although from grounds not entirely amenable to ours:

> An athlete . . .sometimes awakens suddenly to an understanding of the fine points of the game and to a real enjoyment of it, just as the convert awakens to an appreciation of religion. If he keeps on engaging in sport, there may come a day when all at once the game plays itself through him—when he looses himself in some great contest. In the same

way, a musician may suddenly reach a point at which pleasure in the technique of the art entirely falls away, and in some moment of inspiration he becomes the instrument through which music flows. (21:p.172).

This religious form of self-surrender reveals the dynamic, unfolding nature of the structure competition-in which, however, is evoked in a decisive participatory response. The import of its open, actualized synthesis is aptly characterized by Heidegger as a form of "letting be", a revelatory response into the "what-is" of reality as presupposed in freedom. It further signifies, through authentic, conscious countenances, the primordial, asocial temperament of the sport-athletic experience. In sum, the structure competition-in ultimately involves a total spiritual response to the demanding exigencies of the competition, characterized by its authentically transcendent aspiration.

Competition, then, embodies much more than the detached desire to win, to vanquish one's opponent, as realized through the intention of appropriation. As Shorter bluntly observes, concerning the finish of a grueling marathon, "I finished and a great feeling of thankfulness swept through me. There was no sense of conquest, none of this baloney about vanquishing anybody." (28:p.95). Hence, the phenomenological nature of competition belies the putative attempt to ascribe to athletic competition a quasi-military function:

> Patriotic pride and ambition in their military form are, after all, only specifications of a more general competitive passion. They are its first form, but that is no reason for supposing them to be its last form. (20:p.298).

Thus, the *will to win* is itself grounded in the religious-aesthetic ideal of the concept, competition-with. As Weiss and others have noted, competition does not involve merely the subjugation of someone or something but rather the attempt to deal properly with existent realities. It is not, then, primarily an encounter of subject verses object, an intention of appropriation, but more profoundly an attempt to be, a striving towards the ideal and spirit of excellence emanating from within the self in the midst of the contextual situation.

The structure competition-with denotes two complementary elements both fused within the competitive struggle. The first element of the competitive process reveals the agonistic struggle as inherently self-directed. Hence, the introspective phase of self-directed competition forms the fundamental basis of the outwardly projected contingencies of the contest and game. Herrigel notes this contention in his discussion of archery:

> Archery is still a matter of life and death to the extent that it is a contest of the archer with himself; and this kind of contest is not a paltry substitute, but the foundation of all contests outwardly directed—for instance with a bodily opponent. (16:p.19).

The contesting element of the structure competition-with is a self-encountering one which draws the athlete into a primordial quest for self-excellence. In reference to olympic ski racer Tyler Palmer the author relates, ". . . he was relearning what experience taught him at St. Moritz—you do not race to beat someone else, you race against yourself." (27:p.48). Schollander, olympic gold medal swimmer, also comments on this supposition in reference to his swimming career. He delineates two competitive aspirations: one which is characterized by the mundane desire merely not to lose, in this case the sole attempt is to defeat one's opponent, the other intentional act is guided by a quest for excellence in a self-contesting fashion. The latter disposition he regards as the positive foundation of the supreme achievements of his athletic career.

The concept of competition-with also includes the notion of competing with rather than against the significant others of the sport condition. As such, it proceeds directly from the inner quest of the competitive response. In a very real sense the significant others of the athletic context merge in terms of their pursuits, which in turn corroborates the mutual aspiration of being embodied in the contesting nature of competiton: "His opponent is at the same time his partner . . . that is to say, the difference, the antagonism between the other and the self, tends to disappear in sport." The form of this contesting-with is couched in the notion of testimony. Testimony, then, characterizes the heart of the mutual striving exhibited in the competitive strife:

> The concept of 'the good strife' is implicit in the word competition as derived from cum and petere—literally to strive with rather than against. The word contest has similar implications, being derived from con and testare—to testify with rather than against him. (26:pp.41-42).

Hence, the testifying nature of competition is discerned as one against and with oneself and further with the significant others of the athletic situation. Marcel more fully elucidates the quintessence of this form of testimony:

> My testimony bears on something independent from me and objectively real; it is therefore an essentially objective end. At the same time it commits my entire being as a person who is answerable for my assertions and for myself. (25:p.95).

Therefore, the contesting atmosphere of the agonistic struggle reveals the other as a significant aspect of our striving and not as an object of my appropriative attempts. Further, the other is not also merely an important entity to which we feel compelled to respond, but profoundly, the other is our encounter in an embodied sense.

The competitive intent of the multifarious constituents of the athletic contextual situation belies any apparent datum of conflict. The condition of conflict or opposition is itself an arbitrary designation, albeit necessary, which fills the contest with overt purpose but also concealed the reciprocal nature of the contest. The efforts of our endeavors, though, never yield to the security of the social dimension, but ontologically fixate in the personal wombs of human existence. The situation is one basically in which a collective commiseration arises whose sustaining object is located in its intention to be. This "being-for-another" is not a literal and inert surrender to the various concurring forces of the contest but assumes a higher form of actuality in the explicit form of a giving of oneself as presupposed analytically in the structure, competition-in. In terms of the lived experience, both structures cohere in their inner responses and their projected manifestations. Hence, in this context we can speak of a genuine transmutation in that my response embodies my intention of being. The situation involves, then, a fundamental, mutual aspiration in the form of a giving-receiving tension dialectically based in being.

The appeal proffered in the testifying phase of competition is of an ecstatic nature: "Testimony is given before a transcendence." (25:p.94). The object of our intentions becomes, in a lucid fashion, absolute reality. The religious significance of this mutual striving is found precisely in its primal focus on being as the innermost object of its enduring search. The complementary artistic ideal of competition-with again articulates around the primordial finite-infinite polarity in the form of an artistic product, the expedient object of its intentions being an artistic excellence:

> The competitive strife in sport is one with oneself and the seemingly omnipotent forces between one's performance and the most excellent of performances. It is a quest for an over-elusive excellence . . . a perfection of sport performance. (29:pp.22-23).

Yet the perfected artistic product is grounded in the longing for and pursuit of being in an unmediated, spiritual encounter. The latter religious motif is expressed in the athlete's finite quest for being in which the unconditional character of its intended object shatters through the performance rendering it complete. As Tillich relates, "Spirit is only present where existence is impregnated with the unconditional demand that gives it validity." (1:p.137). The object of the espoused, mutual aspirations unveiled in the competitive response is of a decidedly spiritual character and as such the significance of its endeavor is ultimately found in this realm. As Bannister notes, "For the athlete the human spirit is indeed indomitable." (4:p.73).

This brings us to the last element in our analysis, competition-for. The structure of competition-for demarcates the objective of the intentional striving peculiar to athletic competition, namely the contesting for the prize. However, the word prize in this context refers to the ideal founding and accompanying the athletic striving, devoid of its materialistic intonations. It is, then, an ideal not reducible to a tangible, arbitrary entity but rather necessarily remains a non-instrumental quest as artistically realized via athletic excellence and ultimately as spiritually encountered in total striving. Hence, the primordial ideals underlying the structure competition-for remain intangible and utterly based in being.

Thus, the athletic venture as an existent form is bound to the object of its pursuit, being, as envisaged in a symbolic manner. The contest symbolizes the moment of spiritual response in which the ideal becomes palpable. Such striving, then, belies pragmatically conceived ends and is justified only in terms of itself. Athletic competition is, therefore, structured by concern as actualized in and for itself. The generative power underlying the concern exhibited in the athletic contest is expressively manifested as a fundamental act of love. For as Plato used the eros as his word for concern we affirm the constitutive nature of concern as itself love. Love is that which underlies the athletic pursuit in general, enhancing its spiritual disposition. The Love of the athletic contest as a meaningful human form in-itself marks the truly supreme moments of the human spirit in which all forms of spirit ultimately converge:

> Let's be sure that in every competition, however desperate, there is something even stronger than the will to win . . . the desire for sport, the love of sporting competition is an eternal verity of the soul. (2:pp.168-171).

In connection with the structure competition-for, the notion of winning as a mode of interpreting the ideal of competition commands our attention. The agony and ecstasy of athletic competition is linked directly to the dynamic actuality evinced within the athletic realm. Therefore, winning or losing are not merely detached qualities as some would say noting the primacy of athletics as process; nor are they fixated ends as some of the status-quo contingent might assume, implicitly placing the priority of such ends as the essence of athletics. The true significance of winning or losing transcends such a bifurcation. In the former case, the outcome of the contest is inextricably linked to the process of the situation. They are certainly not divorced ends extracted from process for they signify the dialectical unification of intense partaking. Yet, on the other hand, they are not frozen, fixated ends to be blown up in plastic fashion as objective culmination points. For, as culmination points they exhibit a dynamic capacity pointing inward to the spiritually produced excellence and also symbolically pointing beyond to the potentialities of the athlete in his continual quest into the faces of being and nothingness.

Hence, victory is an inward triumph, which points to a lived excellence leading to a fulfillment in terms of the entire contest. This most certainly does not preclude the possibility of fulfillment in the absence of victory. The implications of defeat, though never completely satisfying, are a searching, enveloping movement towards victory. Heed the declaration of British steeplechaser John Disley in response to a rejoinder castigating him for failing to follow advice that possibly could have claimed the olympic victory for him: "Don't talk to me about winning . . . I'm very proud to have been third with such men as these." (2:p.169). Thus, the athletic aristocracy discloses a prestige immersed in excellence which does not necessarily require an external victory, albeit it most certainly does require a subjective striving beyond Kaelin's concept of the "well played game". Yet victory as an exteriorized and concomitantly interiorized achievement is the guiding force of the competitive struggle. Therefore, the fruition of the subjective, intentional strivings of the athlete rests in the corresponding significance of victory as the appropriate object of such intent. The two polar elements of the competitive process, then, are interlocked in a lived tension. Thus, the two aspects of victory, as a bi-polar element and the lived, striving correlative to the inner triumph of athletic-spiritual excellence, are dynamically wed in superb performances attesting to this unity.

In summary, we are led to the following conclusion in consideration of our analysis. The competitive strife indigenous to the sport and athletic sphere is one which can best be characterized as a liberating strife, one that integrates rather than devastates. Hence, the structures delineated in our analysis are reflective by-products of our investigation and therefore are not exclusive forms but permeating structures found in the streaming, unified experiential forces of the competition. The agonistic elements pertinent to the sport and athletic forms of competition are ultimately constructive, unifying forms which belie their satanic appearance. Thus, they are not substantial declarations of war, or microcosmic power struggles attributable to our technocratic society, but in conclusive terms their primal intent is of a spiritual nature. The competitive act, as the tangential, striving element of athletics proper, expressively unveils the athletic contest as a deliberation in which being is the source of all striving attempts.

The ontology of sport herein formulated proceeds along existential phenomenological lines. It is by this view that consciousness and human experience are construed as correlative structures dialectically engaged and unified in being. Consciousness is ascribed an a priori quality in a Kantian sense; that is, the mind is the source of human experience rendering it intelligible through its dynamic, synthesizing capabilities. This view avoids the untenable empiricist position regarding mind as exemplified in Locke's empty container thesis. It is rather the subject that consciously experiences the world and not vice versa. However, human experience is itself more sympathetically viewed in its complete noetic-noematic disposition. By focusing on the pre-reflective base of all reflections concerning conscious experience, the ongoing stream of conscious, structured experience is unveiled in its totality and not merely in its cognitive stance. Hence, the existential perspective enters as a significant aspect of phenomenology as the heart of the lebenswelt, the primacy of the experiential life-world. Reflection is consequently centered on the conjoined entities of consciousness and experience, consciousness as embedded in human experience.

This position, a phenomenological ontology, appears consonant with other proposed ontologies, most notably idealism and its emphasis on the mind's contribution to experience, and certain strains of pragmatism in their treatment of human experience. However, it avoids the former's proclivity to excessive rationalism and the latter's empiricistic, utilitarian tendencies, most conspicuously as evidenced in their theory of truth. In sum, these at best cursory remarks are merely offered in clarification of the expressed contentions of this paper. However, it is to be suggested further that these metaphysical suppositions render the sport-athletic genre intelligible in terms of their all-embracing structures, their essential nature.

In reiteration, it has been contended that the substantive quiddity of sport lies in its primordial, transcendent aspiration. Sport is, then, an activity of the spirit in its highest sense. The resolve of the athlete is itself utterly based in being, beyond analytical and linguistic explication. The constraint to being is the fundamental focus of the intentional structures of sport, a quality that unites the supreme expressions of spirit as found in the arts, philosophy, and religion. Yet, it is also true that sport, as have the other forms of spirit, has been subject to distortion to the point in which its dynamic form lies obscure in the catacombs of mindless exploitation. As Osterhoudt concisely observes, "The mistinterpretation and exploitation of sport as a social, political, pedagogical, militaristic, economic, psychological, and chauvinistic instrument has perhaps irreparably decayed its proper image." (29: p.24). It is, of course, obvious that these exploited innuendos have little to do with sport but rather reveal man's debasement of actitvities of the spirit. Our concern then, begins and ends with sport as it is, in its most compelling and enduring constitutive form. The unity of being attested to in magnificent athletic performances suggests itself, in a provocative manner, the primal import of its intentional form, as that which brings man in his finiteness to the furthest reaches of spirit and meaning. It is to these expanses, into the infinite life of spirit, that we may commit the basic nature of sport and attend to its enamored impressions reflectively.

REFERENCES

1. Adams, James: *Paul Tillich's Philosophy of Culture, Science, and Religion.* New York, Harper-Row, 1965.
2. Baker, Phillip Noel: "A New Understanding of the Phenomenon of Man." *International Research in Sport and Physical Education,* E. Jokl and E. Simon (eds.). Springfield, Thomas, 1964.
3. Bannister, Roger: *The Four Minute Mile.* New York, Dodd, 1958.
4. Bannister, Roger: "The Meaning of Athletic Performance." *International Research in Sport and Physical Education,* E. Jokl and E. Simon (eds.). Springfield, Thomas, 1964.
5. Barron, Frank: "Creative Personality Akin to Madness," *Psychology Today,* Vol. 6, No. 2, 42, 54, 84-85 (July, 1972).
6. Boyles, Robert H.: *Sport-Mirror of American Life.* New York, Appleton, 1967.
7. Camus, Albert: *The Myth of Sisyphus.* New York, Random, 1955.
8. Cassirer, Ernst: *An Essay On Man.* New Haven, Yale Univ. Press, 1970.
9. Copleston, Fredrick: *A History of Modern Philosophy: Ficthe to Hegel, Vol. 7.* Garden City, New York, Doubleday, 1965.
10. Doherty, Kenneth: *Modern Track and Field.* New Jersey, Prentice-Hall, 1963.
11. Doherty, Kenneth: "Why Men Run," *Quest,* No. 2, 60-66 (April, 1964).
12. Forrest, Aime: "Concerning the Aesthetic and Religious Experience," *Humanitas,* Vol. 6, 311-24 (Winter 1971).
13. Fraleigh, Sondra Horton: "Dance Creates Man," *Quest,* No. 14, 65-71 (June 1970).
14. Genasci, James and Klissouras, Vasillis: "The Delphic Spirit in Sports," *Journal of Health, Physical Education and Recreation,* Vol. 38, No. 2, 43-45 (February, 1966).
15. Herberg, Will (ed.). *Four Existentialist Theologians.* Garden City, Doubleday, 1958.
16. Herrigel, Eugen: *Zen in the Art of Archery.* R. Roll (trans.). New York, Random, 1971.
17. Herzog, Maurice. *Annapurna.* New York, Dutton, 1953.
18. Huizinga, Johan: *Homo Ludens: A Study of the Play—Element in Culture.* London, Paladin, 1970.
19. Ingham, Alan and Loy, John W.: "The Structure of Ludic Action." Paper

presented at the Third International Symposium on the Sociology of Sport, Univ. of Waterloo, Ontario, Canada, Aug. 22-28, 1971.

20. James, William: "The Moral Equivalent of War," *Pragmatism and other Essays*. New York, Washington Square Press, 1963.
21. James, William: *The Varieties of Religious Experience*. New York, Collier Books, 1970.
22. Kierkegaard, Soren. *Fear and Trembling and the Sickness Unto Death*. New Jersey, Princeton Univ. Press, 1969.
23. Laing, R. D. *The Politics of Experience*. New York, Ballentine, 1967.
24. Lowenberg, Jacob (ed.): *Hegel Selections*. New York, Scribner, 1957.
25. Marcel, Gabriel: *Philosophy of Existentialism*. New York, Citadel Press, 1968.
26. Metheny, Eleanor: *Connotations of Movement in Sport and Dance*. Dubuque, Wm. C. Brown, 1965.
27. Miller, Peter: "Why U.S. Racers Lose," *Ski Magazine,* Vol. 36, No. 6 42-48, 127 (Jan. 1972).
28. Moore, Kenneth: "Concentrate on the Chysanthemums," *Sports Illustrated,* Vol. 36, No. 19 83-96 (May 8, 1972).
29. Osterhoudt, Robert: "An Exposition Concerning Sport and the Fine Arts." Unpublished manuscript, Lock Haven State College, Penna., 1969.
30. Plimpton, George: "The Mind's Eye," *Sports Illustrated,* Vol. 35, No. 1 50-63 (July, 1971).
31. Putnam, Pat: "A Dream Comes True," *Sports Illustrated,* Vol. 34, No. 21 18-21 (May, 1971).
32. Roberts, David: *Existentialism and Religious Belief*. New York: Oxford Univ. Press, 1968.
33. Sadler, William: "Competition Out of Bounds: A Sociological Inquiry into the Meaning of Sports in America Today." Paper read at the Cultural Section of the A.A.H.P.E.R. Convention at Houston, March 24, 1972.
34. Scheler, Max: *The Nature of Sympathy*. Hamden, Conn., Shoe String, 1970.
35. Scott, Jack: "Sport: Scott's Radical Ethic," *Intellectual Digest,* Vol. 2, No. 2 49-50 (July, 1972).
36. Slusher, Howard: *Man, Sport, and Existence*. Philadelphia, Lea and Febiger, 1967.
37. Tillich, Paul: *The Courage To Be*. New Haven, Yale Univ. Press, 1969.
38. Tillich, Paul: *Theology of Culture*. New York, Oxford Univ. Press, 1969.
39. Wallraff, Charles: *Karl Jaspers—An Introduction to his Philosophy*. New Jersey, Princeton Univ Press, 1970.
40. Wilde, Jean T. and Kimmel, William: *The Search For Being*. New York, Noonday Press, 1967.

THE MOVING "I"

Warren P. Fraleigh

INTRODUCTION

It has been stated previously that the basic purpose of the physical education dimension of the new college is to attempt to actualize the meaning of man as a moving being. (4). This paper is an attempt to contribute to that purpose by identifying and discussing some senses in which meaning of the self-knowledge variety may be available to persons in and by their participation in sports, dance, aquatics and exercise. This is not to stay that each and every identified meaning *will* be in the consciousness of each person who participates in such activities but only that these meanings have been in the consciousness of persons. Discussion of such meanings assumes that verbalizing them *may* "open" our sensitivities so that we may be "present" with them as we reflect upon past movement experiences and as we move in the future.

The idea of self-knowledge needs some attention before meanings are identified. In this context self has three kinds of significance. First, is the self considered as a singular, unique, individual human entity, that is, that which identifies you as yourself and not me or someone else. Second, is the self considered as the unique collection of characteristics which make humans human and not dogs or God. And third, it appears clearly that both of these "selves" are entities formed by relationship; that is, the singular, unique, individual human entity comes into being by relationship with other singular, unique, individual human entities and, likewise, the collective human self comes into being by relationship with non-human entities both earthly and Divine. In both cases the identity of self is developed from relationships which include both similarities and differences.

The concept of meaning of the self-knowledge variety is also in need of further explanation. As mentioned above, the word self means uniqueness in both a singular, individual sense and in the collective, group sense of being human. Meaning of the self-knowledge variety signifies, then, the person coming to awareness of his own identity as an individual and as a member of humanity who is, simultaneously, similar and different from other beings. As meanings which provide personal awareness of identity, such meanings help to provide partial answers to the age-old question, "Who Am I?" This is the reason for titling this paper "The Moving "I".

EXPERIENCES AND MEANINGS
Introduction

This primary section is an attempt to identify certain types of experience which are fairly common in sports, dance, aquatics and exercise and to express and examine some possible self-knowledge meanings which may appear in such experiences.

The Self As Free—The Self As Necessitated

Experiences—There are several ways in which the experience of freedom and necessity occur in sports, dance, aquatics and exercise. It is paradoxical that such seemingly contradictory experiences frequently are intimately related to each other.

In all sports, dance, exercise and aquatics the lived-body experience of the self as necessitated is potential. This is to say that the human body is an entity which, on this earth and without arificial aids, is subject to the same natural forces as any other object. When I jump, I inevitably return to earth. When I assume a vertical position in a swimming pool, lake, river or the ocean, I invariably tend to sink into the water. When continuous physical activity occurs, I arrive at a state whereby my physiological and mechanical powers are diminished by fatigue. When a volleyball is spiked at me, or when a tennis ball or badminton bird is smashed at me, these objects often powerfully overcome me. The lived-body experience of the self as necessitated has two facets. First, is the everpresent necessity of the body as subject to natural forces such as identified by Newton's three laws of motion. Second, is the *relative* necessity of the body as subject to external forces and conditions because of the body's inability, caused by lack of training, to cope as effectively with such conditions as the body's potential will allow. In both of these ways, the bodily experience of movement in sports, dance, aquatics and exercise is that of the self as a necessitated being. This is to say that the "lived-body-self" is aware of himself as a being who is externally controlled.

But paradoxically, as indicated above, the lived-body experience of the self as necessitated is intimately related to the bodily experience of the self as free. When I bounce on a trampoline, I bodily experience a few seconds of freedom as if gravity no longer holds me . When I swing more rapidly and more forcefully around a high bar in gymnastics, I feel as if the force generated is sufficient to propel me into orbit. When I execute several rapid, whirling jumping turns with both arms swinging forcefully in the dance studio, I experience a self which is flung beyond the body and the floor. When my skill develops to the point where the badminton smash which previously overpowered me is now reacted to surely and blocked with my racket, I am aware of a growing independence. When, after sufficient training, I bodily experience the power of "second wind" in distance running, I know myself as a being freer than previously. But again the paradox becomes evident that my lived-body experience of the self as free is intimately related to my lived-body experience of the self as necessitated. I do not experience the two seconds of freedom on the trampoline, the "orbital potentiality" on the high bar, or the self flung beyond the body in dance without the experience of returning to the trampoline bed, without being anchored to the high bar, or without contacting and recontacting the floor with the dancing body. I do not experience my growing independence in badminton without the experience of being overpowered by external objects nor do I experience the flow of power brought by "second wind" without the experience of being rendered powerless because of fatigue. And so the lived-body experience of both necessity and freedom enhance each other as the peaks and valleys define each other.

Another way in which the self is experienced as free is a product of beyond-novice levels of skill development in implement-employing sports. One may observe, for example, the easy assured way that a highly skilled tennis player handles his racket. After development of skill the object called a racket becomes a phenomenal extension of self in the consciousness of the player. The player experiences himself as free in the sense that his intentions and will are extended further into the world by these instruments which have been appropriated into his being.

There is still another sense in which the self is experienced as free and as necessitated. This is a sense in which the particular movements which are actually performed may be perceived to be either as free or as necessitated by the person himself. This is to say that *within* sports, dance, and exercise the experience of self as free or necessitated may be determined by whether the actual movements performed are externally chosen (i.e., necessitated) or internally chosen (i.e., free). To express the concept in still another way, are the actual movements I perform in sports, dance and exercise ones which I am free to choose individually or are they actually chosen by some external agent (necessitated)?

When I participate in most sports, in dance and sport technique drills, or in exercise aimed at a particular physiological purpose, the particular movements which I actually perform are, to a large extent, necessitated movements. That is, if I am to play, say, volleyball, the type of movements which I must perform are to a great extent already chosen for me by the fact that the game is volleyball and not tennis. The movements are determined by the rules and regulations regarding playing area and equipment, specifications for team composition, particulars of point scoring, legalities, of how the ball may or may not be hit and expectancies of behavior which are conventional. In sports, my *choice* of particular movements actually performed is restricted to which kinds of already predetermined movements I will use at any one moment and to my personal style in executing these determined movements. If I choose to perform a particular movement such as kicking the ball in volleyball then either I am confusing soccer with volleyball or I will be penalized for using an illegal movement. If I persist in kicking the ball, then either the game will change to soccer or I will be excluded from the company of players who continue with volleyball or I will be continually penalized to the detriment of my teammates and opponents because I am simply not playing the same game and, consequently, removing the possibility of shared meaning from myself and the other players.

If I wish to exercise for the purpose of developing strength of a particular muscle, the kinds of movements which I can use for such a purpose are necessitated by the physiology of muscular strength and the mechanics of movement which affect that particular muscle. For example, if I wish to develop strength in the biceps muscle then I *must* have some heavy resistance exerted against the movement of flexing my arm at the elbow. Flexing my elbow with little resistance against the movement will do very little for strength development and raising a straight arm straight up from my side to shoulder height will not develop bicep strength.

On the other hand, I may experience performing movements which are relatively free in the sense that I may choose among several possibilities according to my singular purpose. The best examples of this are seen in the personal choreography and movement exploration aspects of modern dance. In these cases, I choose freely the particular movements actually performed to fit a purpose I have chosen myself. Further, I choose the particular movements I actually do from a range of possibilities which I have selected myself. Generally speaking, such movements are necessitated solely by the ever-present time-space restrictions and by my own bodily and movement inadequacies.

But there is still another sense in which the self may experience his own movement as free and this is well identified by Metheny.

> In short, within the complex conditions of life, we are seldom, if ever, free to focus all our attention on one well-defined task and bring all the energies of our being to bear on one wholehearted attempt to perform that task effectively.
>
> In contrast, the rules of sports provide us with a man-made world in which this freedom is fully guaranteed. These rules eliminate the demands of necessity by defining an unnecssary task. They elminate all need for the consideration of material values by defining a futile task that produces nothing of material value. They eliminate all questions about the quality of materials by defining a set of materials of known quality. They eliminate all questions about what we are trying to do and how we can best do it, by prescribing the actions that may be used to perform the task. They eliminate all doubt about what counts by describing how the performance of the task is to be evaluated. And they eliminate all need to debate our own motives and the motives of other people by imposing the same standards of conduct on all performers.
>
> In this sense, the rules of sport provide each performer with a rare opportunity to concentrate all the energies of his being in one meaningful effort to perform a task of his own choosing, no longer pushed and pulled in a dozen directions by the many imperatives he may recognize in his life. (12:p.63).

Accordingly then, although the particular movements performed by the moving self *within* sport may be largely necessitated, his prior free choice (outside of required physical education) to participate voluntarily in the sport environment brings him to the movement experience as a free agent. In amateur sport, since by definition such sport is pursued primarily for its intrinsic meaning and not its instrumental efficacy, the fact of necessitated movements is overarched by the fact of free choice to participate in a movement form constructed and codified by the prior free decisions of men. In this way then, the moving self may experience himself as a free agent who is freely choosing the sport environment within which certain movements are necessitated.

Meanings

Several kinds of experiencing the self as free and as necessitated have been identified. It is now appropriate to explicate some of the meanings which may be derived from such experiences. Again, the attempt will be made to verbalize these meanings in the sense of awareness of human identity. Also, there will be no attempt here to distinguish between meanings of the denotative or connotative variety or to suggest these meanings must be those which come to awareness. In substance, this discussion of meanings of the human identity kind will serve its purpose if it evokes nods of assent, headshakes of negation and/or suggestions of other meanings of the human identity type to the readers.

The lived-body experience of the self as necessitated is a very basic source of human identity meanings. It "tells" me, in a most fundamental way, that my humanness inherently allies me with animals and objects and that, *in this restricted sense*, I am not different from them. It "tells" me that it is an inherent aspect of my personal identity, shared with others, both human, animal and object, that my day-to-day living experience seems to continue at least partially in a deterministic (necessitated) manner. It "tells" me, by direct experience of my own reality and by observation of the reality of others, that my identity does not allow me the God-like interpretation that my existence is *unconditionally* free.

But the lived-body experience of the self as free is also a very basic source of human identity meanings. It "tells" me, in a most fundamental way, that my humanness inherently allies me with freedom and that, *in this restricted sense*, I am not different from God. It "tells" me, by my direct bodily feeling of freedom, and by the fact that I am conscious of this freedom from necessity, that it is a dimension of my personal human identity shared with others and, perhaps with Another. It "tells" me, by the differing, relative physiological and motor abilities of myself and others, that individual freedom in movement activities is variable among different persons and, consequently, becomes an aspect of human personal identity in its singular sense. It "tells" me, by the realized change in relative physiological and motor ability developed by training, that the relative, achieved freedom in movement activities is an individual state of being subject to and modified by individual personal will and, thus, that my personal human identity is at least partially a product of my will to free myself. In short, it "tells" me of a transcendent self who sees an image of himself as a powerful being in the universe and a self who, upon gazing back at his previous self, experiences an "emotion of power" as if he is ". . . not controlled any more by outside sources." (15:p.87).

The experience of the appropriation of sports implements into the phenomenal self gives a different insight into freedom. It "tells" me that my being extends beyond my skin and out into and with the objects of the world. It "tells" me that my personal identity as free results partially from a kind of special relationship with the objects of the world which makes them a positively enhancing part of me rather than apart from me.

The essential freedom of man in voluntarily choosing to participate in his own freely designed movement forms such as sport is very significant in the human personal identity sense. The fact that man is able to construct from his own inventiveness what appears to be a "practically useless" activity may be a symbol of his identity as a being who may build a "world" of his own and, because it is his own self-constructed "world", one in which he is comfortable rather than alien. And it is in entering such a world that man may know himself symbolically as a powerful agent in being since, in that world, he literally uses externally controlling necessities such as space, time and gravity to serve his own purposes which are, themselves, not controlled by necessities such as pursuit of food, clothing or shelter. Further, man in the sports world may modify that world at will.

But human personal identity in movement activities does not always carry an image of positive power. On the contrary, it may present the direct opposite. A few illustrative anecdotes may help clarify the point. Several years ago a physical education teacher was aware of one student (Don) in a badminton class who evidenced considerable frustration with his inability to perform skillfully. Don showed his frustration by several outbursts after losing points in games. At times, he would halt play by turning his back to his opponent or walking to the sideline of the court with hands on hips and a contorted facial mask of violent red. At other times, he would fan the air with vicious, hatchet-like strokes of his racket. In these and other behaviors, Don would often explode with expressions such as "damn it" or "you stink, Don". One day, several minutes after a particularly strong outburst, the physical education instructor, while passing by Don's court casually, said quietly, "Sometimes we just can't seem to do everything we want to do satisfactorily, Don". At this, Don, still fuming underneath, turned and said vehemently, "Yeah, but I don't do anything well!"

In another case, a student in a physical education class discussion made the statement, "Why do physical education teachers take sports so seriously, they just aren't that important!" Subsequently, in a badminton class this same student evidenced considerable frustration by her inability to perform the long serve. In a class discussion later, the instructor related these two incidents and asked the students what they thought was meaningful in the relationship of the incidents. The ensuing discussion developed the point that the student's frustration at being unable to perform a sports skill seemed to deny her previous, adamant statement that sports just weren't that important. Further, there seemed to be some merit to the position that if she really did not feel sports were somehow important she probably would not be frustrated by her inability to perform in them.

Both of these incidents illustrate the lived-body experience of persons having their willed intensions frustrated by the external object, the badminton bird, and by the fact that the person's body is unable to cope with the external necessity of the bird. The personal identity kind of meaning obtainable from such experience lies in the consciousness of a "twoness" of self, that is, one self (the inner, willing self) who intends to hit the bird and another self (the outer, bodily self) who fails to coordinate with the inner self. Two personal identity meanings appear. First, is an awareness of a self who is divided against himself and, second and correspondingly, an awareness of a self who betrays oneself. In this latter instance, the bodily self may become, to the inner self, a foreign and despised agent because that bodily self vividly demonstrates that the person is a being who is unable to control himself to deal with external necessities.

> I never feel my body so much my own than when it makes me suffer. Would it do me harm if it were not me? As a related being, flesh of my flesh, it makes me suffer more than a stranger. But my sick body is infinitely close to me, yet contradictorily foreign. It is me-in a dualistic mode. It is mine, as one suffers an unavoidable traveling companion, chained together for life and death, and to whom one has taken a dislike. Sartre has written, in *No Exit,* "Hell is other people". The sick body, in the same way, is precisely another, beseiging me and clutching me in a deadly familiarity from which I am incapable of extricating myself. (14:p.96).

It is no wonder, then, that persons with a history of such perceived personal betrayal *might* develop deep, unconscious feelings of bodily self-rejection and conscious surface verbalization regarding the insignificance of motor skills in sports.

But experiences of the self divided against himself help to highlight the converse, that is, the self as a unified being. When persons hit tennis balls just the way they want to, when persons dive into a swimming pool in the way they wish and when persons move their bodies in harmony with their image of the desired movements, they experience themselves as being a unity of intention and action, as being a unity of the subjective I and the objective I, as being a unity of mind and body and this experience is the self as free, that is, the self who is now free to fulfill himself in contrast to the self who is divided against himself. The personal identity type of meaning available here is that I am fully functioning and self-actualizing when external behavior is an accurate manifestation of internal intention and when internal intention is in integral accord with external conditions.

The personal identity type of meaning of the unified self in the singular sense, that is, I am in unity with myself, needs to be extended. The related and extended meaning is that of the self as a personal unity who is in a state of accord with totality of being. For example, when I execute a mechanically perfect golf swing and the ball goes exactly where I intend it to go, I experience myself not only as a personal unity of my action and my intention but, simultaneously, as a personal unity who is unified with all that is beyond self. Such experience carries the meaning of the fullest possible self *being with* the fullest possible universe. The feeling of surprising ease and personal effortlessness attained in such experiences can be described as a feeling where the self is no longer controlled (necessitated) or is controlling (free) but exists in a state of being where in there is no controller or controlled but only unity and harmony. (6). The kind of personal identity meaning available here is in the idea that authentic personal identity is achieved in a state of harmonious oneness of being.

The Self As Violent—The Self As Tender

Experiences

There are many, many ways in which violence and tenderness are experienced in sports, dance, aquatics and exercise. Frequently, participants direct explosively violent actions at material objects or receive explosively violent actions through material objects. Executing the smash in badminton or tennis and the spike in volleyball are good examples of this. In this type of experience close to maximum aggression is concentrated into a fleeting instant of time and into a small area of space. For the person executing such violent action the experience is one of intense concentration of one's being to the extent that the self becomes a unity of violent intention and violent action. However, even when the self is experienced as unified violence, there is another aspect of this experience needing clarification. This is the difference between the violent action experience on the part of the beginning, unskilled players and that same experience on the part of the more advanced, skilled player. The unskilled player often executes this action in a practically unrestrained manner wherein he is totally committed to the action. The skilled player, however effective and violent his action is by comparison, executes with a measure of control and restraint.

The player who receives the violent action as it is transmitted through material objects has different experiences. For example, it is

frequently observed that the initial experience of receiving the mediated violence of the badminton or tennis smash or the volleyball spike
result in the recipient quickly turning his back to the violent action
or hurriedly throwing up his hands or racket in desperate protective
moves. Most more experienced participants react quite differently. In
general, the more advanced players meet the transmitted violence
"head on" and attempt to convert it to their own advantage. In the
case of the novice, the mediated violence is an experience of fear while
the skilled player usually experiences a challenge.

The bodily experience of violence obviously occurs in other ways.
At least on the surface, violent action which is directly applied to the
body of another person or received directly from the body of another
person seems experientially different than mediated violence. The
bodily experiences of being hit and hitting another person in boxing
or of being thrown to the mat or throwing another person to the mat
in wrestling and judo are illustrative of this category. The experiential
difference from mediated violence seems to lie in the fact that the
action brings the subjectivity of both the aggressor and the receiver
into direct contact with each other. If in boxing I execute a left jab
to the chin which strikes the mark, then my experience is one in which
my willed intention is in direct contact with another being who wills.
Conversely, if I receive the blow on the chin, then I feel the willed
intention of the other person rather than experiencing the result of
his willed intention. In mediated violence my direct contact is with
an object which does not will or think or feel and is, thus, not responsible or accountable. In direct bodily violence my direct contact is
with a person who wills, thinks, and feels and, accordingly, is responsible and accountable.

There is, furthermore, a bodily experience of violence which does
not separate direct bodily contact between persons from mediated
contact through objects. This type of experience becomes available
probably only to those who are highly skilled in the activities which
use mediating objects for the transmission of violence (such as badminton, tennis or volleyball again). It is the natural outgrowth of appropriation of objects into the phenomenal self referred to earlier.
Highly skilled players in such activities experience the extension of
self into the objects employed to the extent, in some cases, that the

objects are not only physical self-extensions but are infused with personal will. In these instances, violent actions, whether executed or received, become more similar in quality to direct bodily violence rather than solely mediated violence.

The bodily experience of tenderness is also a part of sports, dance, exercise and aquatics. One way in which tenderness is experienced bodily is in executing certain skilled actions which have a tender feel to them. A few examples of such tender feeling skills are the hairpin shot in badminton, the volleyball set and a short putt or some chip shots in golf. Each of these in its own way involves the bodily feeling of tender application of force to objects. In many cases the tender, controlled feeling of the bodily actions involved is highlighted by the presence, either before or after, of a contrasting violent bodily experience. For instance, the hairpin shot might be experienced in close contrast to the smash in badminton, the set might be close to the spike in volleyball and the short putt might be immediately before or after an all-out wood shot in golf. In these cases, and others, the tender and violent feels of the executed skills are enhanced by proximity to opposites.

Interestingly, the tender feel of some executed skills seems, at times, to be mediated through the sports implement and to evoke a similar tender feel skill from an opposing player. This is best illustrated by a sequence of several hairpin shots at the net in badminton where, with skilled players, each successive shot seems to be increasingly tender in execution to the point where too much tenderness in execution results in a shot which does not clear the net.

The bodily experience of tenderness can also be more direct and personal. The modern dancer may select certain movements specifically to emphasize a feeling of tenderness and thus experience that feeling as it is abstracted in the movements. At times in several varieties of dance, the movement patterns and sequences may call for moments when individuals touch each other with exquisite tenderness. Oddly enough, a feeling of direct bodily tenderness in movement can be experienced even in sports which emphasize aggressive force. For instance, in wrestling there are times, such as when one wrestler wishes to turn the other into a certain position but must, at the same time, avoid going beyond that position, when the application of force must be delicately and tenderly balanced so that the resulting movement is neither too large nor too small.

Meanings

Bodily experiences of the self as violent and the self as tender are also productive of awareness of personal human identity. Perhaps the first kind of awareness which may come is the direct bodily realization of a personal capacity for both violence and tenderness. Such realization is self-instructive not simply because it is lived and felt but because living and feeling violence and tenderness provides an experiental basis for persons to react to and reflect upon the personal meanings of such experiences. For instance, if violent action is directed at me, either in a direct bodily way or a mediated way, and my reaction is one of fear of the action, then I become aware of myself in a way which may or may not be acceptable to me. On the one hand if I consider such fear to be indicative of a personal cowardliness, I may be ashamed of my personal identity. On the other hand, if I consider such fear to be a natural human reaction to violence, I may accept my reaction as normal and as one which ties me to mankind in a common human identity. Additionally, if after an initial fear reaction to violence I am able in subsequent experiences to face the violence and overcome the reaction by viewing the violence as a challenge, then I become aware of my personal human identity as a being who, by exertion of will, can overcome barriers and obstacles to fuller self-realization.

> The value of violence in sport to both participant and spectator is not in its expression per se, but in its control towards the achievement of a contested end. Where violence may be sufficient to generate interest in an activity, its control is necessary to sustain our continued interest in its expression. (7:p.18).

There seems to be a fascination with violence on the part of humans which is vividly illustrated in sports. Whereas something of self-identity may be found from the fact of fear of violent physical actions, something else of self-identity may be found from the fact of personal fascination with violent physical actions. How do I react to myself when I execute a particularly violent volleyball spike or badminton smash which goes directly at an opposing player so that he is literally overpowered by the force of it? Am I elated by the effectiveness of my action or am I fearful that he might be injured? Does it make any difference in my reaction to my own violent act if it is directed towards a member of my own sex or of the opposite sex?

The bodily experience of tenderness also gives the experiential basis for me to reflect upon in terms of personal significance. Beyond informing me of my capacity for tenderness, executing or receiving tender actions allows me to reflect on my own reaction to such experience. The bodily experience of tenderness may be reacted to as most enjoyable and fulfilling in that a person may relish the feeling of soft, non-threatening sensitivity. Conversely, the bodily experience of tenderness, particularly in touching or being touched by another person, may be reacted to as a threat. Both of these kinds of reactions are potentially informative of personal identity. If I enjoy the tenderness, then I know something of my identity as a being who is fulfilled in this way. If I am threatened by the tenderness, then I know something of my identity as a being who is fearful that allowing such an expression will question the validity of my own self-image.

In summary, the meanings of a self-identity nature which may be derived from the bodily experiences of violence and tenderness are often ambivalent. This is to say that the positive self-identity meaning of being a powerful agent achieved through the experience of violence is mixed with the negative self-identity meaning of being fearful of the responsibility for the exercise of such power. Also the positive self-identity meaning of being a fulfilled agent achieved through the experience of tenderness is mixed with the negative self-identity meaning of being fearful of one's identity as an agent fulfilled by tenderness. The result of this becomes awareness of human self-identity which is ambiguously joyful and fearful of himself. Here appears a being who both loves and fears himself because he is both exalted and repulsed by his own violence and tenderness alike. To paraphrase Pascal, "To be *man* (beyond animal) is not just to be miserable but to *know* one is miserable. . . ." (2:p.64).

The Self As Competitive—The Self As Cooperative

Experiences

Competition is often defined as two or more persons striving simultaneously for the same object which only one may possess. Cooperation usually means two or more persons striving to achieve and share the same object. The self is experienced as both competitive and cooperative in sports and, upon close analysis, sometimes both cooperative and competitive at the same time.

Surprisingly as it may seem, but nontheless absolutely necessary, the indispensable preface to any sports competition is cooperation. This is to say that the self is implicitly cooperative before he can be competitive by the clear necessity of a mutual agreement between parties that they will meet at a certain place, at a certain time,to share and compete with each other in a given sport. From this base, the self then experiences himself in a variety of ways as competitive and cooperative.

Experience of the self as competitive has many variables which change the experience. One variable is in the kind of opponent faced, such as another individual of the same or the opposite sex, a group of individuals either of the same or opposite sex (a team), or, in the case of nature sports, either an animal or nature itself. A second variable is in the intensity of the competitive setting, ranging from an informal contest after classes in the gym or on a weekend picnic through a school or local tournament to international events such as the Olympic Games. A third variable, related to the first two above, lies in the attitudes of the competitors themselves toward what they expect from the contest itself.

As an individual competitor contesting with another competitor, I may enter a contest with an opponent who is clearly superior or inferior to my skill level or with someone who is approximately equal. If the opponent is clearly superior in skills I may feel either inadequate to the task and somewhat in awe of his ability, indifferent to the contest, or I may feel the challenge of the skill difference. If the opponent is clearly inferior in skills I may feel at ease and very confident, indifferent to the contest, or sympathetic toward the opponent's lack of skill. If the opponent's skill is approximately equal to mine, I may approach the contest with positive anticipation.

During competition with an opponent whose skills are clearly superior to mine, I may experience myself as highly motivated to overcome the difference and, in so doing, may play either much more poorly or much more skillfully than expected. Or I may experience myself as unable to perform well enough and, probably, may play well below my level of skill.

During competition with an opponent whose skills are clearly inferior to mine, I may experience myself as in command of the situation and able to control the contest in any way I wish. I may attempt to execute skills and strategies which I seldom use in more equal contests or I may play my well-tested game in order to establish my superiority clearly. In some instances, I may avoid playing to my opponent's weaknesses and perhaps even play to his strengths.

During competition with an opponent of equal skill, I may experience myself as highly motivated and excited about the unpredictable outcome of the contest. In all of the cases of individual competition cited, the self is experienced as a being who is dependent solely upon his own efforts.

The experience of the self as competitive has some different dimensions when it involves dual or team efforts. Teams enter competition wherein the level of ability of the contestants may be clearly different or equal. Individuals, as members of teams, may experience themselves in ways both similar and different from individual competitors who compete in individual sport. The most general difference is that the self is experienced as a being who is dependent upon the efforts of others as well as his own.

In contests with teams of clearly superior ability, the self may experience himself as a member of a group which feels inadequate, indifferent to the contest, challenged by the difference in ability, or he may find himself at individual variance from the group feeling. In the case of contests with a team of clearly inferior ability the self may experience himself in accord with a team feeling of ease and confidence, indifference, sympathy toward the opponent or at variance from any one of these feelings.

The self may be experienced as cooperative in both individual and team activities. Beyond the previously identified implicit cooperation inherent before any sports competition can be, are the ways in which cooperative experience occurs during a contest. Perhaps one of the most interesting of these experiences appears on those occasions when the actual competition for single points in sports becomes a means to satisfy what is essentially a cooperative objective of the participants.

This experience occurs when participants approach a sports contest with the predominent attitude that they wish to be there primarily for the joy of the game itself rather than the result of the game expressed in winning or losing. In such events, the self is experienced as a co-operative agent in a mutual endeavor wherein all participants may share the rewards of the endeavor. Even though single points may be heartily contested, the competition itself serves to enhance the mutual and cooperative joy, mirth and diversion function of the sport for all participants. (8,9). In this type of experience, the self is both competitive and cooperative simultaneously, however, competition is subordinated to the role of means to a cooperative end.

The self is experienced as cooperative in a different way in team contests where the predominent attitude of the participants is that they wish to be there primarily to determine which team is better. In such contests, team members experience themselves as integral members of a group which has a common competitive objective to overcome a similar group. The self is experienced as a being who relinquishes some individuality in order to enhance the potentiality that he, as a part of a team, may enhance his level of achievement in a way not possible for him alone and that his personal achievement is measured more by team success. In this type of experience the self is both competitive and cooperative simultaneously, however, cooperation is subordinated to the role of means to a competitive end.

Meanings

Experiences of the self as competitive lend themselves to interpretation of meanings of the self-identity variety. In general, the experience of the self as competitive is an experience of the *opposition* of my personal forces and resources (either individually or as a member of a team) against some other type of forceful agent (either another individual, a team, my own aspirations or nature). These competitive experiences of the self in opposition may have several meanings. First, I may come to my own *actual* power, or lack of it, as an effective agent. This is to say that my adequacy in organizing and utilizing my personal resources and expressing them in motor action is subjected to a direct and univocal test. This test is univocal in the sense that it tells me straight and direct (without equivocation) that my actions are effective or ineffective. I may not *really,* verbalization to the contrary, talk my way out of the fact that I am able or unable to perform sports skills effectively or uneffectively. Everytime I hit the ball successfully, it reinforces my identity as adequate to meet and overcome opposition. Everytime I fail to hit the ball successfully, it reinforces my identity as inadequate to meet and overcome opposition. In a very general way, my sense of personal identity as adequate or inadequate to meet external opposition tends to make the "out-there world" a place of personal affirmation or negation; that is, a place which testifies to my being significant, effective force or a place which reminds me of my lack of power.

But a self-identity meaning of adequacy or inadequacy in meeting the external opposition of competition is only part of the picture. Another part of the picture comes from how I feel about my own identity of adequacy or inadequacy in this regard. Still further is how I feel about the identity of others as adequate or inadequate. If my self-identity is adequate in meeting the external opposition of competition, do I accept it as a mark of my superiority for which I am responsible or as an endowment for which I am grateful? If my self-identity in meeting the external opposition of competition is inadequate, do I try to reject it as somehow not being me (and thus reject my own identity as unworthy) or do I accept it as being me (and thus accept my own identity as worthy). In either case, personal acceptance of my identity helps to give me an understanding of the kind of significance which I possess (i.e., either as an agent who makes things happen or as an agent to whom things happen).

And how do I feel about the adequacy or inadequacy of others in meeting the external opposition of competition? If my identity is that of adequacy do I view the adequacy of others as a threat and challenge to me, do I sincerely find joy in the fact of their adequacy, or do I find an ambivalent threat and joy in their adequacy? Honest reflection to supply answers to such questions provide still further insights into who I really am.

Further, if my identity is that of adequacy, do I view the inadequacy of others as a joke, as a barrier to my enjoyment, or as a sign, by its contrast, which helps provide my identity of adequacy? Do I consider others who are inadequate disparagingly as uncoordinated "spastics," as persons who spoil the game, or as persons who provide the needed polarity of contrast which sharpens my own sense of identity? Again my responses to these queries help to define who I am.

The competitive experience of opposition may be interpreted for other types of meaning. For instance, how do I view my opponent or opposition during the competition? One kind of view seems to be more prevalent at highly competitive and publicized athletic events and this is the view in which players tend to view each other in an analytical, objective fashion. This is to say that the view of the opponent is more that of an object to be overcome and dominated. Another kind of view perceives the opponent as an agent who provides the opportunity for the testing and extension of self and for whom the self provides, also, the opportunity for the opponent to test and extend himself. In this latter view, the opponent is regarded as an enabler or facilitator of the self and the self regards himself as an enabler or facilitator of the opponent. Also in this latter view, the opponents view the competition as competition *with* each other while, in the former view where opponents view each other as objects to be overcome and dominated, the mutual view is that of competition *against* each other. (11:pp. 41-42;5).

Simply expressed, the self-identity meaning available to persons is that they literally possess the capacity to stand in opposition to each other as objects and/or to stand in relationship to each other as subjects. Beyond this the self may come to know that it seems necessary and appropriate to view his opponent as an object if the fact of winning or losing the contest is predominant. If, however, the predominant purpose of the competition is mutual joy, then the view of the opponent as a thinking, feeling and willing subject seems necessary and appropriate.

If the experience of competition is essentially one of opposition, the experience of cooperation is one of coordination. Such coordination is one in which the persons involved assume an equality of identity in the mutual endeavor and in which each becomes dependent upon the other. In terms of meaning for self-identity, such experience brings awareness of the possibility of my powers being extended by such coordination with another person while, at the same time, my cooperation extends the powers of the other person. This meaning leads me to realize identity as a being who relinquishes a measure of independence to gain powerful self-extension while accepting dependence upon me to facilitate powerful self-extension of another person. Further, such meaning extends further to the realization that the self-extension power provided by coordination mutually enhances the participants potential to meet effectively the external forces of opposition. This means individuality is subordinated in order to increase its own power. This raises the question if the willingness of the self to place himself in a situation of mutual dependence is always motivated by the desire to enhance effectiveness in meeting external opposition. Or, would I coordinate my efforts with others if there was no opposing external force to meet? Would I cooperate if such cooperation did not enhance my ability to compete?

It was suggested earlier in this paper that competition to overcome opposition of external forces can be subordinated to cooperation, that is ". . . when the participants approach the sports contest with the predominant attitude that they wish to be there primarily for the joy of the game itself rather than the result of the game expressed in winning or losing." This point of view is based in the following which distinguishes between sport, which is essentially a cooperative endeavor, and athletics, which is primarily a competitive endeavor:

"Sport," we are told, is an abbreviation of the middle English *desport* or *disport,* themselves derivatives of the Old French *disporter,* which literally meant to carry away from work. Following this lead, Webster and other lexicographers indicate that "diversion", "recreation", and "pastime" are essenial to sport. It is "that which diverts and makes mirth; a pastime". While the dictionaries reflect some of the confusion and fuzziness with which contemporary thought shrouds the concept of athletics, they invariably stress an element which, while only accidentally associated with sport, is essential to athletics. This element is the prize, the *raison d'etre* of athletics. Etymologically, the various English forms of the word "athlete" are derived from the Greek verb *athlein,* "to contend for a prize", or the noun *athlos,* "contest", or *athlon,* a prize awarded for the successful completion of the contest. An oglique insight into the nature of athletics is obtained when we realize that the word "agony" comes from the Greek *agonia*—a contest or a struggle for victory in the games. Thus we see that, historically and etymologically, sport and athletics have characterized radically different types of human activity, different not insofar as the game itself or the mechanics or rules are concerned, but different with regard to the attitude, preparation, and purpose of the participants. In essence, sport is a kind of diversion which has for its direct and immediate end fun, pleasure, and delight which is dominated by a spirit of moderation and generosity. Athletics, on the other hand, is essentially a competitive activity, which has for its end victory in the contest and which is characterized by a spirit of dedication, sacrifice, and intensity. (8:pp.27-28).

The meaning of all this is that man, in the self-constructed world of sport (as defined immediately above), is able to cooperate with others for the mutual enhancement (i.e., fun, pleasure, and delight) of all involved rather than some being fulfilled while others are not. This is to say that in sport as defined, competition with opposing external forces is subordinated to the role of means, to the dominant cooperative end of providing joy and diversion for all members of both teams equally. In athletics, conversely, cooperation of teammates is subordinated to the role of means of extending personal power to accomplish the competitive end of one team (and its individual members) overcoming the opposing external forces of the other team. In athletics, the positive reward for efforts is restricted to one team. This is not to say that the losing team in athletics cannot have any reward for its effort, but that losing does not bestow upon the loser the kind of reward for which he originally and consciously entered the contest.

In this kind of contrast, the self knows himself as a being capable of using both competition and cooperation as a means and/or an end and as forms of human relationships which can enhance himself and others in differing ways. Again, paradoxically, the self knows himself as a being who is happy with direct evidence of his adequacy to meet opposing external forces while he is sad that his adequacy is attained by overcoming others. Also, he is pleased with his ability to enter into coordinated endeavor which bestows its benefits upon all to the detriment of none while, at the same time, displeased that such endeavor fails to tell him of his personal, relative power.

CONCLUDING STATEMENT

This has been an attempt to explore some few movement experiences which occur in sports, dance, exercise and aquatics and to interpret them for meaning. Hopefully this exploration may stimulate reflections upon personal experience in such movement forms. If such stimulation occurs, then the moving "I" sees, and having seen moves on.

REFERENCES

1. Beisser, Arnold R.: *The Madness in Sports.* New York, Appleton-Century-Crofts, 1967.
2. Come, Arnold B.: *Human Spirit and Holy Spirit.* Philadelphia, The Westminster Press, 1959.
3. Coutts, Curtis A.: "Freedom in Sport", *Quest,* No. 10, 68-71 (May, 1968).
4. Fraleigh, Warren P.: "The Meaning of Man As a Moving Being—The Concept and Structure of Physical Education in the New College of San Jose State College". Unpublished manuscript, San Jose State College, 1968.
5. Gerber, Ellen W.: "Identity, Relation and Sport", *Quest,* No. 8, 90-97, (May, 1967).
6. Herrigel, E.: *Zen In the Art of Archery.* New York, Pantheon, 1953.
7. Kaelin, E.F.: "The Well-played Game: Notes Toward an Aesthetics of Sport," *Quest,* No. 10, 16-28 (May, 1968).
8. Keating, James W.: "Sportsmanship As a Moral Category", *Ethics,* Vol. 85, No. 1, 25-35 (October, 1964).
9. Keating, James W.: "Winning In Sport and Athletics", *Thought,* Vol. 38, No. 149, 201-210 (Summer, 1963).
10. Levine, Jacob: "Humor in Play and Sports," *Motivations in Play, Games and Sports,* R. Slovenko and J.R. Knight (eds.). Springfield, Thomas, 1967.
11. Metheny, Eleanor: *Connotations of Movement in Sport and Dance.* Dubuque, Wm. C. Brown Company Publisher, 1965.
12. Metheny, Eleanor: *Movement and Meaning.* New York: McGraw-Hill Book Company, 1968.
13. Ogilvie, Bruce C.: "The Unconscious Fear of Success", *Quest,* No. 10, 35-39 (May, 1968).
14. Sarano, Jacques: *The Meaning of the Body.* Philadelphia, The Westminster Press, 1966.
15. Schvartz, Esar: "Nietzsche: A Philosopher of Fitness", *Quest,* No. 8, 83-89 (May, 1967).
16. Slusher, Howard S.: *Man, Sport and Existence.* Philadelphia, Lea and Febiger, 1967.
17. Wenkart, Simon: "Sports and Contemporary Man," *Motivations in Play, Games and Sports,* R. Slovenko and J.A. Knight (eds.). Springfield, Thomas, 1967.

SOME MEANINGS OF THE HUMAN EXPERIENCE OF FREEDOM AND NECESSITY IN SPORT

WARREN P. FRALEIGH

INTRODUCTION

For ages humankind has asked the question, "Who Am I?" Additionally, various versions of the dictum "Know Thyself" have been promoted by humans. Each of these refers to the continuing concern of humans with clarifying their own identity. One topical area of interest of humans with regard to identity has been that dealing with the question of human freedom or the lack of it. The intent of this paper is a brief and very simplified examination of the differing senses in which humans may experience freedom and necessity in sport. In addition, interpretations of these experiences in terms of human identity meanings will be attempted. Because of time limitations only skeletal treatment of these themes is presented here.

THE EXPERIENCES OF NECESSITY

Necessity may be experienced in several ways in sport. Among these are necessity as deterministic, necessity as a personal condition of motor inability, necessity as a personal condition of physiological inability, and necessity as restriction on the choice of movements performed.

Necessity As Deterministic

The term deterministic is intended to capture the meaning of the human body as an object which is controlled by natural forces such as those identified by Newton's laws of motion. Humans experience necessity as deterministic in several ways. Gravity is experienced vividly in sports involving jumping, vaulting, and diving. Inertia is experienced directly in sports involving bodily contact with stationary and moving masses as well as sports which demand rapid starts and stops.

In this experience persons may perceive themselves as beings who are controlled externally and have no choice as to whether or not such external control will affect them. This is to say that, on this earth and without artificial aids, persons *always* come down when jumping, vaulting, or diving, persons *always* move when bodily contact occurs, and persons *always* exert great force to start or stop their bodies quickly. The quality of inevitability is present in the experience of necessity as deterministic and it is that qualtiy which characterizes the experience as deterministic. In sport viewed as deterministic necessity, the human self lives the experience of necessity in his participation.

Meanings of Necessity As Deterministic

The lived-body experience of the self as deterministic necessity is a basic source of human identity meanings. It "tells" me that my humanness inherently allies me with animals and objects and, in that *restricted sense,* I am not different from them. It "tells" me that an aspect of my personal identity, shared with animals, objects, and other humans, is that my day-to-day living experience seems to continue at least partially in a deterministic, necessary manner. It "tells" me, by direct experience of my own reality and by observation of the reality of others, that my identity does not allow me the God-like interpretation that my existence is *unconditionally* free.

Necessity As a Personal Condition of Motor Inability

The phrase "personal condition of motor inability" basically means the personal experience of failing to perform motor acts of the sports skills variety effectively. This experience is related to two differing antecedent conditions. One is the experience of motor inability to perform sports skills effectively in the *absence* of prior *practice* of those same skills. The other is the same experience of motor inability, however, *following* extensive opportunities for *practice* of those same skills. In the first instance necessity is experienced as a lack of something which, it may be noted by observation of skilled players, is attainable by practice of the skills. In other words, motor inability that is a necessary consequence of absence of practice may be removed by practice. Thus, the experienced necessity is relative to the condition of practice rather than one of deterministic necessity. In the second instance necessity is experienced as a lack of something which, it may be noted by observation of the development of skills by others, has *not* been attainable by practice of the skills. In other words, the motor inability that is a necessary consequence of absence of practice is *not* removed by practice. Thus, the experienced necessity is no longer *relative* to the condition of practice but becomes a *deterministic* necessity for the person in that he appears to have no control or choice. These two types of experiences allow persons a third kind of experience of motor inability. Namely, the personal condition of motor inability is a *relative* necessity for some while it is a *deterministic* necessity for others.

Meanings of Necessity As a Personal Condition of Motor Inability

The human self who experiences necessity as a personal condition of motor inability has the basis for two identity meanings. First, the potential of persons to overcome relative necessity by their own willed effort is manifest. That is, persons are aware of the function of personal will in the removal of negative-relative necessity. Second, human identity related to individual differences is noted in the varying degrees of ease with which some persons overcome negative-relative necessity when compared with other persons and by the marked contrast between those who cannot overcome (i.e., have no choice) negative-relative necessity with those who can.

In sum, these two types of meanings clarify human identity by way of informing us that individuals, at one and the same time, are both different from and like their fellows. This is to say that human identity involves both individuality and commonality and in relationship to each other. This tells us that we are both unique from and like our fellow humans and that it is precisely human to be so.

Necessity As a Personal Condition of Physiological Inability

This category includes those occasions in which persons experience personal inability to react effectively to sports conditions because of insufficient strength, endurance, or some other physiological requisite. Similar to the previous category, two differing antecedent conditions may be related to the experience. First, is the experience of physiological inability resulting from a lack of athletic condition. This occurs in the context of a sports situation which requires certain physiological qualities in order for effective performance to occur. Second, is the experience of physiological inability despite an athletic conditioning program prior to the sports situation. In the first case, necessity is experienced as a lack of something which, it may be noted by observation of physiologically conditioned players, is attainable by the completion of a physiological conditioning program. In the second case, necessity is experienced as a lack of something which, it may be noted by observation of physiologically well-conditioned players, has not been attained sufficiently despite a program of athletic conditioning.

Meanings of Necessity As a Personal Condition of Physiological Inability

The human identity meanings available here are substantially the same as those of the immediately preceding section of this paper and will not be repeated here.

Necessity As Restrictions on Choice of Movements Performed

The phrase "restrictions on choice of movements performed" signifies the reality of the sports environment. That is, once participants have chosen to engage in sport they *must* perform certain movements which are prescribed by the sport itself. Thus, the sports participant experiences a necessary restriction on the choice of movements he may perform and still be a participant in a particular sport. For example, the volleyball player is restricted from using kicking motions while the soccer player is generally restricted from throwing or batting the ball with his hands.

Necessity here is experienced as a self-chosen restriction. This is to say, when I choose to play volleyball I choose to restrict my movements to those defined by the rules and expectancies of volleyball. Although I may still have some small latitude in the timing of particular movements and in my personal style of performing those movements, I must, nonetheless, restrict my movements to those already prescribed for volleyball.

Meanings of Necessity As Restrictions on Choice of Movements Performed

It is a paradox that "necessity as restrictions on choice of movements performed" carries the identity meaning of freedom. For, the choice to engage in a man-made restricted movement environment is, in essence, the free choice of man to restrict himself in accord with an environment constructed freely by man. The fact that humans are able to construct from their own inventiveness what appears to be a "practically useless" activity may be symbolic of their identity as beings who may build a "world" of their own and, because it is their own self-constructed "world," one in which they are comfortable rather than alien. Upon entering such a "world" persons may know themselves symbolically as powerful agents in being since, in constructing that "world," they literally and freely *use* externally controlling necessities such as space, time, and gravity to serve their own purposes. Further, since the sports "world" is man-made, it is subject to change according to the will of men.

THE EXPERIENCES OF FREEDOM

Freedom may be experienced in a variety of ways in sport. Among these are freedom from deterministic necessity, freedom for the realization of personal intentions, freedom for creating new personal intentions, and freedom to be unified.

Freedom from Deterministic Necessity

Experience of release from deterministic necessity is a fleeting event in sport. It occurs in those occasions when, for a short while, gravity or some other restrictive natural force is overcome. Perhaps the classic example is the few seconds of release experienced in the bounce on a trampoline. The experience is of a negative freedom, that is, a freedom *from* some restriction such as gravity. Such an experience is exhilarating and its attraction is attested to through the rapturous reports of athletes in many sports.

Meanings of Freedom from Deterministic Necessity

The fleeting event of freedom from deterministic necessity provides a personal experience of release from a human condition to a state of supra human condition. This experience "tells" me that my humanness allies me with freedom and that, *in this restricted sense*, I am not different from God. Further, the exhilaration accompanying such experience seems symbolic of man's desire to transcend himself, to become more than he is; that is, a Nietzschean superman or a god.

Freedom for Realization of Personal Intentions

The experience of this positive freedom, that is a freedom *for*, results from the development of sports skills and physiological conditioning. As such, it is the opposite, but intimately related experience, of necessity as a personal condition of motor inability and/or of physiological inability. The experience has two dimensions. One is the experience of a negative freedom, that is, the release *from* the previous restrictions imposed by lack of motor skill and/or physiological conditioning. This release from previous restrictions is a condition from which the positive experience of freedom occurs. The positive experience of freedom may be expressed as the "ability to" rather than the negative "release from."

In sports performance, following release from motor or physiological inability accompanied by a concurrent development of sports skills and physiological conditioning, persons experience increasing ability to realize their personal intentions in the multitude of instantaneous sports challenges which appear. The tennis player now not only hits the ball, but hits it where he intends it to go. The badminton player not only blocks the bird smashed at him but returns it in a way that moves him from a defensive to an offensive position. The mile runner not only withstands the closing sprint of another runner but runs away from the other runner at the finish. In each of these instances the sports performer experiences a positive freedom to actualize (realize) his performance intentions. He is able to achieve congruence between intention and action, between personal will and result.

Still, there is another mode of positive experience of freedom in sport which is related to both skills and conditioning. This is the experience of the extension of the self through sports implements. Highly skilled players develop a type of relationship with sports implements which provides the experience of freedom by extension of the player's intentions further and more forcefully into the world. Rackets, bats, and clubs become phenomenal extensions of the person providing greater range of action as well as increasing the potential for application of force.

Meanings of Freedom for the Realization of Personal Intentions

The lived-body experiences of freedom provided by development of sports skills and physiological conditioning help persons understand two dimensions of human identity. One is variability among individuals in quantity of freedom while another is variability among individuals with respect to personal responsibility for one's own freedom. In the former instance, the relative level of skill and conditioning among different individuals depicts singular, individual identities; that is, each person is free to the extent to which his skill and conditioning allow. Thus, the variances of freedom from one person to another distinguish one person from another in identity in the same way that other developed abilities or conditions do.

Understanding of identity in the case of individual differences in personal responsibility for one's own freedom becomes evident when persons realize that their relative level of skill and physiological conditioning are, at least in part, a product of a person's will to free himself. This kind of understanding notes the fact that variations in skill and conditioning are frequently the result of differences in individual will as it is manifested in effort. In that individual human identity is at least partially dependent upon individual will manifest in effort, persons become aware that their identity is, to some extent, personally constructed. In short, they partially will themselves to be what they become.

The experience of extension of self into the world through sports implements indicates that facet of human identity which allows humans to appropriate the "not self" into the phenomenal self. Such appropriation allows persons to live themselves beyond themselves, that is, their "amplified" and "magnified" phenomenal self allows them to "live" outside their own skin. In other words, the appropriation of sports implements allows persons to project their intentionality into the world.

Freedom for Creating New Personal Intentions

This experience of freedom is an extension of the experience of freedom for the realization of personal intentions. The developments out of which this experience arises are extraordinary sport skill and superb physiological conditioning. From these bases, persons may experience a freedom to create new personal intentions in the forms of entirely new skill techniques, attempts at unprecedented levels of physiological performance, and design of new sport strategies which, without extraordinary skill and superb conditioning, previously were beyond possibility. Similar to the last category discussed, this experience is of both a negative freedom and a positive freedom. The person is released from the negative restrictions of pursuing sports participation armed only with the tools of normal skills accompanied by normal conditioning. In short, the restrictions of "conventional" success with "conventional" tools are overcome. Now the person experiences the positive freedom to intend new skills accompanied by new physiological resources and to construct new strategies.

Meanings of Freedom for Creating New Personal Intentions

The experience of freedom for creating new personal intentions intensifies and deepens a meaning associated with freedom for realization of personal intentions. The person who is free to realize personal intentions understands his identity as a being partly dependent upon his own personal will as manifest in effort. The person who is free to create new personal intentions understands his identity as a being who transcends himself and other humans by his personal will in conjunction with his personal creative ability to devise new skills, new physiological conditioning levels, and new strategies. In short, persons may learn the human identity possibility of transcendence as being a product of not only personal will but of personal will in conjunction with creative intelligence.

Freedom To Be Unified

The experience of freedom to be unified is manifest in two modes in sport. One is the experience of unification of the self with the self. The other is the unification of the self with the "not self."

Freedom for the unification of self with self is provided in two ways. One is well expressed by Metheny.

> In short, within the complex conditions of life, we are seldom, if ever free to focus all our attention on one well-defined task and bring all the energies of our being to bear on one whole-hearted attempt to perform that task effectively.
>
> In contrast, the rules of sport provide us with a man-made world in which this freedom is fully guaranteed. These rules eliminate the demands of necessity by defining an unnecessary task . . .
>
> In this sense, the rules of sport provide each performer with a rare opportunity to concentrate all the energies of his being in one meaningful effort to perform a task of his own choosing, no longer pushed and pulled in a dozen directions by the many imperatives he may recognize in his life. (5:p.63).

This kind of experience may be labeled as freedom for the unification of one's energies.

The second kind of unification of self with self is experienced as the unification of the person's actions with his intentions, the objective with the subjective, the "body" and the "mind." Freedom is experienced as the unity of the person in contrast to the experience of the person as divided against himself.

The second basic mode of freedom to be unified is experienced as unification of the self with the "not self." It occurs when the personal unity of self with self discussed above experiences that personal unity as being in accord with all that is external to the self. Accordingly, this unification goes beyond the unity of personal intention with the results to include the experience of the self no longer being controlled or inhibited by the external, while, at the same time, the self does not feel that it is controlling the external or the "not self." It is the experience that there is neither a controller nor that which is controlled, but only total harmony. The experience may be called the ecstatic feel of oneness with being.

Meanings of the Experience of Freedom To Be Unified

In both modes and sub-types of these experiences there is a common element. It is the sense of reduction or elimination of opposition to the self. In the experience of freedom for the unification of all one's energies to perform in sport, the opposition of conflicting or contradictory focusses is eliminated. In the experience of freedom for the unification of self with self, the opposition of the internal "I" and the external "I" is reduced or eliminated. In the experience of freedom for the unification of the self with the "not self," the mutual opposition of the self to all that is external is eliminated.

This reduction or elimination of opposition appears to be of two kinds, volitional and involuntary. In the cases of the experiences of freedom for unification of one's energies and for unification of self with self the reduction or elimination of opposition appears to be volitional. That is, the person may choose to "throw" himself into sport and, thus, unify his energies. Also, the person may choose to develop his sports skills to the point where unification of self with self is more readily possible, that is, the external "I" has sufficient skill to accomplish the intentions of the internal "I." The human identity meaning available in such experiences is, simply, the understanding that humans are agents who have the potential to unify themselves. This human potentiality may be realized by a person's free choice to "throw" himself into sport or by the free choice to develop effective sports skills.

In the mode of experience of freedom to unify the self with the "not self," the elimination of opposition is of the involuntary type since the experience appears to be unpredictable or even serendipitous. Inasmuch as the experience is ecstatic and, accordingly, is desired by persons, but, at the same time, not controlled by persons, it would seem that the experience places a person in a wholeness of being for which he is not responsible. If such experiences are "caused," the causal agent is other than the person. If that causal agent is nature, then the experience appears to be a result of an uncontrolled (by humans) and unpredictable congruence of the unified self with the "not self." If the "cause" is other than nature, then it seems to be what Christian theology calls grace which, in a secularized version, may be defined as a free and unmerited act through which persons are restored to a state of harmony in being.

The human identity meaning of involuntary freedom to be unified is that the "normal" state of being of humans is, somehow, incomplete. Since the experience of involuntary freedom to be unified is one of ecstatic harmony and wholeness in being, the experience connotes a lack of something in the human condition. This lack may be interpreted as a loss of harmony and wholeness of being or as an indicator of a new future status of the promise of harmony and wholeness. In either case, human identity is understood to be alienated, either from its original status or from its "evolutionary" promise.

CONCLUSION

The several meanings discussed in relation to the experiences of necessity and freedom in sport, taken altogether, appear to establish an ambiguous, paradoxical identity for humans. That is, humans seem to be neither fully necessitated nor fully free but both necessitated and free in variable amounts and combinations. Interestingly, humans appear to lack control over the experiences of deterministic necessity and of unification of the self with the "not self," the two apparent poles of these experiences. Nonetheless, all of the other experiences of necessity and freedom seem to operate to provide the conditions for one another or to clarify one another by contrast. For instance, the experiences of freedom appear to arise out of the enabling conditions of deterministic necessity, necessity as a personal condition of motor inability and physiological inability, and necessity as restriction on the choice of movements performed. At the same time, the experiences of necessity appear to be grounded in the contrasts with images of potential motor skill, physiological condition, and movement choices created freely by sports participants.

In considering all of the above it appears appropriate to conclude that man's freedom and determinism, at least as manifest in sports experiences, are neither of the radical Sartrean variety of total freedom nor of the Marxist concept of ". . . freedom as insight into necessity. . . ." (6:p.10). It is not the function of this paper to argue or debate the adequacy of varying conceptions of freedom, but only to comment upon them as they relate to the experiences and meanings of freedom explored in the text. Accordingly, within the foundations laid by analysis within this paper it appears that conceptions of freedom within sport must take into account ". . . that freedom can be realized only within the confines of certain limitations, and hence that the mystery of this coordination of freedom and limitation must be the first consideration of any doctrine of freedom." (6:p.14).

REFERENCES

1. Coutts, Curtis A.: "Freedom in Sport," *Quest*, No. 10, 68-71 (May, 1968).
2. Fraleigh, Warren P.: "A Christian Concept of the Body-Soul Relation and the Structure of Human Movement Experience." Unpublished manuscript, San Jose State College, 1968.
3. Fraleigh, Warren P.: "The Moving 'I'." Unpublished manuscript. San Jose State College, 1968.
4. Harvey, Van A.: *A Handbook of Theological Terms*. New York, The Macmillan Co., 1964.
5. Metheny, Eleanor: *Movement and Meaning*. New York, McGraw-Hill, 1968.
6. Thielicke, Helmut: *The Freedom of the Christian Man*. John W. Doberstein (trans.). New York, Harper & Row, 1963.

THE CONCEPT OF DOING

Francis W. Keenan

INTRODUCTION

"Learn by doing" is a cherished dictum of pedagogy, especially among those concerned with sport and physical activity. John Dewey, perhaps the most eminent of all American philosophers, provided doing with educational respectability. Doing has become a permanent part of the justification for activity and sport programs, often so overemphasized that the initial meaning and pedagogical logic for doing, intended by Dewey, are ignored or forgotten. This paper shall sketch the Deweyan theory of curriculum found in *Democracy and Education*. The implications of such a theory for sport and physical activity shall be outlined. Doing will then be seen as only the initial thrust of the curricular process.

Doing in sport is patterned and organized as are all experiences. The doing, the action, the experience represents more than may be discovered in the physical doing alone, for ". . . insofar as a physical activity has to be learned, it is not merely physical, but is mental, intellectual in quality." (2:p.38). The "do your own thing" philosophy now so popular is pedagogically unacceptable unless it reaches beyond the sophistry of sensationalism, emotionalism, and sensualism— attitudes widespread among college youth today. Such a philosophy places undue emphasis on the physical and emotional aspects of man while completely neglecting his rational abilities and natural cognitive desires. Dewey, of course, could never have sanctioned emotivist philosophies. He embraced the cognitive approach to knowledge as the best solution to the problems of man. Doing alone was not meant to represent the epitomy of life's experiences. Sensual stimulation was not believed to be replete with value. Dewey warned against this trend in which "... the crowding together of as many impressions as possible is thought to be 'the good life,' even though no one of them is more than a flitting and a sipping." (2:p.45). As Dewey explained: "... nothing takes root in the mind when there is no balance between doing and receiving." (2:p.45). It is this receiving, this cognitive operation which Dewey wished education to foster.

For a physical experience of doing to relate to facts, the values of the experience must be tested and organized. It is possible to be an efficient doer without having a conscious experience of what the doing entails. The player may perform automatically without ever giving his actions a second thought, if indeed, a first one. The doing begins and ends but reaches no closure in consciousness. I contend that we do not need schools to teach this sort of mindless doing separated from its historicity.

Doing in sport and physical activity should culminate in the enhancement of human life by releasing the values potentially available therein. Too many existing activity and athletic programs overlook the humanizing capacities of sport and physical activity. All too often, coaches and physical educationists have misinterpreted the phrase "learn by doing." Too many of our education programs are devoid of educational values. The "throw out the ball" routine is well known in physical education. Doing was meant to serve as a launching pad, an initial learning continuum, rather than just an end in itself. Physical kinds of doing in educational institutions should ultimately lead to an understanding of the total experience undergone, for example, how the self relates to that experience, and what the structure of the experience is. Meanings and relationships among these kinds of experiences should not be ignored; they provide the learner with the richest and most significant educational and intellectual content.

To achieve educational growth, Dewey had intended that the curriculum be constructed around three stages. These were: (1) the doing stage; (2) the information stage; and (3) the science stage.

THE 'HOW TO DO' STAGE

All learning emanates from some experience. Early learning experiences center in learning how to do. Active play and engagement in the skills of the arts and occupations provide learning which possesses a social origin. As Dewey said: "The knowledge which comes first to persons, and that remains most deeply ingrained, is knowledge of 'how to do' . . ." (3:p.184). Unfortunately, physical educators and coaches often never move their students beyond the first stage of the curriculum. We learn by doing, but that is only the initial step toward significant learning. Dewey intended "activity" to mean both mental and physical activity, each conjoined to the other. He had an abiding respect for knowledge as exhibited in organized, structured, and proven subject matter content. It was there, he felt, that the more tangible meanings of experience were to be found.

THE INFORMATION STAGE

When doing is joined in perception with the experience undergone, hidden meanings are discovered. The grasping of these meanings is the objective of intelligence. Doing alone may be intelligent or non-intelligent.

> Zeal for doing, lust for action, leaves many a person especially in this hurried and impatient human environment in which we live, with experience of an almost incredible paucity, all on the surface. (2:pp.44-45).

The second stage of the curriculum should present the social meanings hidden in the cultural life and activities of the student. The information conveyed carries the learner beyond the initial doing to appreciation and an enlarged capacity for insight into social problems and social life. Problems provide the content for further investigation in stage three.

THE SCIENCE STAGE

The science stage is the stellar stage of development in the Deweyan analysis of a curriculum based on doing. It is in this stage that specialization may be allowed to occur, although empirical forms of knowledge should be included in all stages of the curriculum. Study at the third level provides a firmer acquaintance and greater command of the forms of knowledge and methods of intellectual communication and inquiry. This stage, like the other two, is ultimately social in its motive and in its benefit to society.

In stage three, the curricular content is arranged and designed to allow the learner to discover and maintain the continuity of the refined social values of civilization and culture.

The school has an interest in utilitarian pursuits in the curriculum, as does the student. But these marketable skill-type contents are to be used as not only means of achieving a livelihood, but as vehicles for exploration of the effect of the skill on the individual and society. Of educational interest is the value of "doing" type content in conveying the meaning of various forms of culture and their effect on society. The school must move the learner beyond the merely utilitarian stage if it is to serve the values of democracy and insure the continued existence in some form of that democracy. This is no small task, for even today most higher education is employment oriented, as are students. The humanizing content of curricula found in stage two, when required, is largely ignored by students. This must reflect on the quality of teaching to some extent. But the blame is not easily fixed. Blaming students is an academic "cop out." Students, teachers, and administrators, as well as the society are all guilty, to some extent, of allowing curricula to disintegrate, to become watered down in the wrong areas, to proliferate in an uncontrolled fashion, and to become mis-educative generally. Dewey, it is true, placed great emphasis on the utilitarian aspect of curriculum, but he always insisted that it become more than merely utilitarian.

> We may say that the kind of experience to which the work of the schools should contribute is one marked by executive competency in the management of resources and obstacles encountered (efficiency), by sociability, or interest in the direct companionship of others, by aesthetic taste or capacity to appreciate artistic excellence in at least some of its classic forms; by trained intellectual method, or interest in some mode of scientific achievement; and by sensitiveness to the rights and claims of others— conscientiousness. (3:pp.243-244).

The emphasis on a broad and generalized human curriculum, which educates students to perceive the social values of knowledge in all its forms, is eminently practical and pragmatically feasible. The practicality of the "doing stage" motivates the student to learn by capturing his interest in social activity that has significance for him. In stage two the organized disciplines refine perceptions of meanings through problem solution and attentive guidance from the teacher. Stage three provides a more abstract "theoretic plane" which aims at the creation of a better life for man.

Curricula, then, are derived from the social order with no priorities inherently attached to any given mode of experience. All knowledge, of whatever form, may be both intrinsically and instrumentally valuable. The curriculum progresses through stages of activity to appropriation of cultural meanings abiding within the activity, and finally to refined evaluation and reconstruction of experience. This reconstruction is what the conception of education as growth really is about. It is a ". . . modification and corrective to the conception of education as experience . . ." (6:p.200). Experience alone ". . . cannot advance beyond its primary stage of immediate qualitative interaction without criticism, insight, and reflection — without in brief, the stature of growth." (6:p.200). The immediacy of experience derived in activity should culminate in the broader context of qualitative interactions found in stages two and three.

THE THREE STAGES OF CURRICULUM IN PHYSICAL EDUCATION

The strategy of the curriculum should be to develop broad ranges of movement proficiencies in the young so that, as they mature, the selective range of choices will be significantly broad to allow intelligent movement experiences. The best way to supply doing experiences that will not vanish when school years are ended is to aid students in achieving the meanings and understandings of the fundamental structure of human movement phenomena. "This is a minimum requirement for using knowledge." (1:p.137).

Dewey's curriculum plan is designed to "quicken powers of perception" into how movements occur and can be accomplished. "It strives to make the student sensitive to the kinds of problems he will have to meet, in wider contexts, when he is through with formal schooling." (5:p.137). The physical educator and coach should not forget that schooling itself is a part of life, and not just preparation for adult life.

The *doing* stage has rather obvious implications for physical education and sport. The possibilities for human doing are unlimited;

the significance of physical movements for the development of man are just beginning to be understood. Piaget, for example, believes that motor development, which is contingent upon movement, may be the basis upon which *all* later development proceeds. Doing should, therefore, be logically prior to stage two of the Deweyan curricular plan.

Any movement experience has implications within it that go far beyond the immediate involvement. The *information* stage connects the implications of experience to individual and social consequences. (3:p.217). In physical education and sport the following kinds of learning can be pursued at stage two:

1. Knowledge of the body as a part of nature.
2. Knowledge of the dynamics of the human movement phenomenon, physical, mental, and psycho-social.
3. Historical knowledge of past uses of human movement phenomena as a guide to the present and as inspiration for the future.
4. The products of the human movement curriculum including sampling of: individual and team skills, professional preparation, research, teaching, recreation, aesthetic appreciation, coaching, moral development, etc., ad infinitum.

The *science* stage is the culmination of "doing" and "perceiving" which opens new intellectual avenues to the learner. The traits of abstraction, generalization, and definite formulation are developed in the pursuit of knowledge and practice of the human movement discipline. The science stage supplies stages one and two with needed data, resources, and activities. This relationship between theory and practice is binding and reciprocal among the curricular stages. Ideas spring from diverse sources, but providing them with broadness significant to many individuals, and putting them at the disposal of all men is ultimately and philosophically the task of science operating as an organ of general social progress. (3:p.230). All the stages should operate at all levels of education.

SUMMARY

The content of the human movement curriculum in sport and physical education is socially derived and oriented. It acquires meaning as it unifies human movement (means) with socially and morally justifiable outcomes (ends).

The doing stage is important at all levels of education and beyond, since it is the foundation on which later learning is constructed. The information stage relies on "doing" experiences for richness of meaning and social importance. Stages one and two, doing and informing, should occur at all levels of education, early education, middle school, and higher education. The first stage, doing, relates especially to the very young school aged child. Until the child has developed powers of intelligence, he/she is unable to sufficiently perceive the interconnectedness and meanings of events found in doing and informing.

The science stage organized information to solve problems. Teachers, researchers, coaches, students, technicians, and other professional personnel are all necessary for the continual renewal and reorganization of human movement knowledge.

From the undergirding base of doings and meanings, the individual learner may aspire to pursue excellence in specialized forms of human movement. The school, the curriculum, and the teacher/coach should be prepared to focus on the advanced stages of learning in sport and physical activity, but the first two stages of curriculum are logically prior to the development of excellence in individuals desiring to become movement specialists. Physical doing alone, even in its most excellent forms, ". . . results in the acquisition of an additional mode of technical skill." (3:p.275).The reasons for assigning play and sport a place in the curriculum, then, are intellectual and social, rather than expedient. The school should serve society as a laboratory where the conditions of sport and physical activity may be discovered as intellectually fruitful rather than only externally productive.

Reform is needed to alleviate much of the mindless wandering of the traditional curriculum in sport and physical activity which genuflects before the Deweyan concept of doing and then completely ignores the ramifications of such a concept for curriculum. The change is vitally necessary to meet the intellectual, personal, and social demands of student development. This proposal should not be interpreted as advocacy of the so called "child-centered" emphasis which moved curriculum content away from organized subject matter. Quite the contrary, Dewey rejected such an approach to curriculum. Organized content in physical education should serve as the resource for providing understandings relevant to the movement experience. Students and organized content are both important, and doing is an efficient means of bringing the two together.

REFERENCES

1. Bruner, Jerome S.: *The Process of Education*. New York, Vintage Books, 1960.
2. Dewey, John: *Art as Experience*. New York, Minton, Balch and Company, 1934.
3. Dewey, John: *Democracy and Education*. Third edition. New York, Macmillan, 1964.
4. Dewey, John: *Interest and Effort*. Boston, Houghton Mifflin Company, 1913.
5. Hook, Sidney: "John Dewey: His Philosophy of Education and Its Critics," *Dewey on Education,* Reginald D. Archambault (ed.). New York, Random, 1969.
6. Mosier, Richard D.: "Education as Experience," *Progressive Education,* Vol. 29, 200-203 (April, 1952).

(CHAPTER II)

THE ETHICAL STATUS OF SPORT

INTRODUCTION

AXIOLOGY IS THE philosophic sub-discipline concerned with explaining the realm of value, or significance, as distinct from that of
being and knowledge. It is, more directly, the general theory of
value. It considers the nature, criteria, and metaphysical status of
value. Axiology is further distinguished in terms of its three major
subjects of interest: morality, beauty, and the common good. Ethics,
or moral philosophy, is that axiologic sub-discipline concerning judgments of approval and disapproval, rightness and wrongness, goodness and badness, virtue and vice with reference to dispositions of
actions or states of affairs. It is the study of ideal, individual conduct
in view of the nature of good and evil—a prescriptive, or normative,
treatment of moral principles and obligation. Major issues in ethics include the nature of the greatest good, the criteria of moral conduct, the
motivation of moral conduct, and the merit of life. The essays here presented, then, address themselves to these ethical issues as they are
located in the sport condition.

Like the first chapter, this second one begins with a series of
three essays. Also like the first chapter, the first of these essays (by
James W. Keating) presents a view to which the second and third
(by William A. Sadler, Jr. and Robert G. Osterhoudt respectively)
respond.

In "The Ethics of Competition and Its Relation to Some Ethical
Problems in Athletics," James W. Keating opposes those who emphasize the negative effects of competition, choosing instead to concentrate upon its positive contributions. Professor Keating conceives of
competition as an attempt, according to agreed-upon rules, to get or
to keep any thing either to the exclusion of others or in greater

[149]

measure than others; and suggests that this attempt is rather an ineradicable trait of human nature and one that unreplaceably assists in the construction and maintenance of a viable social hierarchy (the common good).

Professor Keating further distinguishes playful activity (a free, creative activity in which the goal of the participants is to maximize the joy or pleasure of the moment, seeking no goal outside the activity itself) from athletics (physical contests designed to determine human excellence through honorable victory in a contest). That is, the two are radically different in terms of their objectives, and since it is the objectives of each which determine the attitude and conduct proper to them, the attitude and conduct proper to playful activity cannot therefore also be suitable to athletics. By this view, then, playful activity is regarded as a cooperative venture in which the participants seek a mutually obtainable goal, and which is consequently dominated by a spirit of generosity and magnanimity. And athletics is conceived as a competitive venture in which the participants seek a mutually exclusive goal, and which is consequently dominated by a spirit of legalism and interpersonal antagonism. Moreover, Professor Keating concludes, the moral problems created by athletics are largely traceable to its highly competitive nature, and to the excessive desire for victory encouraged by that nature. As a result, the moral category of sportsmanship (as herein construed) applies in a strict sense to playful activity only; such that, its application to athletics becomes merely a rather secondary attempt to mitigate the force and ferocity of the competitive struggle.

William A. Sadler, Jr. in "A Contextual Approach to an Understanding of Competition: A Response to Keating's Philosophy of Athletics" opposes Professor Keating's notion (and defense) of competition on the dual grounds that as conceived it is detrimental to the realization of full humanness (it interferes with regarding others more so as persons than material objects), and that it fails to understand competition in its full cultural context. An examination of competition in cross-cultural perspective, it is held, reveals that it (as construed by Professor Keating) is not a universal occurrence, but one appropriate only to a particular form of cultural bias. In support of this view Professor Sadler presents four types of society in which the dominant values, and as a result the view of competition, differ: a being society (past-oriented, submissive to nature, fatalistic, in which competition of the Keatingesque sort has no significant place), a becoming society (present-oriented, cooperative with nature, in which competition within a perspective of moderation and cooperation is tolerated), a doing society (future-oriented, controlling of nature, practical, productive, utilitarian, in which competition performs a highly significant role), and a having society (future-oriented, acquisitive of nature, consumptive, in which a spectatorial interest in competition is primary). According to Professor Sadler, then, Professor Keating's view of the competitive motif in both athletics and playful activity rests in a transitional stage between that appropriate to a doing and that proper to a having society. And he is further convinced that it fails to account for alternative views of competition as occurring in other cultural contexts.

The essay concludes with a proposal which suggests the compatibility of play and competition (though differently construed than in the case of Professor Keating's thesis), and expresses support for a so-termed sharing culture (in which play and competition would converge to create a condition by which self and social development are at once revered and cultivated). In such a culture, sport could well (and in any instance ought to) promote the development of a more humane world.

In "On Keating on the Competitive Motif in Athletics and Playful Activity," Robert G. Osterhoudt grants Professor Keating his disposition to axiologic subjectivism, as well as his notion of competition and its social utility. The essay concentrates instead upon developing a discussion of the implications of these views for a synoptic conception of man, the social substance, and the common good. That is, according to Professor Osterhoudt's position, the competitive motif as located in athletics and playful activity must be carefully examined with respect to its relation to the public interest (the social order), and not be considered in isolation by itself alone.

Professor Osterhoudt argues that the proposed distinction between athletics and playful activity is, in effect, a discrimination between two radically different ways of regarding activities which may be similar in phenomenal appearance, but are necessarily discrete in essence, in terms of their goals, or objectives (the primary intentions of their participants). These ways are, in point of fact, the germ of two radically discrete, indeed opposing, views of man, the social substance, and the common good. Professor Osterhoudt then holds that the notion appropriate to playful activity is best preferred, for it allows the coalescence of self-interest and public interest, and thereby creates a harmony among men which is unknown when they are conceived apart from one another. That is, as an essentially cooperative venture, playful activity entails the genuinely sympathetic regard for other men which we seek openly for ourselves, and which is not apparent in the exclusivity of athletics, wherein other men are regarded rather as objects to be overcome and are employed primarily as means for our own gratification. This latter notion (that with respect to the competitive motif in athletics), it is further argued, is potentially destructive of the whole of humanity and resultantly, of the whole of the social substance as well.

In "The Grasshopper; A Thesis Concerning the Moral Ideal of Man," Bernard Suits shows, through a parable presented in dialogue form, that the activities commonly termed work (activity which is only instrumentally valuable to those who engage in it) are self-contradictory in principle, as they seek in the end their own extinction. That is, by this view a life of play (activity which is intrinsically valuable to those who engage in it) is the only justification for work; as it is principally the opportunity to play that work attempts to secure. Such that, it is a state of idleness (a being at play) that man ought to seek foremost—it is an acting in accord with this Grasshopperian ideal which is most worthy of human allegiance.

Game-playing (as an attempt to achieve a specific state of affairs, using only means permitted by rules, where the rules prohibit more efficient in favor of less efficient means, and where such rules are accepted just because they make possible such activity—a voluntary attempt to overcome unnecessary obstacles) is construed as one intance of play activity. And, irrespective of the phenomenal appearance of such activity, it is the purest form of intrinsic engagement. It is an activity in which what is instrumental is inseparably combined with what is intrinsically valuable, wherein the activity is not itself an instrument for some further end. As such, then, game-playing is regarded as the essential constituent of the moral ideal of man (that thing, or those things, the only justification for which is that they justify all else). According to this view, consequently, it is game-playing which makes Utopia intelligible; and even in our non-Utopian world, it is game-playing that offers us salvation, that allows us insight into a future and better world.

Professor Suits further observes, however, that virtually everyone alive is engaged in the playing of elaborate games, while at the same moment believing themselves to be going about their ordinary affairs. Most persons, then, allegedly do not, nor will not foreseeably, wish to live their lives as game-players. They are rather disposed to regarding life as worth the requisite effort to preserve it, if, and only if, they believe themselves engaged in doing something useful. The essay thereby concludes on a pessimistic note, which portends the implausible prospect of achieving the Utopian state (realizing the moral ideal of man) earlier envisioned.

Jan Broekhoff in "Sport and Ethics in the Context of Culture" examines Huizinga's segregation of ethics and play, and consequently that of ethics and sport (conceived as a contest for something with all of the characteristics of play). Professor Broekhoff holds that play in its transition to sport incorporates some aspects of the work condition, yet maintains its intrinsic, free, extraordinary, and non-rational qualities, thereby continuing to stand outside the valuations of virtue or vice. Even the rules (laws) of sport which determine its boundaries and the terms of conduct proper to players in a game are not themselves regarded as moral laws here; but merely as terms by which the activity in question is distinguished, or defined.

According to Professor Broekhoff, it is rather through the uncertainty and tension located in sport that morality enters its realm, and then largely from without; that is, largely from the emphasis that a particular society places on the winning and losing of sporting contests, or games. Thus a discussion of the ethical status of sport leads rather inexorably to an examination of the cultural context in which sport appears. The greater the emphasis on winning, it is observed, the greater the proclivity of players to interpret the rules in a strict legalistic manner, to regard them as external sanctions, rather than as exhortations to follow the inner conviction of conscience. That is, an excessive emphasis upon the winning of sporting events encourages players to act merely in accord with the rules, to act out of an inner resolve to take even unfair advantage of a situation, in so far as such an act is not explicitly prohibited by the rules. In such a condition, it is concluded, the spirit of genuine fair play, or good faith, among players is sorrowfully lacking.

In "The Pragmatic (Experimentalistic) Ethic as It Relates to Sport and Physical Education," Earle F. Zeigler suggests the general form of pragmatism; its ethical posture, and its implications for education, sport, and physical education. Under the influence of the experimentalistic position, Professor Zeigler discusses the essence of the ethical problem in sport and physical education, ethics in historical perspective, values as construed by Parsons' Action System, contemporary ethical problems, the general nature of the pragmatic (naturalistic) ethics, the educational implications of experimentalism (pragmatic naturalism), the pragmatic (experimentalistic) ethic in sport and physical education, and the strengths and weaknesses of this view.

Emphasized are the themes commonly emphasized by thinkers of this persuasion: the primacy of socio-cultural experience, change (transcience), plurality, relativity, scientific methodology, democracy, ment is a matter of applying human reason to the results of scientific practicality, freedom, and problem-solving. By this view, ethical judg-investigation. The worthiness of an idea is determined by the practical results it realizes in everyday life, by its ability to fulfill useful human purposes. The experimental method is applied to a search for the values of education as a *life experience*. The pragmatic curriculum is, then, an individual (student)-centered program in which a concept of total fitness is promoted. In sport and physical education, it is further argued, skills, knowledges, and attitudes ought to be taught and learned primarily through the medium of movement experiences. Professor Zeigler concludes that pragmatism (experimentalism) offers the best and most humane approach to resolving the problem of new values generally, and those proper to education, sport, and physical education more specifically.

In "The Fiction of Morally Indifferent Acts in Sport," Terence J. Roberts and P. J. Galasso hold that there is no segment of man's voluntary, conscious, and responsible activity which is not morally endowed. That is, there are no such acts/actions which are morally neutral. And in the more specific case of sport, they argue that such acts/actions are necessarily moral. By this view, an act/action is regarded as any activity or performance which is both voluntarily engaged and consciously deliberated; such that, intention and therefore rationality and responsibility are likewise implied. Such acts/actions, then, may be ascribed only to men, as only men perform from a conception of law, and not merely from a response to natural stimulus. This notion which conceives of all acts/actions as either morally right or wrong, and thereby never morally neutral, distinguishes the rational activity of moral intention and conduct from mere bodily movements or other phenomena, which occur by empirical fiat. Mr. Roberts and Professor Galasso further and persuasively demonstrate that there are many instances of such acts/actions in sport, and suggest that a realization of their nature and resultantly of their moral posture may lead us to consider our conduct in sport in more morally persistent and relevant terms.

It is the intent of Robert G. Osterhoudt's "The Kantian Ethic as a Principle of Moral Conduct in Sport and Athletics" to develop a discussion of Kant's categorical imperative as an appropriate principle of moral conduct in sport and athletics; that is, to show the relevance of this principle to moral conduct in sport and athletics, and to thereby reveal an ethical posture proper to men qua sportsmen and athletes. Brief treatments of the general character of Kant's ethical formalism, the various specific formulations of the categorical imperative, and the basic character of sport and athletics provide the basis for establishing that all sportsmen and athletes, once having freely entered the sport-athletic condition, are morally obligated not merely to abide by the laws governing these activities but further, to do so for the sake of duty to the law alone, and thereby to treat their fellow competitors with a sensitivity they themselves would prefer (that is to treat them as an end and not as a mere means to the gratification of their own desires and inclinations). Professor Osterhoudt concludes with the hope that the application of such a principle may serve to encourage an order of ideal conduct which has become increasingly uncommon in the playing of our amateur and professional sports and athletics in recent years.

The second chapter concludes with Carolyn E. Thomas' "Do you 'Wanna' Bet: An Examination of Player Betting and the Integrity of the Sporting Event," in which the general nature and significance of gambling, as well as its more specific place in sporting events are explored. Professor Thomas claims that the essential attraction to gambling is attributable to our interest in the chance factor of success; that is, to our risk-taking propensity. Whereby, stress in the forms of chance, uncertainty, adventure, excitement and challenge is actively sought. Unsurprisingly, then, given this rather natural quality, the excessive focus upon the negative aspects of gambling, common in American society, is regarded as inappropriate. Indeed, it is generally the case, so Professor Thomas argues, that such practice is condemned not for itself, but for the consequences commonly accompanying it—occurrences which interfere with so-termed normal societal duties, or demands. At any rate, the positive psychological and social contributions of gambling have been greatly overlooked, according to this view. It is consequently, to an examination of these contributions that the essay is primarily devoted.

By this account, sport, like gambling, provides man with a fertile arena for expressing his risk-taking affinities. In some sports, however (most particularly the so-termed "better than" sports), unlike yet others (most notably the "conquest" sports), the involvement in the sport itself is not a sufficient gamble. In these cases, player betting introduces the chance that coaching and training practices are increasingly designed to eliminate. Assuming the integrity of the players, then, they may be said to gamble for reasons other than the legal and illegal economic ones most commonly cited; in which case the mere act of making a bet does not destroy individual or game integrity, contrary to fashionable claims. According to Professor Thomas, the authoritarian ethic of those who have categorically disallowed player betting is based, then, upon a suspicion of the player as controlling the game in accord with his bet or outside connection, and denies the player the choice to decide and to know what is right and wrong for himself. All of which raises the question as to the function of law generally wherein the integrity of the constituents to it is unconditionally assumed or assumable. Player betting then, by this view, serves the positive function of introducing a risk and excitement into the game which is not apparent without it, and may even serve to augment performance by offering an additional impetus to it. As such, it is concluded, some means for allowing, even encouraging, player betting ought to be developed.

THE ETHICS OF COMPETITION AND ITS RELATION TO SOME MORAL PROBLEMS IN ATHLETICS

JAMES W. KEATING

COMPETITION DIVERSIFIED

Suppose a person was just beginning an investigation of the subject of competition and he turned to the general catalogue of a large library. What could we safely assume would be his first impression? The chances are overwhelming that he would conclude that "competition" is primarily an economic term and that practically all of its serious investigation has been carried on by economists. Other scholars have, in fact, examined the term but, from the viewpoint of a card catalogue, they appear as rare exceptions.

An investigation, however, soon reveals that we live in a society where other types of competition are almost daily in evidence, obvious in so many different ways. Our political system with its electoral process frequently supplies examples of the most intense competition. Few of us can think of more appropriate alternatives for determining our leaders. How many of you would prefer inheritance as a selective mechanism for choosing our leaders rather than our present form of free elections with all of its short-comings? Our legal system with its advocacy system of law is clearly competitive in many of its aspects and, while it is far from ideal, there has been no mass movement to replace it by another. Even our method of choosing a mate has strong competitive elements whereby prospective suitors often vie with others, similarly motivated, for the attention, affection or marriage of some third person. So natural does this type of competition appear to us that we can hardly conceive of workable alternative methods of selection. Yet for centuries courtship and marriage have been arranged in infancy by parents in Asia and with a high degree of apparent success.

Thus we can see that in addition to the economic sphere, competition is an important ingredient in our political system, our legal system, our method of courtship and in many other aspects of our daily life, but most of all in athletics.

I have been asked to speak on the ethics of competition, particularly as it relates to problems in athletics. Such a request affords me the opportunity to discuss what I regard as the purest type of competitive struggle known to man—athletic competition. By saying it is the purest, I don't desire to assign it any kind of ethical superiority. I simply mean that it is relatively free from problems which beset the other types of competition. Economic competition, as we shall see, often becomes wasteful and unnecessarily destructive or the antidote to the virus of monopoly in the economic struggle. The competition built into the advocacy system of law clearly, at times, turns its back on justice and the man or institution who can hire the best lawyer frequently benefits for this unfortunate fact. In politics it is invariably the unknown or the underdog who cries for a confrontation in the forum while the confident leader seldom if ever is willing to enter the lists. Even in our system of courtships, the real contending parties are often reluctant competitors and may deny that they would stoop so low as to compete for the affections of another. Some of the fainthearted reluctantly choose solitude and loneliness rather than face the humiliation and defeat which a possible rejection magnifies in their minds. But in athletics both competitors normally look forward to and savor the contest and in so far as it is properly conducted, excellence is crowned by victory and the crestfallen loser dreams of and prepares for another tomorrow.

Definition is always difficult. Seeking a definition which will not only be applicable in economics but to all other areas of human life as well is a most difficult undertaking. Consider, however, the remarkable similarity to be found in the definitions of competition offered by outstanding scholars in three different intellectual disciplines. John B. Clark, a noted economist has defined competition in this manner: "Actual competition consists invariably in an effort to undersell a rival producer." (3:p.6). In a somewhat broader anthropological context, Margaret Mead seems satisfied with the definition that "Competition is the act of seeking or endeavoring to gain what another is endeavoring to gain at the same time." (7:p.8). Arthur O. Lovejoy, Professor of Philosophy at Johns Hopkins, did an even more thorough job. Lovejoy characterized competition ". . . as an attempt to get or to keep any valuable thing either to the exclusion of others or in greater measure than others." (6). Notice that in each of the three definitions there is a rival and an attempt to excel or overcome this rival. The only improvement we can make in Lovejoy's excellent analysis of competition is to add a brief qualifying phrase removing competition from the sphere of unbridled or criminal conflict. If we add to Lovejoy's definition the qualifying phrase, "Competition is an attempt (according to agreed-upon rules) to get or to keep any valuable thing either to the exclusion of others or in greater measure than others" we quite properly exclude from the sphere of competition, criminal activities such as burglary, embezzlement, strong-armed robbery and the like.

It is both interesting and important to observe that each of the three definitions considered, if accepted, prevents a common misconception from occurring. Many people commonly speak of competing against themselves. But a proper understanding of the nature of competition makes this impossible. This common misconception is often verbalized in this manner. "When I participate in tennis or golf, my primary objective is to improve upon my own past performance. Victory over my fellow participants is of little or no importance to me." If this is actually the case, and it may very well be, then the person voicing such sentiments is not actually competing. There are far more precise and accurate ways to describe his efforts. He is attempting to improve his skill, to learn, to develop, to grow, to actualize his potentialities. Only when he seeks to exceed, surpass, or go byond the best efforts of others is he actually competing. Competition in all of its forms always presupposes another or others.

If the term competition is used promiscuously in everyday conversation to characterize everything from types of conflict to general processes of growth and development, we are neither surprised nor shocked by the ambiguity. This is par for the verbal course. Many commonly used terms like "sport" have no more specificity. When, however an internationally known scholar in an important book fails to be more precise, we can be understandably disturbed. Georg Simmel, a highly regarded social theorist has devoted the second chapter of an important work exclusively to the subject of competition and his investigation of this subject matter is disturbing. Simmel raises serious questions and doubts when he states that the foremost sociological characteristic of competition is that the "conflict in it is indirect." Linguistic usage, he informs us, reserves the term "competition" for conflicts which consist in parallel efforts by both parties concerning the same prize. (10:p.57). While this position confirms our earlier contention that competition always involves an other or others, his insistence that it consists in parallel efforts by both parties would seem to almost rule out direct competition and to re-inforce his contention that the foremost, sociological characteristic of competition is that the "conflict in it is indirect."

He discusses two types of competition. In the first type, he tells us, where victory is the chronologically first necessity, in itself it (victory) means nothing. The goal of the whole action is attained only with the availability of a value, which does not depend on the competitive fight at all. Presumably the following would be a practical example of what Simmel had in mind. If I challenged several of you to a race and offered $100 to the winner, victory would be the chronologically first necessity and the $100 prize would be the goal of the competitors and its value would in no way be dependent upon the competitive fight.

It is the second type of competition in which Simmel is most interested and which he believes to be of greater sociological value. "In the second type of competition, the struggle consists only in the fact that each competitor by himself aims at the goal without using his strength on the adversary. . . . This type of competition equals all other kinds of conflict in emotional and passionate effort. Yet from a superficial standpoint it proceeds as if there existed no adversary but only the aim." (10:p.58). Simmel gives us three examples of this type of competition in which the competitor proceeds without using his strength on the adversary; indeed as if no adversary even existed. Simmel contends that we find such ideal indirect competition in the case of the religious proselytizer, who only by his zeal and sincere conviction, in the businessman who only by his attractive price, quality merchandise and good service, and in the runner who only by his swiftness, wins the victory. Such competition does, in fact, exist and may provide the greatest social value.

Simmel's failure to treat of direct competition, however, clearly detracts from his study and raises serious questions concerning the depth of his understanding. Most competition does not consist in "parallel efforts" of the competitors. The competition in economics, law, politics is often of a most direct kind. In athletics it is only occasionally indirect. Even in the example which Simmel cites of the runner, the competition is usually far more direct than he believes. Only in the short dashes can it be said that ". . . each competitor by himself aims at the goal without using his strength on the adversary . . . and that he proceeds as if there existed no adversary . . ." In all middle distance and distance races the competitors are keenly aware of the existence of their competitors and usually, by the employment of their strength and speed, attempt to get their opponent to run the type of race for which he is least qualified.

Consider other athletic contests such as baseball, basketball, football, hockey, boxing, wrestling, tennis, etc. and we begin to question whether Simmel's treatment of competition is adequate or only highly esoteric.

While it is only conjecture, it would seem that Simmel's unexpressed attitude toward direct competition is best summarized by the psychoanalyst Ernest Van Den Haag:

> Direct competition is illustrated by games like baseball or football. Each team tries not only to maximize its own score, but also to hold to a minimum the score of the opposing team. Each team attempts to reduce the achievement of the other by directly interfering with it. There is only a relative standard of achievement and no objective, independent one, such as time in a race, or total crop harvested. The extent of the defeat of one team is the measure of the achievement, the victory, of the other team. This is true also of boxing or chess matches. Achievement consists mainly in defeating the opponent, more than in attaining a goal in itself worthwhile. (15:p.133).

Van Den Haag does, however, acknowledge certain values in direct competition.

> The psychological usefulness of competitive games lies both in cultivat-

ing and in absorbing some of our competitive spirit, channeling the need
for superiority feeling into harmless outlets, and above all, in training
us to pursue our aims according to rules that limit the harm we do to
each other. (15:p.135).

THE CASE AGAINST COMPETITION

In *The Greening Of America,* Charles Reich considers the effects
of competition upon the American character during the various stages
of its historical development and in each case finds it wanting.

> . . . There was another side to the American character—the harsh side
> of self-interest, competitiveness, suspicion of others. Each individual
> would go it alone, refusing to trust his neighbors, seeing another man's
> advantage as his loss, seeing the world as a rat race with no rewards to
> losers. Underlying this attitude was the assumption that 'human nature'
> is fundamentally bad, and that a struggle against his fellow men is man's
> natural condition. 'There'll always be aggression and a struggle for power,
> and there'll always be a pecking order,' says Consciousness I. (9:pp.23-
> 24). In Consciousness II, that created by the Corporate State, the same
> outlook prevails: Behind a facade of optimism, Consciousness II has a
> profoundly pessimistic view of man. It sees man in Hobbesian terms;
> human beings are by nature aggressive, competitive, power-seeking; un-
> civilized man is a jungle beast. (9:p.70). Consciousness III, not yet fully
> achieved, is seeking to replace the infantile and destructive self-seeking
> that we laud as 'competition' by a new capacity for working and living
> together. (9:p.387).

One does not have to indulge in the romantic meanderings of Reich
in order to experience qualms concerning a competitive view of
life. Can such a view be reconciled with the Golden Rule, can the
spirit of profit and success be held simultaneously with the spirit of
service? Is not self-interest directly opposed to self-sacrifice? Such
apprehension is obviously not without some foundation when we are
told bluntly by one of America's great economists, Frank K. Knight
that:

> It is in terms of power then, if at all, that competitive economics and
> the competitive view of life for which it must be largely accountable
> are to be justified. Whether we are to regard them as justified at all
> depends upon whether we are willing to accept an ethics of power as
> the basis of our world view . . . (5:p.68).

Knight comes to this emphatic conclusion in a book entitled *The
Ethics of Competition,* a book in which he raises a number of impor-

tant questions. He inquires; "Is emulation as a motive ethically good or base? Is success in any sort of contest, as such, a noble objective?" Ashley Montagu, an anthropologist from Princeton, has a ready answer:

> The first point I would make is that unless he is a gambler, no one should ever play any game in order to win. No one should ever participate in any sport in order to win. I have no doubt that this will be a startling statement to many, but I do not make it in order to startle anyone. I make it as a sober statement calculated from the beginning of the discussion of the meaning and purpose of games to indicate what is wrong with the attitude with which Americans enter into the playing of any game. (8:p.292).

If character development is related to ethics, Montagu attempts to justify this position in the concluding paragraph of the same chapter:

> As Americans we must make up our minds as to the kind of character we would like our citizens to have and to do what is indicated to bring those characters into being, to recognize that a most important preparation for the game of life is the training one receives in playing the game in childhood and youth. We need to realize that the present training we give our children through competitive games tends to bring out the worst rather than the best in them . . . The old adage will always remain true: 'It's not who wins that matters but how you play the game.' (8:p.296).

COMPETITION AND ETHICS

The Ethical Neutrality of Competition Considered In Itself

Competition in and of itself is neither a virtue nor a vice. It can only be ethically evaluated in a concrete situation. Professor Knight errs grievously when he maintains that it can only be justified if we accept an ethics of power as the basis of our world view. Ashley Montagu reveals an abysmal ignorance of athletics when he argues that we should never strive to win, that winning is not important. Competition provides a selective mechanism for assigning position, place, power, productive ability or physical excellence and until its detractors can offer an alternative mechanism that is practical and workable they can only be said to be over-reacting emotionally to many of the evils that do, in fact, follow in the wake of intense competition.

Consider a common, practical example. Ten students are applying for admission to one of our prestigious medical schools. The entire gamut of relevant personal qualifications of each candidate is carefully considered by a screening committee and finally one is selected. Few, if any, of the candidates may be aware of the meticulous efforts of the selection committee to choose the best possible candidate. Yet the very desire of each respective candidate to enter that medical school made him a competitor and while he may not have been aware of the extreme competitive nature of the selective process, this fact of life will eventually become clear to him.

The same difficult question as to how a fair selection is to be made faces those who aspire to political office, or of lawyers who daily seek to win the approval of judge and jury, or, on the social level, of those who seek to win the affection of some popular attractive member of the opposite sex. What alternative to the competitive principle would those who denigrate it offer in the equitable resolution of such problems?

There are few alternatives to competition as a social determinant of position, power or excellence. Historically the chief alternative has probably been some form of status, usually a rule of inheritance. Political preferment has also, at times, been employed but usually found sadly wanting. The chief danger to such methods of selection is that of suppression of personal development. Without a powerful stimulant such as competition human potentialities remain as such, potentialities which will never be actualized.

Despite his stinging criticism of its ethical qualities, Frank Knight seems to concede that the competitive system in economics has produced an abundance of material goods at reasonable prices. Yet if this is so, we find ourselves confronted with the curious paradox that the material welfare of this world is at war with essential morality. Rather than argue for cooperation as a workable alternative to achieve the greatest material advantage, Knight appeals to cooperation on other grounds. He argues that happines, self-realization and personal fulfillment, all basic goals of prominent ethical systems, depend less on material satisfaction than on spiritual resourcefulness and a joyous appreciation of the spiritual things of life, especially the affection for one's fellow creatures:

A strong argument for cooperation, if it would work, would be its tendency to teach people to like each other in a more positive sense than can ever be bred by participation in a contest—certainly in a contest in which the means of life, or of a decent life, are felt to be at stake. (5).

Whereas some isolated individuals and primitive societies may be relatively free from the competitive spirit, an over-all view reveals that competition appears to be an ineradicable trait of human nature. It is true that not all men compete with the same intensity. Some even tend to escape it whenever possible. Still it is difficult to see how any active person can escape all forms of competition for a single day. Competition being therefore an indisputable fact of life, the real question is how to keep it within proper bounds. Men should be esteemed not because they abstain from competition, but because they hold in check that fierce desire for supremacy which threatens the observance of the agreed-upon rules which alone distinguish competition from internecine warfare or deceptive and destructive conflict.

The Intensity of Competition

It is possible to place general limits upon the sphere in which competitive processes are socially beneficial if not absolutely necessary. When this selective process has performed its function, when it has answered the question who is best qualified for the job, who is the best contestant, who can produce the best product at the least cost, etc., then competition has served its purpose and there is little to be gained by its continuance. Where men have common interests it is only reasonable for them to cooperate rather than compete. In those cases where the interests of men are opposed, competition is usually the most equitable way of coping with the problem.

There is another, and quite different aspect to the moral problem of competition. The moral level of competition is largely dependent on the conditions under which it takes place. The more intense the competitive drive, the more significance success carries with it, the greater will be the compulsion to tamper with the agreed-upon rules. Thus a highly developed competitive spirit may result in a whole host of moral ills which are inevitably or essentially connected with it. Deceit, lying, hypocrisy, etc., all too often do follow in the wake of an intense competitive spirit.

Competition is often said to be in its very nature anti-social, a state of war instead of a state of peace, generating hostile passions in the place of sympathy and love. Open and declared opposition, however, is not the thing most likely to give rise to hatred and jealousy. Where a conflict takes place under recognized rules and conditions which are observed by both parties, it does not necessarily give rise to bitter feelings. Bitterness arises when there is, or is believed to be, something unfair, some exception, some infractions of the rules resulting in unjust discriminations. Open competition does not generate hostility. Rather it is among those removed from open and equal competition that hatred and jealousy are most rife.

COMPETITION AND SPORTSMANSHIP

In any discussion of "Sport and Ethics" it would seem that sportsmanship would become a crucial or pivotal point. Yet the term does not even appear in the index of Paul Weiss' book on Sport. (16). Why? Was it consciously and deliberately rejected as of no importance? Or were its complexities and ambiguities too great to unravel? Was he simply being consistent in avoiding the ethical aspects of sport in their entirety? (except for one single indexed reference.)

Whatever the reasons for Weiss' omission, sportsmanship has always had numerous champions who have made remarkable claims for it as a moral category. Albert Camus, Nobel prize winner for literature in 1957 said that it was from sports that he learned all that he knew about ethics. (2:p.242). Henry Steele Commager, Professor of History at Amherst College, argued that it was on the playing fields that Americans learned the lessons of courage and honor which distinguished them in time of war. Commager concluded: "In one way or another, this code of sportsmanship had deeply influenced our national destiny." (4:p.7). For Lyman Bryson of Columbia University, sportsmanship was of extraordinary value: "It could be established, I think, that the next best thing to the rule of love is the rule of sportsmanship. This virtue, without which democracy is impossible and freedom uncertain has not yet been taken seriously enough in education." (1:p.130).

Sportsmanship, when not viewed as the pinnacle of moral perfection, can also be viewed as a moral minimum—one step this side of criminality. In the same vein, the term "poor sportsmanship" is sometimes used as a euphemism for criminal behavior. A recent example of such verbal tomfoolery can be found in the explanation of Commissioner Wayne Duke of the Big Ten Athletic Conference concerning the assault and riot which interrupted the Minnesota-Ohio State basketball game last year. In justifying the suspension of two of the players involved in the assault, Commissioner Duke said that they were suspended for "unsportsmanlike conduct."

It is precisely in difficulties of this type that our functional definitions demonstrate their practical value. The source of the confusion which vitiates most discussion of sportsmanship is the unwarranted assumption that athletics and truly playful activities are so similar in nature that a single code of conduct and similar participant attitudes are equally applicable to radically diverse activities. Not only is such an attempt doomed to failure, but a consequence of this abortive effort is the proliferation of various moral virtues under the flag of sportsmanship, which, thus, loses all its distinctiveness. It is variously viewed as a straight road to moral perfection or an antidote to moral corruption.

Now since I hold that athletics and play are two distinct species under the genus *sport* and that they are easily distinguishable and radically diverse types of human activity, I should be prepared to offer what I have characterized as functional definitions of each. First, consider athletics. Athletics are physical contests designed to determine human excellence through an honorable victory in a contest. Thus they are competitive by their very nature. Professional football, baseball, basketball and hockey are excellent examples of athletic contests. So, also are the various Olympic contests, intercollegiate and inter-scholastic contests. In fact, even most of the highly organized little-league contests must be regarded as athletics. Play, on the other hand, is free, creative activity in which the goal of the participants is to maximize the joy of the moment, seeking no goal outside the activity itself. Good examples of this type of activity are pleasure boating, swimming, and fishing, the three most popular participant *sports* in the U.S.A.

'SPORTSMANSHIP' AS APPLIED TO PLAYFUL ACTIVITIES

In itself sportsmanship as it applies to genuine play is a spirit, an attitude, a manner or mode of interpreting an otherwise purely legal code. Its purpose is to protect and cultivate the festive mood proper to an activity whose primary purpose is amusement, pleasure, joy. The player adopts a cavalier attitude toward his personal rights under the code. He prefers to be magnanimous and self-sacrificing if, by such conduct, he contributes to the enjoyment of the game.

Our insistence that the genuine player is primarily interested in maximizing the pleasure or joy of the moment does not imply that he makes no effort to win the games which he enters. It is common practice for him, once the game is under way, to make a determined effort to win. However, spirited competitor which he apears to be, his goal is joy in the activity itself. Anything which makes the game itself less enjoyable should be eliminated. He *fights* to win because experience has taught him that a determined effort to overcome the obstacles which his particular game has constructed adds immeasurably to the enjoyment of the game. He would be cheating himself and robbing the other partcipants of intense pleasure if his efforts were only half-hearted. Yet there is an important sense in which playful activity is not competitive but rather cooperative. Competition denotes the struggle of two parties for the same valued object and implies that, to the extent that one of the parties is successful in the struggle, he gains exclusive possession of the object at the expense of his fellow competitors. But the goal of playful activity, being the mutual enjoyment of the participants, cannot even be understood in terms of exclusive possession by one of the parties. Its simulated competitive atmosphere camouflages what is, at bottom, a highly cooperative endeavor to maximize the immediate pleasure or joy to be found in the activity itself.

'SPORTSMANSHIP' IN ATHLETICS

Careful analysis has revealed that playful activity, while speaking the language of competition and constantly appearing in its livery, is fundamentally a cooperative venture. Its code for the "sportsman" (player) is directed fundamentally to facilitating the cooperative effort and removing all possible barriers to its development. Mutual generosity is a most fertile soil to cooperative activity. When we move from play to athletics, however, a drastic change takes place. Cooperation is no longer the goal. Competition now becomes the order of the day. The objective of the athlete demands exclusive possession. Two cannot share in the same victory unless they are teammates, and, as a result, the problems of competition are immediately in evidence. "Sportsmanship," insofar as it connotes the behavior proper to the athlete, seeks to place certain basic limitations on the rigors of competition, just as continual efforts are being made to soften the impact of the competitive struggle in economics, politics, international relations, etc. But we must not lose sight of an important distinction. Competition in these real-life areas is condoned or encouraged to the extent that it contributes to the common good. It is not regarded as an end in itself but as the only or most practical means to socially desirable ends. Friedrich A. Hayek, renown economist and champion of competition in economics, supports this position:

> The liberal argument in favor of making the best possible use of the forces of competition, as a means of co-ordinating human efforts . . . is based on the conviction that, where effective competition can be created it is a better way of guiding individual efforts than any other. It does not deny, but even emphasizes that, in order that competition should work beneficially, a carefully thought-out legal framework is required and that neither the existing nor the past legal rules are free from grave defects. Nor does it deny that, where it is impossible to create the conditions necessary to make competition effective, we must resort to other methods of guiding economic activity.

A code which seeks to mitigate the full force of the competitive conflict is also desirable in athletics. While the athlete is in essence a prizefighter, he seeks to demonstrate his excellence in a contest governed by rules which acknowledge human worth and dignity.

For the athlete, being a good *sportsman* is most frequently demonstrated by the self-control he demonstrates in the face of adversity. A festive attitude is not called for; it is, in fact, often viewed as in bad taste. The purists or rigorists are of the opinion that a brief period of seclusion and mourning may be more appropriate. They know that for the real competitor, defeat in an important contest seems heart-breaking and nerve-shattering. The athlete who can control himself in such circumstances demonstrates remarkable equanimity. To ask that he enter into the festive mood of the victory celebration is to request a Pagliacci-like performance. There is no need for phony displays of congratulations. A simple handshake demonstrates that no personal ill-will is involved. No alibis or complaints are offered. No childish excuses about the judgment of officials or the natural conditions. No temper tantrums. To be a good loser under his code, the athlete need not be exactly gracious in defeat, but he must at least *be a man* about it.

After an athlete has trained and sacrificed for weeks, after he has dreamed of victory and its fruits and literally exhausted himself physically and emotionally in its pursuit—after all this—to ask him to act with fairness in the contest, with modesty in victory and an admirable composure in defeat is to demand a great deal, and yet, this is the substance of the demand that *sportsmanship* makes upon the athlete—amateur or professional.

The essence of *sportsmanship* as applied to athletics can be determined by the application of one simple principle—the goal of an activity is the principle determinant of the conduct and attitudes proper to that activity. Honorable victory is the goal of the athlete, and, as a result, the code of the athlete demands that nothing be done before, during, or after the contest to cheapen or otherwise detract from such a victory. Fairness or *fair play,* the pivotal virtue in athletics, emphasizes the need for an impartial and equal application of the rules if the victory is to signify, as it should, athletic excellence. Modesty in victory and a quiet composure in defeat testify to an admirable and extraordinary self-control and, in general, dignify and enhance the goal of the athlete.

Most of the moral problems posed by athletics can be traced to one single source—its highly competitive nature. When competition becomes excessive in athletics, it almost invariably results in moral problems of one type or another. If, however, athletics are competitive by nature, at what point can the competition be said to be excessive? As might be expected, competition loses its social and moral value when it ceases to maintain its judicial role as the determinant of athletic superiority or excellence. This occurs when the desire to win becomes so excessive that it employs immoral means in the quest for victory. Some of these illicit means are hypocrisy, disregard for one's promises or the physical well-being of the fans and participants, incitement to riot, and the abridgement of one's natural rights and freedom.

AMATEURISM AND HYPOCRISY

A careful study of the nature of athletics clearly indicates that the amateur ideal in today's socio-economic world is so impractical that adherence to this Victorian ideal encourages otherwise honorable men and women to all types of ludicrous posturing which can only be characterized as open hypocrisy.

If the competitor is truly an athlete, if his desire is to excel on ever-increasing levels of competence, he must make the sacrifice of complete dedication. Such dedication requires great expenditures of time and effort which, in truth are very expensive commodities. Thus, unless the young athlete is independently wealthy, he will come to see that if he is going to dedicate himself fully to athletics, then it will be necesary for him to earn his living in the process. As a result, the pursuit of excellence in athletics tends naturally and inevitably to some form of professionalism.

In the recent past, the Olympic Games have provided us with international examples of pathetic or tragic cases in which unfortunate athletes, after being forced to sign the Olympic Oath, were rebuked for tampering with the amateur code. Those close to the Olympic scene knew for decades that there were many liberties taken with the Olympic Oath. Finally the explosion came in Mexico City in 1968 with the infamous track shoe scandal. There were pitiful pleas for information concerning payoffs from officials who were totally derelict in their duties if they were, in fact, ignorant of what was transpiring. There were threats of life suspensions and medal forfeitures. But the widespread nature of the fraud prevented any punitive action. In the end it was conservatively estimated that about 200 athletes were paid off. If action had been taken, the U.S. would have been practically medal-less since it was reliably estimated that no more than five U.S. medal winners emerged with clean hands.

Bill Toomey, the U.S. gold medalist in the decathelon summed up the matter. "It is time for athletes to take money and be open and honest or not to take it. The hypocrisy is what's killing us, not the money." (11:p.22).

Hypocrisy is truly the chief culprit where amateurism is concerned. In the Winter Olympics of the same Olympiad, Marc Hodler, the president of the International Ski Federation, sought in vain to get

Avery Brundage to face up to this fact. After threats of their with-
drawal or expulsion, the skiers were permitted to ski in the Olympic
Games but only after Karl Schranz, generally conceded to be the
world's best skier, had been barred as a concession to Brundage. Hodler argued the case for the world class skiers:

> . . . I told Avery that if we could control the manufacturers' temptations
> by having them go legally through our national federations, we might do
> away with much of the hypocrisy that has plagued us. I told him that,
> with the federation's contracts, the manufacturers would feel secure that
> the boys would not run out on using their equipment. And if they felt
> secure they would stop spending all Sundays and Mondays after the races
> in pure bribery to guarantee that they would keep their racers on their
> products. (13:p.15).

Thus it appears that because of Olympic Rule No. 26 which clearly
states: "An amateur is one who participates and has always participated in a sport as an avocation without gain of any kind," European
skiing, according to its own president, is shot through with hypocrisy
and pure bribery. Perhaps U.S. skiers have been more faithful to
the amateur ideal. "Hell, no," says Bob Lange, a highly successful
Colorado manufacturer. "The only skiers on the whole FIS circuit
that I have to pay under the table are Americans. They deserve the
dough as much as anyone else but, by God, the only way to pay
them is on the sly. Talk about hypocrisy." (13:p.15).

The American skiers themselves would seem to agree with Bob
Lange's assessment. Spider Sabich, one of our fine amateur skiers who
turned professional, said:

> It was such a relief to stop as an amateur. I was fed up with the
> hypocrisy. Fed up with racing against guys who were making $50,000
> a year, guys who had other people to wax their skis, sharpen their edges
> and who could go home when they got tired. I was too nervous trying
> to compete with what I thought were insufficient weapons. Now I have
> no worries. (14:p.92).

ATHLETICS AND THE USE OF DRUGS

Wherever the intensity of the competitive spirit burns brightly as
it always does in athletics, there will be a strong temptation to cheat.
To the extent that any given drug promises to enhance an athlete's

performance, he will be sorely tempted to try it. Before, however, we become emotionally involved in the athletic drug scene, we should honestly face up to certain questions. Does the average athlete promise not to use drugs before or during a contest? If so, are such drugs generally regarded by the medical profession as a threat to his physical well-being? Does the use of certain drugs demonstrably enhance an athelete's performance?

If an athlete promises not to use certain drugs or is forbidden to do so by his school or conference, then he is openly in violation of the public trust, even though the drugs have no beneficial effect upon his performance. If an athlete, in order to enhance his performance, uses drugs which the medical profession has pronounced dangerous or harmful, then his actions are highly suspect on the grounds that it is imprudent, if not irrational, to risk one's physical integrity merely for the purpose of performing well in an athletic contest. In the absence of any contrary promise or medical prohibition, an athlete uses a drug to enhance his performance, we are faced with the old moral problem of *drawing the line*. Can he consume aspirin or alka-seltzer to cure a headache or an upset stomach in order to perform better? Can he drink coffee as a stimulant or beer as a depressant? Is there a basic ethical difference between taking a muscle-relaxer like valium whose side effects may not be fully known or giving anabolic steroids when both are done primarily in the attempt to help the athlete perform better?

To the extent that the use of drugs in athletics constitutes a major public health problem or threatens the physical integrity of the athlete who uses them, drugs pose a serious moral problem for athletics. To the extent, however, that the fruits of the pharmaceutical science are openly employed, without documented physical hazards, it is pure romanticism to suggest that the use of drugs destroys the very nature of athletic competition. To hold that "for sport to be of interest, to have emotional impact, to be an artistic or commercial success, the contestants must be as equal as possible," is a myth of great magnitude. Athletic greatness is a triumph of carefully cultivated inequalities. The only equality required is that set by the rules governing the conduct of the contest. The appeal to horse racing with its emphasis on age, sex, past performance and handicapping with extra weight ignores the primary motive for such steps. The motive which calls forth such efforts in horse racing is clearly that of encouraging wagering on the contest—a motive presumably less important in competition between athletes.

There is no doubt that, given their nature as prize fighters, athletes will always be in search of secret drugs which will give them at least a temporary advantage over their competitors. Hal Connolly, a veteran of four U.S. Olympic teams, summarizes succinctly: "My experience tells me that an athlete will use any aid to improve his performance short of killing himself." (12:p.70).

An important difference between athletic and non-athletic drugs can be made. An athlete takes many drugs that he would not take or be given if he were not an athlete. And the rationale for much athletic drug use is unique, for the drugs are not taken either with the intention or effect of improving or maintaining health, or to achieve a pleasurable sensation, but rather because the athlete or those around him believe he will perform better drugged than undrugged. Or the opposite could be the case. If organized gambling interests were involved, the temptation may even be stronger to administer drugs which would adversely affect performance. Administering drugs for this purpose is certainly as probable in horse racing as the attempt to enhance performance through drug usage.

It is a question of motive that directly affects the morality of the athletic drug problem. Athletic integrity is clearly a matter of public interest. It is an accepted moral maxim that an athlete will do everything in his power, coincident with the rules of the contest, to gain victory. If the use of certain drugs will predictably and adversely affect an athlete's performance, then they should never be used unless accompanied by a pre-contest announcement. If, however, any food, exercise or drug not specifically banned by the rules is thought to be an aid in enhancing an athlete's performance, it clearly falls within the bounds of the morally acceptable. The quest for some miracle drug could conceivably result in the unfortunate situation that the winners will not be the best athletes naturally, but the richest, those with the best pharmaceutical resources at their disposal. Such a possibility, however, is so remote that it can cause no legitimate moral concern today.

RESTRICTIONS ON THE FREEDOM OF ATHLETES
TO COMPETE

If too much competition can be a bad thing, it is also true that the absence of competition can also have serious adverse effects. Baseball's "reserve clause" is a good case in point. After Curt Flood had been *sold* or traded to Philadelphia by the St. Louis Cardinals, he decided to test such unique employment practices in the courts. His first step was to appeal to the commissioner of baseball, Mr. Bowie Kuhn in the following words: "After 12 years in the major leagues, I do not feel that I am a piece of property to be bought and sold irrespective of my wishes. I believe that any system which violates my basic rights as a citizen is inconsistent with the laws of the U.S. and of the several states."

Mr. Kuhn was not moved by this argument, however, and Flood's case went through all available legal channels until it reached the Supreme Court. On June 19, 1972, the Court ruled by a vote of 5 to 3 in favor of the "reserve clause" and against Curt Flood. While recognizing the fact that other *sports* have been more sharply restricted, as a result of various judicial decisions, in their control of player personnel, Justice Harry A. Blackmun, writing the majority decision, admitted the inconsistency, but refused to strike down the "reserve clause" as unconstitutional. He pointed to Congress as the proper place for redress.

Justice Thurgood Marshall argued that when the court's ". . . errors deny substantially federal rights, like the right to compete freely and effectively to the best of one's ability we must admit our error and correct it." There would appear to be a form of serfdom involved here under which baseball players are bought and sold. And although the court does not say so, this archaic arrangement does not appear to be in conflict with the constitutional provisions against slavery since the performer can always quit—giving up his only precious and highly marketable talent—and turn to a type of work for which he is far less suited.

While professional football would appear to be far more liberal, the football draft requires that a player go to a city which drafted him despite the inconvenience and hardship it may cause his family. His only alternatives are to skip to the Canadian league or to give up that type of employment for which he is best qualified and which is most lucrative. Once signed it is true that technically a football player can become a free agent by playing out his option, but he is never free to sign with a new team simply by negotiating with it. His freedom, even after his option has expired, is dependent upon the exchange of a player by the new team who is in the opinion of the Commissioner "a player of like quality."

REFERENCES

1. Bryson, Lyman: *Science and Freedom*. New York, Columbia University Press, 1947.
2. Camus, Albert: *Resistance, Rebellion and Death*. New York, Alfred A. Knopf, 1961.
3. Clarke, John B. and Giddings, F.H.: *The Modern Distribution Process*. Boston, Ginn and Co., 1888.
4. Commager, H.S.: *Scholastic*, Vol. 44, 7 (May 8-13, 1944).
5. Knight, Frank H.: *The Ethics of Competition*. Augustus M. Kelley, 1951.
6. Lovejoy, Arthur O.: "Christian Ethics and Economic Competition," *The Hibbert Journal*, Vol. 9 (January, 1911).
7. Mead, Margaret (ed.): *Competition and Cooperation Among Primitive People*. Boston, Beacon Press, 1967.
8. Montagu, Ashley: *The Humanization of Man*. New York, Grove Press, 1962.
9. Reich, Charles A.: *The Greening of America*. New York, Bantam Books, 1971.
10. Simmel, George: *Conflict and the Web of Group Affiliations*. New York, The Free Press, 1950.
11. *Sports Illustrated*, 22 (March 10, 1969).
12. *Sports Illustrated*, 70 (June 23, 1969).
13. *Sports Illustrated*, 15 (March 9, 1970).
14. *Sports Illustrated*, 92 (December 20, 1971).
15. Van Den Haag, Ernest: *Passion and Social Constraint*. Delta Books, 1965.
16. Weiss, Paul: *Sport: A Philosophic Inquiry*. Carbondale, Southern Illinois University Press, 1969.

A CONTEXTUAL APPROACH TO AN UNDERSTANDING OF COMPETITION: A RESPONSE TO KEATING'S PHILOSOPHY OF ATHLETICS

WILLIAM A. SADLER, JR.

In Professor Keating's philosophy of competition and athletics I find a triple objective. First he sets out to provide a definition of competition which will enable him to distinguish athletics from activities which may be associated with them, such as sports and criminal activities. Secondly, on the basis of this definition, he attempts to construct a standard by which to mitigate the potential excess of competition in athletics. Thirdly, in a truly competitive spirit, he presents an argument so inherently provocative that response to it is demanded. I shall acknowledge the achievement of the third objective by calling the first two into question.

There are various levels at which people will want to criticize his argument. Many who spend a considerable part of their lives within the world of sports will argue against his notions on the basis of their own experience. Others will attack his argument on moral grounds; his ethics of competition will disturb the moral sensitivity of many people who are not willing to sacrifice so many primary values for the continuance of his kind of athletics. Philosophers will undoubtedly take him to task for the confusions and dogmatisms that issue from his merging of prescription with description in his definition. While sharing in the intentions of such criticisms, my own approach will operate on a different level. Nevertheless, I should confess at the outset that underlying the following relatively impartial contextual analysis, there are a number of beliefs which might give my response a bias. It will clear the air, and hopefully the argument, if I indicate one of my beliefs about competition.

I believe, though with some reservations, that commitment to a competitive viewpoint as reflected in Keating's philosophy is detrimental to growth towards full humanness. As it becomes part of one's habitual pattern of perception, competitiveness interferes with an individual's way of perceiving others as persons. It functions to obstruct a normal process of critical self-reflection and to produce insensitivity towards personal and social needs. For example, Keating justifies competition in society on the grounds that it is a manifestly efficient way of selecting a candidate for a prestigious medical school. "What alternative to the competitive principle would those who denigrate it offer?" (7) he asks. In view of the drastic shortage of doctors and medical schools to train them, an obvious, immediate and serious answer would be to decrease the competitiveness by increasing the availability of medical training. One might expect from an ethical consideration of competition some critical awareness of the conse-

quences it may have.   Instead, Keating responds to a charge that
competitive games tend to bring out the worst in children with the
irrelevant remark that its author shows himself to be abysmally ignorant of athletics.

I should make clear that I am sympathetic to Professor Keating's
stated aim of establishing a norm by which to regulate and limit the
degree of competition in athletics.   However, I am dissatisfied with his
approach and his norm; his code of sportsmanship does not go nearly
far enough.   Furthermore, his philosophical stance is disturbing; it
appears to be an accommodation to the *status quo*.   I believe that
we still need to work to change our world for the better; to move
towards this goal, we need to reconsider our views of competition
within a context broader than that provided by the sports world.
Keating does acknowledge that competition has played a dominant
role in many aspects of American life, especially in economics.   He
fails to remark, however, that a salient feature in modern economic
theory has involved serious reconsideration of the practical and moral
validity of competition in national and international economies.   The
history of political legislation in twentieth century America involves
lengthy chapters about regulation and restraint of competition.   Recently, even leaders in the business world have expressed doubts about
competition, and some are seeking alternatives to the competitive
principle.   Should not leaders in the sports world also examine competition critically?   Outside of the world of business, there has been
a considerable amount of negative thinking about competition,
especially in view of its consequences per personal and social well-
being.   Keating's ethics of competition are jejune, because he fails
to consider the nature of competition in the context of our society.
Sports and athletics do not take place in a vacuum.   They are permeated by numerous social forces and interpreted in terms of dominant
cultural norms.

Rather than remain on the level of belief and morality, which tends
to heat up quickly, I suggest moving to a cooler level of methodology.
Before prosecuting a contextual analysis, it would be well to expose
a few underlying assumptions associated with competition.   Keating
makes a common American assumption about the naturalness, indeed
inevitability, of competition.   Americans tend to think that competing

is "doing what comes naturally." A little social history is helpful to counteract this unwarranted assumption. (6). During the past century we have so ingested Darwinistic notions about natural selection and survival of the fittest, that we have taken them to be indubitable facts; actually, they were theories meant to account for an order of reality different from modern human life. Americans have been acting out these biological theories in their economic and social lives so that we have seen them as human facts supporting our assumptions about competition. However congruent competition is with our success-oriented life style, we cannot absolutize it as a universally dominant natural, social, and individual force. Biologists have even suggested that dynamics other than competition or aggression are more fundamental to life, such as the tendency towards stabilization and equilibrium. (1,2,3). From this perspective, competition may be unnatural. Social sciences have given ample testimony that competition is not a significant factor in many other societies. In fact, in most societies competitiveness is incompatible with traditional social structures. From a scientific perspective, there are good reasons for being critical of this common American assumption.

There are also reasons for rejecting Lovejoy's definition of competition, which Keating accepts as normative after adding a qualifying phrase. The final version reads: "Competition is an attempt, according to agreed-upon rules, to get or to keep any valuable thing, either to the exclusion of others or in greater measure than others." Both philosophers apparently see competition as an acquisitive stance; it is oriented towards obtaining some thing. As a contextual analysis will indicate, there are other stances within which competition can be viewed. The original meaning of the Latin verb *competo* itself suggests an activity quite different from that prescribed by the above definition. This verb refers to acting together or seeking together; hence, it implies the notion of coming together to reach an agreement. An additional notion, one of contest, infiltrated the term as it was applied to athletic encounters. The original meaning of the Latin term for contest is also significant for our purposes. The verb *contendo* signifies to stretch, to strain or exert oneself. As implied in the Greek term *agon,* a contest is an encounter in which one stretches himself towards his physical and mental limits. A contestant is one who is engaged in an activity that calls forth the full exercise of his powers. By contending, he testifies to his aptitude and ability. Competition signifies an interpersonal contest in which participants testify to their competence as they interact. A quick etymological consideration is enough to indicate how different the classical frame of reference was from that proposed by Lovejoy and Keating.

It is possible to move reflection beyond these alternatives by considering other contexts. We can construct ideal types of cultures and then consider the kind of fit competition will have within them. For numerous reasons, this presentation will have to move on a high level of abstraction. However, these ideal types are not meant to be hypothetical; they have been constructed with specific social and cultural contexts in mind. (5, 9, 12). While some aspects of this analysis will be similar to the work of other students of sport, there will be noticeable differences. I shall not, for example, attempt to assess to what extent competitive sports fit in with the American social system (8); nor shall I suggest some moral ideal which might be sought to guide and correct athletic behavior today. (16). The method employed here is basically a cross-cultural comparison of types of societies in terms of their orientations towards dominant values. Unlike most monographs in this vein, however, the purpose of my article is not to present the findings of a study. Hopefully, this contextual approach will stimulate some empirical studies so that we can have a more comprehensive and realistic framework within which to understand, interpret, and assess competition not only in sports, but in all aspects of human life.

I propose that we consider four cultural constellations to be characterized by their conceptions of normative activity. These four types can be denoted as: *Being, Becoming, Doing,* and *Having.* . There are other types of cultures which could be classified in terms of different dominant behavior patterns. For example, one can think of a Destroying type of culture, where the institutionalized life style is essentially predatory and destructive; but instances of such cultures are rare and not useful to this analysis. One can imagine other types oriented around different types of activity. There could be a Winning culture composed of multiple Vince Lombardis; there could even be Loving cultures. However, these ideas are merely hypothetical and do not serve the purpose of this contextual approach. Each type of cultural constellation will be examined in terms of constants which serve to indicate some distinctive variations between them. The constants to be considered here are: views of time, space, normative activity, interpersonal and social relations, and life goals or aspired final states. Other constants would have to be considered to obtain a fuller understanding of the types themselves; however, these five will be sufficient for our immediate purposes.

The term *being* is here meant to denote a dominant value orientation that may be found in numerous societies throughout history, including both primitive and highly traditional ones. In the modern world, some Eastern societies and some subcultures in Western societies, such as our own Spanish-American and Indian groups, would fall into this category. Within this cultural constellation, time is perceived as either unimportant because it is segregated from eternity, or meaningful in terms of the past. Within the latter view, the *great time* was believed to have been long ago, not now, or yet to come. (4). Today's time is valuable insofar as it recovers, recapitulates, or extends the power and meaning of *that* time. Those who lived long ago are not merely ancestors; they are conceived as heroes or gods. Their time was a golden or sacred era; in contrast, the present is perceived as a degenerate or at least a vapid era. The view of space is correlative to that of time; it similarly lacks a dynamic perspective. As man in time is seen to be heavily dependent upon the past, so he is conceived to be subordinate to nature. The forces of nature are seen to dominate the lived space of this world; consequently, the proper role for man is submission to them. In this perspective, man exists *under* nature. The people of a being culture tend to be fatalistic. Man is dominated by forces of the past and by his environment. There is no reason to attempt to change one's situation. Whatever will be, will be. Quite logically, the view of normative activity is characterized in terms of being. There is a receptive acceptance of things as they are, along with the view that man should not interfere with the present order. A motto for this life style might well read: "Let it be!" In social life, there is great emphasis placed upon lineal relationships, as seen in highly traditionalistic behavior that attempts to preserve the memory and the manners of the group line. Their religions also contain a ritualistic orientation towards the past and a strong emphasis upon yielding to dominant life forces and obedience to old customs.   True piety means submission.   In personal life, emphasis is placed upon finding peaceful accommodation with the cosmos.   Consequently, there is little awareness of the self as an independent unit.   Rather, the self is conceived as an expression of the group or an extension of some primal source.   Conflict must be avoided so as to preserve continuity with one's family, the group, one's environment, and the universe.   A major aspiration for self and reality is continuity, or even an uninterrupted flow of being.

It should be obvious that within this type of value orientation competition simply does not have a logical place.   When we find evidence of competition, it may be regarded as a deviant form of activity; or, it could signify a source of tension and confusion.   Such has been the case when baseball, for example, has been institutionalized in a being type of culture.   In some communities in the American Southwest these games have been experienced as a threat to the entire fabric of the traditional culture.   In other instances, games from other cultures have been refashioned so that the competitiveness in them is greatly reduced.   Within a being perspective, however, anyone who defines competition as a rightful attempt to get or keep any valuable thing to the exclusion of others in his own community would be suitably dispatched and dispensed with.   In the more mystical versions of this cultural type, anyone espousing this view of competition would be told that his way of seeking is ill-conceived.   As T. S. Eliot put it:

> In order to possess what you do not possess
> You must go by the way of dispossession.

The religious language of being cultures is not in terms of grasping but of sacrifice.   One is told to give up in order to receive, to lose in order to attain.   Competition and value simply do not inhabit the same realm in the universe when viewed from this perspective.

A becoming culture evinces a different set of attitudes towards those constants we just examined in a being constellation.   With regard to time, the present is seen to have the greatest reality.   The vitality and significance of the past is seen to fade quickly away, while the future looms uncertainly on the horizon.   *Now* is the moment about which to be concerned.   Why put off until tomorrow what you can enjoy today? The view of space is correlative with the more optimistic temporality. Space provides an area for development of natural and human potentiality. Necessity and the forces of nature are respected; but in addition, there is an awareness of possibility and opportunity. Man's proper relationship to nature is conceived in terms of cooperation rather than subjugation. Within this perspective, man lives *with* nature. Both time and space are more ambiguous than in a being perspective, for they open up to man, providing chances for achievement as well as failure. The cosmos allows for freedom and presents man with challenges for its expression. Normative human activity is here conceived as becoming. In Aristotle's grand conception of this perspective, all of reality is moved by the dynamics of actualization of potentialities. Man is the highest and most complete expression of this fundamental principle. His personal life is to be measured in terms of self-development. Social life is also conceived in terms of becoming. Like individuals, cities have goals as well as virtues and vices. In both interpersonal and social dimensions, there is more concern for collateral relationships than lineal ones. Friendship becomes a virtue challenging filial devotion, and justice is seen to be the aim of social process. Cooperation is emphasized rather than submission and obedience. The goal of life is conceived as the fullest realization of human and natural powers. Individuals and cities should strive for the achievement of excellence.

Competition has definitely found a place within becoming cultures, though it has at the same time been recognized as productive of tension; and sometimes it has been seen to lead to disaster. Consequently, there has often been an emphasis upon limits within which competition must be kept. For example, the well-known *Delphic oracle* commonly rendered "to know thyself" actually meant that one should know his limits and respect them. Within the becoming perspective of classical Athens, the worst sin was *hubris,* the arrogance of unrestrained anger that can so easily emerge in competitive situations. To transgress natural and moral limitations is the essence of hubris. Religion, philosophy, drama, the arts, rhetoric, and the laws collaborated in the classical tradition to keep competition within the framework of moderation and cooperation. There are examples of competition as defined by Keating to be found in classical culture, but they were held to be contemptible rather than normative. Plato went so far as to recommend child's play rather than agonistic activity as the way to lead a good life. Cicero scorned competitive athletic contests as beneath contempt. Even great military leaders singled out co-operation rather than competition as the most natural form of inter-action. Marcus Aurelius, for example, wrote:

> For we are made for cooperation, like feet, like hands, like eyelids, like rows of the upper and lower teeth. To act against one another, then, is contrary to nature. (11).

All of these representative men were competitive in some aspects of their lives. However, they apparently saw competition as a form of becoming. It was a mode of self-actualization and self-expression rather than one of acquisition. Insofar as competition is consonant with a becoming value orientation, it is viewed as an activity *with* another rather than as against him. The aim of competitive activity here is to interact so that participants actualize their fullest potentialities; it is not meant to deprive someone else of something valuable.

A third cultural constellation is oriented around the activity of doing. This type of culture is very activistic, practical, and productive. The United States, especially during its formative years, might be considered a paradigm of this type. Time in a doing culture is future oriented. While the present is important, its significance is seen in terms of its leading to greater opportunities. Americans have typically been future oriented and have viewed time as a ribbon stretching ahead to a brighter tomorrow. In a being culture, change is viewed as a threat; in a doing culture, the lack of change is threatening. For members of the latter cultural type, "time marches on" towards greater progress. The space of a doing culture is also seen in a distinctive way. Space is viewed impersonally as an area within which one might put his time to good use. Nature is neither an oppressive force nor a realm calling for a harmonious relationship. On the contrary, nature represents raw material that man should control for his own purposes. In this perspective, man is seen to be *over* nature. The proper stance towards space is one of mastery. In classical culture, natural limits were emphasized; in America one is told, "the sky's the limit." Athenians were aware of their limits and afraid to go too far; Americans have not known what their limits are and have been afraid of not reaching them. The normative activity within this type of orientation is neither being nor becoming but doing. Just being is viewed negatively; it is laziness as opposed to virtuous productivity. Congruent with time-space notions, truly valuable doing is thought of as getting results. In other cultures, work was viewed as a curse; in this perspective, it is seen as man's highest calling. Hard work is inherently valuable, but even more so when it is productive and useful. This type of culture is production oriented and utilitarian. Its heroes are great producers. The view of self in this perspective is characteristically individualistic. Doing your own work is more important than preserving social and interpersonal relationships. Manners, customs, and even personal sensitivities can legitimately be ignored or suppressed if they stand in the way of getting the job done. Good human relationships are justified not so much as ends but as factors contributing to more efficient operation. Friendly relations are helpful to business. The final objective of this type of life style is success. A primary fear is of failing to "make it."

Competition has played a significant role in the evolution of doing cultures, especially in the United States. The struggle to achieve success has often been supported by the rhetoric of competition as a valuable form of activity. The world is seen as a great arena; wherever one finds himself, he should strive to win. Within this context, the meaning of competition undergoes a transformation. In a becoming orientation, one normally competes with another to develop human potential and to make it manifest. Competition is thus an intrinsic part of the actualization of self and the other person. It is governed by those goals. In a doing orientation, one competes to accomplish results which may be extrinsic to the actual competitive process. The aim of competition in this context is logically to excel, but the boundaries of competition here become confused by extraneous goals. Competitiveness then may be encouraged in the most unlikely areas, such as learning, working, and attracting friends. It is possible that all meaningful doing is eventually interpreted in competitive terms. Thus, competition is conceived as an interminable historical process. Heroes are those who compete constantly. A doer values those people who refuse to quit, who never say die, and who win.

The fourth constellation is clustered around the activity of having.

While this type of orientation may be found among people who have undergone serious deprivation and are thus anxiously motivated to obtain and keep whatever they can, it is also discernible among people in highly successful, affluent societies. For example, this kind of life stance may be found in modern industrial states in which the orientation has shifted from production to consumption. The primary value orientation is in terms of what persons have, rather than what they do. In a doing culture, a man's work defines his status; in a having culture, a person's status is established more in terms of what he can demonstrate he has through manifest consumption. Within a having constellation, time is still future oriented, but the focus is upon an immediate future, and the tempo has increased. A producer will look to the far distant future and wait patiently for his work to come to fruition. A consumer is impatient to have his needs gratified. The temporality of a haver is characterized by a demand for immediate gratification. As a member of the instant generation, he is constantly on the alert for shortcuts to satisfaction. The spatiality of this orientation signifies a transformation of a doing perspective. Here man is also conceived as being over nature. In this instance, however, nature is not merely to be tamed; it is to be "had." A having stance not only dominates a given space, but utterly transforms it. Material eventually is seen as so much potential waste products. A haver's attitude towards space is similar to the "disposal mentality" of the throw-away society portrayed by Toffler. (15). Within a having orientation, space is conceived possessively; one is uneasy until he can own it, that is, get his hands on it. Normative human activity is thought to be acquisitive. Verbs such as get, hold, keep, hand on to, and have resonate the primary value orientation of this type of culture. The mode of social and interpersonal relationships in this orientation continues to be individualistic, but here, too, a shift is noticeable from a doing perspective. The measure of significant individual activity becomes less public and more internalized into a private standard of satisfaction. Valuable activity is assessed in terms of how one feels about what he has rather than how others judge the results of his efforts. There is a marked increase in infantile self-centeredness and relativism. It's good if you like it. Living well is interpreted in terms of feeling good. As the individual becomes privatized, there is a corresponding growth of bureacracy to take care of many responsibilities that doers used to assume. The final state desired within this perspective is a perpetual state of private, individual contentment.

Within a having orientation, competition has no inherent position. If it exists here, it will be extrinsically related to normative activity. That is, competition will be valued if it is seen as an efficient way to increase having, but it can as easily be dropped if other ways of attaining what is desired are believed to be superior. So, for example, vigorous exponents of free enterprise can quickly alter their view and support restrictive tariffs, which eliminate competition that threatens their profits. Within a having orientation, one competes against another in order to have something valuable in greater measure than he has. Corresponding to the aspiration towards contentment, there may be an attempt to regulate competition through technology and an increase in rules so as to keep tension and risk to a minimum. Although excitement will thereby be reduced, these procedures are justified in terms of the primary concerns about having a prize and a satisfied feeling at the end. The interest in competition in athletics here shifts from doing something to gaining satisfaction by watching others do it. Thus competition is perceived more as a satisfying form of entertainment, something to give thrills and pleasure to millions of spectators. A code of competition emerges that emphasizes the need for competitors to observe rules so as not to spoil a good show. Within this orientation, competitive activities, like everything else, become extremely vulnerable to commercialization. When the value of an activity is measured by what you can take away from it, its inherent worth is suppressed in favor of utilizing the activity to obtain money by satisfying customers. Even the competitor sees his activity as oriented towards more having, for wealth is the primary means toward greater consumption. Competitors and the competitive activity become commodities to be consumed within a life style that is oriented towards having more and more.

This typology of cultural contexts is useful in several ways. First, it suggests the cultural bias that has influenced Keating's definition and his philosophy. His conceptualization fits best in a context that is in a transitional stage between doing and having orientations. While he emphasized that his philosophy is descriptive and functional, it should be recognized that it is so only within his specific context. There is no reason to accord it universality. His insistence that competition requires seeking to excel or surpass is essentially a prescriptive statement; it may be considered descriptive within a doing context. His notion that competition is an attempt to get or keep something to the exclusion of others best fits a having orientation. Such a view is appropriate for an acquisitive society but not other types. His rigid distinctions between athletics and play are further indication of his value orientation. Unless one chooses to absolutize Keating's goals, it is unnecessary to insist upon these distinctions. For example, one can indeed compete to beat somebody and obtain a prize. But within another orientation, the goal might be personal and social development. If that seems incredible, then one is simply not stepping outside the context of his cultural bias. To make a workable definition of a significant human activity, it is important to consider the full socio-cultural context within which it occurs rather than just an immediate manifest goal. The advantage of this typology of contexts is that it provides a broad, flexible framework within which to understand and assess the meaning of competition in a given situation.

Another advantage of this approach is that it provides an incentive for reassessing our understanding of other relevant activities, such as play. Keating's conceptualization of play patently exhibits a doing-having orientation. From that perspective, the play phenomenon, is simply delightful; the essence of play is pleasure. That is a traditional interpretation of play from within the perspective of a Western work ethic. By reducing play to pleasure, the worker robs it of serious significance. However, careful study of play in various contexts has revealed that it is a much more complex and important activity than workers and athletes might suspect. (14). In addition to being fun, play can constitute a very important form of learning. In a child's world, for example, where there is a dominant orientation towards growth, play represents a significant form of testing and discovery. In therapy and numerous ordinary situations, play can be a mode of attaining important personal and interpersonal insight. Within an aesthetic context play can be a primary mode of developing creativity and enhancing productivity. In various situations, especially those associated with a becoming orientation, play can be a vital mode of self-expression in which one displays his true self. A serious question which needs to be faced is whether or not authentic play can tolerate competition. The inclination of many play theorists thus far seems to indicate a negative answer.

However, a positive assessment of competition with a play orientation has recently been provided by Scott Kretchmar. (10). From within a phenomenological perspective that manifests strong inclinations towards a becoming orientation, Kretchmar sees play as emerging from existential fullness. While his view of work is suspiciously negative, he has a point. Within his view work proceeds from an encounter with necessity. You work because you have to; you do not need to play. Thus characterized, play is seen to have its own time; its temporality is constituted by a full present. The space of play is open, providing players with a sense of adventure and challenge. It is an activity that is expressive of the self. It views relationships to others in terms of opposition. At this point in his argument, Kretchmar makes some very important distinctions relevant to the above question. One's opponent is not necesarily viewed as a threat to one's own attempts to acquire something valuable. On the contrary, an opponent primarily provides the challenge necessary to express oneself and to develop one's capacities to the fullest. Consequently, competitive play can be recognized as constituting an interdependence between opponents whose contest mutually testifies to their personal worth. From this perspective, a true sportsman is not a hard worker who is legalistically concerned about *his* attainment but a good player who cares about *our* experience of our game. If one views competition and play consistently within the same value orientation of becoming, then apparently both modes of activity may converge to form an intrinsic element of self and social development.

One general lesson to be learned from this approach is that words and deeds have different meanings according to the cultural contexts within which they occur. Only if we insist upon the superiority or necessity of one context over all the others should we become dogmatic in our interpretations of human action. Consequently, competition and sports, work and play will take on different meanings within diverse cultural contexts. Competition in a doing or having culture will perform a different function from that within a becoming culture. Similarly, competition in a warlike perspective will be directed towards surpassing another and acquiring valuable things exclusively. An opponent is thus viewed as an obstacle to be overcome. From within a self-actualization perspective, competition might be viewed as a form of encounter that occurs for mutual benefit. These are not the only alternatives, however. Another goal towards which competition might be oriented is the formation of friendships and community. Within a sharing orientation, people might compete in order to evoke a world of play in which bonds of reciprocity are established. In this context, one could compete with another not merely to do his best but to create a playful situation in which to interact freely, totally, and honestly with other persons. In most perspectives, it is difficult for opponents to be good friends; but in a sharing orientation, it would be possible for competitors to become the best of friends, because they would compete with, rather than against, each other.

The purpose of this article has been to suggest a contextual approach with which to understand and assess important forms of human action, such as competition, sports, and play. I have suggested that definitions and philosophies should be worked out not only in view of their own context but of alternatives. Furthermore, it has become apparent that different types of competition may be delineated by considering the framework of various ideal types of dominant value orientations within which competitive behavior takes place.

In view of the increasing aggravation of problems in the modern world, there is also a need for substantial moral considerations. Towards that end, types of value orientation other than those already delineated may be necessary. At least a fifth type of culture should be considered as a viable alternative towards which to work and play. This type can be denoted as a sharing culture in which the dominant form of care is for the well being of the total context; as such, its care would be inclusive of the other types. If competition is to survive in this kind of culture, then I propose that it be understood in the following way within the specific context of sports. Here competition would be a form of social and/or interpersonal encounter in which participants interact in a contest wherein the goals are to test abilities, increase in competence, express freedom, and share in a common endeavor to create a more playful environment in which bonds of friendship and community are strengthened. Admittedly, this is an idealistic notion. But unless one opts for a materialistic view of history, he must recognize the importance of ideals as formative social forces influencing the shape of human destiny. It is just possible that if the institution of sports were reoriented towards a sharing value constellation, it might function to counter the trend towards greater having and foster the development of a more humane world. At least that is something for an ethics of competition and sports to take into consideration.

REFERENCES

1. Dobzhansky, Theodosius: *The Biological Basis of Human Freedom.* New York, Columbia University Press, 1960.
2. Dubos, Rene: *A God Within.* New York, Scribner's, 1972.
3. Dubos, Rene: *So Human an Animal.* New York, Scribner's, 1968.
4. Eliade, Mircea: *The Sacred and the Profane.* New York, Harper and Row, 1961.
5. Hall, Edmund: *The Silent Language.* Garden City, Doubleday and Co., 1959.
6. Hofstadter, Richard: *Social Darwinism in American Thought.* Revised edition. New York, George Braziller, Inc., 1959.
7. Keating, James W.: "The Ethics of Competition and Its Relation to Some Moral Problems in Athletics." Essay presented at the Symposium on Sport and Ethics, Brockport, New York, October 26-28, 1972.
8. Kenyon, Gerald S.: "Sport and Society: At Odds or in Concert?" Unpublished manuscript.
9. Kluckhohn, Florence and Strodtbeck, Fred: *Variations in Value Orientations.* Evanston, Row, Peterson and Co., 1961.
10. Kretchmar, Scott: "Ontological Possibilities: Sport as Play." Essay presented at the Symposium on the Philosophy of Sport, Brockport, New York, February 10-12, 1972.
11. Marcus Aurelius: *Meditations, Book II.* Harmondsworth, Penguin Books, 1967.
12. Parsons, Talcott and Shils, E.A. (eds.): *Toward a General Theory of Action.* New York, Harper and Row, 1961.
13. Sadler, William A., Jr.: "Competition Out of Bounds: Sports in American

Life." Essay presented at the Annual Meeting, AAHPER, Houston, March, 1972.

14. Sadler, William A., Jr.: "Creative Existence: Play as a Pathway to Personal Freedom and Community," *Humanitas,* Vol. 1 (1969).
15. Toffler, Alvin: *Future Shock.* New York, Random House, 1970.
16. Zeigler, Earle F.: "Putting the Greek Ideal in Perspective in North American Athletics Today." Unpublished manuscript.

ON KEATING ON THE COMPETITIVE MOTIF IN ATHLETICS AND PLAYFUL ACTIVITY

ROBERT G. OSTERHOUDT

I

In accord with the principle of charity, we must allow Professor Keating his conception of competition as: ". . . an attempt, according to agreed-upon rules, to get or to keep any thing either to the exclusion of others or in greater measure than others." (4:p.3). That is, such a phenomenon has been frequently and accurately observed it seems, and it is thereby not a vacuous concept (an idea without an object, or fact) we have of it, irrespective of the term employed to represent, or signify, it. We are also given to take as unproblematic, as Professor Keating claims, that such a phenomenon provides a socially useful mechanism (assists in the construction and maintenance of a viable social heirarchy) for determining our place, or position, in relation to others with respect to any particular ability. It, in effect, provides for an amicable testing of powers and is in this sense helpful in terms of its encouraging self-discovery and thereby contributing to the public interest. We acknowledge as well Professor Keating's disposition to axiologic subjectivism, allowing that this competition is in and of itself ethically neutral, that its ethical status waits upon human objectives for, and experiences of, it.

The crucial question here, then, the one upon which the very preservation of athletics may well rest, is that concerning the nature of man, the social substance, and the common good as located in athletic competition. That is, this competition is in the end justified by Professor Keating himself as contributing to the common good; such that, an adequate understanding of the competitive strife requires an explanation of it in view of the common good, and not in isolation by itself alone. Professor Keating's treatment while instructive in itself fails to secure a tenable conclusion largely because it does not consider the consequences of such a treatment in terms of its implications for a synoptic view of man, the social substance, and the common good. If Professor Keating's examination is lacking in any respect, then, it is apparently lacking in the vision of the metaphysician to carry the inquiry further, and to set out its first principles and plausible consequences more explicitly, comprehensively, and systematically. The dispute here, then, is one with respect to the order of generality at which these various phenomena operate. And more so than a disputation, or refutation, of Professor Keating's theses, it is rather the hope to offer an interpretive extension of them.

The major observation we wish to make here is that Professor Keating's conception of competition does not, and ought not, commit us inexorably to the notion that it is the excelling, or vanquishing of others which is of primary significance in this process. For Professor Keating himself rather allows that we encourage this sort of activity in the economic and political spheres, as it operates in the end to the common good. It is the common good, then, which we seek foremost, and not the victory of one at the destructive expense of others. The question here is not whether or not competition performs a socially useful function or whether or not it is an indisputable fact of life (notions to which we have already submitted), but more fundamentally how it is that one ought to regard other men generally and one's so-termed athletic opponent more specifically. The keeping of the competitive urge in proper bounds must entail not only the mere observance of rules and regulations (laws), but the genuinely sympathetic regard for others necessary to the elimination of deceit, hatred, and jealousy among athletes, and to the constructive respect for humanity generally.

The spirit of profit and success is coextensive with the spirit of service, if they are both kept confluent with the common good, in which case profit and success are construed in terms of public service. An act is profitable, a person successful, in virtue of it or him contributing to the commonweal. The material welfare of the world is not, then, itself at odds with essential morality, though it is rather clear that an unsatisfactorily inequitable distribution, or treatment, of it is.   In this preferred condition, self-interest and public interest coalesce and produce a harmony (a synthetic unity) among men, which is unknown when they are conceived in exclusive terms, or independently of one another.   If all compete in the end for the same thing, which may be mutually held, the great cleavages between men dissolve, as Professor Keating admits.   The difficulty here, and that to which the substance of our response to Professor Keating speaks, arises from a general conception of the world which allows the rival, the other or others, to be construed as means to an end, and not as ends in themselves, thereby promoting a view of man which serves principally to divide particular men irreconcilably, and which is potentially destructive of the whole of humanity, let alone athletics.   This instrumental treatment of other men comes in large measure to regarding them as empirical objects to be employed in the service of our own egoistic satisfactions and aspirations, and is at utter odds with Kant's exhortation: "Act so that you treat humanity, whether in your own person or in that of another, always as an end and never as a means only." (3:p.47).   Each man is hereby regarded as a free moral agent, and not a mere object bound to, and thereby exploited by, the self-interested desires and inclinations of others.   The use of men to produce ends beyond, even alien to, themselves is, so it would appear, self-destructive of them, in the sense in which it requires of them action which is contrary to the cultivation, even preservation, of their human distinctiveness and integrity.

Our rivals are perhaps best conceived not as other men, but as standards of excellence to which we are assisted by other men (our so-termed opponents).   The ends of such a quest are exclusive in only a superficial sense.   That is, they provide the necessary constraint to excellence which allows one to achieve that which he seeks foremost, self-fulfillment, or an acting in accord with the common good (a transcendence of exclusivity, a bringing of the self-interest to one with the common good, a unification of all ends).   Contrary to what superficial inspection may have led us to believe, then, the victory sought is not a victory over, so much as a victory with, others.   Consequently, we may most properly be said to be competing against others for an exclusive prize only in terms of our unreflective, or superficial, apprehension of the character of athletic competition. In terms of the larger scheme, the whole, of things and the normative preferences reported here, Professor Keating's notion, if raised to all-embracing (metaphysical) perspective without further modification, leads us to a distasteful, a self-destructive view of man, the social substance, and the common good; and nothing well-disposed, it seems, can be said to actively favor its own demise. This objectionable view, in effect, refuses to allow other men the humanistic regard we seek openly for ourselves. There is, then, as James suggests, no sufficient reason to hold that the destructive, military form of competition is its only, nor its last, form:

> Patriotic pride and ambition in their military form are, after all, only specifications of a more general competitive passion. They are its first form, but that is no reason for supposing them to be its last form. (2:p.298).

II

In his discussion of the attitude and conduct proper to playful activity (a free, creative activity in which the goal of the participants is to maximize the joy of the moment, seeking no good outside the activity itself) and that appropriate to athletics (physical contests designed to determine human excellence through honorable victory in a contest), Professor Keating argues that these forms of activity are radically different in terms of their objectives, that the nature of the activity (its goal, or objective) determines the attitude and conduct appropriate to it, and that the attitude and conduct proper to playful activity cannot therefore also be suitable to athletics. But his treatment here appears to proceed on an equivocal notion of competition, and in the case of athletic competition leads once again to a potentially self-destructive view of man, the social substance, and the common good.

It would appear that Professor Keating wishes to regard the competitive motif as located in playful activity as an essentially cooperative venture in which the participants in the end seek a mutually obtainable goal (namely, the immediate joy of all participants) and which is therefore dominated by a spirit of generosity and magnanimity. This process is not productive of listless competition, Professor Keating argues, but is rather the source of an arduous competitive undertaking. Apparently, however, the competitive theme as located in playful activity differs from that appropriate to athletics in three very crucial ways.

Firstly, in the case of playful activity, competition is an intermediate involvement; that is, one of interest only in terms of that which it allows beyond itself, namely, a heightened joy and pleasure for all disputants. It functions in this instance as a means to achieving a yet more venerated end. And in the case of athletics, conversely, it appears to function as an end in itself. Secondly, since playful activity generally may include particular activities which are in no evident manner similar to athletic forms of competitive activity, even in phenomenal appearance (e.g., stamp collecting, reading, and the like), the competitive strife itself appears altogether accidental to playful activity, while a necessary condition for athletics. And thirdly, competition as construed in athletic terms is not consonant with the ends sought for playful activity; such that, the sort of so-termed competition appropriate to playful activity is not competition in the strict sense at all. That is, in playful activity, we have a so-termed competitive endeavor conducted in accord with the form and spirit of a cooperative enterprise, or an activity which is not essentially competitive at all; that is, an activity in which exclusive ends are not sought foremost. In point of fact, then, competition in its athletic form is so radically different from that appropriate to playful activity that the two phenomena are not properly signified by the same term. For, insofar as the activities are both genuinely (in the same sense) competitive, and we are not operating under an equivoval notion of competition, they are essentially the same, at least with respect to their competitive aspects, and we have seen rather clearly that they are not. Such a use, consequently, comes to an equivocation with respect to the term, competition.

The distinction proposed by Professor Keating between athletics and playful activity is, in effect, a discrimination between two radically different ways of regarding activities which may be similar in phenomenal appearance, but are necessarily discrete in essence, in terms of their goals, or objectives (the primary intentions of their participants). What we have here as well, then, it seems, is the germ of two radically discrete manners of conceiving man, the social substance, and the common good—two inclinations which are so clearly and distinctly different as to be incompatible. That is, the principles supporting these two codes of moral conduct are so incongruent as to oppose one another. It is not a mere difference in degree, but one of a substantial sort. Professor Keating's case may be more effectively argued, it appears, by opting for one of the two general conceptions, for a hybrid form of one of the two views, or for a thorough reconciliation of them. We cannot tenably regard other men both as the strict competitive notion would have us, and as the strict cooperative notion (competitive in only a superficial sense, as suggested previously: competitive only in the sense in which one is constrained by some thing in his quest for excellence, and therefore has no free, cavalier path to its realization) would suggest. As per our previous discussion, then, we conclude that the cooperative notion native to playful activity is the one which ultimately yields the most appealing general account of man, the social substance, and the common good. For, it is a conception which yields not merely a jurisprudential justice, but one of a genuinely altruistic order; and is therefore preferable to its major alternative.

Sportsmanship, when regarded as the moral category appropriate to playful activity, and to the whole of life, becomes the all-embracing moral principle Professor Keating holds that it is not. It becomes one with the sentiments of generosity and magninimity proper to all forms of human activity. The moral qualities absolutely essential to the sportsman are resultantly those absolutely essential to all humanity. The application of sportsmanship to athletics, then, is not so much an attempt to soften the force of the competitive struggle as it is an attempt to reorder and reform it.

It has been the intent here to offer a brief critique of James W. Keating's "The Ethics of Competition and Its Relation to Some Moral Problems in Athletics." Clearly, issues have been more so raised than resolved. Nothing has been set to rest absolutely. If this attempt has done no more than provoke thought with respect to notions alternative to those expressed by Professor Keating and to the larger consequences of his view, then it has likely achieved all that might be plausibly expected of it.

REFERENCES

1. Herrigel, Eugen: *Zen in the Art of Archery.* Hermann Tausend (ed.). New York, Random House, Inc., 1971.
2. James, William: "The Moral Equivalent of War," *Pragmatism and Other Essays.* Joseph L. Blau (ed.). New York, Washington Square Press, Inc., 1963.
3. Kant, Immanuel: *Foundations of the Metaphysics of Morals.* Lewis White Beck (trans.). Indianapolis, The Bobbs-Merrill Co., Inc., 1959.
4. Keating, James W.: "The Ethics of Competition and Its Relation to Some Moral Problems in Athletics." Essay presented at the Symposium on Sport and Ethics, Brockport, New York, 26-28 (October, 1972).
5. Keating, James W.: "Sportsmanship as a Moral Category," *Ethics,* Vol. 85, No. 1, 25-35 (October, 1964).
6. Metheny, Eleanor: *Connotations of Movement in Sport and Dance.* Dubuque, William C. Brown Co., Publishers, 1965.

THE GRASSHOPPER; A THESIS CONCERNING THE MORAL IDEAL OF MAN

Bernard Suits

It was clear that the Grasshopper would not survive the winter, and his followers had gathered round him for what would no doubt be one of their last meetings. Most of them were reconciled to his approaching death, but a few were still outraged that such a thing could be allowed to happen. Prudence was one of the latter, and she approached the Grasshopper with a final plea. "Grasshopper," she said, "a few of us have agreed to give up a share of our food to tide you over till spring. Then next summer you can work to pay us back."

"My dear child," responded the Grasshopper, "you still don't understand. The fact is that I will *not* work to pay you back. I will not work at all. I made that perfectly clear, I thought, when the ant turned me away from his door. My going to him in the first place was, of course, a mistake. It was a weakness to which I shall not give in again."

"But," continued Prudence, "we don't begrudge you a portion of our food. If you like, we will not require you to pay us back. We are not, after all, ants."

"No," replied the Grasshopper, "you are not ants, not any more. But neither are you grasshoppers. Why should you give me the fruits of your labor? Surely that would not be just, when I tell you quite clearly that I will not pay you back."

"But *that* kind of justice," exclaimed Prudence, "is only the justice of ants. Grasshoppers have nothing to do with such 'justice'."

"You are right," said the Grasshopper. "The justice which is fairness in trading is irrelevant to the lives of true grasshoppers. But there is a justice which prevents me from accepting your offer. Why are you willing to work so that I may live? Is it not because I embody in my life what you aspire to, and you do not want the model of your aspirations to perish? Your wish is understandable and to a certain point even commendable. But at bottom it is inconsistent and self-defeating. It is also—and I hope you will not take offense at my blunt language—hypocritical."

"Those are hard words, Grasshopper."

"But well meant. My life, you must understand, was not intended to be a sideshow, yet that seems to be what you want to make of it. You should value me because you want to be like me, and not merely so that you can boast to the ants that you are an intimate of the Grasshopper, that oddity of nature."

"We have never done that, Grasshopper!"

"I believe you. But you might as well have done so if you believe that your proposal is a good one. For it amounts to working so that I may be idle, which is the opposite of the wisdom to which I have tried to lead you. The whole burden of my teaching is that you ought to be idle, but now you propose to use me as a pretext not only for working, but for working harder than ever, since you would have not only yourselves to feed, but me as well. I call this hypocritical because you would like to take credit for doing something which is no more than a ruse for avoiding living up to your ideals."

At this point Skepticus broke in with a laugh. "What the Grasshopper means, Prudence," he said, "is that we do not yet have the courage of his convictions. The point is that we should not only refuse to work for the Grasshopper, we should also refuse to work for ourselves. We, like him, should be dying for our principles. That we are not is the respect in which, though no longer ants, we are not

grasshoppers either. And, of course, given the premise that the life
of the Grasshopper is the only life worth living, what he says certainly
follows."

"Not quite, Skepticus," put in the Grasshopper. "I agree that the
principles in question are worth dying for. But I must remind you
that they are the principles of Grasshoppers. I am not here to persuade you to die for my principles, but to persuade you that *I* must.
We ought to be quite clear about our respective roles. You are
not here to die for me, but I for you. You only need, as Skepticus
put it, the courage of my convictions up to a point; that is, courage
sufficient to approve rather than to deplore my death. Neither of you
is quite prepared to grant that approval, though for different reasons.
You, Prudence, because, though you believe the principles are worth
dying for, you do not believe they need to be died for; and you,
Skepticus, because you are not even sure that the principles are worth
dying for.

"Although," replied Skepticus, "I believe you to be the wisest
being alive—which is why I have never left your side during the
whole summer of your life—I have to admit that I am still not convinced that the life of the Grasshopper is the best life to live. Perhaps if you could give me a clearer vision of the good life as you see
it my convictions would approach yours, and my courage as well.
You might do this by one of the parables for which you are justly
esteemed."

"Parables, my dear Skepticus," replied the Grasshopper, "ought to
come at the end, not at the beginning, of serious inquiry; that is, only
at the point where arguments fail. But speaking of parables, you
may be sure that the ants will fashion one out of my career. They
will very likely represent my life as a moral tale, the point of which
is the superiority of a prudent to an idle way of life. But it should
really be the Grasshopper who is the hero of the tale; he, not the ant,
who should have the hearer's sympathy. The point of the parable,
that is, should not be the ant's triumph, but the Grasshopper's tragedy.
For one cannot help reflecting that if there were no winters to guard
against, then the Grasshopper would not get his comeuppance nor
the ant his shabby victory. The life of Grasshopper would be vindicated and that of the ant absurd."

"But there *are* winters to guard against," Prudence protested.

"No doubt. Still, it is not only possible, but on the whole more likely than not, that with accelerating advances in technology the time will come when there are in fact no winters. We may therefore conclude that although my timing may be a bit off, my way of life is not wrong in principle."

"The operation was successful but the patient died," put in Skepticus.

"No," replied the Grasshopper, "it's not quite like that. That my way of life may eventually be vindicated in practice, is, now that I think of it, really beside the point. Rather, it is the logic of my position which is at issue. And this logic shows that prudential actions (e.g., those actions we ordinarily call work) are self-defeating in principle. For prudence may be defined as the disposition (a) to sacrifice something good (e.g., leisure) if and only if such sacrifice is necessary for obtaining something better (e.g., survival), and (b) to reduce the number of good things requiring sacrifice, ideally to zero. The ideal of prudence, therefore, like the ideal of preventive medicine, is its own extinction. For if it were the case that no sacrifices of goods needed ever to be made, then prudential actions would be pointless, indeed impossible. This principle, knowledge of which I regard as an indispensible first step on the path to wisdom, the ants seem never to have entertained. The true Grasshopper sees that work is not self-justifying, and that his way of life is the final justification of any work whatever."

"But surely," replied Skepticus, " you are carrying your point to an unreasonable extreme. You talk as though there were but two possible alternatives: either a life devoted exclusively to play or a life devoted exclusively to work. But most of us realize that our labour is valuable because it permits us to play, and we are presumably seeking to achieve some kind of balance between work input and play output. People neither are, nor want to be, wholly grasshoppers or wholly ants, but a combination of the two; people are and want to be (if you will forgive a regrettably vulgar but spooneristically inevitable construction) asshoppers or grants. We can, of course, all cease to work, but if we do then we cannot play for long either, for we will shortly die."

"I have three answers to make to what you have said, Skepticus, and I fear I shall have to make them quickly, for the sun has set and the frost is already creeping through the fields. First, evidently I was put on earth just to play out my life and die, and it would be impious of me to go against my destiny. That is, if you like, the theology of the case. But second, there is also a logic of the case, which is as inescapable as fate or, if you like, a fate of the case which is as inescapable as logic. The only argument against living the life of the Grasshopper arises from the contingent fact that at present one dies if one does not work. The answer to that argument is that my death is inevitable in any case. For if I am *improvident* in summer, then I will die in winter. And if I am *provident* in summer, then I will cease to be the Grasshopper, by definition. But I will be either provident or improvident in summer; there is no third alternative. Therefore, either I die or I cease to be the Grasshopper. But since I am just the Grasshopper, no more and no less, dying and ceasing to be the Grasshopper are one and the same thing for me. I cannot escape that logic or that fate. But since I am the Grasshopper and you are not, it would seem to follow that you are not compelled by this logic. As I intimated earlier, I often think that I was put on earth just to die for you; to bear that heavy but inevitable cross. But I confess that that is when I am in something of an early Christian—that is, late pagan—frame of mind. At other times (and this brings me to my third and final answer to your objection, Skepticus) I have the oddest notion that both of you are Grasshoppers in disguise; in fact, that everyone alive is really a Grasshopper."

At this Prudence whispered to Skepticus, "The end must be near; his mind is beginning to wander." But Skepticus just looked keenly at their friend and teacher as he continued to speak.

"I admit that this is a wild fancy," the Grasshopper was saying, "and I hesitate to tell you my thoughts. Still, I am used to being thought foolish, so I shall proceed, inviting you to make of my words what you will. Then let me tell you that I have always had a recurring dream, in which it is revealed to me—though how it is revealed I cannot say—that everyone alive is in fact engaged in playing elaborate games, while at the same time believing themselves to be going about their ordinary affairs. Carpenters, believing themselves to be merely pursuing their trade, are really playing a game, and similarly with politicians, philosophers, lovers, murderers, thieves, and saints. Whatever occupation or activity you can think of, it is in reality a game. This revelation is, of course, astonishing. The sequel is terrifying. For in the dream I then go about persuading everyone I find of the great truth which has been revealed to me. How I am able to persuade them I do not know, though persuade them I do. But precisely at the point when each is persuaded—and this is the ghastly part—each ceases to exist. It is not just that my auditor vanishes on the spot, though indeed he does. It is that I also know with absolute certainty that he no longer exists anywhere. It is as though he had never been. Appalled as I am by the results of my teaching I cannot stop, but quickly move on to the next creature with my news, until I have preached the truth throughout the universe, and have converted everyone to oblivion. Finally I stand alone beneath the summer stars in absolute despair. Then I awaken to the joyful knowledge that the world is still teeming with sentient beings after all, and that it was only a dream. I see the carpenter and philosopher going about their work as before . . . But is it, I ask myself, just as before? Is the carpenter on his roof-top simply hammering nails, or is he making some move in an ancient game whose rules he has forgotten? But now the chill creeps up my legs. I grow drowsy. Dear friends, farewell."

The rest of my remarks will consist in an elucidation of Grasshopper logic, an examination of Grasshopper ideals, and an interpretation of Grasshopper dreams. I hope to accomplish these tasks with the help of a definition of game-playing. Here is the definition:

> To play a game is to attempt to achieve a specific state of affairs, using only means permitted by rules, where the rules prohibit more efficient in favor of less efficient means, and where such rules are accepted just because they make possible such activity.

In high-jumping, for example, the contestants strive to be on the other side of a barrier. But certain means for achieving this goal are ruled out, for example, walking around the barrier, ducking under it, or using a ladder or catapult to get over it. The goal of the contestants is not to be on the other side of the barrier *per se,* since aside from the game they are playing they are unlikely to have any reason whatever for being on the other side. Their goal is not *simply* to get to the other side, but to do this by using only means permitted by rules; namely, running from a certain distance and then jumping. The players accept the rules, furthermore, just because they want to act within the limitations the rules impose; that is, they accept rules so that they can play a game, and they accept these rules so that they can play this game.

There is thus a sharp difference between the ways in which we justify ordinary rules and the ways in which we justify the rules of games. To the question why there are traffic rules we respond, so that automobiles will not be continually crashing into one another. While to the question why Smith is hitting a ball with a funny stick we respond, because he is playing golf. But we do not justify Jones's obedience to the traffic rules by the fact that he is driving a car, and we do not justify Smith's hitting a ball with a funny stick by the fact that he wants to get the ball into a hole.

For convenience, I have formulated a one sentence version of my definition: Playing a game is the voluntary attempt to overcome unnecessary obstacles.

Now let us return to a proposition which was advanced by the Grasshopper as a basic principle; namely, that the life of the Grasshopper—that is, a life of play—is the only justification for work, so that if there were no need for work, we would simply spend all of our time at play. Now, if playing and playing games are the same thing, and if I have correctly defined game-playing, then it would follow that the Grasshopper is recommending a life devoted to the kind of activity I have defined. But it does not seem to be the case that playing, as the Grasshopper uses that term, can be the same as game-playing. The Grasshopper uses the terms "work" and "play" as logical complements of that class of things which we may call "intentional behaviour." His assumption is that if an action is not work then it is play, and *vice versa.* But *prima facie,* at least, this is an unconvincing dichotomy. For example, passing the time of day with a colleague seems to be neither work nor play, and attempting to solve a double crostic seems to be both work and play. As descriptions, therefore, the words "work" and "play" do not designate sub-sets of intentional behaviour which are either exclusive of each other or exhaustive of the set which includes them. My conclusion, however, is not that the Grasshopper has given us poor descriptions, but that he has not given us descriptions at all. He is using the words "work" and "play" stipulatively rather than descriptively. He means by "work" activity which is instrumentally valuable, and he means by "play" activity which is intrinsically valuable.

It may be wondered how I can be sure that that is what the Grasshopper intended. The answer, of course, is that he is *my* Grasshopper, and that he intends precisely what I intend him to intend. By "play," then, the Grasshopper intends to designate all those activities which are intrinsically valuable to those who engage in them. Game-playing, as I define it, *is* one such activity, but not all such activities are game-playing. Thus one may value for their own sake— value instrinsically—things like scratching an itch or listening to a Beethoven quartet, but their being instrinsically valued does not make such things games.

The thesis I would like to advance has three main elements. They are (1) play as the Grasshopper uses that term, (2) game-playing, as I use that term, and (3) what I shall call the moral ideal of man. I take it that what the Grasshopper means by "play" and what I mean by "game-playing" are sufficiently clear, so let me just say a word about the moral ideal of man. By the phrase I mean that thing or those things whose only justification is that they justify everything else; or, as Aristotle put it, those things for the sake of which we do other things, but which are not themselves for the sake of anything else. The Grasshopper is making the claim that play as he defines it is identical with the moral ideal of man. I shall attempt to establish a position which is, in effect, an interpretation or modification of the Grasshopper's claim. This position can be expressed by two related contentions. The first is that Grasshopperian play is necessary but not sufficient for an adequate account of the moral ideal of man. The second is that game-playing performs a crucial role in delineating that ideal—a role which cannot be performed by any other actvity, and without which an account of the moral ideal is either incomplete or impossible.

In order to support these contentions I would like to borrow from Plato, as I have already borrowed from Plato in creating a Socratic Grasshopper. This time I would like to use the kind of device Plato used in trying to get at certain characteristics of the human psyche. If we look at the state, said Plato, we will find there the magnified extensions of the characteristics of the psyche that we are seeking; and, being magnified, they will be easier to recognize. Somewhat similarly, I would like to begin by representing the Grasshopper's version of the moral ideal of man as though it were already instituted as a social reality. We will then be able to talk about a Utopia which embodies that ideal—that is, an actual state of affairs where people are engaged only in those activities which they value intrinsically.

Let us imagine, then, that all of the instrumental activities of human beings have been eliminated. All of the things ordinarily called work are now done by wholly automated machines which are activated solely by mental telepathy, so that not even a minimum staff is necessary for the housekeeping chores of society. Furthermore, there are so many goods being produced so abundantly that even the most acquisitive cravings of the Getty's and Onassis's of society are instantly satisfied, and anyone who wishes may be a Getty or an Onassis. Economically, the condition of man is a south sea island paradise, where yachts, diamonds, racing cars, symphonic performances, mansions, and trips around the world are as easily plucked from the environment as breadfruit is in Tahiti. We have, then, eliminated the need for productive labour, for the administration of such labour, and for a system of financing and distributing such production. All of the economic problems of man have been solved forever. Are there any other problems? There are indeed. There are all of the inter-personal problems which do not depend upon economic scarcity.

Let us, then, further imagine that all possible inter-personal problems have been solved by appropriate methods. Let us suppose that psychoanalysis has made such giant strides that it actually cures people, or that all the various kinds of group treatment have proved successful, or that some quite new development in socio- or psycho-therapy or in pharmacology has made it possible to effect 100 per cent cures for all psychic disturbances. As a restult of these developments there is no longer any competition for love, attention, approval, or admiration, just as there is no longer any strife in the acquisition of material goods. Perhaps a single example will serve to illustrate the state of affairs in question. Let us take the case of sex. Under present conditions, or at least under conditions of the relatively recent past, there is a short supply of willing sexual objects relative to demand. The reason for this is the prevalence of inhibitions in the seekers of such objects, in the objects themselves, or in both, such that great expenditures of instrumental effort are required in order to overcome them and thus get at the intrinsic object of desire. But with everyone enjoying superb mental health the necessity for all this hard work is removed, and sexual partners are every bit as accessible as yachts and diamonds.

At this point I would like to cast the presentation of my argument in dialogue form once again, and for that purpose I would like to resurrect the Grasshopper. Besides being useful for my exposition, such resurrection is also dramatically fitting, since the Grasshopper seems a bit undecided as to whether he is Socrates or Jesus Christ. Let us imagine, then, that the Grasshopper is once again discoursing with Skepticus and Prudence. Prudence, by the way, will have only one line in this renewed colloquy. To resume, then. The point has been made that sex would not have to be struggled for in Utopia. Skepticus then raises another question.

S. But what about love, approval, attention, and admiration, Grasshopper? Even in Utopia people would have to work to achieve these.

G. On the contrary, Skepticus, many people seem to believe that the kind of love, attention, and admiration alone worth having is just the kind that one ought *not* to work at.

S. Yes, but many other people, such as marriage counselors, take a quite different view. They are always saying things like, "You have to *work* at your marriage, you know."

G. Yes, but what does this "working at" mean in the case of marriage or, for that matter, in the case of any other intrinsically valued relationship between people? Does it not mean, essentially, being tolerant of, and helpful with respect to, one another's social and psychological short-comings? But in Utopia we are supposing that there are no such short-comings to be tolerant of. Furthermore, whether it is or is not the case that in Utopia one will have to work at something in order to gain love and admiration, it cannot be love and admiration at which one works. We admire a person who works hard, let us say, at teaching. But we admire him because he works hard at teaching, not because he works hard at being admired. I suggest that for convenience we lump together under the word "approval" all of the pro-attitudes we have been talking about, and then ask whether there is anything at all that our Utopians could do to gain approval.

S. Very well. First, then, it is clear that they cannot gain approval by their economic industry, since there is no need for such industry. And I take it that we must also rule out approval for governing well, since with no competing claims for goods requiring legislation, adjudication, and execution, there is no need for government. What seems to be left for approval is excellence in moral, artistic and intellectual accomplishment. Do you agree?

G. For our present purpose, at any rate, I think your list will do. Let us consider moral goodness first. Will you agree with me that moral action is possible only when it is morally desirable to prevent or to rectify some wrong or evil that is about to be or has been done somebody?

S. Yes, I agree with that.

G. But we are also agreed, are we not, that in Utopia no evil or wrong can befall anyone?

S. Yes, that is true of Utopia by definition, since Utopia is just a dramatization of the ideal of human existence, and evil and wrong-doing are obviously inconsistent with such an ideal.

G. Well, then, if no evil can befall anyone in Utopia, there will simply be no demand there for the performance of good deeds. They will, in fact, be quite impossible, and therefore not a means for gaining approval. Morality is relevant only to the extent that the ideal has not been realized, but there is no room at all for morality in the moral ideal itself, just as there is no room for revolution in the ideal which inspires revolutionary action.

S. What about excellence in art? We admire superior artistic creators, good critics, and accomplished connoisseurs.

G. You will no doubt find what I am about to suggest very hard to accept, but it strikes me that there is no place in the moral ideal for any of the skills you have mentioned.

S. I must admit, Grasshopper, that I find your suggestion positively staggering. How on earth do you arrive at such a strange conclusion?

G. I believe that these skills would not exist in Utopia because art would not exist there. Art has a subject matter, which consists in the actions and passions of men: with human aspirations and frustrations, hopes and fears, triumphs and tragedies, with flaws of character, moral dilemmas, joy and sorrow. But it would seem that none of these necessary ingredients of art could exist in Utopia.

S. Perhaps a good deal of art would be impossible for the Utopians, but surely not all of it. There is, or at least there used to be, a school of aesthetics which regarded art as essentially consisting in pure forms, such that content was either adventitious and therefore dispensable or, preferably, not present at all. Art as shape or design or form does not require the kind of subject matter you are talking about.

G. My own belief is that form is not separable from content in the way you suggest, but if it were, then the creation of designs, whether in tones, shapes, colours, or words could, and presumably would, be turned over to computors, since the products to be turned out would be, by hypothesis, uninspired by human emotion.

S. Even if the Utopians could not admire workers in the field of the arts, they could still admire accomplished thinkers: scientists, philosophers, and the like. Persons, that is, who are engaged in the acquisition of knowledge. Suppose we consider that possibility.

G. Very well, let us do so. Now, by hypothesis, we are supposing that our Utopians have completely eliminated the need for any instrumental activity whatever. But the acquisition of knowledge, just like the acquisition of anything else, is an instrumental process; that is, acquisition is instrumental to possession, no matter what it is that one is seeking to possess—food and shelter or knowledge. And just as we have supposed that our Utopians have acquired all the economic goods they can use, we must assume that they have acquired all the knowledge there is. In Utopia, therefore, there are no scientists, philosophers, or any other intellectual investigators.

S.   Then it seems that there is nothing that one could do in Utopia in order to gain approval. But we were talking about approval only to try to discover whether such things as love and friendship could exist in Utopia. But human relationships like love and friendship include more than approval. Just as important, surely, is the *sharing* which is generally recognized to be very prominent in love and friendship. And mutual interest in something does not imply a deficiency to be overcome on the part of those who have such an interest.

G.   True enough, Skepticus, but in Utopia what is there left to share? The sharing which admittedly plays a large part in love and friendship cannot be the sharing of love and friendship themselves. There must be something else; something like success and failure, adversity and prosperity, the enjoyment or creation of art, intellectual inquiry, respect for the moral qualities each possesses, etc. There is simply nothing of any importance in Utopia to be shared, so that if love and friendship could exist in Utopia, it would have to be kinds which contained neither approval nor shared interests; at most, therefore, extremely attenuated forms of love and friendship.

S.   Grasshopper, let me collect my wits. In Utopia man cannot labour, he cannot administer or govern, there is no art, no morality, no science, no love, no friendship. The only thing which our analysis has not utterly destroyed is sex. Perhaps the moral ideal of man is just a supreme orgasm.

P.   Don't complain, Skepticus. It's a lot better than nothing.

G.   Of course, we mustn't forget game-playing. That has not been ruled out.

S.   No doubt, no doubt. Are we then to conclude that the moral ideal of man is sex and games or, as we might say, fun and games?

G.   Actually, now that I think of it, I am no longer all that sure about sex.

S. Oh, come now, Grasshopper!

G. No, Skepticus, I am quite serious. The obsessive popularity that sex has always enjoyed is, I suspect, inseparably bound up with man's non-Utopian condition. Sex, as we have come to know and love it, is part and parcel with repression, guilt, naughtiness, domination and submission, liberation, rebellion, sadism and masochism, romance, and theology. But none of these things has a place in Utopia. Therefore, we ought at least to face the possibility that with the removal of all of these constituents of sex as we value it, there will be little left but a pleasant sensation in the loins—or wherever. People like Norman Browne in his book *Life Against Death* take the view that sex is something which has been distorted and corrupted by the repressions and restraints of civilization, and that with the end of civilization (which Browne looks forward to with great keenness), sex will re-emerge as the unsullied item that it was in our infancies. We will then all become happy children once again, enjoying without inhibition our polymorphous perversity. But if, as I believe, sex is the product rather than the victim of civilization, then when civilization goes, sex—at least as a very highly valued item— goes as well.

S. If not convinced I am for the moment silenced.

G. Very well. Then we appear to be left with game-playing as the only remaining candidate for Utopian occupation, and therefore the only remaining constitutent of the moral ideal of man.

S. And now I suppose you are going to rule out game-playing as well. Grasshopper, I begin to suspect that what you are really up to is to show that the concept of Utopia itself is paradoxical, as philosophers from time to time try to show that the alleged perfections of the Deity entail paradoxes.

G. Quite the contrary, Skepticus. I believe that Utopia is intelligible, and I believe that game-playing is what makes Utopia intelligible. What we have shown thus far is that there does not appear to be anything to *do* in Utopia, precisely because in Utopia all instrumental activities have been eliminated. There is nothing to strive for precisely because everything has already been achieved. What we need, therefore, is some activity in which what is instru-

mental is inseparably combined with what is intrinsically valuable, and where the activity is not itself an instrument for some
further end. Games meet this requirement perfectly. For in
games we must have obstacles which we can strive to overcome
just so that we can possess the activity as a whole, namely, playing the game. Game-playing makes it possible to retain enough
effort in Utopia to make life worth living.

S. What you are saying is that in Utopia the only thing left to do
would be to play games, so that game-playing turns out to be
the whole of the moral ideal of man.

G. So it would appear, at least at this stage of our investigation.

S. I don't think so.

G. I beg your pardon?

S. I don't think that conclusion follows.

G. You don't.

S. I believe we made a mistake earlier on.

G. A mistake.

S. Yes. Earlier on.

G. Perhaps you would be good enough to point it out to me.

S. I shall be happy to do so. When you were advancing the view
that science, or any kind of intellectual inquiry, was an instrumental activity and thus could have no place in the moral ideal
of man, I had some misgivings, and now I believe I know why.
You know, Grasshopper, as well as I do, that people who are
seriously engaged in the pursuit of knowledge value that pursuit
at least as much as they do the knowledge which is its goal.
Indeed, it is a commonplace that once a scientist or philosopher
after great effort solves a major problem he is very let down,
and far from rejoicing in the possession of his solution or discovery, he cannot wait to be engaged once more in the quest.
Success is something to shoot at, not to live with. And of course,
now that I think of it, this is true not only of intellectual inquiry,
but it certainly can be true of any instrumental activity whatever, and frequently is. We might call this state of affairs the
Alexandrian condition of man, after Alexander the Great. When
there are no more worlds to conquer we are filled not with satisfaction but with despair.

G.   How do you think we could have made such an elementary mistake, Skepticus?

S.   I think we failed to take note of the fact that an activity which is, from one point of view, instrumentally valuable can, from another point of view, be instrinsically valuable. Thus, we would agree that carpentry is an instrumental activity; that is, instrumental to the existence of houses. But to a person who enjoys building for its own sake, that otherwise instrumental activity has intrinsic value as well. And the same could be true of anyone who really enjoys his work, whatever that work might be. It seems to follow from this that we may now re-instate most of the activities we thought we were obliged to banish from Utopia. The ideal, therefore, does not consist wholly in game-playing.

G.   I believe you are correct, Skepticus, in pointing out that otherwise instrumental activities can be valued as ends in themselves. But I am not convinced that it follows from that fact that game-playing is not the only possible Utopian occupation. Let me see if I can persuade you of this. Let us continue to think of the moral ideal of man as an actual Utopian community, then, but where, instead of supposing that all—so to speak—*objectively* instrumental activities have been banished—physical and intellectual labour, and the like—what has been banished is simply all activity which is not *valued* instrinsically, thus leaving it open to any Utopian to enjoy the exertions of productive endeavor. Thus, just as some Utopians will be able to pluck yachts and diamonds off Utopian trees, others will be able to pluck off opportunities to fix the kitchen sink, to solve economic problems, to push forward the frontiers of scientific knowledge, and so on, with respect to anything a Utopian might find intrinsically valuable.

S.   Yes, Grasshopper. That seems a much more satisfactory picture of Utopia and of the moral ideal of man.

G.   Splendid. Now, to continue. It is clear, I should think, that the opportunity to work—or whatever other instrumental activity it might be which is desired—should not be left to chance in Utopia. If, at any given period of time, *everyone* in Utopia wanted to work at something, then such work should be available for them all. And if nobody wanted to work, then it would not follow (as it surely would in our present non-Utopian existence) that society would collapse. And similarly, of course, with intellectual inquiry. That is to say, with respect to any objectively instrumental activity whatever, it would have to be the case that such activity *could* be undertaken, but it would also have to be the case that no such activity *need* be undertaken. For another way of saying that the Utopians only do those things which they value intrinsically is to say that they always do things because they want to, and never because they must.

S. Yes, that seems correct.

G. Very well. Now let us consider two cases that would inevitably arise in Utopia. Case One: John Striver has spent his first decade in Utopia doing all the things that newcomers to Utopia usually do. He has traveled round the world several times, loafed a good deal in the sun, and so on, and now, having become bored, he wants some *activity* to be engaged in. He therefore makes a request (to the Computor in Charge or to God or whatever) saying that he wants to *work* at something, and he selects carpentry. Now, there is no demand for houses which John's carpentry will serve, because all the houses of whatever possible kind are already instantly available to the citizens of Utopia. What kind of house, then, should he build? Surely it would be the kind whose construction would give him the greatest satisfaction, and we may suggest that such satisfaction would require that building the house would provide enough of a challenge to make the task interesting while not so difficult that John would utterly botch the job. Now, what I would like to put to you, Skepticus, is that this activity is essentially no different from playing golf, or any other game. Just as there is no need, aside from the game of golf, to get little balls into holes in the ground, so in Utopia there is no need, aside from the activity of carpentry, for the house which is the product of that carpentry. And just as a golfer could get balls into holes much more efficiently by dropping them in with his hand, so John could *obtain* a house simply by pressing a telepathic button. But it is clear that John is no more interested in simply *having* a house than the golfer is in *having* ball-filled holes. It is the *bringing about* of these results which is important to John and to the golfer rather than the results themselves. Both, that is to say, are involved in a voluntary attempt to overcome unnecessary obstacles; both, that is to say, are playing games. This solution, it is interesting to note, was also open to Alexander the Great. Since he had run out of worlds to conquer by impetuously conquering the only world there was, he *could* have given it all back and started over again, just as one divides up the chess pieces equally after each game in order to be able to play another game. Had Alexander done that, his action would no doubt have been regarded by his contemporaries as somewhat frivolous, but from the Utopian point of view his failure to take such an obvious step would indicate that Aleaxnder did not really place all that high a value on *the activity of conquering worlds.* Case Two: The early experience of William Seeker in Utopia is very similar to that of John Striver. William, too, after a time, wishes to be able to achieve something. But whereas John's abilities and interests had led him to choose a manual art, William is led to choose the pursuit of scientific truth. Now again, how much scientific inquiry there is to undertake at any given time cannot be left to chance, since the interest in doing scientific research might far exceed the amount of research that could logically be undertaken at any given time. It is even conceivable that there would come a time when all scientific investigation had come to an end; a time, that is, when everything knowable was in fact known. Since, therefore, there could be no guarantee that there would always be an objective opportunity to do scientific research, it follows that it would be undesirable to have Utopian scientists stop doing research on a problem simply because the problem had already been solved. For what is important in Utopia is not the objective state of scientific knowledge, but the *attitude* of the Utopian scientist, which may be described in the following way. If the solution of the problem he is working on were readily retrievable from the memory banks of the computors, the Utopian scientist would not retrieve the solution. This is just like the devotee of crossword puzzles, who knows that the answers to the puzzle will be published next day. Still, he tries to solve the puzzle today, even though there is no urgency whatever in having the solution today rather than tomorrow. And just as the dedicated puzzle-solver will say, "Don't tell me the answer; let me work it out for myself," William Seeker will have the same attitude toward his scientific investigations. Even if other means of coming to know the answer are readily available, he voluntarily rejects these means so that he will have something to do. But this is again, I submit, to play a game.

S.　What you seem to be saying is that a Utopian could engage in all of the achieving activities that normally occupy people in the non-Utopian world, but that the quality, so to speak, of such endeavors would be quite different.

G.　Yes. The difference in quality, as you put it, can be seen in the contrast in attitude of a lumber-jack when he is, on the one hand, plying his trade of cutting down trees for the saw-mill and, on the other hand, when he is cutting down trees in competition with other lumber-jacks at the annual wood-cutter's picnic. Thus, all the things we now regard as trades, indeed all instances of organized endeavor whatever would, if they continued to exist in Utopia, be sports. So that in addition to hockey, baseball, golf, tennis, and so on, there would also be the sports of business administration, jurisprudence, philosophy, production management, motor mechanics, *ad,* for all practical purposes, *infinitum.*

S.　So that the moral ideal of man does, after all, consist in game-playing.

G.　I think not, Skepticus. For now that the Utopians have something to do, both admiration and sharing are again possible, and so love and friendship as well. And with the re-introduction of the emotions associated with striving—the joy of victory, you know, and the bitterness of defeat—emotional content is provided for art. And perhaps morality will also be present, possibly in the form of what we now call sportsmanship. So, while game-playing need not be the sole occupation of Utopia, it is the essence, the "without which not" of Utopia. What I envisage is a culture quite different from our own in terms of its *basis.* Whereas our own culture is based on various kinds of scarcity—

economic, moral, scientific, erotic—the culture of Utopia will be based on plenitude. The notable institutions of Utopia, accordingly, will not be economic, moral, scientific, and erotic instruments— as they are today—but institutions which foster sport and other games. But sports and games unthought of today; sports and games that will require for their exploitation—that is, for their mastery and enjoyment—as much energy as is expended today in serving the institutions of scarcity. It should behoove us, therefore, to begin the immense work of devising these wonderful games now, for if we solve all of our problems of scarcity very soon, we may very well find ourselves with nothing to do when Utopia arrives.

S.   You mean we should begin to store up games—very much like food for winter—against the possibility of an endless and endlessly boring summer. You seem to be a kind of ant after all, Grasshopper, though, I must admit, a distinctly odd kind of ant.

G.   No, Skepticus, I am truly the Grasshopper; that is, an adumbration of the ideal of existence, just as the games we play in our non-Utopian lives are intimations of things to come. For even now it is games which give us something to do when there is nothing to do. We thus call games "pastimes," and regard them as trifling fillers of the interstices in our lives. But they are much more important than that. They are clues to the future. And their serious cultivation now is perhaps our only salvation. That, if you like, is the metaphysics of leisure time.

S.   Still, Grasshopper, I find that I have a serious reservation about the Utopia you have constructed. It sounds a grand sort of life for those who are very keen on games, but not everyone *is* keen on games. People like to be building houses, or running large corporations, or doing scientific research to some purpose, you know, not just for the hell of it.

G.   The point is well taken, Skepticus. You are saying that Bobby Fischer and Phil Esposito and Howard Cosell might be very happy in paradise, but that John Striver and William Seeker are likely to find quite futile their make-believe carpentry and their make-believe science.

S.   Precisely. (pause)   Well, Grasshopper, what answer do you

have to make to this objection? (There is another pause).
Grasshopper, are you dying again?

G. No, Skepticus.

S. What is it then? You look quite pale.

G. Skepticus, I have just had a vision.

S. Good lord!

G. Shall I tell you about it?

S. (Skepticus glances furtively at his wrist watch). Yes. Well.
Certainly, Grasshopper, please proceed.

G. The vision was evidently triggered by your suggestion that not
everyone likes to play games, and it was a vision of the downfall
of Utopia, a vision of paradise lost. I saw time passing in Utopia,
and I saw the Strivers and the Seekers coming to the conclusion
that if their lives were merely games, then those lives were scarcely
worth living. Thus motivated, they began to delude themselves
into believing that man-made houses were more valuable than
computer-produced houses, and that long-solved scientific problems needed resolving. They then began to persuade others of the
truth of these opinions, and even went so far as to represent the
computors as the enemies of mankind. Finally they enacted
legislation proscribing their use. Then more time passed, and
it seemed to everyone that the carpentry game and the science
game were not games at all, but vitally necessary tasks which
had to be performed in order for mankind to survive. Thus,
although all of the apparently productive activities of man were
games, they were not believed to be games. Games were once
again relegated to the role of mere pastimes useful for bridging
the gaps in our serious endeavors. And if it had been possible
to convince these people that they were in fact playing games,
they would have felt that their whole lives had been as nothing—
a mere stage play or empty dream.

S. Yes, Grasshopper, they would believe themselves to be nothing
at all, and one can imagine them, out of chagrin and mortifica-
tion, simply vanishing on the spot, as though they had never
been.

G. Quite so, Skepticus. As you are quick to see, my vision has solved
the mystery of the dream I was telling you about earlier, just be-

fore I died. The message of the dream now seems perfectly clear. The dream was saying to me, "Come now, Grasshopper, you know very well that most people will not want to spend their lives playing games. Life for most people will not be worth living if they cannot believe that they are doing *something* useful, whether it is providing for their families or formulating a theory of relativity.

S. Yes, it seems a perfectly straight forward case of an anxiety dream. You were acting out in a disguised way certain hidden fears you had about your thesis concerning the moral ideal of man.

G. No doubt. But tell me, Skepticus, were my repressed fears about the fate of mankind, or were they about the cogency of my thesis? Clearly they could not have been about both. For if my fears about the fate of mankind are justified, then I need not fear that my thesis is faulty, since it is that thesis which justifies those fears. And if my thesis is faulty, then I need not fear for mankind, since that fear stems from the cogency of my thesis.

S. Then tell me which you feared, Grasshopper. You alone are in a position to know.

G. I wish there were time, Skepticus, but again I feel the chill of death. Goodbye.

S. Not goodbye, Grasshopper, *au revoir*.

SPORT AND ETHICS IN THE CONTEXT OF CULTURE

JAN BROEKHOFF

Play lies outside the antithesis of wisdom and folly, and equally outside those of truth and falsehood, good and evil. Although play in itself is a non-material activity it has no moral function. (7).

I

In the course of our discussions of play theory, many of my students have expressed puzzlement about Huizinga's segregation of play from the realm of ethics. This is not surprising, since play has hardly ever been free from valuations of virtue or sin. To Friedrich von Schiller "man is only whole when he plays," to Paul Weiss ". . . a man is normally most a man only when he stops playing and tries to do some justice to his responsibilities." (15). Even Huizinga himself could be *accused* of posing play as an ethical standard when he states that, in a sense, culture will always be played according to given rules based on mutual agreement. In the terminology of the game, *fair play* has become here the equivalent of good faith.

It is well known that Huizinga viewed sport as a higher form of play, as a contest *for* something with all of the characteristics of play. The critics of *Homo Ludens* have not convinced me that this view is logically inconsistent. I thought, therefore, that it might be profitable at a symposium on sports and ethics to probe the extent to which sport *sui generis* lies outside the categorical antithesis of ethics. It seemed to me, moveover, that such an excursion would lead me of necessity to the cultural context in which sport appears and hence to the topic of this presentation.

In contrast to biological interpretations of play as a means to an end, Huizinga finds play an absolutely primary category of life characterized by its fun-element, its standing apart from the seriousness of ordinary life. The purpose of play lies in its own existence and it does not have its root in a rational nexus. The non-rationality of play confirms for Huizinga the supra-logical nature of the human condition. Formally defined, Huizinga calls play:

> . . . a free activity standing quite consciously outside "ordinary" life as being not "serious," but at the same time absorbing the player intensely and utterly. It is an activity connected with no material gain, and no profit can be achieved by it. It proceeds within its own proper boundaries of time and space according to fixed rules and in an orderly manner. It promotes the formation of social groupings which tend to surround themselves with secrecy and to stress their difference from the common world by disguise or other means. (7:p.13).

So defined, play lies originally outside the domain of good and evil, right and wrong. At most one could assign to it a quality of ontological ambivalence. (5).

The question arises whether play in its transition to sport maintained this basic non-rationality which defies ethical categorization. There is no doubt that in the transition some of Huizinga's formal characteristics have lost significance. Heidemann (5:p.74) for example, considers this transaction as a dialectic development in which originally "pure" play has incorporated aspects of the world of work (*Arbeitswelt*). In this particular view, work can even be construed as a special form of play in which the economy principle of the straight line has replaced the indeterminacy and multiplicity of the original play situation. For Rijsdorp (12:p.191) sport is the development of antithetical play in the direction of competition. In sport, the competitive element has become so powerful that it functions as an independent force which stands in polar tension opposite the vital moment of pure play. Sport that lacks the element of competition and does not emphasize performance, is no longer sport; sport, however, which has lost the element of playfulness has degenerated into mere production, has become toil, according to Rijsdorp. The differentiation of play into sport can be extended by pointing out the institutionalized character of sport, the conscious and planned preparation for contests and games, and the material rewards reaped by professional athletes. (10). It seems to me, though, that all of these elements in the differentiation from play to sport do not alter the fact that sport *as such* remains non-rational.

The fact that sport is basically non-rational is not always evident to those who are totally absorbed in it. Often it will take an outsider to point out that the idea of sport cannot very well be explained in rational terms. A delightful example of this is provided by the Greek writer Lucian of the second century B.C., who takes us back to the Lyceum of Athens in the early sixth century. Solon, the great Athenian lawgiver, tries to explain the Greek athletic contests to the Scythian Anacharsis who takes a dim view of the things that go on in the gymnasium. First, Solon defends the rigorous training on the basis that it may lead to a prize in the Olympics. The Scythian is far from impressed with the Games in general and the prizes in particular:

> So these athletes are all the more ridiculous if they are the flower of the country, as you say, and yet endure so much for nothing, making themselves miserable and defiling their beautiful, great bodies with sand and black eyes to get possession of an apple and an olive-branch when they have won! (11:p.15).

Solon next turns educator and tries to convince Anacharsis that the contests are admirably suited to build the bodies and the characters of the young athletes. He particularly stresses the practical advantage

in the preparation for warfare. Once again, Anacharsis proves hard
to convince as is evident from this reaction:

> Then if the enemy attack you, Solon, you yourselves will take the field
> rubbed with oil and covered with dust, shaking your fists at them, and
> they, of course will cower at your feet and run away, fearing that while
> they are agape in stupefication you may sprinkle sand in their mouths,
> or that after jumping behind them so as to get on their backs, you may
> wind your legs about their bellies and stangle them by putting an arm
> under their helmets. Yes, by Zeus, they will shoot their arrows, naturally,
> and throw their spears, but the missiles will not affect you any more than
> as if you were statues, tanned as you are by the sun and supplied in
> abundance with blood. (11:p.51).

Against such scepticism, Solon puts up a desperate argument, but in
the end he is no closer to converting Anacharsis to his point of view
than when he started.

Lucian may not have been interested enough in atheltics to end
the discussion with the conversion of the Scythian. Through it all
The Anacharsis shows that sport *as such* still escapes the valuations
of virtue or vice. For Solon, the pedagogue, sport may be a means
to an end, but that in itself does not signify that sport *sui generis* has
been subordinated to the purposes served by other human activities.
For Anacharsis, the sceptic, sport may have been ridiculous, but the
Olympic Games went on.

> Sportmanship is probably the clearest and most popular expression of
> morals. Morals are the rules of the game, and sportmanship means that
> cooperation according to the rules is more important than ruthless com-
> petition. (9).

II

If the *idea* of sport does nothing to help us discover the ethical
function of sport, it might be appropriate to examine the function
of the rules that govern sport. Is it the rules of the game, as Link
(9:p.7) claims, that reveal the ethical character of sport? There is
no question that sport is more rule-oriented than play. The rules in
sport are binding and absolute; in an ontological sense, as Heidemann
indicates, they are laws. But are they also moral laws? At this point
I would submit that they are not.

Many of the rules in sport deal with the definition of boundaries of time and space. Contrary to the dance, for example, in which time and space as extension and gestalt become themselves thematic, these dimensions in sport merely constitute that what is attainable; they point toward an *Erreichbarkeit*. (5:p.35). For each sport, the preconditions of time and space define what is attainable dependent on a complex network of interactions of human capabilities vis-a-vis the objects and the immanent purpose of the game. Anyone who has ever played soccer on an American football field knows about the loss of possibilities, the "motoric shortening" that takes place as a result of the reduction in space from a normal soccer pitch. There is a great need for a phenomenological study of the time-space relationships in individual sports, but clearly such investigations would not touch ethical dimensions.

It appears more likely that the ethical dimensions of sport will be revealed by the rules that define, often in an indirect fashion, the conduct of the players in the game situation. I am thinking especially of those rules that pertain to the physical interaction of the participants. But even here it seems tenuous to read moral precepts into what mostly appears to be a further delineation of what is appropriate for a particular sport. For example, the soccer rule that outlaws the pulling down of an opponent can hardly be viewed as a general "ought-not" statement, since the same behavior is perfectly legal and even desirable in the games of rugby and American football. Link's observation that morals are like the lanes in a swimming race, because they are the guides that permit each individual to make the most of himself without doing injustice to his neighbors, seems therefore overly simplistic. The lanes as such define the contest; they do not portend to make a moral ought-statement.

Perhaps I have strained the moral neutrality of *sport sui generis* far enough and it is time that I consider the question how morality enters into the domain of games and contests. Huizinga himself supplies the answer to that question in his discussion of the element of tension that attends play. Play, and even more so sport, is accompanied by a feeling of uncertainty that has its root in the fact that the final outcome of the game remains in doubt. In fact, one could say that the rules and other preconditions of the game must guarantee a "lawful-

ness of chance" (*Freie oder offene Determination*). (5:p.64).
Through the elements of uncertainty and tension, morality enters into
the realm of sport. Huizinga expresses it in the following words:

> Though play as such is outside the range of good and bad, the element
> of tension imparts to it a certain ethical value in so far as it means a
> testing of the player's prowess: his courage, tenacity, resources and, last
> but not least, his spiritual powers—his "fairness;" because despite his
> ardent desire to win, he must still stick to the rules of the game. (7:p.11).

Although it is apparent that the ethical dimensions of sport spring
in part from an emotion that is constitutive of sport itself, it is also
clear that morality enters into sport largely from the "outside" and
that it depends greatly on the emphasis that a particular society puts
on winning contests or games.   In this respect I must agree with
Heidemann that the ethical dimensions of sport do pertain not so
much to the cheater or the spoilsport, but rather to the higher demand
(*ubergeordneten Anspruch*) of moral responsibility and the historically
or individualy existing *Ethos.* (5:p.56).   For Huizinga this is the
Ethos of *fair play,* the sportive equivalent of good faith.

Fair play presupposes the acceptance to play a game or engage in
a contest under a certain set of rules, but it clearly transcends the
mere playing according to the rules.   It is based on an inner resolve
not to take unfair advantage of the situation, to make it on one's
own strength.   The concept of fair play is generally attributed to the
British, although certain of its characteristics were clearly present in
the sportive behavior of the medieval nobleman.   Jacques Ehrmann
finds it an ideal of nobility marked by moral and esthetic detachment
and perhaps also by indifferences.   He draws support from Roger
Caillois who writes:

> It is understood that the good player is one who can envisage with
> distance, detachment and some appearance at least of composure the
> unhappy results of the most sustained effort, or the loss of exorbitant
> stakes. The decision of the arbiter, even if unjust, is approved on prin-
> ciple. Corruption of the agon begins where no arbiter and no arbitra-
> tion is recognized. (4:p.53).

This definition of fair play I cannot totally endorse.   There is no question that fair play necessitates a measure of detachment, but it seems
to me that the spirit of fair play is better exemplified by spontaneous

acts not prescribed by the rules than by a detached or even calculated acceptance of the rules.

Now, I am convinced that the *Ethos* of fair play could only have emerged in what anthropologists call a "guilt culture." Ruth Benedict (1:p.222) defines a "guilt culture" as a society "that inculcates absolute standards of morality and relies on man's developing a (personal) conscience." In such cultures, good behavior is based on an internalized conviction of what is right and wrong and not on a set of external sanctions. A society in which behavior is largely regulated by sets of external sanctions is called a "shame culture." Shame is a reaction to other people's criticism, usually one of acute chagrin, but not rooted in a personal feeling of sin. As a consequence, one would not expect the spirit of fair play to pervade sport in a shame culture.

Come along, stranger, have a try at the games yourself, if you ever learned them. A man ought to know about games, for nothing brings a man greater renown throughout his life than what he does with hands and feet. (6).

III

In *The Greeks and the Irrational,* Dodds (3) convincingly argues that the Homeric society was a "shame culture." The *summum bonum* for the Homeric Greek was not a good conscience, but the enjoyment of public esteem. Werner Jaeger points out that in effect the early Greeks did not conceive of anything like the personal conscience of our modern western society. He also indicates how difficult it is for us to imagine how entirely public the conscience of the archaic Greek was. (8).

The ideal of the Greek nobleman was to gain *arete,* the glory and honor that is gained through a showing of physical prowess, but also deeply colored by a courtly morality. In this ethics of honor as an agonistic ideal, sport could emerge as a concept of life. Since *arete* was chiefly measured by success in battle and contest, winning became all important to the Greek nobleman. Segal (13:p.606) calls it a protean morality: if you must resort to shady tactics, do so, as long as you win.

An interesting example of this morality, at a much later stage of Greek society is given by Statius, an epic writer of the second century A.D. He describes a footrace at the first Nemean Games, in which Idas of Pisa manages to finish first by pulling his opponent Partheno-paeus back by the hairs. Instead of disqualifying the former Olympic victor, the referee Adrastus, likely influenced by Idas' raucous supporters, decides to have the two run the race over on opposite sides of the track. This time Parthenopaeus wins handily, but Idas is awarded second prize, an honor he does not deserve by our standards of fair play. (14).

During the chariot race in honor of the slain Patroclus, Homer (6:pp.427-428) relates how Antilochus, youngest of the participants, fouls the horses of Agamemnon's brother Menelaus. Antilochus finishes in second place, ahead of Menelaus and clearly shows not the slightest feelings of guilt for having cheated until Menelaus challenges him in public. The way the younger man defers to his elder and superior is typical of a "shame culture:"

> Bear with me now, for I am much younger than you, my lord Menelaus; you are my elder and my better. You know that a young man always goes too far. His mind is too hasty, his wits are flighty. Then let your heart forgive me. I will hand you willingly the horse I won. And if you demand something of my own besides, something greater, I will give it at once rather than be out of favor with you, my lord. . . . (6).

Menelaus' *arete* is restored and magnanimously he offers the mare to Antilochus, not without warning him, though, aganst playing tricks on his superiors in future contests. In a similar vein, rank interferes with fair play when Achilles declares Agamemnon winner of the javelin contest before the king and his lowly opponent, Meriones, have had a chance to compete. Meriones gets the actual prize, but Agamemnon's *arete* has shrewdly been safeguarded from possible defeat. (6:p.436).

In Greek athletics, one can always observe the strange mixture of *ponos,* the Pindaric concept of hard work, perserverance, and tenacity with *poneria,* the concept of cunning and resourcefulness. If Achilles is the archetype of *ponos,* Odysseus personifies the principle of *poneria.* (13:p.606). Many times it is his cunning and not his physical prowess which helps Odysseus get out of a difficult situation. The ancient

Greeks apparently had great admiration for a man who could pit craft against strength, even if the means were slightly devious. It should give physical educators something to think about that Hermes, among other things, was the patron of thieves and cheaters as well as gymnastics!

When the one Greater Scorer comes to write against your name,
He marks not that you won or lost but how you played the game.

Grantland Rice

IV

For the ancient Greeks, sport was but an extension of life; seriousness and play were never easily distinguished. Sport was a perfect fit for a "shame culture" in which man had to show physical proof of his worth. The battle fields often resembled the sport arenas and the sport contests rivaled the battles in fierceness. Competition was part and parcel of ancient Greek education. Twice in Homer, an educator admonishes his pupil ". . . always to strive for first place and to be superior to others." Small wonder that the Greeks were so concerned with finesse and victory in competition. (2:p.80).

If sport fits perfectly within the framework of a "shame culture," it is most likely because sport itself has many of the features that characterize the structure of such a culture. In sport, infractions of the rules are punished according to predetermined, uniform, and unchanging penalties. One may look at these penalties as the external sanctions for unruly behavior. The whistle of the referee may show up the cheater and keep the violator in check in much the same way as a "shame culture" checks its members by sets of external rules. It follows, then, that our modern concept of fair play, based as it is on an internalized set of convictions of what is good and bad game behavior, can only be a very frail superstructure in the realm of sport. It would seem that the more emphasis a society puts on winning games, the more the players will fall back on the external sanctions of the rules rather than following the inner conviction of their conscience.

In our own society, with its increasing insistence to produce winners in all kinds of sports, the fair play *Ethos*, if it is more than just a detached acceptance of absolute arbitration, must be very vulnerable indeed. Ruth Benedict (1:p.223) remarks that shame is becoming an increasingly heavy burden in the United States, that guilt now is less extremely felt than in earlier generations. This shift toward a "shame culture" no doubt has many ramifications but it may in part explain the attitudes and forms of behavior one can observe in the world of sports. Perhaps it is proper to close with Huizinga's powerful finale of *Homo Ludens* in which he resolves the antithesis of play and seriousness with his belief in man's moral conscience. It seems a belief that is fading rapidly:

> Play, we began by saying, lies outside morals. In itself it is neither good nor bad. But if we have to decide whether an action to which our will impels us is a serious duty or is licit as play, our moral conscience will at once provide the touchstone. As soon as truth and justice, compassion and forgiveness have part in our resolve to act, our anxious question loses all meaning. One drop of pity is enough to lift our doing beyond intellectual distinctions. Springing as it does from a belief in justice and divine grace, conscience, which is moral awareness, will always whelm the question that eludes and deludes us to the end, in a lasting silence. (7:p.213).

REFERENCES

1. Benedict, Ruth: *The Chrysanthemum and the Sword.* . Boston, Houghton-Mifflin Co., 1946.
2. Bloch, Raymond: "The Origins of the Olympic Games," *Scientific American,* Vol. 219, No. 2 (August, 1968).
3. Dodds, E.R.: *The Greeks and the Irrational.* Berkeley, University of California Press, 1966.
4. Ehrmann, Jacques: "Homo Ludens Revisited," *Game, Play, Literature,* Jacques Ehrmann (ed.). Boston, Beacon Press, 1968.
5. Heidemann, Ingeborg: *Der Begriff des Spieles.* Berlin, Walter de Gruyter and Co., 1968.
6. Homer. *The Iliad:* E. V. Rieu (trans.). Baltimore, Penguin Books, 1963.
7. Huizinga, Johan: *Homo Ludens.* Boston, Beacon Press, 1955.
8. Jaeger, Werner: *Paideia: The Ideas of Greek Culture.* Second edition. Gilbert Highet (trans.). New York, Oxford University Press, 1962.
9. Link, Henry C.: *The Rediscovery of Morals.* New York, E.P. Dutton and Co., 1947.
10. Loy, John W.: "The Nature of Sport: A Definitional Effort," *Quest,* No. 10, 1-15 (May, 1968).
11. Lucian: "Anacharsis, Or Athletics," *Lucian, Vol. IV,* A.M. Harmon (trans.). Cambridge, Harvard University Press, 1961.
12. Rijsdorp, Klaas: *Sport als Jong-Menselijke Activiteit.* Utrecht: Stichting Jan Luiting Fonds, 1966.

13. Segal, E.: "It Is Not Strength, But Art, Obtains the Prize," *The Yale Review,* Vol. 56 (1966-1967).
14. Statius. *Thebaid*: J.H. Mozlcy (trans.). Cambridge, Harvard University Press, 1961.
15. Weiss, Paul: *Sport: A Philosophic Inquiry.* Carbondale, Southern Illinois University Press, 1969.

THE PRAGMATIC (EXPERIMENTALISTIC) ETHIC AS IT RELATES TO SPORT AND PHYSICAL EDUCATION

Earle F. Zeigler

The fundamental theme underlying this presentation is that the pragmatic (experimentalistic) ethic may be related to sport and physical education in Western culture in such a way that those holding this philosophical position will be enabled to employ these cultural forces as "socially useful servants." The intent is to present these ideas in as logical and scientific a manner as possible, even though to some who embrace a different outlook and approach it may emerge as a polemic. The writer sees no way to avoid this dilemma because the discipline and sub-disciplines of philosophy seem to be presently incapable of "eschewing obfuscation."

With apologies to no one, therefore, the following sub-problems of the topic, phrased as questions, will be discussed in this order: (1) what is the essence of the ethical problem in sport and physical education in the present context? (2) what is the problem of the "good" and "bad" viewed in historical perspective? (3) what insight about values may be gained from an examination of Parsons's Action System? (4) what appear to be the problems of ethics today? (5) what answers are provided by pragmatic (naturalistic) ethics? (6) what seem to be the implications for experimentalism (pragmatic naturalism) as an educational philosophy? (7) what may be considered as the pragmatic (experimentalistic) ethic in sport and physical education? (8) what are the strengths and weaknesses of this position? (9) what conclusions may be drawn from this analysis and interpretation?

THE ETHICAL PROBLEM IN SPORT AND PHYSICAL EDUCATION

The essence of the ethical problem in sport and physical education in present context cannot be delineated without an analysis of the social system and culture in which it is taking place. (The writer regrets his inability at present to separate the terms "sport" and "physical education," or at least the fact that for him no *one* term adequately describes this aspect of culture being considered. The following definition has merit currently: the art and science of human movement as related to the theory and practice of sport, dance, play, and exercise.)

The problems in sport, dance, play, and exercise appear to be legion. The amateur ideal has long since been shattered in Olympic competition, and most recently we have witnessed a display of Canadian nationalism as a group of top professional, U.S.-oriented hockey players of Canadian origin barely won over a group of Russian "amateurs" who finished second to Czechoslovakia in the Olympic Winter Games. If dance may be classified as human movement with a purpose, it is obvious that all is not well here either. Certainly this form of aesthetic expression has not yet found its rightful place within the educational pattern of the culture, and one does not need to travel far to hear that freedom in various dance forms undermines the moral fibre of youth. The term *play* is one of the most ambiguous in the English language, the average unabridged dictionary offering about sixty-eight different definitions for the reader's consumption. Still further, at almost any age too much play in one's life in the eyes of many implies shiftlessness and lack of purpose and direction. As for the subject of exercise, some say it is excellent, others say it is beneficial in moderation, and a third group warns that too much of it is bad, that it is not essential or right in a school curriculum, and that an excess of exercise can cause very ill effects. Is it any wonder that the common man exhibits a large amount of confusion, and that there is a strong tendency to follow the line of least resistance and to do "what comes naturally" depending upon the exigencies of the moment?

It must be completely obvious that such diversity of opinion and belief could exist only in a social system within a culture characterized by pluralistic philosophies, philosophies of education, and philosophies of sport and physical education. Such a state is, of course, not necessarily bad, and it undoubtedly requires a political state in which a considerable amount of participatory democracy exists. And yet the opinion is often expressed that North America functions materialistically despite an overarching, inherent philosophical idealism. Many people are absolutely convinced that all of the old standards and morals have been completely negated, and that only a return to earlier halcyon days can prevent impending disaster. They decry what they believe are the prevailing "situation ethics," because they sense an uncharted course ahead on the way toward the year 2,000.

Oddly enough, at the very time when people seem to need guidance, a large percentage of the profession of philosophy—in the English-speaking world at least—seems to have abandoned them for a more strictly disciplinary approach to their work. (Of course, it it difficult to be too condemnatory when a similar phenomenon seems to have taken place in educational philosophy, and more recently a "similar infection seems to be spreading" within the philosophy of sport and physical education at an alarming rate.) To make matters worse, the general public has taken such words as pragmatism, idealism, realism, and now existentialism and given them other than their original philosophical meanings. The result is that correct use now requires extensive qualification.

All of this adds up to the conclusion that society has now "progressed" to the point where unanimity is largely lacking in regard to "what's good," "what's bad," and what lies somewhere in between. And this problem is present no matter what phase of life and/or society is under consideration. Writing somewhat editorially about these developments of recent years, Cogley explains how in his opinion:

> . . . every major institution in the land and most of the minor ones as well seemed to have been caught up in an identity crisis. Upheavals in the church were front-page news for almost a decade. The revolt against the prevailing idea of a university which began in Berkeley in 1964 kept erupting with dismaying frequency. Veteran army officers found themselves at a loss as to how to deal with rebellious troops. The Democratic debacle at the Chicago convention four years ago dramatized a widespread disillusionment with the political parties. The once sacro-

sanct public school system came under severe attack. Working newsmen who took to producing their own underground papers after hours voiced bitter disenchantment with the established press employing them. So prevalent was the discontent inside the academic and professional communities that the 'radical caucuses' within them were given semi-official status. Bishops, university presidents, military brass, publishers, politicians, school principals, and other established 'leaders,' it became increasingly clear, were no longer leading . . . (27:p.2).

Thus, it should be obvious that values, morals, and ethical standards are undergoing an *identity crisis* from which they may never recover. If this is true, the implications for sport and physical education as a microcosm of the culture are that turmoil would inevitably be present there as well. This brings the reader directly back to the point made above that all is far from well in the realm of sport, dance, play and exercise.

THE "GOOD" AND THE "BAD" IN HISTORICAL PERSPECTIVE

In a paper such as this, there is obviously not time to review the problem of the "good" and the "bad" in great detail so that the reader will have available even an outline history of that branch of philosophy known as "ethics." In a language where even the word "meaning" has eight different meanings, the term "ethics" is employed typically in three different ways (each of which has a relation to the other). First, it is used to classify a general pattern or "way of life" (e.g., Christian ethics). Second, it refers to a listing of rules of conduct or a so-called moral code (e.g., professional ethics). Lastly, it has come to be used when describing inquiry *about* ways of life or rules of conduct (e.g., that sub-division of philosophy now known as metaethics).

The primary focus here should be on metaethics and its central questions. What is meant when one searches for the "good" or the "bad"? What guarantee is there that any such intent is correct? Can there be right standards for use in judging actions or things to be good or bad? If such value judgments are made, how do they differ, if at all, from judgments that are value free (or value neutral) in nature? In any such search or investigation, it is also difficult to know whether to proceed from the general to the specific or vice versa (i.e., from the good in general to right conduct or justice in particular, or in the opposite direction).

Even a cursory examination of the history of ethics substantiates that it is a description of ". . . irregular progress toward complete clarification of each type of ethical judgment." (51:Vol.III:p.82). It is indeed difficult to judge exactly, or even generally, how much "irregular progress" has been made since the development of Greek ethics starting with the fifth century B.C. contributions of Socrates. It could be argued presumably that the changing political, economic, and other social influences of the time required the development of a new way of conduct just as there is a need for altered standards of conduct today. The emergence of professional teachers of philosophy were in a sense the by-product of greater civilization. As Sidgwick stated,

> If bodily vigour was no longer to be left to nature and spontaneous exercise, but was to be attained by the systematic observance of rules laid down by professional trainers, it was natural to think that the same might be the case with excellence of the soul. (112:p.21).

Time and space do not permit a detailed consideration of the ideas of Socrates, Plato, and Aristotle, nor later Hellenistic and Roman ethical tendencies that have come to be known as Epicureanism, Stoicism, and Neoplatonism. Socrates began the development of standards for the qualities of goodness, justice, and virtue. Plato gave a spiritual orientation to such thought as he believed that these timeless qualities or ideals had been defined in a world beyond the ken of man. Aristotle, conversely, sought his answers in what now have been designated as the sciences and social sciences. Plato's approach to goodness was through comparison with so-called universal ideals, while Aristotle's "happiness" resulted from the accomplishment of more natural goals. Individual good was related to social good, but the ideas of moral responsibility and free will were not viewed with the same importance as was to become the case later in Christian thought.

For the next two thousand years ethical thought was oriented much more to practice than to theory. This is why the meanings of the various ethical terms or concepts were not altered to any extent, even though moral codes and life purposes were viewed quite differently.

The Hellenistic and Roman ideas were lacking in the necessary scientific insight required to advance beyond the intellectual genius of the earlier Greeks. It was during this period that the seedbed of later, all-encompassing Christian philosophy was established. As a result the Western world went into a long period during which time philosophy and religion were most closely interwoven. During this new period in the history of ethics there was one system in which man's reason and God's purpose for man were combined to produce one ultimate purpose for man—his eventual union with his Creator.

It was during this period of so-called medieval ethics that Thomas Aquinas brought together Aristotle's scientific and philosophic thought with the theology of St. Augustine. A highly significant and fundamental concept of the ethical system created by St. Thomas was his doctrine of natural law. Here he invented an accommodation of two different ethical systems so that there was a "natural domain" and a "theological realm." Reason and conscience were somehow fused inherently in man's nature; natural law contained God's ethical standards to which man could elevate himself by the application of God-given reason. The apparent weakness here is that religious dogmas, being infallible, could presumably negate valid scientific advances.

So-called modern ethics flourished during the marked period of social change of the sixteenth and seventeenth centuries. The philosophical watershed seems to be created immediately after a series of major social changes have occurred. Thus, when many considered the prevailing ethical system to be in a "state of disarray," various attempts at reconstruction began. Thomas Hobbes made a strong effort to release ethics from its complete servitude to theological law. He postulated that ethics was unreliable unless it was grounded on the objective laws of biology and psychology. If it turned out that the experimental analysis of nature was to be ethically neutral, then he argued that ethics should indeed be contrasted with science. Such thought brought reaction and counter-action from the early intuitionists (e.g., Henry More), Benedict Spinoza, John Locke, Bishop Butler, David Hume, and the so-called Common-sense Intuitionists (e.g., Thomas Reid). A similar "theoretical struggle" was being carried on in eighteenth century France through the efforts of

Voltaire, Jean-Jacques Rousseau and the Encyclopedists (e.g., Diderot), although some feel that their political orientation often distorted the objectivity of their arguments. Montesquieu did add to a more scientific approach, however, by viewing values more as sociological and historical facts.

Special mention must be made of the monumental role played by Immanuel Kant in the German Enlightenment. His complex and often perplexing nonutilitarian analysis based moral principles on a priori laws by which man's "practical reason" is guided. He postulated that man feels no obligation to obey laws of nature, but that he does sense subjectively a duty to respond to moral laws that are inherent in the universe. Kant's ethical system has three basic premises: (1) analysis of the evidence of moral experience, (2) consideration of the underlying logic, and (3) construction of metaphysical principles undergirded or presupposed by ethical analysis that is in contra-distinction to generalizations from science. He distinguished sharply between naturalistic ethics and moral law. His *categorical imperative* implied a moral code above and beyond any law of nature (e.g., man's strong desire for happiness). He postulated a *universalizability criterion* as the most fundamental moral principle ("Act only on that maxim which you can will to be a universal law"). This more precise statement of the "golden rule" represents perhaps Kant's greatest addition to the theory of ethics despite its apparent weakness. Lastly, he envisioned an autonomy of the will which placed man in a position to defy causal determinism grounded in regulative scientific principle. Man was conceived as part of, and yet distinct from, the laws of nature and science.

The nineteenth century in the Western world witnessed a sharp struggle between the two great traditions of utilitarianism and idealism, the former looming large in England and France and the latter predominant in Germany. So it is not surprising that both developing systems met with favorable responses from different quarters in the United States. Idealism was welcomed by certain philosophers and literary figures and, of course, the Christian Church. Utilitarianism blended with the drive for greater technological advancement, and then was joined or supplanted by the pragmatic ethics of Peirce, James, and Dewey. The developments in England, Germany, and the rest of the continent will not be catalogued here. They are quite well known, and the essential battle lines have already been drawn. The main concern in this paper is the pragmatic philosophy devised by James and Dewey in which ethical considerations relate to all of human knowledge. They were able to avoid the almost ageless, perennial distinction between value and fact by a type of reinterpretation that blurred the controversial issues for those who were willing to disavow Kantian ethics and the traditional outlook toward scientific knowledge as including only value-free facts. With this approach ethical judgment was simply a matter of applying human reason to the results of scientific (empirical) investigation by ascribing value to those human acts so designated as valuable.

At this point the historical thread will be broken and picked up later with a discussion of modern metaethical problems. In the meantime a short digression will be made to discuss the role of values in Parsons's Action System, thereby placing this problem in sociological perspective as well.

THE ROLE OF VALUES IN PARSONS'S ACTION SYSTEM

A student of the history of ethics, or the history of anything for that matter, soon realizes the importance of the major social forces as determinants of the direction a society may take at any given moment in its history. It is the opinion of the writer that both philosophers and historians would be well advised to avail themselves of the knowledge about cultures and social systems that is becoming available in a spiralling growth pattern through advancing sociological theory. Although it is current fashion in some quarters to debunk the complex "theory of action" developed by Talcott Parsons and others, it often appears that many of these critics have not even made a solid effort to understand his work. Because this theory is so firmly grounded in the descriptive and experimental methods of science, it seems both logical and consistent to review the role of values of Parsonian theory with an eye to any insights that may be gained for use in this analysis of ethics in pragmatism. It is also possible, of course, that the pragmatic outlook on values may in time strengthen the Parsonian theoretical structure.

Parsons's general action system may be regarded as a type of empirical system that is composed of four subsystems (culture, the social system, the personality, and the behavioral organism). The theory is that these subsystems compose a hierarchy of societal control and conditioning. (75:pp.46-58. The writer is grateful to Professor Johnson, an authority on Parsons, for his generous willingness to assist in this interpretation of this theory; any errors or omissions, of course, rest with this writer.)

Culture as the first subsystem of the action theory provides the basic structure and its components ". . . and, in a sense, the 'programming' for the action system as a whole." (75). The structure for the "social system," of course, "has to be more or less attuned to the functional problems" of social systems, and the same holds for the structure and functional problems of the personality and the behavioral organism, respectively. Further, the subsystem of culture exercises "control" over the social system, and so on up and down the scale. Legitimation is provided to the level below or "pressure to conform" if there is inconsistency. Thus, there is a ". . . 'strain toward consistency' among the system levels, led and controlled from above downward." (75).

The terms "conditioning" and "strain" are used by Parsons to explain a hierarchy of conditioning. The higher systems depend on the lower ones, and the "strain" that may occur at the lower level "works" to change the very structure of the system above. Of course, "incipient strain" at the lower level may be resolved prior to the creation of such an effect that change takes place above. Generally speaking, a change in culture is apt to take place when important scientific or religious beliefs are challenged or negated. This can in fact bring about structural change in larger social systems, while change in personality could well bring about change in somewhat smaller social systems.

Running the risk of inadequate treatment, it seems most important in this paper on ethics to consider the four levels of structure within the social system itself. Here we are referring to the United States or to Canada as social systems. Proceeding from the highest to the lowest level, from the general to the more specific, they are designated as (1) *values,* (2) *norms,* (3) *the structure of collectivities,* and (4) *the structure of roles.* The reader should keep in mind that all of these levels are normative in that the social structure is composed of sanctioned cultural limits within which certain types of behavior are mandatory or acceptable.

Note that values are at the top—the highest level, and there are

many categories of values (scientific, artistic, and values for person-
alities, etc.). *"Social* values are conceptions of the ideal general character of the type of social system in question." (75). As Johnson explains,

> For the United States as a society, important societal values are the rule
> of law, the social-structural facilitation of individual achievement, and
> equality of opportunity. (75:p.48).

It is most important to keep in mind the difference between values
and the shared sanctioned norms that are the second level of the social
structure. In the U. S. social system, for example, the basic norms
are the institutions of private property, private enterprise, the mo-
nogamous conjugal family, and the separation of church and state.
At this time no detailed discussion of collectivities or roles will be presented. The Democratic Party, or Liberal Party in Canada, would
be examples of collectivities, and the fourth-level roles would in these
instances would be the unique influence of a George McGovern or a
Pierre Trudeau, respectively.

This brief abstract from sociological theory will cease at this point,
hopefully after having whetted the appetite of the philosophically-
oriented reader. Without going into detail about the interchange processes and the various subsystems of the larger social system, it can be
stated that Parsons's action theory suggests that the most important
cultural aspect of any society is its value system. In the United States,
for example, there has been (according to Parsons) a remarkably
stable value system with gradual value generalization such as that
which accompanies structural differentiation.

Progress toward these so-called United States' values obviously has
not been a straight-line movement, mainly because of various types
of resistance that have risen "along the way." Johnson (75:p.55)
outlines four of these obstacles as follows:

1. Many mistakenly identify norms with values and react indignantly
   to reform because to them this represents a subversion of values.
   Parsons calls this "fundamentalism."
2. Reform is most difficult because it comes into conflict with vested
   interests bent on preventing a redistribution of the benefits and
   burdens of the system.
3. So-called ideological distortion often develops, a situation in which

many citizens hold a distorted view of the state of the system and of the probable effect of the proposed changes.

4. Because of the rapid change in the culture and the social systems of the United States, there exist a great many needs for change. Some of these needs are not being met, or are being met insufficiently at best. This is producing strain with a resultant "need" to restore solidarity (an integrative problem).

It is interesting to note that truly significant change can take place at the three lower levels without actually "doing violence" to the value level itself. The reason for this is the hierarchy of control and conditioning that prevails. It takes a "true" social revolution—in which a new value system becomes the source of legitimation, guidance, and control—to bring about a sufficient amount of disequilibrium to force the social system to adopt new or basically altered values.

Parsons's action system does not state that history is the unfolding of a predetermined cultural value system—the possible error of those who hold teleological beliefs, or who may even believe in some type of an idealistic philosophy of education. What is important for this paper is the evident relationship and actual identity of the scientific methodology underlying Parsonian theory and that of James and—particularly—John Dewey. Both Parsons and Dewey envision an actor-situation frame of reference in a world characterized by ever-present change and novelty. The crucial position and importance of values, and especially the approach to the determination of specific values, is paramount and undoubtedly lends strength to the case for pragmatic (naturalistic) ethical theory.

THE PROBLEMS OF ETHICS

As anxious as the writer is to move ahead to a consideration of pragmatic (naturalistic) ethics, it is only reasonable that the problems of metaethics be put into perspective first. This brief treatment will include a very short discussion of what has gone before in the history of ethics and moral philosophy.

As has been indicated earlier, there are almost as many views of ethics and/or moral philosophy as there are philosophers—an obvious exaggeration, of course, but a definite indication that there is no single, non-controversial foundation stone upon which the whole structure of ethics can be built. In fact, it can even be argued that the nature and function of the subject are themselves topics upon which there is vigorous dispute. This is not to say that there are not some aspects of this branch of philosophy upon which there is fairly wide consensus. For example, in the past moral philosophers tried to offer general guidance as to (1) what to do, (2) what to seek, and (3) how to treat others. (100).

Philosophers as a rule have not tried to "preach" to their adherents, although many have made strong efforts to offer fairly practical advice that included important pronouncements on the subject of good and evil. Many early philosophers believed that there was indeed a true moral code—a normative ethical system upon which people could and should base their conduct. In this sense, therefore, philosophers saw their task as the enunciation of basic principles of morality (usually with supporting justification). What is good? What is the good life? What are the limits of moral justification? How shall people live their lives? These were the types of questions to which philosophers spoke.

Others have offered such advice freely down through the years. Theologians, dramatists, novelists, poets, and even comedians have offered considerable insight into the question of good and evil, but such counsel was often viewed as dicta, and usually differed from distinctly philosophical accounts in that it was specific, unsystematic, and lacking in proof.

As was stated above, there is strong disagreement within the so-called traditional conception of the philosopher's task. Some believed that philosophers should not discover new truths (e.g., Kant), while others felt just the opposite to be the case (e.g., Bentham). There was an effort to systematize the knowledge that men already have and to demonstrate the ultimate rationale for these beliefs. Some were concerned with objective justification of any moral claims, whereas others (known as subjectivists) argued that true objectivity was simply not possible or reasonable. One group was extremely skeptical, therefore, about any body of knowledge which purported to tell men how they *should* live. Their opponents—the objectivists—worked away at the creation of a true moral code. In this struggle Nietzsche was a "true revolutionary" in that he contradicted previous objectivistic thought violently—even the common-sense moral principles unchallenged by most skeptics. In summary, therefore, the battle lines were drawn: one group of ethical theorists agreed with the traditional task (so-called) of the philosopher, and the "enemy" denied that moralists could ever hope to achieve such an objective goal as a truly justifiable moral code.

It is very difficult if not impossible to gain historical perspective on the philosophical trends and developments of the past fifty to seventy-five years. So-called philosophical analysis has been a most interesting and important development during this period of time. Despite the fact that scholars in the Western world have been engaged in philosophical thought for more than two thousand years, there is still controversy over what the exact nature of philosophy is. And so into the struggle between the ethical objectivists and subjectivists came a third combatant—the contemporary analytic philosopher of the twentieth century who asked himself the question, "What kind of activity am I engaging in?" Searching for the answer, he began to develop three different analytic approaches that became known as (1) logical atomism, (2) logical postivism, and (3) ordinary language philosophy. Each looked at analysis somewhat differently, but there was agreement that philosophy must be approached through the medium of language analysis to a greater or lesser extent. Logical atomists struggled to rearrange our ambiguous language so that more logically arranged sentences would become crystal clear. Logical positivism's aim was to subject statements to a verifiability principle. This meant that ordinary language statements were to be arranged in logical, consistent form to see if they were empirically verifiable either through mathematical reasoning or scientific investigation. The main goal of so-called ordinary language philosophy was to decide what the basic philosophical terms were, and then to use them correctly and clearly so that all might understand. Obviously, these developments were a far cry from the efforts of the ethical subjectivists to get the objectivists on the run!

Thus, at the very time when the world is in such a turmoil full of "hot and cold" wars, at the very time when people of all ages are highly concerned about ethical values—about "what to do, what to seek, and how to treat others," brilliant philosophical scholars are relatively silent, avoid the rational justification of any type of moral system, and spend their time and energy analyzing the meaning and function of moral concepts and statements. The result is that there has developed a sharp distinction between the *normative ethics* of the moral philosophers and the analytic or critical or theoretical approach of that branch of philosophy now known as *metaethics*. Thus, it is possible to distinguish between a normative ethical statement and a meta-ethical statement as follows: "Harsh coaching methods have no place in amateur sport" would be an instance of the former, while "A coach knows through intuition whether his statements about sporting ethics are fundamentally true" is an example of the latter type of statement.

Obviously, it is of considerable concern to those of us interested in the philosophy of sport and physical education to ascertain in quite exact fashion what the relationship between normative ethics and meta-ethics should be. There are extremists on both sides, but a more reasonable approach would seem to be one in which a moral philosopher or ethical theorist engages in metaethical analysis, but at the same time works toward the elimination of irrational ethical beliefs while attempting to discover a truly sound ethical system. The one would not seem to be incompatible with the other so long as the scholar is fully aware of the interrelationships between the two research approaches or techniques.

It must be recognized, however, that the task of normative inquiry is most difficult, especially when complex issues and conclusions tend to stray into the realm of metaethics. For example, when a normative ethical theory such as hedonism includes a statement such as "Competitive sport is good because it brings pleasure," the non-hedonist might challenge this statement solely on the meaning of the terms "good" and "pleasure." The obvious dificulty of justifying a normative ethical theory brings to the fore questions about meta-ethical relativism and subjectivism, questions which when pursued carefully point up the severity of the "subjectivistic threat."

Basically and fundamentally, then, justification of an ethical theory, or even an incomplete set of ethical statements about sport (or any other aspect of life), revolves around the ability of the theorist to state correctly, elucidate sufficiently, and defend adequately his moral and/or ethical claims and arguments. Is a moral judgment objective or subjective? Does a moral judgment differ from a factual judgment?

Is an ethical statement about correct conduct in sport, for example, "publicly warrantable?" In other words, is there some publicly acceptable procedure for verification which reasonable men would be willing to accept? Finally, then, ethical claims or judgments should be objectively verifiable; they should be universalizable; they should be practical for use in everyday life; and—ideally—they should be autonomous in that the structure or "fabric" of the theoretical statements does not rest on solely nonnormative statements.

ETHICAL NATURALISM (PRAGMATISM)

The various metaethical theories are propounded, therefore, by philosophers who are striving to account as best possible for each of the four, so-called ideal features of sound moral or ethical discourse as listed immediately above (objectivity, universality, practicality, and autonomy). The reader will have to decide for himself to what extent the various ethical theories of the twentieth century satisfy the demands indicated for ideal ethical discourse. Since this paper is designed to focus on ethical naturalism (pragmatism), no effort can be made, other than incidental comments, to cover the nonnaturalism of G. E. Moore; the deontological nonnaturalists (e.g., C. D. Broad) who are typically intuitionistic; the phenomenological intuitionists (e.g., Max Scheler); the noncognitive emotivists (e.g., A. J. Ayer); the non-cognitivist existentialists who imply normative value theory through what has been called philosophical anthropology on the Continent (e.g., Albert Camus); the linguistic philosophical approach of a R. M. Hare which states that moral dicta are much like imperatives; and, finally, what has been called a "good-reasons approach" in that moral precepts should be justified on the basis of which resulting social practices would cause the least amount of suffering (e.g., Stephen Toulmin).

The focus in this section will be on the answers (or "answers") that seem to be provided by pragmatic (naturalistic) ethics. Space will not permit a *detailed* discussion of the various subdivisions of this philosophical position although the broad outline will be presented. The point must be made immediately that Dewey's ethical theorizing was different than anything which had been heard of since the Greeks. As Rucker explains,

... for Dewey there are no fixed ends, either psychological, sociological, or theological; no authoritatively decreed moral laws; and no externally specified virtues or vices ... Dewey states in a variety of places that the job of philosophy is to restore the long-broken connection between the realms of science and value. Hence his insistence upon a science of ethics: the procedures of the natural sciences are the procedures of any search for knowledge and understanding. The analysis of the act of reflective thought yields the ground for science and for ethics, the distinction between them being one of the primary interest at the time: knowledge or action, truth or goodness ... (107:p.116).

Even before the turn of the century, therefore, Dewey realized that morality should not be compartmentalized and considered in a different way than other aspects of life. This point is a sine qua non which must be understood by any who would evaluate his efforts.

Interestingly enough, further substantiation of the "peculiar" approach comes from an analysis of the functions of the philosopher in American pragmatism written some twenty years ago by a young Catholic philosopher at the Catholic University of America in Washington, D. C. In an evident early effort to establish himself as a freethinker, Keating compared the function of the pragmatic philosopher with that of the philosopher in Thomism. His major findings help to set the stage for this present treatment:

1. It is the negative or critical function of the philosopher to dismiss make-believes, to clear the air of erroneous premises and attitudes.
2. The primary duty of the philosopher is to aid in the advancement of the common good.
3. The function of the philosopher is to provide the average man with a more rational conception of the framework of things and to aid in the creation of realization of human ideals.
4. The primary function of the philosopher is the application of the pragmatic test ... If a proposition has no practical meaning, what difference does it make whether we call it true or false?
5. It is the function of the philosopher to aid in the construction of a new science of human values.

Finally, in summary, he stressed that the philosopher ". . . should organize and integrate the specialized results of the various sciences, . . . [and in the process he should take great care] to delineate fundamental concepts which, if left vague, inevitably cause unnecessary wrangling and dissension between special sciences and philosophy." (77:pp.9-19).

Naturalism has been called the oldest philosophy in the Western world. It has been said further that it is the most elusive. Naive naturalism can be described quite accurately, but it tends to become either more pragmatic or realistic as it moves from questions about reality into theory about the acquisition of knowledge. For this reason many have felt that its place had been usurped in the twentieth century by these two major philosophical positions or tendencies. And yet it represents an attitude that we cannot escape even today, just as the philosophy of idealism is ever present to influence our thoughts and actions.

Nature is reliable and dependable according to naturalistic metaphysics. From an early belief that nature was composed of one substance, naturalistic philosophers later accepted the idea that energy was the "substance" out of which the universe was constructed. Now nature is viewed as a process exhibiting continuity. The epistemology of naturalism, starting with the idea that objects presented images of themselves in the mind, advanced to a greatly improved understanding of sensory knowledge. The observation of specifics in nature (induction) was suggested as complementary to the earlier idea of deduction. Still later, scientific investigation was recognized as the only true means of gaining knowledge about the world. The logic of naturalism relies heavily on induction—the "method of science." Generalizations about nature become self-evident when facts are amassed carefully and painstakingly. The axiology of naturalism is based on the many values inherent in Nature itself. *Ethically,* naturalism is hedonistic—the achievement of the highest type of abiding pleasure for all is basic. Experiences that are purely natural bring aesthetic pleasure. Religious value is identical with over-all realization; life now is what is significant. Social goals are secondary values; the relationship of the individual to the physical universe is paramount. A social system is accepted since it is better than anarchy. (125:pp.45-46,52-53).

Moving ahead to a consideration of Deweyan pragmatism, which was subsequently designated by Dewey himself and others as "experimentalism," it should be kept in mind that other terms such as instrumentalism, pragmatic naturalism, and progressivism have been employed almost interchangeably by many educational philosophers (at least). Generally speaking, pragmatism proceeds on the assumption that it is possible to find out if something is worthwhile only after it has been tested in experience. Of course, this approach is not new to mankind, but Peirce, James, Dewey, Mead *et al.* were the first to organize this type of (or approach to) thinking to a philosophical position or tendency that has been accepted by many in both scientific and educational circles. It has been argued that epistemology looms so large in the consideration of pragmatism that this aspect of the total position—the study of how man acquires knowledge—should be considered first in any presentation. This approach will be followed here in keeping with an early statement by James that knowledge is the result of a process of thought with a useful purpose. According to pragmatism knowledge is wrought in the action of experience.

Epistemology

An adequate definition of knowledge has tried the ingenuity and insight of scholars for many centuries. If knowledge is fact, and fact is truth, then truth is knowledge. Knowledge has been described as a "knowing about something," an "awareness," a "comprehension," or an "understanding." Here it becomes a subjective matter, and it has to do with the "inner workings" of the mind. Still others believe in a type of knowledge called *objective*—knowledge existing in a world outside of the individual that is there to be known (possibly) by man's intellect.

Modern scientific development, after Darwin's evolutionary theory, opened the way for a new theory of knowledge—the pragmatic or experimentalistic idea of knowledge and truth. Truth was to be tested by its correspondence with reality *and* also by its practical results. This pragmatic treatment of knowledge lies between the extremes of reason and sense perception with some ideas that are not included in either rationalism or empiricism. This approach, interestingly enough, has quite a bit in common with a great deal of contemporary philosophy, because it revolves about those conditions under which a statement does have meaning, and what specific meanings it has in the light of such conditions. Thus, if a proposition truly has meaning, it must make a difference in people's lives. This relates, of course, to the verifiability theory of meaning promulgated by the logical positivists (and related so effectively to sport and physical education recently by Patrick:101).

The meaning develops, therefore, because such knowledge has been earned through the experience of people for whom such knowledge serves repeatedly in their lives as an "instrument for verification." Viewed in this manner we can appreciate what James called the "cash value" of an idea—the import that it has for the fulfillment of human purpose. Knowledge is knowledge only if it works to help man in the battle for survival.

Such an approach "naturalizes" mind and implies that intelligence is a "relatively late-comer" on earth. Such a function of mind gives man a more flexible means of adapting himself to life. If his mind were not functioning, man would lose control of his earth. Mind serves to form knowledge or truth by undergoing experience. It must be adaptable because of the possibility of novelty and the consequent precariousness of man's relation with the world.

Pragmatism is based on a behavioral psychology which is now conceived in a considerably different way than heretofore. This is not the position which dispensed with consciousness on the assumption that the mind and the central nervous system were identical. If the mind is simply another bodily organ, man could simply stop thinking and "do what comes naturally" according to impulse! That kind of behaviorism simply did not take into account that meaning (and, therefore, mind) must have a social context in which to develop; it is a social phenomenon, and it "expands" when meaningful interaction occurs between organisms because of their identification with each other. Mind ". . . is an abstraction derived from the concreta of intelligent behavior." (76:p.26).

Mind, through evolution, has become part of the whole of man which enables him to cope with the surrounding world and all the creatures living in it (hopefully). Through experience, man's many problems have been, are, and will be solved as he encounters new ones in the future. An intelligent mind makes this possible. This theory of knowledge leads to Dewey's experimental method for the solving of problems, which is characterized by the following steps:

1. Life is characterized by movement, the smoothness of whose flow may be interrupted by an obstacle.
2. This obstacle creates a problem; the resultant tension must be resolved to allow further movement to take place.
3. Man marshals all available and pertinent facts to help with the solution of the problem.

4. Data gathered falls into one or more patterns; subsequent analysis offers a working hypothesis.

5. This hypothesis must be tested to see if the problem may be solved through the application of the particular hypothesis. When the problem is solved, movement may begin again. A hypothesis which turns out to be true offers a frame of reference for organizing facts; subsequently, this results in a central meaning that may be called knowledge.

Note: The experimentalistic (pragmatic) theory of knowledge acquisition merges with its value theory at this point, inasmuch as such knowledge acquired frees man to initiate subsequent action furthering the process of movement and change indefinitely into the "future." (125:pp.72-74).

Logic

There is rather general agreement that logic is primarily concerned with the methods of reasoning that man employs in his search to find answers to the problems that confront him daily. As the reader might expect, pragmatism departs radically from traditional logic because ideas are viewed typically as instruments to be used for the solutions of problems. This is why the term "instrumentalism" was coined to explain an approach designed to meet the challenge of a universe which seemed to be boundless—and perhaps even expanding! Dewey calls this revised system ". . . a unified theory of inquiry through which the authentic pattern of experimental and operational inquiry science shall become available for regulation of the habitual methods by which inquiries in the field of common sense are carried on." (42).

Such a pattern of logic bears a strong resemblance or relationship to the learning theory (experimental method for solving of problems) described above under epistemology. Again we see terms and phrases such as "indeterminate situation," "institution of a problem," "determination of a problem-solution," "reasoning," and "operational character of facts-meanings." Such a pattern of logic, of course, appears to bridge the gap between traditional logic and modern scientific inquiry, while at one and the same time providing an approach to reasoning that can be employed by any man with daily problem-situations. (18:p.464). That such an approach is innovative hardly needs restatement. The typical patterns of thought peculiar to induction and deduction cannot be applied arbitrarily because of the uniqueness of each problem-situation. Secondly, there is a very close relationship between this pattern of logic and life on earth as we know it—"man and Nature are continuous." Thirdly, such a pattern of logic seems to fit man's sociological development as well as his biological progress. Lastly, it is important and interesting to note that pragmatic logic has application for individual as well as group and societal problems. (18:pp.264-266).

Axiology

The system of values of the philosophy of pragmatism is consistent with the other departments of this philosophical tendency and stems directly from the pattern of logic described above. A value is a fact which, when applied to life, becomes useful. An experience is adjudged as valuable by the human organism which is attempting to adapt itself to the environment in the best and most profitable manner. The comparison of values to determine the best ones is a problem of deciding which value or values will help achieve life's purposes in the best way ("the good life" that a man consciously or unconsciously chooses for himself). We should not forget, however, that these goals or human values may be (and, in many instances, will be) only temporary ones.

What are the main values? For the pragmatist, that depends on when, where, and how the individual is living. The pragmatist believes that ". . . values must be closely related to the world in which man finds himself." (55:p.142). Man must choose which means and ends he will accept and which he will reject. His progress depends upon critical examination of values prior to intelligent selection. Our society has traditionally made the mistake of contrasting facts and values; the contrast that should be made is between *old* values and *new* ones! "The radical dualism which besets our culture is the institutionalization of a faulty philosophy. When we try to defend values by declaring them out of bounds to inquirers into fact, we succeed only in dehumanizing science and technology and in deranging politics, religion, morality, and art." (76:pp.36-37). The pragmatist believes that man is perhaps dangerously unrealistic and romantic when he doesn't appreciate the instrumental quality of values lying on a "means-end continuum."

Ethically, the pragmatist (experimentalist) finds himself facing continually new situations in which he must exercise wise judgment in keeping with the apparent elements of the indeterminate situation. It is argued that pragmatism offers the possibility of avoiding a typically troublesome ethical problem—how to resolve a situation where one's motives are presumably pure, and yet his actions violate currently acceptable standards. When the pragmatic steps of logic are employed, it is possible to blend inner motives and outer behavior in planned, purposeful action to meet each new situation in a fresh, unbiased manner.

Aesthetically, men are concerned with experiences which convey beauty and meaning of an enduring nature to man. For the pragmatist, aesthetic appreciation is closely related to the nature of the experience. In life man fluctuates between tension and pleasure depending on whether indeterminate situations are resolved to our satisfaction. When the answers to problems are found, tensions are eased and enjoyment results. There is no state of aesthetic pleasure that may be designated as permanent for man, however, since life's rhythm of experience does not function so as to make this possible. Thus, aesthetic satisfaction comes when close identification is maintained with the ebb and flow of life's indeterminate situations. We are all anxious to preserve a state of enjoyment and release; yet, if it is held too long and life's rhythm is disturbed, troublesome difficulties arise. The psychological problems arising from life in a dream world are only too well known. Fortunately, various types of artists help us to "freeze" many of these aesthetic values for possible subsequent enjoyment. The man who would achieve the greatest amount of aesthetic enjoyment for himself must possess and continue to develop those habits which promote keen insight. It should be mentioned that Dewey assigned a lesser role to values which are the opposite of beauty. Tragedy and horror, for example, may be preserved as art forms, so that man will be able to look back at these past experiences, still "feel" the experience but with some perspective, and perhaps accept it as a form of beauty despite its earlier impact.

Religiously, the pragmatist assumes a completely naturalistic approach. For him religion would not involve any worship of the supernatural, and hence would be considered unorthodox by many. The religious pragmatist would be a person who is most anxious to reach pragmatic values whenever and wherever possible by living purposefully. Man's task is to thrust himself into life's many experiences; only *there* will he find the opportunity to give his life true meaning.

Socially, the pragmatist (experimentalist) places great emphasis on this aspect of life. Social values are fundamental, since life (or society) is ". . . an organic process upon which individuals depend and by which they live." (18:p.475). Any person who would withdraw from relationships with his fellow man in order to devote himself to the realization of so-called other values in his life makes a drastic error. Recluses injure society by withdrawing from their responsibility to it, and it is quite possible that they do themselves still greater harm. Such social values as loyalty, cooperation, kindness, and generosity can hardly be achieved in a vacuum. The pragmatist envisions the relationship between the individual and the society as being of the highest type, and this applies especially to life in a democracy. Pragmatic values are most in evidence when the individual has the opportunity to develop to the highest of his potentialities, so long as such development does not interfere with the good of the whole. It is impossible to develop social values in the same way in societies that are undemocratic, although to a degree such value realization may occur.

Metaphysics

The reader will understand now why it seemed legitimate to the writer to remove metaphysics from its usual position at "the head of the list." Followed through to its logical conclusion, the epistemological theory of pragmatism makes it clear that it is beyond man's power to speculate accurately about the infinite or to do anything about the fundamental course of the physical universe. Man's problem is to interpret what he finds. He looks at nature, and he asks questions about its interpretation. Is nature an inexorable process which is advancing according to a universal plan? Is the onward surge of nature a kind of emergent evolution? The pragmatist takes what he finds and functions from that point. He doesn't know whether nature is functioning inexorably. He tends to believe that nature is an emergent evolution, but he can't answer the question—emerging toward what? So this philosophy limits man's frame of reality to nature as it functions; any assumptions made are only hypotheses to be held tentatively.

The future is always to be considered, because situations are continually changing. The ongoing process cannot be dealt with finally at any one time.

Even these preceding statements are not entirely free from inferences about the nature of reality. The world is characterized by activity and change. All that is known about the human response to nature can be known without first definitely making a final statement about the universe (multiverse?) as a whole. Thus, experience or interaction with the environment is all that the experimentalist has by which to live his life. If his environment doesn't give him an accurate account of reality, then he would conclude that humans could well be the victims of a fantastic hoax.

The pragmatist believes further in organic evolution, and that rational man has developed in this process. The logical conclusion to draw from this assumption is that the world is yet incomplete. This doesn't mean, of course, that *everything* is in a state of change. Some elements and structures appear to be relatively stable, but this quality of seeming stability is often deceiving. The experimentalist finds that he must look upon the world as a mixture of things relatively stable and yet incomplete. This makes all life a great experiment. It is the task of education to make this experiment an intelligent one.

A theory of emergent novelty makes great sense to the pragmatist if the universe (reality) is constantly undergoing change. An excellent example of novelty is explained by Brubacher:

> This is true about the individuality of any particular boy or girl. It is inescapably unique since any given offspring of bisexual reproduction is the only one of its kind. Such a child commences and lives his life at a juncture of space and time which simply cannot be duplicated for anyone else. (13:p.35).

The concept of freedom of will is a very strong point in favor of the pragmatic position. He can argue that man's future *must* allow for true freedom of will. He does not conceive of free will as a motiveless choice. His contention is that all beings are in process of interaction with other "existences." He inquires about the quality of this interaction and how great a role the individual can play in this process. Man should determine the character of this process from within (meaning through intense and intensive social intercourse in life experiences). Freedom developed in this manner is achieved through continuous and developmental learning from experience. As Childs states,

> In a changing world the only person who can become free and who can maintain his freedom is the one who has 'learned to learn.' A democratic society can hope to succeed only if it is composed of individuals who have developed the responsibility for intelligent self-direction in co-operation with others. (21:p.168).

IMPLICATIONS FROM PRAGMATISM FOR EDUCATION

The possible implications from pragmatism (experimentalism) for education have been spelled out in such great detail by so many different people, educational philosophers included, that it hardly seems necessary to repeat this pattern ad nauseam for the reader at this point. Further, as the analysis movement in philosophy gathered strength on this continent, it began in the 1950's to influence educational philosophy to a great extent as well. Thus, it was only a matter of time before those interested in sport and physical education would "get the message and catch up." Well, this has indeed happened, and the profession of physical education and sport is now beginning to reap the benefits of this "new wisdom" that is being made available to it. Fortunately or unfortunately, even though such effort was undoubtedly most worthwhile, the analytical "excursion" of educational philosophy in the fifties and sixties has certainly not influenced the conduct of education very much, and it can be argued also that the "structural analysis technique" and normative educational philosophizing may not have had the desired effect either. It seems quite safe to make exactly the same statement about the recent history of sport and physical educational philosophy as well.

The battlelines were quite clearly delineated in the presentations by Sterling McMurrin and B. Othaniel Smith at a symposium entitled "Philosophy of Education" held at the 59th Annual Meeting of the American Philosophical Association in December, 1962. Mr. McMurrin stated that ". . . the chief deterrent to the advancement of the philosophy of education as a respectable discipline, beyond its identification with such a considerable number of persons lacking in adequate philosophic competence, is the obstinate assumption that from different metaphysical premises differing educational systems and methods can and should be logically derived." (95). Mr. Smith in reply pointed out that McMurrin used the term "philosophy of education" in three of four different possible ways, and that such usage made it difficult to respond. Granting that ". . . the path from the metaphysics of the system to the classroom is long and tenuous, and anyone who tries to travel it is apt to lose his way," Smith's response was that,

> . . . any philosophical system will include a picture of man and society. Insofar as it deals with man's nature, his development, and his destiny, the system will necessarily have implications for the education of man . . . (113:p.639).

Then he went on to argue that McMurrin's latter two questions went to the heart of the matter: (1) should prospective teachers study the philosophy of education, and (2) if not, what philosophical pursuits are relevant to their preparation as teachers?

Obviously, this present paper cannot address these questions seriously, but it is important to note that Soltis has recently most strongly challenged ". . . the efficacy of the analytic approach for both theorists and practicing educators alike who would realistically face problems concerning the proper description and adequate understanding of the learning process and the unescapable normative quations to be found in thinking deeply about education today." (90:p.29). A reply to Soltis by McClellan is most straightforward, even if arrogant, but it will serve to bring the present paper back to its purported progression. McClellan asserts that Soltis's historical analysis ". . . ignores the overwhelming influence of John Dewey and his very talented collaborators and colleagues." (90). Young educational philosophers were "impelled" to ". . . abandon the Deweyan synthesis and start in pursuit of new ways of doing philosophy of education. "(90). Now there is a new generation upon us, so to speak, and educational philosophers may indeed not be ready to serve them either emotionally or intellectually. That the same may be said for sport and physical education philosophers ought to be apparent from the results of the last two symposia, and it is to be hoped that this present meeting will get them back on target. It is important to seek guidance from colleagues in related disciplines in an effort to gain strength, but even more important to avoid their mistakes in direction.

Thus, the position to be taken in the remainder of this paper regarding research methodology and technique is that of the Deweyan synthesis—the problems of ethics are problems of "developing the habits and skills to act intelligently." It is not being argued that educational philosophical systems—or sport and physical education philosophical "systems"—should or can be slavishly and completely logically deduced from metaphysical positions. It is being argued that certain philosophical systems still extant do include "a picture of man and society," and that such systems ". . . will necessarily have implications for the education of man." (113). The important point here, however, is that pragmatism (experimentalism) does *not* deduce educational aims from a metaphysical position; the *tentative* metaphysical outlook is a result of the application of the experimental method to the search for educational values. It is on this basis that some of the educational implications of pragmatism (experimentalism) are presented briefly prior to the offering of implications for sport and physical education.

Society, School, and the Individual

There is no doubt but that pragmatism (experimentalism) has exercised influence on education on this continent, not to mention lesser influence elsewhere. An investigation would indicate, however, that it has not had nearly as much influence as its opponents would have educators and the public think it has. The reader is reminded that Parsons claims that the United States has had a remarkably stable value system over the years. (75:p.13). The experimentalist views education as a social institution and, as a social phenomenon, education is presumably one of the basic means by which society progresses and regenerates itself. Further according to this position, education is a moral affair—a *value* enterprise. To carry out its role best, there is no escaping the fact that the school, of necessity, must maintain an extremely close connection with society. (125:p.78). Today there are many people who claim that such a "connection has all but severed!"

A belief in democracy (whatever that means!) as a way of life seems practical because of the opportunity for the free growth of the individual, as well as for the sharing of the cultural and social heritage. Furthermore, a democracy tends to have an economic system which allows children and young people to enjoy some form of so-called higher education.

In experimentalism, the school has a creative function—to guide the student as he develops an understanding of and an ability to cope with the new and changing factors of his environment. Whether today's schools and universities are meeting this goal can be most vigorously debated; it is most difficult to preserve that which is useful from the social heritage, while at one and the same time to provide competencies, skills, and knowledge that will prepare youth for the uncertain future in the "new world" of tomorrow. The home and the school should play the leading roles in the education of most children, and the place of the private school in a democracy of an ideal nature is doubtful. Comparative religious education belongs in the public schools, and it deserves a place of importance. The church as a social institution appears to leave much to be desired at present, but religious freedom should be preserved so long as separation of church and state can be successfully maintained.

Process of Education

The individual not the subject matter is placed at the center of the educational experience. Pupil growth through actual problem-solving in life experiences is the typical pattern employed to bring about learning. The unity of the human organism must be recognized, and mind is viewed as a function rather than as a structure. The "mind" reaches out to make its own knowledge from experience. Learning takes place when interest and effort combine to produce the desired result. The temporal order of the experimentalistic curriculum may follow both a *logical* arrangement (from the simple fact to the complex conclusion) and a *psychological* order (problem-solving as explained through scientific method). The latter approach is to be preferred, since it enables thinking to become actual problem-solving in a life experience. The pragmatic experimentalist has unusual difficulty in evaluating, because his aims and objectives are likely to change somewhat as experience indicates the need for such change. It can be determined partially when learning has taken place through the use of educational measurement. In the final analysis, the individual's ability to adjust to a changing environment is the best method of knowing whether learning has been effected. (125:p.78).

Educational Aims and Objectives

Aims and objectives (tentatively held) are the result of a meaningful educative process. Experimentalism suggests that ". . . education in the broadest sense can be nothing less than the changes made in human beings by their experience." (55:p.144). For Dewey social efficiency—the competency, skill, and knowledge to adapt to a changing environment—was the general aim of education. (42:p.90). If these instrumental educational goals are realized, the child will be prepared for present-day life, and future aims can and should grow out of continuing experience. The curriculum which develops from such an instrumentally-oriented problem-solving approach to education cannot be gleaned from the traditional subject-matter approach of today. It should state which competencies, skills, and knowledge are needed to live life today (and looking toward the future). Dewey would agree with Alvin Toffler that "future shock" has already set in and that man is poorly prepared to counteract its effects.

THE PRAGMATIC ETHIC IN SPORT AND PHYSICAL EDUCATION

Any analysis of the pragmatic ethic in sport and physical education must take cognizance to the longstanding fact vs. value dualism. Dewey's cognitive theory of value is one in which value judgments are determined experimentally in the light of experience. When an ethical problem, or moral dilemma, arises it is always within a social context. Wisdom accumulated from past experience is employed as an "intellectual instrumentality" or tool to aid in the verification of a moral hypothesis advanced to help in the solution of today's problem. In the process new definitions of ethical terms emerge as judgments are made in response to problematic situations that occur in unique social situations. Thus, problematic situations involving ethical theory in sport and physical education are resolved in this same fashion.

(It should be stated parenthetically at this juncture that the writer has been typically employing the term "physical education and sport" to describe the field as it exists today in educational institutions. He recognizes further that some wish to retain the term "physical education," while others are using "sport" or "sport sciences." Many will recall that much earlier Staley recommended the use of "sports education." At any rate, the writer recognizes the need for a new name for the profession, and also for the disciplinary aspect of the field. The art and science of human movement as applied to the theory and practice of sport, dance, play, and exercise seems to be a helpful definition presently. Furthermore, because of a tri-partite professional development within health, physical education, and recreation, health and recreational consideration per se will not be discussed here, *even though* the writer's pragmatic leanings over a thirty-year period caused him to use the term "physical, health, and recreation education" in earlier writings. Lastly, acknowledgment must be made to the careful and insightful analysis of Deweyan progressivism made recently by Francis Keenan (78), a study in which the writer shared slightly and which served to renew his conviction that experimental method applied to value theory in sport and physical education was being grossly neglected.)

Knowledge Acquisition in Sport and "Physical Education"

The process of sport and physical education will be considered first because of the fundamental nature of this approach. It is vitally important that aims and methods go hand in hand. As Larkin stated decades ago, "Trading the drill master of calisthenics for the domineering coach of football does not appear to be enough." (85:p.67). The salient qualities of the experimentalistic teacher of sport and physical education were further listed as follows:

> In restating the desirable methods in a physical education program the pattern appeared to be this: a broad social outlook, great consideration for the learner, well prepared teachers, and a minimum of inherited technique as such. (85:pp.37-38).

The experimentalistic teacher and coach should aid the student and/or player in the development of skill for problem-solving. This skill is more than a conditioned reflex; the learner needs to develop insight into the nature of the anticipated outcome whether it be in the movement experience of sport, dance, play, or exercise. Keenan expresses it well as follows: "Man should not only learn to move, and learn about movement, he should also learn about himself and his culture through the medium of movement experience." (78:p.136). This implies that attitude development is most important along with the learning of competencies, skills, and knowledge.

Such an approach means that there will be a new conception of the curriculum (or of the "curricular or co-curricular" experience in sport). "As teachers we must make ourselves progressively unnecessary," says Kilpatrick, because ". . . we face thus a new conception of the curriculum as consisting properly of such a succession of school experiences as will best bring and constitute the continuous reconstruction of experience." (79:p.123). It is important to start at the student's level and to give him ". . . as much freedom as he can use wisely. And again the test is the learning that results." (79:p.129). A coach who subscribed to this position could employ this line of reasoning quite nicely.

An experimentalistic educator has a responsibility to order the learning experience so that it is interesting and significant to the learner/performer. The idea here is that teachers and coaches will find a greatly different attitude if they involve the individual as "an agent or participant" rather than as a spectator. It could be argued that the coach has an advantage over the teacher in this regard because in competitive sport there is the possibility of quite complete psycho-physical integration for the player. This is true, but it fails to take into consideration the way that the coach involves the player in the total plan and operation. A quarterback who very rarely calls a play for his team seems to be expected to function as a "conditioned reflex." And then there are all those players on the squad who may never get in the game, or who play only a few moments, or who stand around even during practices and may indeed serve as "dummies" or members of the taxi squad.

The teacher/coach as the agent of the school or university should create an environment in which ". . . play and work shall be conducted with reference to facilitating desirable mental and moral growth." (33:p.230). Obviously, the mere introduction of games and sporting contests is not sufficient. "Everything depends on the way in which they are employed." (33:p.230). There must be an environment offering great opportunity for interaction between the individual and his "natural and social" surroundings. For Dewey it is the *interaction* that is vital, because it ". . . will effect acquisition of those meanings which are so important that they become, in turn, instruments of further learnings." (33:p.320).

Standardization of the curriculum or coaching plan from year to year is something that the pragmatic experimentalist is most anxious to avoid. There should be opportunities for changes in plan and program involving student choice. Morland (97), for example, explained that an experimentalistic curriculum should be flexible and not systematically arranged. The avoidance of direct prescription of —say—a syllabus in a course was recommended so that the student would have the chance to use and thereby develop his own judgment. How often is such an approach adopted in the coaching of an individual, dual, or team sport?

Too often today the teaching and coaching methods employed in overlay commercialized varsity sports have brought criticism of a most sharp and intense nature against the entire athletics establishment. As Keenan forthrightly states,

> . . . the evils of athletics often receive more attention than the values. Athletics in some instances have been 'a cancer in the side of physical education.' This refers to the growing immorality which has its base in the individualism of coaches and athletes, and the effort to win at any cost. Under such conditions, valid educational values have no chance for survival. There are those who think that the 'metastasis of this sort of educational disease' is too widespread; the cancer is incurable! This view must be avoided since it is this pessimism that allows perpetuation of immoral systems. Educators should speak out for removal of 'cancerous athletic growth' while physical education is still alive. If the malpractices cannot be discontinued, then athletics ought to go its own way as separate from physical education aimed at desirable educational practices. There is an optimum level of athletic activity which can serve educational priorities. Uninhibited quests for victory leave little time for reflection and evaluation of athletics in terms of educational objectives. (78:pp.139-140).

The recommendation is, therefore, that the best possible learning occurs when the student/player aids in the origination and planning of his own educational experience, when he has a fair share in the execution of the enterprise, and when he has the opportunity to evaluate the success or failure of the whole venture. Measurement of individual growth by grades, term marks, testing, and other evaluative devices deserves most careful consideration. Is it more important to evaluate individual pupil growth than it is to measure whether an overweight, sensitive student comes up to a national norm in pull-ups for his age or grade? How does such objective testing take into account that there may be as much as a four-year difference in the physiological maturity of two students at the same age? Furthermore, there is evidence to support the position that certain students "go to pieces" in situations where the psycho-social factors are such that the performer feels unusual stress. It would seem much more sensible to consider the individual's body type, his continuing health record, and his past performances before testing him to determine whether individual pupil growth has taken place. Competitors in athletics learn to live with stress or they are confined to the bench. One wonders how much consideration is given to the question of whether young people can gradually learn to have so-called stress immunity.

There is an element of uncertainty with a considerable measure of contingency when an experimental problem-solving approach is employed in the teaching of a class. Dewey placed great emphasis on the idea of education as "life experience." Presented with a problem, the student, guided by the teacher, searches for ways and means to solve it. A desirable third stage is when the student—not the teacher—comes up with a proposed solution which he proceeds to test by putting it into practice (a fourth stage). If the plan of action works, or it appears that it might work after a reasonable amount of practice, then learning is the result of the experience. This particular learning experience should enter upon a fifth stage when it is correlated with previous experiences to give broader meaning and perspective to the entire educational process. (13:pp.255-256). During this process any disciplinary measures, if absolutely necessary, should arise from the actions of the class itself. The teacher's role is to be ready to help out in management; he should be ". . . a responsible leader as well as a thoughtful follower upon occasion." (120:p.273).

Lastly under this heading is the recognition that there may be a variety of learnings in a class or coaching experience. There is the *technical* learning of how to bring a man to the mat in wrestling, but there is also the *associated* learning that the wrestler will have to fol- low—a rigorous training routine and possible dieting in order to be fit and make his ideal weight. In addition, there are other important *concomitant* learnings that accompany the sport (e.g., no punishing holds are allowed, and a young man should "give the best" that is in him).

Sport and Physical Education Aims and Objectives

Very briefly, then, as this paper draws to a close, what meaning do people obtain as they understand what the learning process of experi- mentalism is supposed to do (i.e., how it works to fulfill its purpose)? The most fundamental goal for philosophy ought to help man ". . . as- similate the impact of science on human affairs." (76). Is man to be the "master of the machine?" As Kaplan states,

> The business of philosophy today is to provide a system of ideas that will make an integrated whole of our beliefs about the nature of the world and the values which we seek in the world in fulfillment of our human nature. (76:p.16).

Applied to sport and physical education, the experimentalist af- firms the priority of man over athletics and physical activity. He is much more interested in promoting the concept of total fitness rather than physical fitness alone. Sport and physical education can provide excellent problem-solving experiences to children and young people. Students should have the opportunity to select a wide variety of useful activities, many of which should help to develop social intelligence. The activities offered should bring natural impulses into play. Physical education classes and intramural sports are more important to the large majority of students than interscholastic or intercollegiate ath- letics and deserve priority if conflict arises over budgetary allotment, staff available for guidance and instruction, and use of facilities. The experimentalist can, however, give full support to team (as well as to individual and dual) experiences in competitive sports, because they can be vital educational experiences if properly conducted.

Man should be a strong, healthy animal—a standard which can

apply to girls as well as to boys in today's world. Health should be a primary objective of education; a child needs health instruction. Although the basic responsibility for health education and recreation education ideally should not rest with the physical educator-coach, he can give full support to a unified approach whereby the three specialized areas of health, physical education, and recreation would provide a variety of experiences that will enable the individual to live a richer, fuller life through superior adjustment to his social environment.

The school program of health, physical, and recreation education may be administered as a unified program even though three separate professions are now emerging in society. The success of the school health education program depends on the degree of cooperation among home, school, and community, and much the same can be said about the cooperation necessary for a successful physical education and sport program or a recreation education program. All these aspects of the total program may be coordinated because they are related in so many ways.

Education for the worthy use of leisure is basic to the curriculum of the school—a curriculum in which pupil growth, as defined broadly is all important. Play should be conducted in such a way that desirable moral growth will be fostered. Overly organized sport competition is not true recreation education, since the welfare of the individual is often submerged to other more materialistic goals. It is a mistake to confuse the psychological distinction between work and play with the traditional economic distinction that is typically recognized. All citizens should have ample opportunity to use their free time in a creative and fruitful manner. A person who watches others with a high degree of skill perform should not be condemned for this recreational pursuit. The important point is that the individual keeps such viewing in a balanced role in his life pattern. (125: pp.107-108).

THE STRENGTHS AND WEAKNESSES OF PRAGMATISM (EXPERIMENTALISM)

Generally speaking, experimentalism is strong because it encourages man to meet each daily experience fully—one step at a time. In an age when scientific discoveries are legion, emphasis on experimental method can accomplish much good more rapidly in the world. If it is indeed a changing world, experimentalism would appear to be a highly practical approach to life.

In education, experimentalism breaks down the distinction between life *in* the school and life *outside* the school by keeping teacher and student close to experience and by making every effort to eliminate much of what might be called "academic artificiality." The aim, as had been heard so often, is to place the student at the center of the educational process, not the teacher or the subject matter. Freedom for the pupil—at least as much as can be used wisely—is certainly appealing to the individual; yet in experimentalism there is undoubtedly great concern for society and the social implications of the educational process. If initiative and self-reliance are desirable educational goals, pupil freedom might well bring about these qualities more quickly and much more fully. This approach should have great appeal to a people presumably devoted to the concept of an evolving political democracy. Stress on interest as the basis for motivation of instruction should bring greater involvement on the part of the student and should, therefore, be a strength. Furthermore, as we move toward Asimov's concept of a "global village," a philosophy such as experimentalism is desirable because it promotes easy interchange of diverse cultural viewpoints; this is vital as man seeks to promote better understanding among various races and creeds at home and throughout the world.

The experimentalistic position offers a great deal of strength to the profession of physical education and sport. Physical education viewed in this context can become an integral subject in the curriculum if it realizes its educational potentialities. Secondly, despite present efforts toward separate professionalization by health education and recreation, experimentalism at least encourages these fields to remain allied and closely affiliated within education so that the needs and interests of the student may be met. Thirdly, a teaching method based on an effective combination of interest and effort affords strength for the educational task in today's schools.

From a general standpoint, many have argued that experimentalism is weak because it doesn't provide the stability that many people seem to need. Critics say that it is a house built on sand. The thought of no fixed aims in advance can be very disturbing to men who are fearful for the future. How does experimentalism speak to the decade of the 1960's during which time so many problems arose that experimental method does not seem equipped to solve? Many argue that progressivism in education has served its purpose and run its course. Such an approach may be helpful with certain types of youngsters, but we don't have enough good teachers equipped to use this approach. In addition, teachers are typically swamped with large numbers of students, and this approach can only work with small, select groups.

Other critics assert that the application of the experimental method in physical education classes would mean chaos and lowered physical fitness. Coaches, who tend to hold an essentialistic orientation in educational philosophy, would have to learn to be "good losers" if they adopted such an approach with their squads. Youth needs to be guided by "a strong hand"; experimental teaching is "soft," and indeed may be at least partially responsible for the general weakening of moral fibre of youth today. These ideas, critics say, arose from observation of experimentalism in action!

WHAT REASONABLE CONCLUSIONS MAY BE DRAWN?

Drawing "reasonable" conclusions from a presentation such as this is probably the most difficult and risky phase of the entire project. One hesitates to be too bold; on the other hand, these appear to be unusual times. Certainly a type of world transformation is taking place as the tempo of civilization increases almost exponentially. People are frightened as they look to the future. Societies have become increasingly complex, and sociologists until most recently were in great demand so that they might serve as "psychoanalysts" of society. The "dialogue of freedom," we are told, may go on indefinitely, but the ". . . solutions to our problems are not primarily ideological but structural . . . They constitute a new political direction in the world, not left or right, but human and forward." (102:pp.21-22). We are exhorted further to prepare for the continuing and advancing technological thrust, and that ". . . the only indispensable human component is the mind component for design, redesign, complex evaluation, and control." (102:p.26). If these predictions be even approximately true, then as Platt states,

Yet millions of the older generation, alternately disgusted and terrified by these developments, will have to learn new values and a new language . . . (102:p.26).

In the same vein Callahan writes about searching for an ethic in a new culture that is on its way here, but that still does not yet exist. (19:p. 4). It will need to be "one in which human beings can live (and die) securely, harmoniously, and humanely in the presence of constant advances in the medical and biological sciences." (19:p.4).

The general conclusion of the writer is that pragmatism (experimentalism) offers the best and most humane approach to the problem of new values—and possibly a new culture—that is quite evidently being thrust upon us. Pragmatism has always been a philosophy of social protest from the moment of its conception; ". . . a pragmatist is always dissatisfied, always striving for betterment." (76:p.41). By its very nature and approach it is receptive to innovation and change. Its method relies upon the application of human intelligence to problems that arise in social planning for the future. It offers man not a philosophy *of* life, but a philosophy *for* the living of life today and tomorrow.

The reader is undoubtedly familiar with the general and specific conclusions that have been drawn on behalf of pragmatic philosophy applied to the educative process. Thus, only a few brief conclusions will be drawn. Basically, the writer concludes that social conditions are presently such that the school and society must maintain a very close connection. The pragmatic philosophy of education is founded upon its premise! Creative answers to life's problem now and in the future will most certainly be needed, and it is this experimentalistic position which is based on an educative process that provides pupil growth through actual problem-solving in life experiences. If "future shock" has already set in, the provision of competency, skill, and knowledge necessary to adapt to a continually changing environment is required.

Most important for this study are possible implications from pragmatic educational philosophy for sport and physical education. Early in this paper certain exemplar problems in sport, dance, play, and exercise were cited. In regard to the amateur-professional controversy, a pragmatist would most certainly search for alternatives based on a world situation that has changed sharply in the past one hundred years. The amateur ideal of Olympic competition has failed miserably; it is simply not adequate today. A pragmatic answer to the problem of dance in North American society would be to encourage its introduction into an articulated curriculum in such a way that the movement experience would relate to the child's growth and development pattern. It brings natural impulses into play and thereby can contribute to man's total fitness for life. Aesthetic experiences convey beauty and meaning to life's rhythm of experience—in the ebb and flow of its indeterminate situations.

The experimentalist has an answer to the traditional distinction between the concepts of work and play. Just because children and youth usually take part in play outside of school proper is no reason why educators should think that something completely different should take place when school is in session. The psychological distinction between work and play has been confused with the economic one. Thus, when the play instinct is introduced into school activities, the complete psycho-physical organism exhibits a type of integration not normally present in activities that have been typically designated as "work."

The question of exercise awaits some definitive answers as well. One great problem confronts many physical educators today who are armed with a seeming abundance of literature emphasizing the life-preserving qualities of regular exercise. The problem is how to motivate people to take part in this important aspect of the "life of an amphibian." The conclusion to be reached from pragmatic naturalism (experimentalism) is that the element of artificiality must be reduced in proportion to the introduction of the play element and freedom of choice. People now appreciate that they *should* exercise, but that is all too logical. The task is, therefore, to devise a psychological order of learning which will "lure the human animal into the trap."

These are obviously only a very few of the conclusions that might well be drawn. Many of the points made earlier (Cf. pp. 38-47) could be reiterated, but the essence of these conclusions should be clear by now. Sport and physical education must serve as "socially useful servants" to man in the world of today and tomorrow. Man should use these activities for his own welfare, individually and collectively. The individual must not be "used" by anyone else. Sport and physical education activities should provide excellent problem-solving experiences for children, young people, and adults. Professional ethics and standards can be successfully developed with the philosophical undergirding of the ethical naturalism of the pragmatist.

REFERENCES

1. Archambault, Reginald D.: "The Philosophical Bases of the Experience Curriculum," *Harvard Educational Review,* Vol. 26, No. 3, 263-275 Summer 1956.
2. Bair, Donn E.: "An Identification of Some Philosophical Beliefs Held by Influential Professional Leaders in American Physical Education." Unpublished Doctor's dissertation, University of Southern California, 1956.
3. Barton, George E. Jr.: "John Dewey: Too Soon a Period Piece," *The School Review,* Vol. 67, No. 2, Summer 1959.
4. Belth, Marc: *Education as a Discipline.* Boston, Allyn & Bacon, 1965.
5. Berkson, I. B.: *Preface to an Educational Philosophy.* New York, Columbia University Press, 1940.
6. Bode, Boyd H.: *Conflicting Psychologies of Learning,* Boston, Heath, 1929.
7. Bode, Boyd H.: *Progressive Education at the Crossroads.* New York, Newson, 1938.
8. Bode, Boyd H.: *How We Learn.* Boston, Heath, 1940.
9. Brameld, Theodore: *Toward a Reconstructed Philosophy of Education.* New York, The Dryden Press, Inc., 1956.
10. Brameld, Theodore: "Imperatives for a Reconstructed Philosophy of Education," *School and Society,* Vol. 87, 18-20, (Jan. 17, 1959),
11. Brameld, Theodore: *Patterns of Educational Philosophy: A Democratic Interpretation.* New York, Harcourt, Brace & World, 1950.
12. Brameld, Theodore: *Philosophies of Education in Cultural Perspective.* New York, The Dryden Press, Inc., 1955.
13. Brubacher, John S.: *Modern Philosophies of Education.* Fourth edition. New York, McGraw-Hill, 1969.
14. Brubacher, John S. (ed.): *Eclectic Philosophy of Education.* Second edition. Englewood Cliffs, Prentice-Hall, 1962.
15. Brubacher, John S. *et al: The Public School and Spiritual Values.* New York, Harper & Row, 1944.
16. Burke, Roger K.: "Pragmatism in Physical Education," *Philosophies Fashion Physical Education,* E. C. Davis (ed.). Dubuque, Wm. C. Brown, 1963.
17. Burton, W. H.: *Introduction to Education.* New York, Appleton-Century-Crofts, 1934.

18. Butler, J. D.: *Four Philosophies*. Revised edition. New York, Harper & Row, 1957.
19. Callahan, Daniel: "Search for an Ethic: Living with the New Biology," *The Center Magazine*, Vol. 5, No. 4, 4-12, July/August, 1972.
20. Cassidy, Rosalind: *New Directions in Physical Education for the Adolescent Girl in High School and College*. New York, A. S. Barnes & Co., 1938.
21. Childs, John L.: *Education and the Philosophy of Experimentalism*. New York, Appleton-Century-Crofts, 1931.
22. Childs, John L.: *Education and Morals: An Experimentalist Philosophy of Education*. New York, Appleton-Century-Crofts, 1950.
23. Childs, John L.: "Boyd H. Bode and the Experimentalists," *Teachers College Record*, Vol. 55, No. 1, 1-9 (October, 1953).
24. Childs, John L.: *American Pragmatism and Education*. New York, Holt, Rinehart & Winston, 1956.
25. Clark, Margaret C.: "A Program of Physical Education in a State Teachers College." Unpublished Doctor's dissertation, New York University, 1943.
26. Cobb, Louise Staples: "A Study of the Functions of Physical Education in Higher Education." New York, Teachers College, Columbia University Press, 1943.
27. Cogley, John: "The Storm before the Calm," *The Center Magazine*, Vol. 5, No. 4, 2-3 (July/August, 1972).
28. Counts, George S.: *Education and the Promise of America*. New York, Macmillan, 1946.
29. Cowell, C. C. and France, W. L.: *Philosophy and Principles of Physical Education*. Englewood Cliffs, Prentice-Hall, 1963.
30. Curti, Merle: *The Social Ideas of American Education*. New York, Scribner, 1935.
31. Davis, E. C.: *The Philosophical Process in Physical Education*. Philadelphia: Lea & Febiger, 1961.
32. Davis, E. C. (ed.): *Philsophies Fashion Physical Education*. Dubuque, Wm. C. Brown, 1963.
33. Dewey, John: *Democracy and Education*. New York, Macmillan, 1916.
34. Dewey, John: *Reconstruction in Philosophy*. London, University of London Press, Ltd., 1921.
35. Dewey, John: *Human Nature and Conduct*. New York, Holt, Rinehart & Winston, 1922.
36. Dewey, John: *Experience and Nature*. Chicago, The Open Court Publishing Company, 1925.
37. Dewey, John: *The Quest for Certainty*. New York, Minton, Balch & Co., 1929.
38. Dewey, John: "From Absolutism to Experimentalism," *Contemporary American Philosophy, Vol. II*, G. P. Adams and W. P. Montague (eds.). New York, Macmillan, 1930.
39. Dewey, John: *How We Think*. Boston, Heath, 1933.

40. Dewey, John: *Art as Experience.* New York, Minton, Balch & Company, 1934.
41. Dewey, John: *A Common Faith.* New Haven, Yale University Press, 1934.
42. Dewey, John: *Experience and Education.* New York, Macmillan, 1938.
43. Dewey, John: *Logic, The Theory of Inquiry.* New York, Holt, Rinehart & Winston, 1938.
44. Dewey, John: *Intelligence in the Modern World.* New York, Modern Library, Inc., 1939.
45. Dewey, John: *Education Today.* New York, Putnam, 1940.
46. Dewey, John: *Problems of Men.* New York, Philosophical Library, Inc., 1946.
47. Dewey, John and Tufts, James H. (eds.): *Ethics.* New York, Holt, Rinehart & Winston, 1908.
48. Dewey, John, *et al*: *Creative Intelligence.* New York, Holt, Rinehart & Winston, 1917.
49. Downey, Robert J.: "An Identification of the Philosophical Beliefs of Educators in the Field of Health Education." Unpublished Doctor's dissertation, University of Southern California, 1956.
50. Edman, Irwin. *John Dewey: His Contribution to the American Tradition.* Indianapolis, Bobbs, 1955.
51. *Encyclopedia of Philosophy, The.* New York, Macmillan and The Free Press, 1967.
52. Esslinger, A. A.: "A Philosophical Study of Principles for Selecting Activities in Physical Education." Unpublished Doctor's dissertation, State University of Iowa, 1938.
53. Feibleman, James: *An Introduction to Peirce's Philosophy.* New York, Harper & Row, 1946.
54. Frederick, Mary Margaret: "Naturalism: The Philosophy of Jean Jacques Rousseau and Its Implications for American Physical Education." Unpublished Doctor's dissertation, Springfield College, 1961.
55. Geiger, George R.: "An Experimentalist Approach to Education," *Modern Philosophies and Education,* N. B. Henry (ed.), Chicago: University of Chicago Press, 1955.
56. Groos, Karl: *The Play of Animals.* New York, Appleton-Century-Crofts, Inc., 1898.
57. Groos, Karl: *The Play of Man.* New York, Appleton-Cent., 1901.
58. Hansen, Kenneth H.: *Philosophy for American Education.* Englewood Cliffs, Prentice-Hall, 1960.
59. Henry, N. B. (ed.): *Philosophy of Education, Forty-first Yearbook of the National Society for the Study of Education.* Chicago, University of Chicago Press, 1942.
60. Henry, N. B. (ed.): *Modern Philosophies and Education, Fifty-fourth Yearbook of the National Society for the Study of Education.* Chicago, University of Chicago Press, 1955.
61. Hess Ford A.: "American Objectives of Physical Education from 1900-

1957 Assessed in the Light of Certain Historical Events." Unpublished Doctor's dissertation, New York University, 1959.

62. Hetherington, Clark: *School Programs in Physical Education.* New York, Harcourt, Brace & World, 1922.
63. Hobbes, Thomas: *The English Works of Thomas Hobbes.* Sir Wm. Molesworth (ed.). London, John Bohn, 1889.
64. Hook, Sidney: *The Metaphysics of Pragmatism.* Chicago, The Open Court Publishing Company, 1927.
65. Hook, Sidney: *Education for Modern Man.* New York, The Dial Press, 1946.
66. Horne, Herman Harrell: *The Democratic Philosophy of Education.* New York, Macmillan, 1932.
67. Huxley, Thomas Henry: *Science and Education.* New York, Appleton-Century-Crofts, 1896.
68. James, William: *Pragmatism.* New York, McKay, 1907.
69. James, William: *A Pluralistic Universe.* New York, McKay, 1909.
70. James, William: *Essays in Radical Empiricism.* New York, McKay, 1912.
71. James, William: *The Will to Believe.* New York, McKay, 1912.
72. James, William: *Talks to Teachers.* New York, Holt, Rinehart & Winston, 1946.
73. James, William: *The Philosophy of William James Drawn from His Own Works.* New York, Modern Library, Inc.
74. Johnson, Glen: *Some Ethical Implications of a Naturalistic Philosophy of Education.* New York, Bureau of Publications, Teachers College, Columbia University, 1947.
75. Johnson, Harry M.: "The Relevance of the Theory of Action to Historians," *Social Science Quarterly,* 46-58 (June, 1969).
76. Kaplan, Abraham: *The New World of Philosophy.* New York, Random House, 1961.
77. Keating, James: "The Function of the Philosopher in American Pragmatism." Unpublished Doctor's dissertation, Catholic University of America, 1953.
78. Keenan, Francis W.: "A Delineation of Deweyan Progressivism for Physical Education." Unpublished Doctor's dissertation, University of Illinois, 1971.
79. Kilpatrick, William H.: *Education for a Changing Civilization.* New York, Appleton-Century-Crofts, 1926.
80. Kilpatrick, William H.: *Philosophy of Education.* New York, Macmillan, 1951.
81. Kilpatrick, William H.: *The Educational Frontier.* New York, Appleton-Century-Crofts, 1933.
82. Kozman, H. C. (ed.). *Democratic Human Relations, First Yearbook of the American Association for Health, Physical Education, and Recreation.* Washington, D. C., AAHPER, 1951.

83. Krikorian, Yervant H.: (ed.). *Naturalism and the Human Spirit.* New York, Columbia University Press, 1944.

84. Lange, Frederick A.: *History of Materialism.* E. C. Thomas (trans.). Boston, Osgood, 1877.

85. Larkin, Richard A.: "The Influence of John Dewey on Physical Education." Unpublished Master's thesis, The Ohio State University, 1936.

86. Lucretius: *Of the Nature of Things.* W. E. Leonard (trans.). London, J. M. Dent & Sons Ltd., 1921.

87. Lynn, M. L.: "Major Emphases in Physical Education." Unpublished Doctor's dissertation, The University of Pittsburgh, 1944.

88. Maccia, George S.: "The Educational Aims of Charles Peirce," *Educational Theory,* Vol. 4, No. 3, 206-212 (July, 1954).

89. Mayhew, K. C. and Edwards, A. C.: *The Dewey School.* New York, Appleton-Century-Crofts, 1936.

90. McClellan, James E.: "In Reply to Professor Soltis," *Philosophy of Education 1971: Proceedings of the 27th Annual Meeting of the Philosophy of Education Society,* 55-59 (Dallas, April 4-7, 1971).

91. McCloy, C. H.: "Physical Education as Part of General Education," *Journal of Health and Physical Education,* 45 (November, 1928).

92. McCloy, C. H.: *Philosophical Bases for Physical Education.* New York, Appleton-Century-Crofts, 1940.

93. McCloy, C. H.: "A Half Century of Physical Education," *The Physical Educator,* Vol. 17, No. 3, 83-91 (October, 1960).

94. McMurray, Foster: "The Present Status of Pragmatism in Education," *School and Society,* Vol. 87, 14-17 (Jan. 17, 1959).

95. McMurrin, Sterling M.: "What About the Philosophy of Education?" *Journal of Philosophy,* Vol. 59, No. 22, 629-637 (October, 1962).

96. Mills, C. Wright: *Sociology and Pragmatism.* New York, Oxford University Press, 1966.

97. Morland, Richard B.: "A Philosophical Interpretation of the Educational Views Held by Leaders in American Physical Education." Unpublished Doctor's dissertation, New York University, 1958.

98. Mosier, Richard D.: "School and Society in Experimentalism," *School and Society,* Vol. 89, 106-109 (March 11, 1961).

99. Nash, Paul: "The Strange Death of Progressive Education," *Educational Theory,* Vol. 14, No. 2, 65-75 (April, 1964).

100. Nowell-Smith, P. H.: *Ethics.* Harmondsworth, England, 1954.

101. Patrick, George: "Verifiability of Physical Education Objectives." Unpublished Doctor's dissertation, University of Illinois, 1971.

102. Platt, John: "What's Ahead for 1990," *The Center Magazine,* Vol. 5, No. 4, 21-28 (July/August, 1972).

103 Ratner, Joseph. *The Philosophy of John Dewey.* New York, Holt, Rinehart & Winston, 1929.

104. Raup, R. Bruce, *et al: The Improvement of Practical Intelligence: The Central Task of Education.* New York, Harper & Row, 1950.

105. Rousseau, Jean Jacques: *Émile*. London, J. M. Dent & Sons, 1943.
106. Rousseau, Jean Jacques: "Social Contract," *Social Contract: Essays by Locke, Hume, and Rousseau,* Sir Earnest Barker (ed.). New York, Oxford University Press, Inc., 1948.
107. Rucker, Darnell: "Dewey's Ethics (Part Two)," *Guide to the Works of John Dewey,* Jo Ann Boydston (ed.). Carbondale and Edwardsville: Southern Illinois University Press, 1970.
108. Sayers, E. V. and Madden, W.: *Education and the Democratic Faith.* New York, Appleton-Century-Crofts, 1959.
109. Schilpp, P. A.: *The Philosophy of John Dewey.* Evanston and Chicago, Northwestern University Press, 1939.
110. Shepard, Natalie M.: "Democracy in Physical Education: A Study of the Implications for Educating for Democracy Through Physical Education." Unpublished Doctor's dissertation, New York University, 1952.
111. Shivers, Jay S.: "An Analysis of Theories of Recreation." Unpublished Doctor's dissertation, The University of Wisconsin, 1958.
112. Sidgwick, Henry: *Outlines of the History of Ethics.* London, 1886.
113. Smith, B. Othaniel: "Views on the Role of Philosophy in Teacher Education," *Journal of Philosophy,* Vol. 59, No. 22, 638-647 (October, 1962).
114. Spears, Betty M.: "Philosophical Bases for Physical Education Experiences Consistent with the Goals of General Education for College Women." Unpublished Doctor's dissertation, New York University, 1956.
115. Spencer, Herbert: *Education: Intellectual, Moral and Physical.* London: C. A. Watts & Co. Ltd., 1949.
116. Tenenbaum, S.: *William Heard Kilpatrick.* New York, Harper & Row, 1951.
117. Van Dalen, D. B.: "Philosophical Profiles for Physical Education," *The Physical Educator,* Vol. 21, No. 3 (October, 1964).
118. Wegener, Frank C.: "The Philosophical Beliefs of Leaders in American Education." Unpublished Doctor's dissertation, University of Southern California, 1946.
119. White, Morton G.: *The Origin of Dewey's Instrumentalism.* New York, Columbia University Press, 1943.
120. Williams, J. F.: *The Principles of Physical Education.* Seventh edition. Philadelphia, Saunders, 1959.
121. Wood, T. D. and Cassidy, Rosalind: *The New Physical Education.* New York, Macmillan, 1927.
122. Wynne, John P.: *Philosophies of Education.* Englewood Cliffs, Prentice-Hall, 1947.
123. Zeigler, Earle F.: "Naturalism in Physical, Health, and Recreation Education," *The University of Michigan School of Education Bulletin,* Vol. 34, No. 2, 42-46 (December, 1962).
124. Zeigler, Earle F.: "The Implications of Experimentalism for Physical, Health, and Recreation Education." Essay presented at the American

Association for Health, Physical Education, and Recreation Convention, May 3, 1963.

125. Zeigler, Earle F.: *Philosophy of Physical, Health, and Recreation Education.* Englewood Cliffs, Prentice-Hall, 1964.

126. Zeigler, Earle F.: *Problems in the History and Philosophy of Physical Education and Sport.* Englewood Cliffs, Prentice-Hall, 1968.

127. Zeigler, Earle F. and VanderZwaag, H. J.: *Physical Education: Progressivism or Essentialism?* Revised edition. Champaign, Stipes, 1968.

THE FICTION OF MORALLY INDIFFERENT ACTS IN SPORT

TERENCE J. ROBERTS AND P. J. GALASSO

Stanley B. Cunningham has recently written the paper "The Language of Morally Neutral Acts" (1) which is the foundation of the concepts contained in this paper. The purpose of Cunningham's essay is to illustrate that quite possibly all acts or actions performed consciously and voluntarily by men are "inescapably" (1:p.3) moral. It is the present paper's intent to reaffirm and to make more clear that this concept is true in the area of sport. Indeed, it can be argued that because Cunningham's treatment is universal (dealing with all acts) that it necessarily includes sport. Such a claim is conceded, but the purpose here is to show further that acts occurring in sport can be elucidated more positively and with more force than actions in general.

Cunningham's attack on the popular "neutrality thesis" (1:p.1), which is implicitly included in many ethical theories, must be centered on those who make outright attempts to defend it, namely: Mabbott (4), D'Arcy (2), Singer (7), and Mayo (5). These authors contend that there is a segment of man's conscious activity which is morally neutral. We are made aware of weaknesses in this theory by Cunningham's thesis. But his attack is necessarily a negative type argumentation and in his paper we must be satisfied with the tentative universal statement that: ". . . the following analysis leaves open the possibility of viewing all conscious voluntary activity as being in varying degrees inescapably moral." (1:p.3).

Because Cunningham's argument is being specifically applied and continued in the field of sport we could be criticized for presenting a duplication that does not benefit either philosophy or physical education. Hopefully it will become more apparent that the following analysis does not follow along the same negative lines as Cunningham's. Due to the nature of sport it can be more forcefully claimed that every action occurring in its participation is not only *possibly* in the moral sphere, but *necessarily* so.

To avoid confusion, as does Cunningham, the term "moral" (moral sphere, moral realm, morally relevant)is being used to refer to that whole segment of acts/actions that we are able to describe in such terms as "right" or "wrong" and "good" or "bad". As such, the term's proper opposite is "non-moral" or "amoral", rather than "immoral", a term which is usually used to describe only one of the two types of actions contained in the moral sphere. The term "immoral" (and its proper opposite) is being eliminated from the discussion, and instead we shall use the terms "morally wrong" (opposite is morally right) and "morally bad" (opposite is morally good).

The term "sport" for the ensuing discussion, has a very broad meaning. It represents play, games, sport, athletics and professional competition. It may be criticized that the term is being used very loosely, and not according to the legislative defining techniques of some of our colleagues. But purely for the sake of convenience, the term shall represent all those activities with the exceptions of sports of a gaming nature, board games and child's play.

An understanding of the use of the word "action" (act) as it is used in the paper is vital to the conclusions. Quite commonly, as Cunningham uses it, it represents ". . . any activity or performance which is both voluntary and attended by conscious deliberation." (1:p.1). Although this definitioin is likely adequate, to facilitate understanding it is desirable to elaborate further by illustrating some of the implications derived from the definition.

To use the criteria of "voluntary" and "conscious deliberation" is to be able to ascribe actions to individuals. It implies responsibility because it implies intention, rationality, and reason giving. John Wilson in *Introduction to Moral Education* explains that,

    . . . if an action is to fall within the moral sphere, . . . it must be rational:

and this implies that it must be done for a reason (not just as a result of a cause). But this means more than that the agent must in principle be able to say why he did it. It means that the reason must also be causally operative: it must not be a rationalization. (8:p.51).

Here Wilson implies that there are actions based on reason and actions that are non-rational. It is somewhat questionable, however, whether we can call unconscious movements actions. It is the present position that an action in sport falls within the moral sphere precisely because it is rational, by definition. And if it is rational, then it means that one is performing that action for a reason, reasons, or to satisfy an end, goal or desire. If one is acting, or performing an action he is either rational, or irrational, but never non-rational. Thus, actions imply responsibility.

A. I. Meldon in "Action" (6) distinguishes between actions and mere bodily movements. He contrasts the activity of an infant (who does not know the rules of chess) and of a chess player, who perform the identical movement of changing the position of the knight in the accepted manner. The child's movement is not considered to be an action, but rather a mere bodily movement, because the infant was unaware of the rules of chess. Obviously the player's movement is considered to be an action because it was made from a rational or irrational conception of the rules. The non-chess player's movement is not an action only in the context of the chess game however, for he could perform the same movement with very good reasons such as simply to move it out of his way. Again, because it was performed with reason, we call it an action.

It appears then that action cannot be discussed without a consideration of its context. That is, in what situation did it occur, and what was taking place in the agent's mind when the action took place. In reference to descriptions of actions in only physiological, kinesiological, or biochemical terminology, Meldon states that: "The underlying mistake is that what occurs when an action is performed can be understood independently of its context . . ." (6:p.93).

We are concerned, in the area of sport, with those activities that are voluntary and consciously attended to—that is, those that are rational (as opposed to non-rational), done for a reason, and for which the agent is responsible (in this restricted sense). At first glance, one may think that this statement encloses virtually all activity which takes place in sport, but, with further observation however, one comes to the realization that this is not so. A description of an offensive drive block from the line of scrimmage will illustrate the misconception. The only activity which can be called an action, when such a block is performed by a moderately skilled individual, is the total block. The conscious attention paid by the individual is directed toward such thoughts as: "Where shall I make contact?"; "Shall I hit high or low?"; and "Should I move him left or right?" These are thoughts concerning the whole action.

The moderately skilled individual does not consciously attend to all the sub-activities, such as moving the left leg first, pumping the knees, bulling the neck, and rotating the arms upward and forward. These make up the total action, but, because they are not consciously and individually attended to, they are not actions, but merely bodily movements. They can *only* be described in physiological- or neurological-type language, but, to describe the *total* action in only these terms however, would be to take the action out of its context of being consciously deliberated on.

These same sub-actions of pumping the knees, bulling the neck, and so on, become actions in a lesser skilled football player. The young player first learning the drive block is very aware of all the minor movements which make up the whole. He tries to follow exactly the coach's intricate descriptions of a well performed block. Here there is conscious attention, and therefore action.

It has been stated that all actions in sport by definition are based on a reason or reasons. The next question that needs considering here is: "Is there very much of this conscious-type action, or are we speaking of a relatively small segment of sport activity?" One is led to believe in the prevalence of conscious attention and deliberation because for a vast number of movements or activities in sport we can rationally answer the question: "For what reason (s) did you do that?" If we are unable to (as opposed to not wishing to) answer such a question about a particular action then either we were not conscious of it, or it was not voluntary.

Why, even the whole general involvement of oneself in sport is always done for a reason or a combination of several reasons. Some such reasons are: a desire to become more fit, to enjoy oneself, to develop one's potential, to prolong one's life and many many more. It seems incredible that an individual would perform in sport for absolutely no reason. There must be one of some sort or other.

Another indication of the presence of much conscious deliberation in sport is that much of our activity can be traced back to the desire to achieve and fulfill these initial predisposing reasons for participation. A possible objection here is that often a person's actions appear to be completely unrelated to his supposed reasons. But what the objection should be is that quite often we are unable to know whether the reasons that one tells us he has for participation are the real ones. Because of this discrepancy there often appears to be differences between the action and the supposed reason, but quite likely the actions in question are truly representative of the real reasons for which one performs.

The next step in the paper is the most crucial in the argument and the most difficult to illustrate properly. It is that every reason or motive for involvement in sport has moral significance and that every action in sport (that is consciously deliberated upon) is either morally right, or it is morally wrong—it is never morally neutral. It must not be assumed here that we are saying that we can show how particular actions are either morally right or morally wrong. Instead of saying which they are, we are merely saying they are in the moral sphere. The paper is not concerned with or limited to the rightness or wrongness of particular actions.

Some will object here and state that this maneuver has broadened the moral realm so that it includes many actions in sport that are purely prudential, merely personal or simply trivial. But, when we examine a "moral" action what do we find? It seems that it usually concerns an activity which we feel we *should* or *ought to* do. It has a certain compelling or binding effect upon us. When we investigate to see why this is so we arrive at the conclusion that the reasons for doing such an action seem to be convincing ones. We perform such "moral" actions because the reasons behind them have led us to believe that we *should* perform such actions.

W. D. Falk, in his article "Morality, Self, and Others," comes to the conclusion that the discussion of the proper use of the term "moral" is merely semantic and academic. His is a reaction against those who state that purely personal or prudential oughts are not moral because they do not involve others. He states:

> Your view comes to saying that if an ought is to be moral it must satisfy two conditions: it must seriously bind one in every way, and it must do so for other-regarding reasons. On your showing, a personal ought cannot be moral, as it cannot satisfy one of these conditions simply by having personal grounds. But it still may satisfy the other condition, and be as cogently binding and action-guiding in its force and function as a moral ought. (3:pp.25-67).

To become more fit, although often considered merely personal and thus non-moral, is a common enough goal among sport enthusiasts. However, there is a certain compellingness attached to such a reason. Individuals with such an aim probably realize that physical fitness leads to a more healthy life and greater effectiveness in their occupation. These can conceivably be personal oughts if the agent has no one depending on him, but yet they still do have a "nagging" effect on one. Falk, discussing one who is concerned for his health, future or self-respect states that,

> Surely these are respectable aspirations and there may be things he ought to do on account of them without violating other claims. His health requires that he be temperate, his self-respect that he live without evasion. Would it not then be positively remiss of him not to act in these ways? If he did not one would say that he had failed to do what a man in his position really ought to have done. . . (3:p.30).

An interesting example arose in a recent discussion concerning the choice of ends just prior to the commencement of a football game. The captain, after winning the toss of the coin, takes into consideration the wind, the sunlight and the field conditions, etc. He decides that because of all these circumstances that end A is better and chooses for the advantage of his team. Is this a moral action? It is voluntary and consciously deliberated on. He chooses that particular end for reasons which he has taken into account and been influenced by. We think this choice offers itself as a good example because it illustrates three different types of choice. It is one that is correct (or incorrect), that one wants to make, and that is moral as well. Why is it moral? Not only does the individual usually naturally want to do what would be best for the team by choosing end A, but he should make that choice. It is his duty to try to choose the end that is going to be more advantageous to his team. If he consciously endeavors to fulfill this duty, then he has performed a moral action. Suppose the captain took all these circumstances into account, realized that end A was more beneficial to the team, and then, in spite of all these, for some reason or other, chose end B? This example points out that quite often in sport the moral thing to do coincides with what we wish to do and even what we should do for our own best interests. But, this does not make it any less morally relevant.

Another line of argumentation, pointed out by Cunningham, concerns the misleading abstract terms "society" and "individual". Neither of the words seem to represent any thing . . . actually real. Although the terms are definitely useful, if we try to find the thing called society we fail, and yet there is no such thing as a competely isolated individual either. The point being made is that actions can never help but be partly social or other-affecting in some degree. This seems especially true in sport where generally our actions determine other's successes and failures to a great degree. We agree that this is true in the main for team and competitive sports, but to some degree a case can be made for all sport. Perhaps this line of attack is weak in the respect that some examples may be presented that are hardly other-affecting, but we think overall, it adds strength to the paper's major contention.

It is true that many actions in sport appear hardly important enough to deserve the title of "morally relevant". But, the point is that they are morally trivial, not too trivial to be moral. An example of a trivial action could be that which occurs when baseball players come to bat and consciously dig a little hole beside the plate with their lead foot. Is this within the moral sphere? They could perform this action to get a firmer stance, to upset the pitcher's rhythm or simply to relax themselves. These three reasons are directed toward the end of satisfying a goal of the player and the team and have moral significance because of it. They could also perform such an action to cover up the edge of the plate or to kick dirt in the catcher's direction. Again, such actions may appear too trivial on the surface level, but when we delve into the consciousness behind them they do appear to be morally significant.

It is our contention that all actions in sport are morally relevant.

Some people still ask "Well how can you say that—just because you have presented us with a few examples does not mean you can make that universal statement does it? Our first reaction is to state that we can make that statement simply because we have not yet come across an example that cannot be placed within the moral sphere. One that seems to come very close to being neutral is the example of the mountain climber being asked: "Why did you climb the mountain?" The offhand reply was "Because it was there." Now that reason certainly seems to present itself as non-moral all right, but, we still do not think that the action of climbing the mountain was. According to Wilson, the just-mentioned reason would appear to be a rationalization, instead of a causally operative reason. (3:p.32). Suppose we had asked him instead, "Did you want to reach the top?" or "Did you try very hard to reach the top?" We think it can now be seen that the orginal question and reply did not represent the situation correctly. Surely now that action can be seen to be morally relevant as well.

For the sake of discussion try to conceive of a morally indifferent end or reason for action that an individual could have. Do not think of a particular, actual end because it would be too difficult, but just reflect for a moment on the concept of an individual having a wish or desire from sport that is neither, one way nor the other, morally right or morally wrong. He goes about his way through participation to acquire such an end, and finally with effort, he achieves it. But do we not describe individuals who work towards ends without giving up, with such adjectives as "diligent" and "assiduous". Sport is filled with this conscious subjugation of the self to an end. Thus even if there is such a thing as a morally indifferent reason (which we highly doubt) its diligent pursuance and its resultant action (which is our major concern) is still not exempt from the moral category.

The significance of all this, again due to Cunningham, is that it makes us more aware of the great breadth of the moral sphere. It leads us to realize that sport is full of morally relevant activity which we all come into contact with in some degree whenever we participate. It may lead some to become more morally aware of their actions or at least to reflect on their activity in such a manner. Perhaps there can even be an implication for moral education which is thought to occur from the mild stress of making numerous moral decisions. If sport is full of these moral situations, then an aware coach or teacher perhaps can make his students come under the pressure of this mild stress.

Voluntary, conscious and responsible activity seems to be prevalent in sport participation. Because sport is so goal—or end—orientated, it is characterized by actions which are performed from one's conception of reasons. This ability to give reasons for one's actions means that one has been influenced or convinced to perform such actions. To some degree one feels as though one *should* or *ought* to perform such actions. Since "should" and "ought" talk is vital to "moral" talk, we think the next progressive step to the statement that all actions in sport are morally relevant, is quite a natural one.

REFERENCES

1. Cunningham, S.B.: "The Language of Morally Neutral Acts." Essay presented at The Canadian Philosophical Association Meeting, Montreal, 1972.
2. D'Arcy, Eric: *Human Acts.* London, Oxford University Press, 1963.
3. Falk, W.D.: "Morality, Self, and Others," *Morality and the Language of Conduct,* Hector-Neri Castaneda and George Nakhnakian (eds.). Detroit, Wayne State University Press, 1970.
4. Mabbott, J.D.: *An Introduction to Ethics.* London, Hutchinson University Library, 1963.
5. Mayo, B.: *Ethics and the Moral Life.* London, Macmillan, 1958.
6. Meldon, A.I.: "Action," *The Philosophical Review,* Vol. 65, 529-541, 1956.
7. Singer, M.G.: *Generalization in Ethics.* New York, Knopf, 1961.
8. Wilson, John; Williams, Norman and Sugarman, Berry: *Introduction to Moral Education.* Baltimore, Penguin, 1967.

THE KANTIAN ETHIC AS A PRINCIPLE OF MORAL CONDUCT IN SPORT AND ATHLETICS

ROBERT G. OSTERHOUDT

INTRODUCTION

It is the intent of the present inquiry to develop a discussion of Kant's categorical imperative as an appropriate principle of moral conduct in sport and athletics. The atttractions of the Kantian ethic to sport and athletics will not be established via an explicit comparison of it with alternative views (e.g., voluntarism, hedonism, personalism, or evolutionism), however.   That is, there will be no attempt to suggest the advisability of its adoption relative to the advisability of adopting others—no attempt to suggest its adequacies and inadequacies as over and above those of other such principles.   Though this comparison is itself a worthy consideration and may be tacitly achieved here (that is, its mere presence indicates its being regarded as the doctrine by which our moral judgments are best and most sensitively rendered and understood), the preference is rather to concentrate upon an interpretation of the ethic; such that, its relevance to moral conduct in sport and athletics becomes at once evident and revealing of an ethical posture proper to men qua sportsmen and athletes. Prior to such a treatment, however, it will be necessary to develop a brief discussion of the general character of Kant's ethical formalism.

THE FUNDAMENTAL NATURE OF KANTIAN ETHICS

Given the identified purposes of this essay, it will not be feasible to attempt a full blown account of the metaphysical and axiologic postulates (first principles, basic assumptions, basal axioms), or their intricate consequences, upon which Kant's supreme principle of morality has been constructed.   Though crucial to a satisfactory understanding of the categorical imperative itself, as well as the issues directly at hand, such considerations as the three propositions of morality; the good will as the singular unconditional, indefeasible good; the principle of the autonomy (freedom) of the will (a notion which serves as the foundation of the Kantian morality in terms of its providing a singular universal, necessary, unconditional, a priori imperative, which guides moral conduct: the categorical imperative), as contrasted with that of the heteronomy of the will (a notion regarded by Kant as the source of all particular, contingent, empirical, conditional, a posteriori, and thereby spurious principles of morality: all hypothetical imperatives); man's membership in a variant world of sense determined by natural law, and in an invariant world of understanding by which laws of reason are self-appropriated (man is then at once a sensuous and a rational being); and the relationship of the moral imperative to ordinary conceptions of morality and to practical moral principles (or maxims) which guide specific actions, exceed the scope of the present effort. A cursory overview of Kant's position may prove helpful, nevertheless.

In his *Foundations of the Metaphysics of Morals* and *Critique of Practical Reason,* Kant views morality as conduct guided by reason, a reason unsullied by empirical fiat, example, or imitation. He regards pure reason, or non-emipirical activity of the mind, as the ultimate arbiter of moral concerns:

> Thus not only are moral laws together with their principles essentially different from all practical knowledge in which there is anything empirical, but all moral philosophy rests solely on its pure part. (1:p.5).

For Kant, ethics proper may not, therefore, describe the manner in which men actually conduct themselves, but prescribe the manner in which they ought to act. The formulation of a metaphysics of morals is consequently prior to a popular assent to it.

According to Kant, all imperatives are expressed by an 'ought'; that is, they command either conditionally, contingently (those being hypothetical) or unconditionally, necessarily (those being categorical). The categorical imperative functions as a universal principle to which we refer as governing our action, as a principle of ideal moral judgment and conduct, a principle by which we live a moral life. Demonstration of the possibility of the categorical imperative is neither possible itself, nor is it necessary for its (that of the moral imperative) establishment. It is not, strictly speaking, a proof Kant offers in this regard, but simply an observation as to that which the moral imperative presupposes; namely, a freedom which is not further accessible to reason:

> Thus categorical imperatives are possible because the idea of freedom makes me a member of an intelligible world. Consequently, if I were a member of only that world, all my actions would always be in accordance with the autonomy of the will. But since I intuit myself at the same time as a member of the world of sense, my actions ought to conform to it . . . (1:p.73).

We, thereby, apprehend moral principles as constraining, even though self-addressed by reason; constraining given our sentient passion to do other than that which reason exhorts us.

FORMULATIONS OF THE CATEGORICAL IMPERATIVE

We will begin, then, with the categorical imperative; that is, take it as given, and thereby it, and much that went to establish it, as unproblematic; preferring to direct our attentions instead to a consideration of its applicability to moral conduct in sport and athletics.

Although Kant suggested there to be but one categorical imperative, several formulations of it were developed so that it might be applied more easily. He speaks specifically of three such formulations. The first and primary form indicates most directly the criterion for establishing moral relevance:

> Act only according to that maxim by which you can at the same time will that it should become a universal law. (1:p.39).

The second formulation is very much like the first:

> Act as though the maxim of your action were by your will to become a universal law of nature. (1:p.39).

And the third formulation reveals the supreme limiting conditions of the freedom of each man to act as he will:

> Act so that you treat humanity, whether in your own person or in that of another, always as an end and never as a means only. (1:p.47).

It commands that we respect each man as a free moral agent, and not as a mere object bound to, and thereby exploited by, our own desires or inclinations. Such a respect entails ". . . the idea of the will of every rational being as making universal law." (1:p.49). Kant here proposes, then, a union of all rational beings through a realm of common law, or a 'realm of ends' in which the ends of all become the ends of all others: the individual and common goods coalesce.

The adoption of a single such universal principle, as opposed to several of a particular character, allows us to apply that principle without need of yet another (as well as the criteria for choosing it) to indicate which principle ought appropriately be applied in whatever circumstance. In such a case, we have before us not a categorical imperative, but one of a hypothetical disposition; that is, one, or several, which waits upon conditions. A commentator on Schelling's *System of Transcendental Idealism* has noted well the necessity of such a single principle, as the categorical imperative:

> . . . if we are to proceed by such a necessary method, we must start with a single principle, since otherwise we should have two or more disconnected systems; and this principle must be one higher than which we cannot go, since from it all others are to be derived. (9:pp.105-106).

The rightful singularity of the categorical imperative as a moral principle entails it accounting for all conditions, all circumstances; that is, entails its necessity and universality. We must either, then, have such a rigorous, absolutistic guide to our moral conduct, or no normative guide whatever. In the case of all hypothetical imperatives we have need of a moral principle which dictates the circumstances in which different (relative) moral principles are appropriate; that is, we have need of a moral principle either very much like the categorical imperative or greater than the supreme principle of morality, in which case we have either what we have argued all along that we must have, or a logical impossibility which we can never have. In the case of hypothetical imperatives we have as many imperatives as variegated circumstances; such that, the imperatives themselves are ad hoc, and thereby not actually principles at all; that is, they are entirely uninstructive in terms of providing us with a guide to our moral conduct.

The formulations of the categorical imperative come, in large measure, it would appear, to specific philosophic restatements of what Runes has come to regard as: "Perhaps the oldest ethical proposition of distinctly universal character." (6:p.VII); that is, the Golden Rule: "Whatsoever ye would that men should do to you, do ye even so to them. —Jesus of Nazareth." (6:p.VII). The Rule itself appears very much like: each of us acting such that the principle of our action become universal law; that is, treating men always as an end and never as a means only. Being members of the culture that we are, we need perhaps be reminded that, this proposition is not the exclusive possession of Christian dogma, but is an important feature of many of the other major religious faiths of both East and West (e.g., Buddhism, Classical Paganism, Confucianism, Hinduism, Jainism, Judaism, Sikhism, Zoroastrianism) as well. As a bit of an aside, then, we might observe that it (the Golden Rule, and what we have regarded as a philosophic restatement of it) is not merely universalizable, but has achieved in some very important respect, a glimpse of universal acceptance.

THE BASIC CHARACTER OF SPORT AND ATHLETICS

James W. Keating has proposed a distinction between sport and athletics, which serves to explain the diverse orders of intent associated with involvement in such activities and the conduct appropriate to each:

. . . historically and etymologically, sport and athletics have characterized radically different types of human activity, different not insofar as
the game itself or the mechanics or rules are concerned, but different
with regard to the attitude, preparation, and purpose of the participants.
. . . In essence, sport is a kind of diversion which has for its direct and
immediate end fun, pleasure, and delight and which is dominated by a
spirit of moderation and generosity. Athletics, on the other hand, is
essentially a competitive activity, which has for its end victory in the
contest and which is characterized by a spirit of dedication, sacrifice,
and intensity. (3:p.28).

The present inquiry proposes that we may allow, even encourage, the
appropriate ontological distinction suggested by Keating, while at the
same moment bringing the general conduct appropriate to both sport
and athletics under a singular principle.

THE CATEGORICAL IMPERATIVE AS A PRINCIPLE OF MORAL CONDUCT IN SPORT AND ATHLETICS

Kant's claim as to the universalizability of his moral imperative
commits our interpretation of his view to the thesis that this imperative
is not only applicable to moral judgments in such seemingly disparate
forms of human movement activity as sport and athletics, as well as
more primitive forms of such activity, namely, play, exercise, and
recreation; but to such orders of judgment in all of life. With respect to the supreme principle of morality, then, there are no moral
encounters to which it does not rightfully apply. According to our
interpretation of Kant, its application to moral concerns in sport,
athletics, and the like presupposes its proper application to the whole
of our moral confrontations. Our adopting it as appropriate to our
lives in their most general constitutions necessarily commits us to its
adoption with respect to our involvement in sport and athletics. We
have allegedly before us, then, a single, universal moral principle to
which we might appeal in seeking a guide to moral judgment in sport
and athletics.

Such a principle requires that once having freely entered the sport-
athletic condition, a stringent adherence to the rules and regulations
(laws) of that condition be sought. And presupposed by a free
entry into such a condition is a regard for its laws as self-regulated.
These laws serve, in most important measure, to define the condition
(e.g., of soccer, track and field athletics, gymnastics, etc.) in question,
and to insure an equal opportunity for the success of all those partici-

pating in that condition. The categorical imperative, in its multiple formulations, dictates that we abide by these laws for their own sake (for the sole sake of duty to them) and that we treat our fellow competitors with a sensitivity we ourselves would prefer; that is, treat them as an end and not as a mere means to the gratification of our own desires and inclinations. Since we have willed that our acts are proper for all who locate themselves in these circumstances, to do otherwise is to destroy the condition into which we have freely entered, to destroy sport-athletics, to destroy the laws we ourselves have legislated, to destroy our unique participation in the world of understanding (of pure reason), to deny an essential aspect of our being. For all to willfully disobey the law is to destroy the integrity of the condition in question; such that, we are no longer engaged in wrestling, let us say, but in brawling, or the like. Such conduct is likewise destructive of the humanistic spirit of sport-athletics, of the general humanistic dispositions of sportsmen and athletes. The relations among competitors becomes one of an antagonistic, military order, one without sympathy and mutual concern for the public interest, as in Metheny's characterization of 'the bad strife:'

> Thus, in 'the good strife' men treat each other as partners in a common enterprise; in 'the bad strife' they treat each other as animals or things.
> The concept of 'the good strife' is implicit in the word competition, as derived from cum and petere—literally, to strive with rather than against. The word contest has similar implications, being derived from con and testare—to testify with another rather than against him. The concept of 'the bad strife' is implicit in the idea of 'beating the opponent' as distinguished from 'winning the contest.' (4:pp:41-42).

In 'the bad strife' as contrasted with 'the good strife' an exclusive order of egoism prevails at the expense of the common good—an egoism which is potentially destructive of all of humanity (the community of spirits, realm of ends of which Kant speaks), let alone sport and athletics. We could not, then, according to our interpretation of Kant's moral imperative, opt for the disregard, or even instrumental treatment, of law in sport and athletics, or for the unsympathetic, hostile treatment of our fellow competitors so as to exploit them in effect; for to do so is to will that such conduct become universally legislated, in which case sport-athletics, and man himself for that matter, become sterile instruments of something we know not what. That is they become what they are not. A clear view of their distinguishing features (those which make them what they are: themselves proper) is obscured in deference to an indulgence in the manner in which they might be used to produce ends beyond themselves. According to our interpretation of Kant, the anticipation of such conduct in sport and athletics would not allow us to freely and thereby rightfully enter their conditions; for we would enter with the intent of overturning the integrity of those conditions—we would enter with a motive of deceit, a motive destructive of the self-legislated law.

In terms of specific indications of moral conduct in life generally and in sport-athletics more specifically, all of this is not to suggest that, because it is appropriate that some of us in some circumstances do something, that all of us in all circumstances do the very same thing; to wit, it is obvious that not everyone ought to build houses, make clothes, produce food, play baseball, block the defensive right tackle, even though it is desirable that some do these things. (7:p.4). For Kant, the general law must avoid self-contradiction and must be such that one may freely become a member of such a system. The inference of universalizability (from 'not everyone has the right' to 'no one has the right,' from 'it would not be right for everyone' to 'it would not be right for anyone'—7:p.5) in the Kantian ethic,

> . . . is mediated, and therefore qualified, by the principle that what is right (or wrong) for one person must be right (or wrong) for any similar person in similar circumstances. (7:p.5).

and further from Singer:

> . . . the categorical imperative is advanced as a principle for determining whether any act is right or wrong. But it cannot be applied to an action taken apart from any determinate context. It must always be applied to an action considered as taking place in certain circumstances, or for a certain purpose. The proof of this is that a reference to the circumstances and purpose of an action is necessarily involved in the 'maxim' of an action. And it is the maxim of an action that Kant continually insists is what must be willed to be a universal law, not the action taken apart from some determinate maxim, that is, apart from some determinate purpose or circumstances. (7:p.237).

In conclusion Singer asserts that:

> . . . the rule derived from the application of the categorical imperative holds only for the circumstances to which it is applied, and, of course,

for anyone in the same or similar circumstances, and does not thereby hold for all possible circumstances. (7:p.238).

Thus, hopefully, the frequent rejection of Kant's view, and others of a similar character, on the basis of their being ". . . vacuous and hence devoid of significant application" (7:p.5) has been, in small measure at any rate, dismissed. Certainly, where the consequences of one's acting in a certain fashion are problematic, so is the application of the categorical imperative, though we must also note that it is not the intended nor feasible function of the categorical imperative to provide automatic solutions to moral problems, as Singer observes:

> In saying that an ethical theory should be relevant to the solution of moral problems, I do not mean that it must provide automatic solutions to them. (7:p.7).

CONCLUSION

The fundamental nature of Kantian ethics, the multiple formulations of the categorical imperative, the basic character of sport and athletics, and the categorical imperative as a principle of moral conduct in sport and athletics have been herein discussed. Though the major themes and arguments have been more so posited than well developed, the principal intent of this inquiry has been to indicate what the application of the Kantian ethic achieves with respect to encouraging an order of ideal conduct which has become increasingly uncommon in the playing of our amateur and professional sports and athletics in recent years.

REFERENCES

1. Beck, Lewis White (trans.): *Immanuel Kant: Foundations of the Metaphysics of Morals.* Indianapolis, Bobbs-Merrill, 1959.
2. Friedrich, Carl J. (ed.): *The Philosophy of Kant: Immanuel Kant's Moral and Political Writings.* New York, Random House, 1949.
3. Keating, James W.: "Sportsmanship as a Moral Category," *Ethics,* Vol. 85, No. 1, 25-35 (October 1964).
4. Metheny, Eleanor: *Connotations of Movement in Sport and Dance.* Dubuque, William C. Brown Co., 1965.
5. Paton, H.J.: *The Categorical Imperative: A Study in Kant's Moral Philosophy.* Sixth edition. London, Hutchinson and Co. Ltd., 1967.
6. Runes, Dagobert D.: *Pictorial History of Philosophy.* New York, Bramhall House, 1959.

7. Singer, Marcus G.: *Generalization in Ethics*. New York, Knopf, 1961.
8. Smith, Norman K. (trans.): *Immanuel Kant: Critique of Pure Reason*. New York, St. Martin's Press, 1965.
9. Watson, John: *Schelling's Transcendental Idealism: A Critical Exposition*. Chicago, S.C. Griggs and Co., 1882.

DO YOU 'WANNA' BET: AN EXAMINATION OF PLAYER BETTING AND THE INTEGRITY OF THE SPORTING EVENT

CAROLYN E. THOMAS

Gambling is often presented to the public as a specific social problem, a source of tension, and a stimulus to deviant behavior. This would appear to stem from the presentation of its more negative features and the concern for the pathological and bizarre rather than the conventional modes of gambling behavior. Such a preoccupation with its pathological effects on the individual and/or the social order, the interest in losers rather than in winners, and the often made connection between gambling and crime, cloud both the quantity and quality of gambling in this counrty. There is a dichotomous view by both church and secular elements regarding the morality of gambling. According to sociologist William Whyte (14), the church, with its bingos and raffles, considers gambling immoral only when the gambler cheats, uses money which is not his own, or deprives his dependents of what is needed for their maintenance. The recognition of the potential of such deprivation associated with gambling thus causes the church to look with suspicion rather than condemnation on gambling in its various forms.

Gambling emerges as a form of social pathology only when there is widespread resentment against it because of the psychological and social problems it creates. The individual who becomes psychologically addicted is condemned largely for his failure to perform the personal, social, and family responsibilities expected of him rather than for the actual bet or for the nature of gambling, *per se*. Since even the most avid gambler does not suffer the deleterious effects that other "vices" such as drugs, alcohol, or tobacco impart, its danger to the social group lies in its interference with normal assumption of the duties which society demands. The agrarian ethic remains with us in the form that leisure, of which gambling may be considered a form, may be respectably enjoyed only when work is finished.

A second resentment is that gambling is essentially an exploitation. "Gambling is merely a method whereby wealth is redistributed from the hands of the many to the hands of the few." (9:p.17). This attitude toward gambling perceives the business of gambling as being entirely parasitic and existing for the sole purpose of exploiting a human "weakness." The odds and the mathematical probability always favor the "house." "House" exploitation is compounded by the criminal connections that the house may have even in states where gambling is legal and by the contribution that the average gambler naively makes to few hands which operate chains of illegal activities.

The gambler is in an anti-social position because he can gain only as others lose. Therefore, as he becomes more efficient and wins more frequently, the loser's hostility increases, morality is questioned, and the rest of the world organizes to restrain such anti-social (winning) behavior. It may be possible to consider the athlete in the same anti-social position and despite the fact that *his* morality, by virtue of winning, is rarely questioned, the means by which he comes to be a winner is questioned. Recruiting, scouting, scholarship, player draft procedures are all scrutinized, policed, and appropriately penalized indirectly on the moral assumption that: to win too much must mean "they" are doing something illegal. Nobody can be *that* good without having bent the rules somewhere. However, moral condemnation of non-pathological gambling cannot rest on its economic irrationality for it may be defended as rational either on the ground that the bet is so small as to entail no real loss or on the basis that the amusement is worth the cost. Rather, such condemnation rests on our judgment of the effects it produces on man's integrity and on his willingness to co-operate with and preserve the social structure.

According to Bloch (2:p.217), the essential basis for all gambling seems to inhere in the chance factor of success irrespective of the type of game or device which is employed. Although the chance element may vary from some games which demand some skill such as cards to others which are pure chance such as dice, the element of chance is always present. Klausner has pointed out that empirical observations suggest:

> . . . some individuals seek danger and search for problems resistant to solution, and even seek the stress, fear, or anxiety engendered by such encounters. In this activity, these negative emotions swept up in excitement, adventure, or challenge. Individuals and groups promote stress through the play conflict of sports and through the 'real' social conflict of business, war, and crime . . . (6:p.VI).

If we accept the premise that people do seek stress in the forms of chance, uncertainty, adventure, excitement, challenge and "worthy opponents," what outlets exist for these stress-seekers? Klausner suggests one such outlet is manifested in the conflict of sports which we will return to later in the paper. Sociologist Block suggests that ". . . gambling provides a function in a well-organized society where the stress of competition (with its lack of predictability) is great, and where, in contrast, the regimen of economic and social life is rigorous." (2:p.221). Hedged by stereotyped employment and its attendant regularities (the professional athlete qualifies in this category), the fear of insecurity or loss of job, the pressures of family financial responsibility and the opinions of others, the average individual fears taking the chances which may mean riches and prestige or even the satisfaction at having taken the "risk." Such a society placing a premium on risk and "taking a chance" provides through gambling an outlet for many individuals to experience suspense, insecurity, momentary thrill and hope. Campbell's study on "The Vocational Interests of Beautiful Women," (3) and Malumphy's study on the "Personality of Women Athletes" (7) both indicate that women are as stress-seeking as men and that their risk-taking behavior parallels that of men, at least in terms of outlets.

The risk-taking propensity, particularly as it relates to the uncertainty of betting, is subject to the presence of both economic and psychological variables. Non-pathological betting on horse races, in sports pools, and in state lotteries is a genuine economic possibility for most people providing an acceptable psychological and social means for escaping the routine of work and family to "take a chance." Whether there is such a thing as the "sporting nature of man" that has been or will be developed by instinct theorists, sports events seem to provide a fertile ground for man to explore and display his gambling nature. With the elaborate handicap systems which have been developed, albeit informally and somewhat haphazardly, the spectator and the player can be assured of an even chance, a moment or an hour of uncertainty.

In sport, risk-taking situations may be dichotomized into those whose outcomes are contingent upon skill plus a couple of "good breaks" which would be the case in most athletic contests; and those where skill and chance are corollary and complementary such as those found in McIntosh's (8) "conquest" sports of man versus environment. Skill tasks, structured to be achievement oriented, are quite likely to involve ego involvement and emotional involvement. The spectator's arousal, despite the absence of actual skilled participation, is either promoted by his perceiving the game situation as one which requires his skill, i.e., how informed he is about each competing team and how adept he is at picking winners, or by the introduction of actual monetary rewards. Usually it is a combination of the two since money will reinforce his perception of his skill or his lack of it. Most non-pathological risk-takers are not foolhearted and seek to control the risks which they take. This rationale may, in part, explain why spectators, or non-participants, seldom bet on participants in "conquest" sports. The chance element which the environment creates in these kinds of sport is too much of a risk for the bettor.

In addition to the hope for material reward which is implicit in any form of betting and the ancillary "sports" skill of picking a winner, betting has allowed the spectator to become involved in a simulated stress-risk situation. "He has now identified himself with one of the agonists and thus becomes a participant as well as a spectator." (1:p.16). The spectator now has a definite commitment to the game. Even the casual sports observer who makes only the seasonal bets on the World Series, Super Bowl, Stanley Cup, or Rose Bowl can suddenly be transformed into an avid "fan" capable of calling the plays, sending in the substitutes, and analyzing the instant replays. However, spectator betting is not restricted to professional sports. Sports betting is implicitly associated with the "old school spirit." Betting on the home team from Pop Warner to the pros is not an uncommon phenomenon since even if they are the underdogs, there is the handicap system which makes all men equal in the world of competition. In other countries, the "school spirit" syndrome is recognized in various extremes of nationalism in which millions of dollars are wagered legally and illegally on teams in international competition.

On the one hand where spectator betting is condoned and even promoted by a risk-oriented society, betting by players is condemned. Historically, there is a perspective for this attitude. Amateur sportsmen, at least until 1863 when various governing bodies began to outlaw player betting, were supposedly dedicated to the deCoubertin ideal and the Grantland Rice adage that "how one plays the game" is primary. The player was a gentleman and a "lover" of sport as the word derivation of "amateur" would imply. "Between 1870 and 1890 the amateur came to be defined no longer in terms of social status but in terms of rewards and payments." (8:p.179). There was an increasing fear of professionalism and one of these fears was the ethically questionable practice of bribing competitors and arranging results in advance. The Black Sox Scandal of 1919 did nothing to improve on an already colored Puritan attitude about sport, professional sport, and gambling. As the number and kind of professional and collegiate sports increased with its corollary increase of spectator betting, the involvement and/or control of gambling by illegal syndicates became increasingly apparent.

Carol Vance, representing the commissioners of the nation's four major professional sports who are opposing the extension of legalized gambling into their sports, told a news conference recently, "We are convinced that legalized gambling will ruin the integrity of team sports, place teams under a cloud of suspicion and increase the possibility of scandal. From our investigations into organized crime, there is no question that the national crime syndicates would welcome legalized gambling as a bed partner." (13:p.4). It is interesting to note that in some other countries in which we can assume there is some degree of organized crime, gambling is an ancillary industry to sport. In Norway science and education are supported by monies from sports gambling. Great Britain's allocations for public sports facilities and programs are made, in part, from taxes on sport, including betting.

Athletes who have placed bets on games in which they are involved have been judged guilty of a potential "fix" by the mere act of placing the bet since the "connection" the player must make to place such a bet would obviously be one of less desirable repute. There is a somewhat ambivalent attitude about participant betting and the policing and surveillance of such betting. There is very little concern with what millions of Americans do, in terms of betting, on the sports in which they themselves participate. Rather, the concern is with those players in sports which they watch, i.e., professionals and heavily promoted amateurs and collegians. Commissioners and franchise owners and managers have assumed the responsibility for the protection of some very expensive business enterprises while an omnipresent news media has lessened the chance that dishonest money can be made in a sporting situation by either sportsman or spectator. Proponents of Off-Track Betting (OTB) and legalized gambling urge the extension of horse race betting to other sports contending that the state and local governments would reap the revenues now being channeled into illegal betting. Opponents maintain that legalized gambling will not end illicit bookmaking since ". . . no substantial better wants Uncle Sam to know how much or how often he bets." (10:p.4). Sports commissioners argue that legalized gambling would entice more players to bet on games and "Rozelle told newsmen he didn't want to see the day when a quarterback could be accused of holding down a score to protect the gambling point spread . . ." (10:p.1) presumably on his bet or for someone else who would later pay-off.

The assumption underlying arguments against legalized gambling and player betting is that the player is able to, or will, control the game in accordance with his bet or in accordance with the desires of an outside "connection" that will provide some "kick-back." However, in light of the social and psychological rationales that individuals gamble, it may be feasible to suggest that there are legitimate reasons other than the obvious legal and illegal economic ones noted by the guardians of player morals. Underwood's (12) account of Paul Hornung and his suspension for betting on games may provide an opening clue for the reasons a player would wish to make a bet other than for some financial gain. "Hornung himself is not a criminal; his football play is unassailable, and he has not thrown a game, taken a bribe, or sold his soul to Frankie Carbo." (12). Hornung's "mistake" was not criminal but as Underwood says "naive and irresponsible." His "friends" and the fact he made bets with such friends could do nothing but arouse suspicion. More recently, Rozelle's insistence that Joe Namath take definite actions to limit his association with less desirables is another form of preventive medicine. Hornung and Namath, like other star athletes, come in for special treatment in a society that holds them up as heroes and which could be considered in the current rock vernacular as a "mass groupie." They become accustomed to favors most of which demand no answer. The money, as Hornung himself noted, meant very little yet the possibility of having to return a "favor" exists and must remain a consideration.

Like much of the sporting world that maintains the athlete shall have no political views, the authoritarian ethic which manifests itself in the rulings of commissioners also denies man the choice to decide and to know what is right and wrong for himself. It assumes the individual cannot or will not make such decisions and if he does, he may not make them "appropriately." The authoritarian ethic answers the question of good and bad in terms of the interests of the authority which in reference to sport could be either money or prestige or both. However, in terms of the individual, it is exploitative because it assumes the action is bad, bans it or sets up barriers before it is actually experienced. It is true that for the integrity of the sport to be maintained it is imperative that the man on the field be ethically straight to the degree that no one will doubt his sacrosanctity. However, the fact that a player makes a bet does not destroy individual or game integrity.

If we can put aside, at least for the balance of this paper, the potentially negative ethical aspect of player performance as determined by betting, it may be fruitful to examine player betting in another light. As noted earlier, man seeks risk and sport has the potential for allowing man to take chances by providing a risk, or uncertainty, in a situation. However, it is interesting to note that both player and spectator betting are not universal occurrences in all sports. Returning again to McIntosh's classification of sport, in sports that classify as "conquest" sports, i.e., man versus the environment, there is no betting and if there is it is nominal, tertiary, and not taken very seriously by those involved in the bet. Sports such as skiing, surfing, skydiving, and mountain climbing are essentially non-competitive in terms of "other." The "other" is the environment which provides an infinite number of risks and chances. The "conquest" sports demand skill because despite the risk-seeking and the risk inherent in conquest sports, no one seeks uncontrollable risks, especially where one's life is at stake. However, no amount of skill will eliminate the chance element of conquest sports. Involvement in the sport is a sufficient gamble. The addition of a material bet is almost irrelevant, and for some, even ludicrous. Man's sense of game, his competitiveness, his need for challenge and achievement, and his "sporting instinct" are satisfied within the boundaries of the sporting situation. No external motivation is needed or sought. In a sense, it is a complete experience. Mallory's often quoted reaction to his successful climb of Everest suggests this completion: "Have we vanquished the enemy? None but ourselves. Have we gained success? That word means nothing here. . . . We have achieved the ultimate satisfaction."

In contrast to the "conquest" sports, we have the category of "better than" sports. These, of course, presuppose others either singly or in groups. In considering the significance of the player bet in this category of sport, it seems appropriate to consider the duffer and the "beer frame syndrome" on the one hand and the very highly skilled and/or professional player on the other hand. For the once-a-week player in games which necessitate skill, the lack of skill, despite handicaps, may provide a very great chance element in the game. However, the very fact that he is not committed to the game in terms of skill development may cause him to seek motivation and satisfaction from something outside the game. The player, like the spectator, seeks the tension of a close game and is willing, in most instances, to spot or be spotted pins, shots, or points in order to make the bet more meaningful, i.e., more uncertain and more risky. Fromm (4:p.32) has noted that uncertainty is the condition which impels man to unfold his powers. If this is the case, the handicap system stemming from the betting situation the players have created may provide an incentive to "overachieve" in terms of skill. For the player who is not motivated by external reward nor desirous of the pressure of the bet, his alternative is simply not to make sidebets but to derive his risk from the elements of the game. Most likely, he has assumed a commitment to develop skills and the closer he gets to having a reasonable command of the necessary game skills, the more the "game" becomes the challenge and the less significance the sidebet holds. The non-serious and/or poorly skilled player cannot pit himself against the chance elements of the game for he is not adequately prepared to "compete."

While the sport itself may inherently hold factors of risk of which the player is unaware, e.g., injury, the skills and abilities which individual participants bring to the sport situation determine the extent of risk or chance in the sport. In contrast to the duffer, the professional athlete brings a high degree of commitment, at least in terms of skill, to the sport situation. Improvements in training, scouting, and coaching coupled with the use of media and the perfecting of sports equipment have produced athletes who come to the man-to-man "better than" encounters with skills specifically geared toward eliminating chance in performance and increasing the probability of victory. Attemps are made to eliminate extraneous and contingent elements of performance. Multiple option offenses and defenses are developed and practiced always presenting the performer with a calculated alternative. However, unlike the "conquest" sport where the environment presents infinite chance elements, the "better than" sports find that the offensive and defensive options are finite. Where each wave or each climb is different and holds a risk for the performer, there are only X number of offensive and defensive possibilities as well as X number of legal techniques and variations all of which are known by all players. Even the creative invention of a new strategy is soon filmed, analyzed, practiced, and performed until it becomes part of the finite game possibilities. Hence, the very structure of the game limits chance and the development of skill has, for the athlete, eliminated another chance-risk element.

The "conquest" sportsman is repeatedly called upon to make decisions involving his participation in the sport; decisions for which *he* must be responsible. There is the chance he may be wrong and he gambles on his own knowledge and skills to be "better than" the infinite conditions he faces. Even in the classic "better than" athletics, the individual engaged in various individual and dual sports retains this decision-making option since coaching is forbidden either as a written or unwritten rule. Although there are no statistics or even valid empirical data, it seems to me that there is less sidebetting by highly-skilled players in individual sports than in team sports. Since prize money rides on each contest, this may serve as a game chance factor not available to the salaried team player. This is not to suggest individual and dual sportsmen do not make sidebets but it is to suggest that the side bet may fall into the same perspective that it does for the "conquest" sportsman. The prize money may supplant the necessity for the sidebet. However, in the team sports such decisions which possibly involve the outcome of the game are taken out of the domain of the participant and become the responsibility of the coaching staff. As John Silber (11) has noted, "The way coaches call the shots and the way substitutions are made now, things like spirit, conditioning, and mental capabilities mean very little." With the exception of a few college and professional athletes, the player is bound to play out decisions which coaches make. Such conforming behavior is an abdication of the opportunity to take chances in the game situation. The coach takes the risk and it is interesting to note that the concern with betting has usually ignored coaching staffs and centered around key players when in actuality, the coaches may be in a better position to control the outcome and point spread of a game than is any player including the quarterback. The player cannot risk venturing out on his own for to err is to be censured by crowds and coaches, to be benched for not following directions, or to be traded for being uncooperative. Perhaps, as Silber recommends, coaches should be sent up into the stands during the games not for the educational values he wishes to reinstate in the game by such action but to replace the risk-taking aspect of "sport" back into the players domain.

The opportunity to place sidebets on games may, aside from providing a chance element, serve as an extrinsic motivator in a situation which has become routine and boring for the good long-term player. Ryan has classified stress-seekers as either reducers or augmenters. Athletes have been classified generally as reducers who have high tolerance to pain and who tend to reduce their perception of stress, risk, and anxiety in a situation. We may then speculate that the better they get in terms of skill, the more it takes to "turn them on" or upset them. Psychologically the bet may serve to reinforce self-doubt by becoming a personal vote of confidence. Or, in the context of the McClelland achievement syndrome, the participant may experience a certain degree of cognitive dissonance when he sees a difference between his level of aspiration and his level of achievement in which case he places a sidebet to create a secondary chance of achieving if he wins. In other words, after having achieved an ultimate in skill, he aspires for greater achievement which the bet may satisfy.

We are drawn to the contention here that betting can serve as a positive function for the players because in a "better than" sport situation, it is possible to believe that the game is not enough. The game fails to satisfy a need that betting does satisfy, i.e., risk for the highly-skilled and a commitment-motivation that the duffer lacks. In this instance it may be feasible to suggest that some means be established by which the player, particularly the professional with whose morality the public is so greatly obsessed, could make sidebets on games. Since the right "connections", close surveillance, improper use of monies, and the handicap system are priorities among many ethical concerns, it might be feasible to suggest further that the various players' associations institute some betting system for its players perhaps patterned after the New York OTB system in which these concern priorities could be accommodated.

Facilitation and encouragement of player betting may provide the player with a complete game but it casts some question on the purpose and nature of "better than" sporting games *per se*. If the duffer or the pro need something like a bet outside the actual contest, it becomes obvious that the "game" definitely lacks something. The individual who achieves excellence in a sporting game creates an aura of routine and boredom forcing him outside the game for his excitement and to find complete satisfaction. The betting duffer "uses" the sport as a means to some other goal, a satisfaction which is outside his game. This is reminiscent of aggression theorists who seek to vent aggression and use sport as the supposed cleansing agent, or of the man who plays only out of fear that he will die of a coronary if he does not play with some regularity. The ultimate satisfaction is not in the doing but in what ends the doing may serve. The quality and integrity of the sporting games we have developed must be questioned if they are not inherently and intrinsically satisfying on their own merits by anyone who engages in them. Perhaps the removal of *any* betting by *any* player in *any* contest would force a re-examination and a re-structuring of our sporting games in such a way as to make them self-sufficient and complete, and re-affirm the integrity which seems to be inherent in "conquest" sports. As it is now, the bet does a great deal for the player but nothing for the game. Rather than the common notion that betting is a potential degradation of the player, perhaps it is really more accurate to state that it is an actual degradation of sport, at least to these sports in which it is possible to diminish the chance element.

REFERENCES

1. Bernard, Jessie: "The Eudamonists." *Why Man Takes Chances,* Samuel Klausner (ed.). New York, Anchor Doubleday, 1968.
2. Bloch, Herbert A.: "The Sociology of Gambling," *American Journal of Sociology,* Vol. 57 (November, 1951).
3. Campbell, David: "The Vocational Interests of Beautiful Women." Essay presented at the Midwestern Psychological Association Meeting, May, 1966.
4. Fromm, Erich: *Man for Himself.* New York, Holt, Rinehart and Winston, 1947.
5. Keating, James W.: "Sportsmanship as a Moral Category," *Ethics,* Vol. 85, No. 1, 25-35 (October 1964).
6. Klausner, Samuel (ed.): *Why Man Takes Chances.* New York, Anchor Doubleday, 1947.
7. Malumphy, Theresa: "The Personality Characteristics of Women Athletes in Intercollegiate Athletics." Unpublished Doctor's dissertation, Ohio State University, 1966.
8. McIntosh, P.C.: *Sport and Society.* London, Watts, 1968.
9. Peterson, Virgil: "Obstacles to Enforcement of Gambling Laws," *Annals of the American Academy of Political and Social Sciences,* May, 1950.
10. *Rochester Democrat and Chronicle,* September 29, 1972.
11. Silber, John R.: "Bench the Coach," *New York Times,* Septmber 17, 1972.
12. Underwood, John: "The True Crisis," *Sports Illustrated,* May 20, 1963.
13. Vance, Carol: *Rochester Democrat and Chronicle,* September 29, 1972.
14. Whyte, William: *Street Corner Society.* Chicago, University of Chicago Press, 1943.

(CHAPTER III)

THE AESTHETIC STATUS OF SPORT

INTRODUCTION

Aesthetics, or the philosophy of art, is that axiologic sub-discipline which concerns the nature and significance of the arts; and, consequently, of aestheic value. It entails a prescriptive treatment of the first and most general principles of the arts and aesthetic value. It is, in effect, the standards of taste and artistic judgment, the discipline concerned with the nature and significance of ideal form, beauty, and the beautiful, most particularly in the arts. Most important among the major issues in aesthetics are: the metaphysical status of the arts; the form, content, and subject matter of the arts; the criteria of aesthetic judgment (criticism); the relation of the arts to natural phenomena (the role of representation, or imitation, in the arts); the role of intellectuality (contemplation) and emotionality (feeling) in the arts; the nature of aesthetic experience and pleasure; the moral, social, political, didactic, and cultural significance of the arts; the relation of the art product (work of art) to the process by which it is created; the role of technique and expression (creativity) in the arts; the role of the artist, performer, and audience in the arts; the nature of artistic media and notative form; the role of training (education) in the arts; and the nature and distinctions among the individual arts (architecture, sculpture, painting, literature, poetry, drama, theater, cinema, opera, dance, and music). The essays here presented, then, address themselves to these aesthetic issues as they are located in the sport condition.

This third chapter begins with Paul G. Kuntz' "The Aesthetics of Sport." Following Camus' insight, Professor Kuntz likens sport to the theater and ascribes unusually high value to it. The similarities between sporting and artistic performance, between athlete and artist receive foremost attention here. These similarities are drawn principally on the basis of a general conception of performance (as the doing of an activity largely for the pleasure of another individual or group) which is applicable to both. That is, more specifically, both sporting and artistic forms of performance arise in a special, contrived world (an idealization of the everyday) governed by freely chosen rules and values and persisting in exclusive and isolated times and places. And further, both are productive of a beauty and excellence vicariously available to the spectator (audience), and both are a vital part of human life occurring quite apart from work. Professor Kuntz concludes his essay with an appeal that would have sport cultivate more fully its likeness to the arts.

Francis W. Keenan's "The Athletic Contest as a 'Tragic' Form of Art" interprets Aristotle's model of dramatic tragedy in terms of its implications for the athletic contest. Aristotle's *Poetics* lends itself particularly well to such interpretation. Professor Keenan begins his investigation by observing that athletic contests are potentially dramatic events; that is, a dramatic tension is created by an athlete attempting to perform excellently under conditions which constrain, or limit, his expression in some respect. While victory as quantitatively evidenced has been commonly regarded as a necessary condition for achieving excellence in athletics, this essay argues that qualitative, or aesthetic, measures are more appropriate criteria.

As in the case of the arts, the process, or effort, of becoming in, and not the quantitative result, or product, of the athletic contest is of primary concern here. Also like the arts, the athletic contest creates an illusion of facility, raises human limits of insight and expectancy, and operates under the constraint to excellence. And like dramatic tragedy, more specifically, the athletic contest envisions beauty in the pain and suffering of conflict and competition, in man's struggle with the inequities and paradoxes of life, in man's attempt to overcome the hostile forces of the world to which he must in the end yield, and in man's display of courage in the face of this adversity. These common attributes of the athletic contest and the dramatic tragedy lead Professor Keenan to the adoption of the Aristotelian paradigm of the tragedy as a model for explaining the tragic elements (plot, character, thought, diction, melody, and spectacle) as they are located in the athlete's and the spectator's perspectives of the athletic contest. This analysis equates the imitation of action and life, and the evocation of pity and fear inherent in the dramatic tragedy to that apparent in the athletic contest; and it allows for a more humanistic notion of athletic competition than is currently fashionable.

The present volume concludes with Robert G. Osterhoudt's "An Hegelian Interpretation of Art, Sport, and Athletics." In this essay Professor Osterhoudt attempts to develop a discussion of Hegel's general philosophic commitments, most particularly those of an aesthetic dimension, and to suggest the implications of these views for regarding sport and athletics as an art form; that is, to propose what might be made of sport and athletics as an art form given the philosophic foundations of Hegelianism. The inquiry includes a brief, introductory treatment of the specific nature of sport and athletics, by which they are distinguished from other entities with which they are commonly confused; namely, movement, play, work, recreation, dance, exercise, games, and physical education. These foundational examinations then provide the basis for suggesting the fundamentally spiritual (idealistic) disposition of sport and athletics, as well as for demonstrating the measure of unity between the sensuous and the spiritual apparent in sport and athletics which is essentially identical to that apparent in the arts generally. It also serves to establish the enduring, rational, intrinsic, and disinterested intent in sport and athletics to embody themselves in a particular fashion in a particular medium as in the case of the arts. Discussed as well are the amateur-professional controversy, the competitive motif (agonistic element), and training and records in sport and athletics, as well as the distinction between true and spurious sport-athletic forms.

THE AESTHETICS OF SPORT

Paul G. Kuntz

Clamence in *La Chute* couples athletic games with stage plays and ascribes to them the same role in his experience. Doubtless we hear the conviction of Albert Camus, a football goalkeeper who unlike most philosophers and most artistic geniuses, ascribed high value to sport. "I was only really sincere and enthusiastic during the period when I played games, and also in the army when I acted in plays which we *put on for our own enjoyment* . . . . Even today, the stadium crammed full of spectators for a Sunday match, and the theatre which I loved with unequal intensity, are the *only places in the world where I felt innocent.*" (3:p.13).

Several prominent American aestheticians have singled out the aesthetic aspects of sport, the similarities of sporting performance to artistic performance, the similarities between the athlete and the artist: Thomas Munro, Monroe C. Beardsley, Virgil C. Aldrich, Paul Weiss. Munro considers sports *"fields which border on the arts,"* showing such characteristics as being enjoyed for their own sake. (8:pp.147-150). Beardsley notes this also, coupled sometimes with "consummatory conclusion . . . tied closely to sensuous presentations." (2:p.530).

These powerful incentives to inquiry have not yet produced significant results. This is the case, I believe, because we have neglected the general conception of *performance,* under which sports and such arts as theatre, dance and music are specific kinds. (5).

A very striking and profound theory of performance that links theatre to play, games and sports as well as to ritual is from Richard Schechner. He invites us to compare these: ". . . each autonomous form shares characteristics with the others: methods of analysis of one may be useful in the analysis of the others. Together these five comprise *the public performance activities of men."* "Theatre" covers dance and music as modes and will be so used here, for sake of brevity. (11:pp.26-27).

"Performance" is not, according to Schechner, and this is true of the other analysts, so general that it covers all human interaction. It is specifically "the doing of an activity by an individual or group largely for the pleasure of another individual or group." The *audience,* then, is essential to most sport and to all theatre, a strong similarity. (11:p.27).

That sport and theatre are apart from economic institutions (which may be their "innocent" character referred to in Camus) is not trivial for both live in *"a special world."* "A special world is established where men can make the rules, re-arrange time, assign values to things, and work for pleasure. This 'special' world is not gratuitous but a vital part of human life. No society can do without it. It is a special world only when compared to the 'usual' activities of productive work." (11:p.32).

Each of the great modes of performance requires a special place and most require a *special building.* "Theatre" and "church" are both the names of buildings as well as activities. Arenas and stadiums are similarly costly especially because they are used ony a few hours a week. They are quite unlike factories. Their arrangement springs from the relationship between performer and audience: many may watch a few. Here a celebration or ceremony takes place. Hence comes ". . . an expressive rejuvenation and reaffirmation of the moral values of the community." Indeed, without "having" a religion, "rooting for" the team, and "going to the theatre" we are not a community. (11).

Is it useful to consider sport and theatre in the same category, *performance?* It is, because both employ props that help *create symbolic reality.* It is otherwise silly to contend, in sport, for a ball or defend territory, or to pretend that a costume makes a king. (11:p.31).

Another very striking way in which sport and theatre, along with ritual, is each a special world, is that their *time* is as frequently symbolic or adapted to the events and not strictly correlated, as is economic activity, to unilinear and uniform clock time. (11:pp.28-29).

Even though sport and theatre take place in special places, an athletic or artistic "church," and create a special reality in its own time, as do rituals, and depend upon a crowd of witnesses who participate in the rite, are not the *rules* very different? Whereas rules of ritual symbolize external divine authority and in play we may invent games by fiat, ". . . games, sports, and theatre mediate between these extremes. It is in these activities that we often express our *social* behavior. Certainly these three groupings constitute a continuum: however, differences in degree become differences in kind." (11:p.36).

A great difference that here distinguishes theatre from sport is that only the former has a text, a score, or choreography, in one word, *a performing art is based on a text, but a sport has no text.* (11:p.35).

The questions of rules and the question of text are related to the question about the control of the actor in the theatre, the performer in sport: what kinds of *direction and control limit their freedom?*

Because these questions have not been asked, we have not considered data as relevant answers. Sometimes it is said that whereas the *arts symbolize reality, sports cannot do so.* But if mountain climbing is a sport rather than an art, then we must qualify this judgment. Climbing a mountain from Petrarch on, has been profoundly symbolic. It is man raising himself against obstacles, enduring hardship, scorning dangers, and triumphantly occupying the place of great vision. (10:p.10).

The experience of a bullfight is not only *formally divided into acts,* as Ernest Hemingway says, the *trial,* the *sentencing,* and the *execution.* Here is *a ritual symbolizing man living in scorn of death,* a life ". . . in which disregard of consequences dominates." (4:p.101).

It is sometimes said that beauty is only accidental in sport. But this is not so in figure skating and diving. *Grace is deliberately aimed at,* as in dancing. In swimming and skiing perhaps *grace is a by-product of the training in skill.* But we respond here to the ". . . beauty of movement [that] depends on the success of [the athlete's] muscular economy." (7:p.140).

Very few aestheticians have speculated upon the pleasure of the many forms of ball games and putting a missile wherever we can see. Virgil C. Aldrich makes these activities enjoyed for their own sake, examples of *marksmanship.* It is *not simply* ". . . *pretense nor the spilling over of surplus energy."* We might develop this line of thought as the experience of power. Perhaps the great public acclaim of the late Bobby Jones was his superb mastery of the golf ball. All of us could *share vicariously in excellence* and were lifted to heights comparable to those of great dance, music and theatre. (1).

A great debate now rages over the moral justification of sport, because many see its corruption, the anxiety to win, the brutality of American football, the exploitation of the athlete, particularly the limitation of the game to what can be presented on television (without the community of live performer and live audience). But if the *moral argument fails, there is the aesthetic argument.* (6).

Perhaps the sports of the future will be more like the arts: "Eventually, the world of sport is going to take the emphasis off winning-at-any cost. The new direction will be towards helping athletes make personally chosen modifications of behavior: *towards the joyous pursuit of aesthetic experience. . . ."* (9:p.63).

If our topic has suffered from gross neglect in traditional aesthetics, the broadening of aesthetics to consider sports is now required. Happily the questions raised philosophically are questions which are considered good ones by performers in sports and the arts, and they are questions which ordinary men know are relevant to daily life.

REFERENCES

1. Aldrich, Virgil C.: "A Theory of Ball Play," *Psychological Review,* Vol. 44 395-403 (1937).
2. Beardsley, Monroe C.: *Aesthetics: Problems in the Philosophy of Criticism.* New York, Harcourt, Brace, and Co., 1958.
3. Cruickshank, John: *Albert Camus and the Literature of Revolt.* New York, Oxford University Press, 1960.
4. Hemingway, Ernest: *Death in the Afternoon.* New York, Scribner's, 1932.
5. Jenkins, Iredell: "Performance," *Aesthetic Concepts and Education,* Ralph A. Smith (ed.): Urbana, University of Illinois Press, 1970.
6. Kempton, Murray: Sports in America: Jock-Sniffing," *New York Review of Books,* Vol. 16, No. 2, 34 (February 11, 1971).
7. Langfeld, Herbert Sidney: *The Aesthetic Attitude.* New York, Harcourt, Brace, and Co., 1920.
8. Munro, Thomas: *The Arts and Their Interrelations.* New York, The Liberal Arts Press, 1949.
9. Ogilvie, Bruce C. and Tutko, Thomas A.: "Sport: If You Want to Build Character, Try Something Else," *Psychology Today,* Vol. 5, No. 5 61-63 (October, 1971).
10. Roberts, David: "Deborah: A Wilderness Narrative," *The New York Times Book Review,* 10 (February 7, 1971).
11. Schechner, Richard: "Approaches to Theory Criticism," *Tulane Drama Review,* Vol. 10, No. 4, 26-36 (Summer, 1966).
12. Weiss, Paul: *Philosophy in Process, Vol. V.* Carbondale, Southern Illinois University Press, 1971.

THE ATHLETIC CONTEST AS A 'TRAGIC' FORM OF ART

FRANCIS W. KEENAN

INTRODUCTION

Athletic contests have become increasingly significant as forms of human expression. Performer and spectator alike understand that athletic contests involve drama. Dramatic tension is created when athletes are able to overcome the limitations placed on freedom through superlative action. Many kinds of controls and restraints are placed on the competitions of various orders, and winners are determined by their ability to use movement forms within those given confines. Unfortunately, at least from an aesthetic appreciation posture, excellence in athletics has been equated with quantitative measures. Winning has become the necessary condition for achieving excellence. This constraint to victory would be a restriction on the freedom of the aesthetician to perceive other forms of beauty and excellence in athletics.

One may ask, how many wins are necessary to prove excellence? Apparently, necessary quantitative grounds for excellence exist when one is able to hold a portentous forefinger aloft and proclaim "number one" status. In the qualitative realm of aesthetics, I submit that such is not the case. The process becomes more important than outcome, or product.

Art involves a transformation. Excellence in art is a becoming, a changing of reality, and not an achieved state. Reality is perceived in a new perspective by the artist, a perspective which is aesthetically significant. It is true that we can be guided by paradigm cases in art, but what is beautiful, like who is best, always remains an "open question." There are always borderline cases to be considered and necessary conditions are useful, if not sufficient, in drawing attention to processes which may be candidates for inclusion in the aesthetic domain.

As you all know, Aristotle set forth the necessary conditions for tragedy in his *Poetics*. His form of tragedy is of interest to those concerned with beauty in athletics because Aristotle viewed process as greater in philosophic import than the emphasis on outcome. Singular and factual historical events relate what "has been." The concern with process is a concern for what "can be." (2:9;1451b, 1-12).

This paper shall explore some possibilities from Aristotle's model for the athletic contest. New ways of looking at athletics are needed if we are to understand the phenomenon. The win-lose approach is not the only viable method of judging excellence in athletics. New perspectives have a way of jarring us out of some of our conformity.

COMMENTS ABOUT AESTHETICS AND ATHLETICS

In describing the aesthetic qualities of sport, critics usually illustrate the similarities between art and the beauty in movement. Beauty in sport has been recognized in the grace and skill of the gymnast, in the coordination and style of synchronized swimming, in the acrobatic mastery displayed in diving, and in the symmetry and fluidity of dance, to give only a few examples. In team sport, the beautiful, in large measure, is contingent on the skill of players to be sure; but also of importance are the precisioned movements of teams, the coordination of effort, and unity of purpose, all of which affect an illusion of facility, as does all art.

Athletic art is a process of doing, of craftsmanship which becomes artistic as it becomes "loving," (3:pp.47-48) and as it becomes an "endeavor after perfection in execution." (15:p.467). Athletic competition qualifies as art as it raises the limits of insight and expectancy and by creating ever new levels of human achievement. The athletic contest also functions culturally. Like the drama, it functions as a mechanism for the celebration and enforcement of traditions of race and group; it instructs people by commemorating the glories of the past and by strengthening communal pride. (3:p.7).

The struggle and conflict of athletics is agonistic. We normally do not associate the pain and suffering of competition with beauty. The dramatic tragedy is unique in this respect. Even painful experience, both physical and mental, can be beautiful. When the distasteful can be perceived as a means for further developing and cultivating an experience, it may be viewed as aesthetic and enjoyable. (3:p.41).

Pleasurable, or painful, or both, athletic sport has the power to excite us. It is not only the excitment that attracts us; as in art, it is excitement about something. To generate this indisposable excitement something must be at stake and the odds concerning outcome must be doubtful. Lopsided athletic contests are as unexciting and aesthetically unpleasant as canvases that provide the "artist" with numbers and lines to follow in painting a picture. The resut is known prior to the experience. Sure things do not arouse us aesthetically or emotionally. It follows then, that all athletic contests, like all painting, are not aesthetically pleasing.

To discover the aesthetic in athletics is to be concerned with the action and movement of the medium, for athletics is necessarily process oriented. Overemphasis on the product of athletics—some fixed, final structure like winning—obscures the aesthetic qualities. Too often an appreciation of the aesthetic character of an athletic contest escapes player and spectator alike. (9:pp.19-20). With the player the problem may be attributable to an inability to achieve the "psychological distance" necessary to evaluate objectively. Some athletes have, however, claimed the ability to concentrate on the exigencies of the contest while entertaining an awareness of the aesthetic properties of the dimension.

Lack of artistic appreciation for the athletic contest may also be attributed to lack of knowledge of aesthetic qualities. Both player and spectator must possess some understanding of aesthetic qualities to judge a contest's artistic form. Another difficulty is that aesthetic perception is also partly an affair of readiness on the part of motor equipment. (3:p.98). A movement is appreciated to the extent that it is understood. The athlete must train and perfect his skills until he is able to cope with a variety of situations successfully on the spur of the moment. Athletic contests provide him with the opportunity to improvise and transform his movement talents. Despite what some coaches may believe, as witnessed by their so called "bibles," the highly electric events of athletics often have not been previously experienced by the athlete in quite the same context. There is an element of newness, of uniqueness associated with the exciting situations in a contest. Perhaps it is the ability to cope with the novel immediately and skillfully which provides us with an aesthetic quality in the athletic contest.

Returning to the perception of the spectator, only the skilled recognize the extreme difficulty and fully appreciate the artistry of another's performance. The competent observer can follow a performance sympathetically, if not overtly, in his own body. He has prior movement experience of a similar nature. The knowledge which comes from motor preparation plays a prominent role in aesthetic appreciation in any particular art form. (3:p.98). Yet even with this sort of knowledge aesthetic qualities may escape notice because of engrossment in the immediacy of events. However, while the aesthetic movement dimension is most readily available in the act itself, it is also rationally accessible to player and spectator ex post facto.

Drama and Athletics

The drama is an art form developed with spectators in mind. It is perhaps in the drama that sport reaches its closest affinity with art as process. The audiences at athletic contests behave similarly to those at dramatic stage productions; there is applause for performers who are skillful as well as overt manifestations of disapproval for poor performances. We speak of "players" in both athletics and drama. The attitudes and experiences surrounding stage and arena are also similar in that we take pleasure and delight in exciting performances which deliver an organized sequence of action executed with skill. If attendance at contests is any indication, athletics appear to have become the modern theater.

One of the most powerful members of the dramatic genre is the tragedy. The tragedy symbolizes mans' struggle with the inequities and paradoxes of life. In tragedy, man is featured in an attempt to overcome hostile forces to which he inevitably must succumb. The display of courage in the face of adversity is prized because it reflects something beautiful about man—the spirit with which he enters marvelous combat with an overwhelming and unpredictable world. The tragic athlete's call to the contest may be likened to Unamuno's call ". . . to live, seeing that we all have to die; to live, because life is an end in itself." (16:p.393). It is the tragic sense, the profoundest sense of our common humanity, which provides us with a positive inspiration. (16:p.152).

Tragedy applauds the same fighting spirit that is found in the athletic contest. It commends the insuperable fortitude and gallantry of the underdog who fails to recognize that he is the underdog, who fails to relent even when seemingly controlled by athletic powers greater than his own. It is this conflict between the inevitable power of "necessity," and the reaction to it by conscious effort which is dramatic.

Dramatic tragedy and athletics appear to have more in common than conflict resolution. In ancient Greece the theater and the stadium were often located adjacently. The Greek word "theatron" literally means "a place for viewing a spectacle." (6:p.152). The historical antecedent of tragedy was a competitive movement form, in quest of a prize at the ancient Greek festival rites. Aristotle informs us that the tragedy originally was an improvisation by the leaders of the dithyramb. (2:p.4.1449a,10-12). A literal interpretation of dithyramb renders it as a leaping, inspired *dance,* a dance performed to implore the gods to come to Athens and dance flower-crowned. (7:p.77). The flower-crown is interesting because it was also an award given to athletes at athletic festivals. The frenzied dancing of the dithyramb evolved into a kind of dramatic competition which was composed and enacted by performers called "tragedians." The tragedians, or poets, competed for a prize which was awarded for the best performance. The original prize for the poet who best illustrated tragedy was a goat. This explains why the word tragedy has often been interpreted to mean "goat song." (5:pp.56-57). Isn't it interesting that even today the tragic athlete who commits the fatal "faux pas" during the course of the contest is referred to as the "goat!" It is in the origin of tragedy as dance, a strenuous movement form, and in the competition for a prize that tragedy relates most vividly to athletics. During the tragedies enacted at the Feast of Dionysus, ". . . the whole public understood all the allusions and reacted to the subleties of style and expression sharing the tension of the contest like a crowd at a footfall match." (8:p.145). It is to the matter of the style of tragedy that we now turn.

TRAGEDY: THE ARISTOTELIAN PARADIGM

The changes in the early form of Grecian tragedy led to a more stabilized form which Aristotle described with an air of certainty. The medium is designed primarily, to have an emotional impact on the audience, a reaction resulting from critical action. Aristotle's most concise definition reads as follows:

> Tragedy, then, is the imitation of a good action, which is complete and of a certain length, by means of language made pleasing for each part separately; it relies in its various elements not on narrative but on acting; through pity and fear it achieves the purgation of such emotions. (1:p.6;1449b, 25-30).

This passage, as Aristotle explains, describes six formal elements which provide the structure of tragedy as an art form. These six are: (1) plot (mythos); (2) character (ethe); (3) thought (dianoia); (4) diction (lexis); (5) music (melopoiia); and (6) spectacle (opsis). Each shall be briefly discussed before applying them to the athletic contest.

The Plot

Of the six elements, plot is by far the most important. Four kinds of plot were identified by Aristotle, the first three of which he rejected as unsuitable for tragedy.

The primacy of plot is essential and the one favored by Aristotle finds a "common man," that is, one who is neither good nor bad in the Aristotelian sense, falling from a state of happiness to misery, unhappiness, and perhaps even death. The "common man" is one who is not outstandingly endowed with "virtue." We can readily identify with the actions of this plot for the hero is to be one much like ourselves.

In the plot there is a "mimesis" of action. "Mimesis" is commonly interpreted as "imitation." Kaufmann suggests that "representation" may be a better meaning of "mimesis." (10:p.42). It does seem to be a better word for the context of athletics.

The plot has a beginning, middle, and end, and the action is of sufficient length and quality to give it magnitude and dimension, and to illustrate a human predicament.

The language of plot is not seriously considered at any length by Aristotle. He stresses *action* rather than narrative. "Tragedy, then, is essentially an imitation not of persons but of action and life, of happiness and misery." 2:p.6;1450a, 15-16).

The major qualification for language is that it be made pleasing.

The plot progresses through an arrangement of events which display tragic consequences that result from the hero's "hamartia." "Hamartia" has proven equally difficult to translate to English. It has been translated as: a moral weakness; a mistake; a flaw in character; and, as an error due to inadequate knowledge of particular circumstances. Interpretation is hindered by the fact that there are no exact equivalent words for many Greek words. However, all interpretations of "hamartia" seem to point to a *failing* of one kind or another. (10:pp.72-80). It is because of some memorable and seemingly unavoidable failing that tragic man falls into unhappiness. His "mistake" may occur at any point in the plot. (10:pp.49-50). When it occurs at the end of the plot, the cathartic effect is stronger.

Catharsis is the final element that must be considered by the poet in his plot. The true test of any tragic plot is whether it has the power to evoke the emotions "eleos" and "phobos," pity and fear. The drama serves the cathartic function of purging the spectator of these emotions. The aesthetic interest lies in the sobering of the spectator to the reality of the frailty of human existence.

Character

The second element of tragedy is character. Character is that which reveals the purpose of the agents and the intentionality of the action. (2:p.6;1450a,10-15). Characterization is successful when the "players" are capable of depicting the purpose of the drama accurately during a series of events.

Thought

Thought, the third element of tragedy, is the capacity to *express* what is involved or suitable to the situation. (10:p.62). Thought is reflected in language. It is the outward manifestation of what the "player" believes is the correct response. Thought is revealed in all that is said in proving or disproving some particular point. (2:p.6; 1450b,10-12).

Diction

Diction is the use of language to express the thoughts of the characters accurately and precisely. (2:p.6;1450b,12-14).

Melody

Melody, of course, refers to music. Aristotle held music to be the most "pleasurable accessory" of the tragedy.

Spectacle

The final element of the tragedy is the spectacle. It involves the actual staging or public performance of the tragedy. Aristotle felt it to be the least important of six attributes of dramatic tragedy. It depended on the services of those other than the poet, like the customer and the ticket seller, for example, and had little to do with the formal structure of the action in the drama.

TRAGEDY AND THE ATHLETIC CONTEST

There is no doubt that athletic contests, like other human endeavors, provide drama. No one would question whether Bannister's effort which produced the first sub-four minute mile was dramatic. Drama seems to pervade every contest in which there is doubt about the outcome. The question is, when does the drama of athletics reach tragic proportions? Was Bannister's effort tragic because he knew his record was not to receive tenure, because records are transient rather than eternal occurrences? When is the athletic contest tragic in the aesthetic sense? Here Aristotle is instructive. His form is considered as a guide suggestive of tragic elements recognizable in the athletic contest. First, let us consider plot again.

Plot: The Will to Win

In the athletic contest, two aspire to what only one may possess. The athlete's dedication to training and excellence is motivated by the urge to win. (11). Athletes feel a kind of compulsion to train, practice, and compete to the limits of their ability. They seek perfection through practice. They abhor losing—the symbolic death of the contest. It is this sort of compelling force which grips the mind of the tragic hero in the staged drama as well. It is the will to overcome that provides the tragic impetus.

These qualities endear the athlete to all men. As a man of action the athlete has a universal appeal. His actions become "good actions" as he is able to perform well.

Good action is more than excellence of performance. There is an emotional expectancy. The aura of the "big game" is one of anticipation, of excitement. It is a serious encounter in which the stakes are high; the Super Bowl is a current example. But even Super Bowls can fail to reach tragic proportions. "Laughers" just don't count! There must be a portrayal of will, a comeback, a persistence where lesser men would relinquish; tragedy must be an insistence in the face of adversity. The tragic athlete continues to assert his freedom in an attempt to disturb the impending forces of necessity. Such action is good action in the tragic sense.

The primacy of interest does not lie in defeat; we are directed to the circumstances surrounding and precipitating it, the qualities which reflect a particular contest as an example of mans' plight in an uncertain world.

The mimetic feature of athletic tragedy lies partially in its portrayal of life in microcosm. The action of the arena both represents and presents the man of action because the action is real. The stage must rely on imitation; athletics presents life first hand and thereby increases the drama.

Aside from presenting an image of life, the mimetic feature of tragedy can take another form more directly related to the spectator. Lenk states that:

> . . . the seriousness of sport is stressed by the presence of spectators. The spectator has a 'connection' with the athlete, a 'participation,' which might be understood as a sort of imitation of the movements he makes. (12:p.12).

Along the same line Maheu relates that:

> In the theatre the audience involves itself in the drama being enacted before it, thus becoming, after a fashion, actor as well as spectator, and similarly in the stadium, an intense empathy develops between spectators and performers. (13:p.31).

Watching spectators provides us with insight to a second order of "mimesis." They seem to be trying to enter the bodies of the athletes they watch. They lean, twist, rise, wriggle and squirm. The mimetic feature of tragedy transfers from the arena to the stands both in terms of physical manifestations and mental gymnastics. The arm chair quarterback plays a game of wits. He anticipates action and attempts strategic decision as if he were coaching or actually playing. He parades his expertise by announcing proper actions in advance of actual occurrences. When his pronouncements find consonance with real events, the spectator is fulfilled and delighted with the drama. The action becomes, in a sense, imitative of his forecasts and representative of his will.

Elias and Dunning, discussing the mimetic effect of events, point out that the strict interpretation of "mimesis" as "imitation" is not wholly justified. "Mimesis," they assert, ". . . refers to all kinds of artistic forms in their relation to 'reality,' whether they were representational in character or not." (4:p.41). The implication here is that all art forms, athletics included, are in some sense imitative of other art forms.

Athletic contests, like dramatic tragedy, are divided into time periods of varying length. Periods, quarters, halves, and innings are the counterpart of the "acts" of drama. The action of the athletic tragedy, like the action of the stage tragedy, is enhanced when the plot includes what Aristotle calls anagnorisis and peripeteia—recognition and reversal.

Recognition involves what a player has done, or what he has become. (10:p.68). The athlete suffers from an identity crisis. He seeks to know or recognize himself as an athlete through competition with other athletes. When his competitive aspirations and achievements are in harmony, he is fulfilled. Even in defeat fulfillment is potentially available. To the athlete, the contest is that which permits him to approach the truth of his being as an athlete. The aesthetician, however, sees the actions and their intent as indicative of the actions of man. (12). The dilemma of the athlete is that recognition of personal excellence is not always forthcoming; it is attainable only for a few athletes. The quantitative restrictions which the athlete accepts have absolute limiting powers. Each athlete can "measure" himself objectively under these conditions. Often he is brought quickly to an awareness of self that he finds undesirable. The realization that one is not a great athlete, the best, "number one," can be traumatic for those who come close but fail. In this case, recognition is becoming abruptly aware that one is another person. The contest is a vital aspect of existence which opens the self to the mystery of one's being as an athlete. (19:p.8).

As previously mentioned, recognition can involve the discovery that an action thought to be proper is indeed "tragic." This sort of "recognition" is reminiscent of Roy Riegels, the 1929 Rose Bowl football player who ran the wrong way with a fumble. His All-American teammate, Bennie Lom, stopped him just short of the goal line. This action resulted in an eventual safety which decided the game. Tragic? One might claim that this situation illustrates comedy, not tragedy:

The difference between tragedy and comedy is not in essence one of subject matter, but depends upon our point of view. The same action, involving the same people, can be represented as tragic or comic. (10:p.45).

Peripeteia, or reversal, is a sudden flip flop of advantage during the contest. John Brodie's pass into the arms of a surprised Dallas Cowboy reversed the tenor of the game. It was a crucial turning point. Advantage seemed to shift almost completely to Dallas when previously the precarious nature of the game was evident.

Aesthetically speaking, the most tragic end of an athletic contest occurs when the outcome is decided on the final play or in the last few seconds, with both recognition and reversal occurring simultaneously. A team on the way to an apparent victory is suddenly defeated. A crazy turn of events, some unforeseen and apparently unpreventable incident, a long shot gamble succeeds and glory turns to gloom. The end comes just as the final seconds tick away. There is no opportunity to recoup, no choice in the matter—freedom seems lost—there is no possibility of retaliation, only resignation and the unhappiness that accompanies the loser stricken by recognition and reversal. Excitement in these closing moments peaks as the scoreboard clock initiates furious bits of action aimed at the recovery of a lost image. The athlete, demanding perfection of himself, seeks the fulfillment of his capacities even in the face of impending failure. Athletic tragedy inevitably trembles on a thin line between victory and defeat. Examples of this nature are legion in the annals of sport. In 1966, Milt Plum tossed a desperation 60 yard pass to Amos Marsh in the last 25 seconds to defeat Minnesota. The play so upset Van Brocklin that he retired the next day. He could not believe what he saw. The unreality of the event provided it with the quality of power. It changed an existent situation into its opposite. The sudden death battle between Baltimore and New York, the first in professional football, seemed tragic, saddening, even pitiful. One of those great teams had to lose, yet in defeat was made beautiful by the nature of the action leading to defeat.

Fear always accompanies athletes in these situations. The excellence of athletes permits them to rise to the occasion, knowing that the future may hold the promise of disaster as well as the fulfillment of dreams. We can truly sympathize with classic efforts of athletic excellence that end in tragedy. They parallel the difficult episodes of life.

The beauty resides in the effort, not the result. I am thinking of the performance of Dorando Pietri, an Italian entry in the Olympic marathon of 1908. The amazing Pietri entered the stadium with an enormous lead on the field, needing only to negotiate the last 385 yards to win. His effort had left him in an obvious state of extreme physical fatigue. On rubbery, wobbly legs, he somehow agonizingly circled the the track while swerving across several lanes as if drunk. The crowd cheered lustily for him to continue, to fight off the fatigue, to win. His final collapse came near the finish line as the eventual winner, an American runner named John Hayes was just entering the stadium. Pietri in defeat had given the spectators more than 300 yards of raw human courage—the kind of effort that even in defeat exemplifies the spirit of man at his best.

But reversal need not occur at the end. The kind of event referred to as a "pivotal point," or a "turning point," usually carries the kind of impact that is referred to by the concept of reversal. These events carry the premonition of impending defeat. While the contest must yet run its course, one senses that the outcome has been decided. In the Liberty Bowl football game of 1971, a field goal was disallowed that would have made the score 16-7, Arkansas. The tenor of the game was such that it was obvious points would be scarce. The field goal would have lifted the Razorbacks to relative security. But the penalty voiding the kick served as a premonition which was felt by player and spectator alike. One could almost predict what was to happen. The Tennessee team scored a late touchdown; the final score was 14-13, Tennessee, although Arkansas had dominated the game. Coach Broyles could be seen squeezing his head as if it were impossible for him to believe or accept the result.

Tragedy does not preclude the possibility of a happy end. (2:p.7; 1451a,12-16). This is necessarily the case in athletics for while defeat brings unhappiness, victory brings joy to the same contest. Aesthetically, both winner and loser are appreciated for having "played the tragedy" so to speak. In the humanistic sense, the winner is tragic for he denies the "other" what both hold supreme; that is, victory in the contest, and victory for the athlete is synonymous with fulfillment. The "other" athlete, the loser, is not "another," but rather, he is the universal athlete. As such he is a participant in the same order of consciousness as are the victors. Both "achieve" and fail to "achieve."

"Hamartia" is a crucial part of the plot in a tragedy. You will recall that "hamartia" is a tragic failing. It is the necessary mistake or flaw which eventuates defeat. It may be a physical shortcoming, an inability to perform a certain skill at a sufficient level to avoid defeat. The quarterback looks for a weakness of this nature in the defense which he can attack and exploit; wishing to hasten the fall, he initiates action aimed at a formation which is not appropriate—a sort of mental failing by the defensive coordinator. Scouting reports are aimed at uncovering such weaknesses, mental and physical. Such information may not be used until the most opportune moment—the instant when its use will inflict the most telling damage to the opponent.

The "failing," the fateful flaw, does not always occur on the defensive side. At the crucial moment, with 31 seconds left to play, Jan Stenerud was called upon to kick a 31 yard field goal against Miami in the waning seconds of the game. He had not missed from that distance all season, but this one—the most important goal of his career—was not to be. His identity as the premier kicker in the NFL was besmirched. Kansas City lost in the longest football contest in history.

Mental and emotional failings may take the form of "blowing one's cool," or losing concentration. Often the one-upsmanship strategy is employed in a calculated effort to cause a failing. Athletes with low "boiling" points are goaded in an attempt to get them ejected from a game, at least to rattle them. Coaches will call for a "time out" to allow a poor free throw shooter time to think about missing a crucial attempt. Another example of "hamartia" in the tragic athletic contest is the athlete or team that habitually practices with exceptional skill, but always seems to deliver a manque performance in the contest itself. A defect is exposed which Weiss calls a defect in character. (20:p.168). Just as in the drama, "hamartia" takes many forms in the athletic contest.

The final concept that must be given attention to complete the discussion of plot is "catharsis." Catharsis is concerned with reactions of spectators. The curative effect Aristotle attributed to tragedy is a product of the release of pleasurable excitement at events of a serious and critical nature. The knowledgeable spectator is aware of the seriousness of athletics: "No one at any time likes to lose, but the athlete performing before an audience is forced to 'win' instead of playing for 'play's sake.' Winning becomes the primary motivation." (18:p.698). Losing is a kind of evil to be avoided. We are symathetic for those athletes who seem to deserve a more just reward than fate has in store for them.

The plot with recognition and reversal near the end causes cathartic upsurges of pleasurable excitement and emotional release. The psyche is liberated of tensions that often stretch beyond the perimeters of the contest. The contest provides for a maintenance of mental tonus. (4:p.41).

The tragic plot spins out a web of episodes complicating the recognition process. Reversals increase the tensions. With winning as the "raison d'etre" of the contest, any hint of defeat elicits fear. It is this kind of dramatic plot which evokes emotions and produces the cathartic effect. (21:p.403).

> Like culture and the arts in general, sport exteriorizes those feelings and emotions in the player and, by empathy, in the spectator, thereby assuming the function of 'catharsis,' of purification. (13:p.32).

The aesthetician is wary of the trend in athletics of viewing an opponent as an enemy to be literally destroyed. Such a plot does not evoke pity and fear. As you all know, Aristotle plainly believed that when enemy crushes enemy as in war, pity and fear were not forthcoming. We tend to justify the conquering of an enemy as a deserved fate. The warlike model of athletics is reminiscent of the Roman gladiatorial games in which the loser often received "thumbs down" and paid with his life. There is no longer a "mimesis" of pleasurable action in such events, only the stark reality of depravity and terror.

Character

The "character" of the tragic contest is conveyed through plot, through adversaries vying with a necessity which decrees that one side shall win and one lose. When the players are excellent performers, as actors are excellent performers, they bring greatness to their roles. Good athletes give us good action in the plot. They characterize well the purposiveness and seriousness of the plot. But what of the tie? What of that contest that provides good action, elicits the emotions of pity and fear, and ends in a draw? Can it be considered tragic?

At the festivals of ancient Greece a drawn contest was called "no contest," or a "sacred contest." In a "sacred contest" the prize for victory was offered to the gods. (6:p.167). In crucial contests, those of great magnitude, the rules are amended to allow a decision. There is precedent for this procedure among the beauty-loving ancient Greeks. Races ending in a tie were repeated until a decision was reached. One runner defeated his opponent in the stade race (200 yards) on the fourth repeat. (6:p.160). The implication is that the true character of an athletic contest is that winner and loser are inexorably sought.

A tie is not tragic. Such contests cannot qualify aesthetically. Crisis passes without a solution to dilemma; a temporal end is achieved; a definite aesthetic end is not. A draw does not cause the intense sort of emotional suffering that accompanies defeat; it doesn't arouse that pleasurable catharsis. The standard line in athletics is that a tie is "like kissing your sister." Remember, it is the *quality* of action attending a tie which concerns us and not the quantitative result alone.

Thought and Diction

Language portrays the thinking of the players as well as the character of the plot. For the aesthetician the language or medium of the athlete is bodily movement. These movements represent the mind of the athlete. The athlete's movement has a visual impact on spectators in the way that an actor's language has mental impact on the audience. The athlete's movements indicate his thoughts, you might say. Movement symbolizes his existence and possesses meaning for him as an avenue to knowledge in the athletic medium. (14). Movement reflects not only the thoughts of athletes, but of coaches as well. Like a choreographer, his thoughts can be read in the strategies released through movements. Meaning of underlying thought accompanying movement is released and understood when the execution of movements is skillful. Execution is the diction of the athlete's language.

Melody and Spectacle

The athletic contest has a circus atmosphere. The "big game" has its pre-game, half-time, and post-game music, entertainment, appetizers, color, pageantry, costuming, exhibitions and displays. These things are not essential to the tragic contest. They provide pleasure in a trivial sort of way. Spectacle has nothing to do with the actual struggle. It is a technical fabrication as are stage backdrops. The integrity of the contest as a tragedy remains intact without either music or spectacle.

SUMMARY

In summary, an athletic tragedy has plot, character, thought, diction, melody, and spectacle. The plot is fundamental. It must be of sufficient length to allow for the development of pleasing action. The plot illustrates a good athlete coming to a state of unhappiness. His unhappiness is precipitated by a failing on his part that appears unavoidable. The plot that has the strongest cathartic effect is one which presents recognition and reversal concurrently near the end of the contest.

The tragedy seems to be an essential element in our universe. (10: p.352). It teaches us that for many men, the ultimate achievement is defeat and that the highest level of performance, the most noble effort, may end in defeat. The athlete who is second best symbolizes both excellence and failure. If the athletic contest has reached its apotheosis in the quantitative realm, the qualitative domain awaits discovery. I have suggested that an understanding of Aristotelian tragedy affords a stylized aesthetic perspective of the athletic contest understood primarily in terms of process rather than outcome. Dramatic tragedy is proffered as a method for understanding the beauty in the process of athletics and for extending our human sympathies to "tragic" athletes. The beauty of the "tragic" athlete is found in his ability to seize a "spiritual" victory from a natural defeat.

REFERENCES

1. Aristotle: *On Poetry and Style.* Translated with an introduction by G.M.A. Grube (trans.). Ann Arbor: University of Michigan Press, 1967.
2. Aristotle: "Poetics," *Introduction to Aristotle,* Richard McKeon (ed.). New York, The Modern Library, 1947.
3. Dewey, John: *Art as Experience.* New York, Minton, Balch and Company, 1934.
4. Elias, Norbert, and Dunning, Eric: "The Quest for Excitement in Unexciting Societies," *The Cross-Cultural Analysis of Sport and Games,* Gunther Luschen (ed.). Champaign, Stipes, 1970.

5. Else, Gerald F.: *The Origin and Early Form of Greek Tragedy.* Cambridge, Harvard University Press, 1965.

6. Harris, H.A.: *Greek Athletes and Athletics.* Bloomington, Indiana University Press, 1966.

7. Harrison, Jane E.: *Ancient Art and Ritual.* New York, Greenwood Press, 1969.

8. Huizinga, Johan: *Homo Ludens: A Study of the Play-Element in Culture.* Boston, Beacon Press, 1955.

9. Kaelin, E.F.: "The Well-Played Game: Notes Toward an Aesthetics of Sport," *Quest,* No. 10, 16-28, (May, 1968).

10. Kaufman, Walter: *Tragedy and Philosophy.* Garden City, Doubleday, 1969.

11. Keating, James: "Winning in Sport and Athletics," *Thought,* Vol. 38, No. 149, 201-210, (Summer, 1963).

12. Lenk, Hans: "The Philosophy of Sport." Unpublished manuscript, University of Karlsruhe, 1971.

13. Maheu, R.: "Sport and Culture," *Journal of Health, Physical Education, and Recreation,* Vol. 34, No. 8, 30 (October, 1963).

14. Metheny, Eleanor: *Movement and Meaning.* New York, McGraw-Hill, 1968.

15. Mill, John Stuart: *The Oxford English Dictionary.* Oxford, Clarendon Press, 1933.

16. Muller, Herbert J.: *The Uses of the Past.* London, Oxford University Press, Inc., 1952.

17. Raphael, D.D.: *The Paradox of Tragedy.* Bloomington, Indiana University Press, 1961.

18. Slovenko, Ralph, and Knight, James A.: *Motivation in Play, Games and Sport.* Springfield, Thomas, 1967.

19. Slusher, Howard: *Man, Sport and Existence: A Critical Analysis.* Philadelphia, Lea and Febiger, 1967.

20. Weiss, Paul: *Sport: A Philosophic Inquiry.* Carbondale, Southern Illinois University Press, 1969.

21. Wenkart, Simon: "The Meaning of Sports for Contemporary Man," *Journal of Existential Psychiatry,* Vol. 3, No. 12, 397-404, (Spring, 1963).

AN HEGELIAN INTERPRETATION OF ART, SPORT, AND ATHLETICS

ROBERT G. OSTERHOUDT

INTRODUCTION

It is the intent of the present inquiry to develop a discussion of Hegel's general philosophic commitments, most particularly those of an aesthetic dimension, and to suggest the implications of these views for regarding sport and athletics as an art form. It ought to be clear, then, that we are not expressing an interest in Hegel's interpretation of sport and athletics as an art form, an interpretation not forthcoming from the great philosopher himself, but an interest in an independent interpretation of sport and athletics as implied by Hegel's reflections upon art. The major purpose of the treatise consequently becomes an attempt to suggest what might be made of the nature and significance of sport and athletics given the philosophic foundations of Hegelianism, and to further propose what might be made of the relation of sport and athletics to the fine arts given these foundations. The preference here, then, is to concentrate upon an interpretation of the Hegelian aesthetic; such that, its relevance to sport and athletics becomes at once evident and revealing of an aesthetic posture proper to sport and athletics.

An inspection of the literature concerning the philosophy of sport and athletics reveals that little of an authentically idealistic disposition is to be found there. It also reveals that little has been written to suggest the relation of sport and athletics to the fine arts. The present inquiry is in some measure intended to eliminate both of these oversights. The scope of such an effort is so unmistakably great that this essay ought be regarded as little more than an introduction to the enterprise at hand.

For one inclined to idealistic-tending world views a reflection upon Hegelian notions of art, as well as those with respect to the whole of reality, come easily and are perhaps more instructive than deliberations over alternative notions. For Hegel must clearly be regarded as among the purest and grandest exponents of such views, as among the greatest civilizers of Western culture. As Carritt observes, Hegel's high place in the history of philosophy is secure:

> Hegel was the last great speculative genius who has appeared in the history of philosophy, a genius of the class of Plato and Aristotle, of Descartes, Vico and Kant. (8:p. 13).

And Kaufmann holds him in similar high esteem:

> It is generally agreed that Hegel was one of the greatest philosophers of all time, and no philosopher since 1800 has had more influence. A study of Hegel enriches our comprehension of subsequent philosophy and

theology, political theory and literary criticism. Indeed, recent intellectual history cannot be understood apart from him. (19:p. VII).

All such investigations, it is suspicioned, are in the end reducible to metaphysical foundations (a mosaic of basic assumptions and their rational, intuitive, and empirical consequences concerning the nature and significance of reality), or are, at any rate, fundamentally based upon such frameworks. All else, then, is derived or inferred from these bases; such that, an attempt to make the basic assumptions of the discourse explicit, to posit and defend them, to put forward their origin and development appears advisable. Otherwise, these first principles are allowed to flow tacitly into and out of the discussion without explicit attention or defense, or without due explanation concerning the origin of the problems with which they deal. Indeed, Hegel himself was of the view that propositions of speculative philosophy can be properly understood only in the context of a comprehensive, all-embracing system of thought, and not by themselves as fragmented bits of knowledge. And since the aesthetic views of Hegel, like those concerning all other dimensions of his thought, are so intimately bound to his metaphysical system, the offering of a brief overview of that system, prior to developing an exposition of his aesthetic platform, is well recommended.

THE GENERAL FORM OF IDEALISM AND THE FUNDAMENTAL NATURE OF THE HEGELIAN ENTERPRISE

Hegel must be counted among the major participants in the philosophic tradition of idealism. His view, like all others of an idealistic cast, proceeds on the notion that reality is best conceived, explained, understood in terms of ideas, thought, spirit, soul—that the fundamental interpretative principle of reality is ideally, or intellectually, constituted. Idealism, then, is regarded as a philosophic system emphasizing mind or what is characteristically of pre-eminent value to it. By it, the explanation of all things is sought in terms of the mind, in terms of the spiritual. Reality, by this view, is spiritually disposed, idea-centered, of the stuff of mind: the nature and significance of knowledge and reality are one. In a phrase, idealism posits the primacy of mind. It regards the mind as philosophically primary, as that from which an apprehension of all else is derived. In so doing it does not deny the existence of the phenomenal (material, external) world, but rather construes and explains that world in terms of idea. Idealism consequently claims that, that world is derivative of mind. For the idealist, then, reality is itself a spiritual order. Such that, it is the charge of man to pursue a harmony with that order (a harmony with his most perfect, his unsullied aspect), to act in accord with it, to seek its realization, to cultivate its will to intellectual and creative perfection, to establish his likeness to it.

Though it is not the explicit, nor feasible, intent of the present inquiry to argue exhaustively for the general virtues of idealism, or the specific attractions of its Hegelian forms, as over and above those of alternative inclination, a brief statement as to its major strengths and weaknesses does appear appropriate. Idealism begins, and ends for that matter, with our most immediate and indubitable apprehension, and best accounts for it; namely, the mind or that which is constituent to it. We have no distinctly human civilization, no academy, no philosophy without the triumphs of intellectual activity. In this respect the metaphysical, epistemological, and axiologic focus of idealism is intuitively appealing. The system also generally advances a synoptic account of reality—one which makes a noticeable attempt to explain and understand all that might be explained and understood. That is, of all major philosophic systems the vision of idealism is perhaps greatest, its order of scepticism least abiding and intolerant.

This expansive perspective common to idealistic systems of thought has led many antagonists of idealism to argue that its comprehensiveness is arbitrary, dogmatic, contrived, schematic, and, as a result, bogus, or ingenuine; suggesting that an explanation of the whole of reality, or of as large a part of it as idealism commonly undertakes, may not be obtainable. Of course, an exhaustive review of the evidence employed by such systems as appropriate would need be made in order to determine the force of this objection. Quite obviously, such a review far exceeds the scope of the present effort. Though the feasibility of achieving an explanation of the sort generally sought by idealism is certainly open to serious question, an overzealous dismissal of its attainability seems also unwise. A superficial inspection of the matter, the only sort available to us here, reveals no more evidence to suggest its infeasibility than to support its feasibility. Since, then, it is the general charge of philosophy to approach this ideal of the synoptic as best it might be approached, the ardor of idealism to do so apparently comes to no more a weakness than a strength. That is, the greatness of a philosophic system is measured by its ability to plausibly account for the whole of reality in its most general, accessible constitution; and idealism, so it would appear, has taken the most fearless strides toward achieving this objective.

Another charge popularly levelled against idealism concerns the great difficulty with which it is understood, and, resultantly, the enormous number of its misconceptions. We ought not be surprised to learn, however, that the popular appeal of such a complex doctrine concerning such complex affairs is limited. And it does very much appear to be the case that its popular appeal is not so much in question here as the persuasive force of its arguments. For one of a sceptical disposition similar to that reported by idealistic views the adoption of such a system of ideas, as opposed to other such systems, seems well advised.

Given the identified purposes of this essay, it will not be feasible to attempt a full blown account of the Hegelian enterprise. A cursory overview of Hegel's general philosophic stance may prove helpful, nevertheless.

Much in the spirit of harmonization characteristic of Greek thought, which he greatly admired, Hegel protested the philosophic fragmentation of man. In accord with the insight of Fichte and Schelling, his rejection of Kant's material thing-in-itself as unduly speculative and in violation of Kant's own premises, defined his complete commitment to monism, and allowed his system to cohere in a fashion virtually unknown to his predecessors of pluralistic persuasion. He held, much in agreement with the predominant line of thought in modern Western philosophy from Descartes to Kant, that the source of all knowledge is experience. His allegiance to Kant's transcendental method of argument, however, led him to the view, as Friedrich contends, that, though ". . . all knowledge commences with experience, . . . it does not flow from it. The higher knowledge of philosophy has to be applied to it as a measuring rod." (10:p.XXVII). Hegel would have asked, in effect, what must be presupposed of art, sport, and athletics, in this case, so as to explain the indubitable character of experience associated with them? What must art, sport, and athletics be so as to be an object of this experience? Hegel was, as a result, committed to a circular view of knowledge in which an interaction among elements which refine one another occurs. In which case one must use all parts to understand the whole, and the whole (the Idea) to understand all parts.

Much as had Kant, then, Hegel avoided both the strict rationalist thesis by which the world is construed as conforming to a rigid mathematical or natural scientific model, as most notably in Descartes, Leibniz, and Spinoza; as well as the strict empiricist thesis in which the mind is construed in terms of conforming to the impressions of a mindless world, as most notably in Locke, Berkeley, and Hume. His view accounts for both the contributions of the mind to experience, thus escaping a hyper-empiricism which fails to explain much of life; and for the contributions of the world to experience, thus avoiding an equally as limited a priorism. As a clear advance to the Kantian enterprise in this regard, however, Hegel was also successful in explaining the creative flow and record of this experience throughout history with his notion that truth is historically unfolded in the dialectic of the Spirit. He also overcame the tacit dualism of Kant, and Kant's paradoxical allegiance to the material thing-in-itself as the causal agent of perception (sensation). In point of fact, Hegel never did engage himself in reflections concerning cosmological origin, as the Kantian antinomies themselves persuade. He also avoided the sort of God erected by Berkeley to explain perceptual causation.

We must conclude, then, that Hegel successfully overcame all of these difficulties while at the same moment retaining the impulse to metaphysics. His triumph over previous ages, therefore, is not one of a sceptical order, not one which simply rejects the problems and issues he inherited as philosophically inaccessible (a fashionable twentieth century tactic); but one of a genuinely creative character, one which drew those problems and issues into a new and more comprehensible unity. He offered a remarkable summary of that which preceeded him, and launched an entirely new epoch in the history of human thought.

It must be admitted that much of Hegel's metaphysics, if taken by itself, appears hopelessly bizarre, even nonsensical. In view of the philosophic tradition to which it responded, and out of which it emerged, however, it is actually quite plausible and yet remains a thesis of compelling proportion for the author. Indeed, Hegel's conciliation of the philosophic difficulties he inherited leads him rather inexorably to the sort of view commonly attributed to him. His discrete brand of rational, objective idealism committeed him to seek the harmony of universality and particularity, reason and nature — to the view that a single Spirit permeates all individuated forms, to a belief in the unity of reason. What exists, by this account, is consciousness and nothing but consciousness. All existence reduces itself to conscious events; such that, reality is construed as a mosaic of laws which regulate and explain these events.

For Hegel, the fundamental structure of reality, the essential nature of things, is spiritually constituted; that is, conceived in terms of a single complex, rational system, or Idea, the concrete manifestations of which become idealized (perfected, or progressively more adequately embodied) in time. These manifestations thereby become self-conscious of their universal participation, their Spiritual membership. It is Hegel's contention that the form of truth is at one with this system of rationality, and that only by the rational process proper to philosophy may the Idea be apprehended, may we account for the full-realization, the self-actualization, of the world. It is the task of philosophy, then, to reveal the characteristic of reason in all things, to reveal the pattern of development inherent in the Idea, which the world merely copies. Hegel demonstrates that all concrete existence may be understood by this view. By it the actual is the rational and the rational the actual; for the course of reality is shaped and implicity guided by this rational network of laws, by this Logic. Philosophy, then, becomes the self-apprehension of Spirit, Thought thinking itself, and as such is considered the highest manifestation of Spirit.

As the previous discussion rather indicates, various forms are assumed by Spirit throughout its development. These forms represent a series of succeeding stages, from primitive forms of consciousness in which all things appear differentiated to absolute forms of consciousness in which all things are apprehended as a unity. Each of these stages is necessarily dependent on the previous one, and each develops toward pure rationality; that is, all stages, but the final one, are both a product (themselves discrete) and a prophecy (only an intermediate stage which leads to a yet higher one). And each is therefore concerned, in some respect, with natural, biological, psychological, social, political, economic, historical, artistic, religious, and philosophic developments. According to Hegel, then, the Idea acquiring bare inanimate existence becomes the physical world, which in turn acquires animate existence becomming life, which in turn acquires subjective, or idiosyncratic, consciousness becoming what Hegel terms Subjective Spirit, which in turn acquires interpersonal (intersubjective) existence becoming for Hegel Objective Spirit, which in turn acquires self-knowledge (reflection upon one's own, essentially rational nature) becoming the denouement, termed by Hegel Absolute Spirit.

He held that Absolute Spirit, or God, is the attainment of Spiritual Self-Consciousness. It is only here that Spirit becomes conscious of itself, and exists in and for itself. As revealed in his *The Phenomenology of Spirit,* Absolute Spirit is consciousness knowing itself, qua Spirit:

> The last embodiment of spirit—spirit which at once gives its complete and true content the form of self, and thereby realizes its notion, and in doing so remains within its own notion—this is *Absolute Knowledge.* It is spirit knowing itself in the shape of spirit, it is knowledge which comprehends through notions. (12:pp. 797-798).

That is, the world in the form of Absolute Spirit comes to adequately embody the system of reason. To be sure, the world exists for Hegel prior to becoming fully rational, but develops toward a collapse of the distinction between object and subject, substratum and attribute, subject and predicate, existence and essence, as so-termed material objects become invested more thoroughly with Spirit, or Subject. For according to Hegel, there is only consciousness and nothing but consciousness in its various forms, and this consciousness is exhausted by the multifarious specifications of these forms. Subject and substance are thereby reconciled in an enduring, rational unity.

It is additionally instructive to observe at this juncture that Hegel hasn't in mind here an orthodox Christian, mystic, or romantic notion of Absolute Spirit, or God; views he himself regarded as excessively speculative and worthy of disdain, but rather a philosophic conception of God existing as the perfection of the world and man, as Copleston observes:

> Absolute Spirit exists only in and through the human spirit, but it does

> so at the level at which the individual human spirit is no longer a
> finite mind, enclosed in its own private thoughts, emotions, interests and
> purposes, but has become a moment in the life of the infinite as an
> identity-in-difference which knows itself as such . . . man's knowledge
> of the Absolute and the Absolute's knowledge of itself are two aspects of
> the same reality. For Being actualizes itself as concretely existing self-
> thinking Thought through the human spirit. (6:p. 271).

The significance of man, as well as all else, consequently rests with his
being a manifestation of consciousness, and not his being a unique
human subjectivity, or a participant in the socio-political order. What
is essential to man, by this view, is not his unique particularity, itself
regarded as a form of Subjective Spirit by Hegel, or his facility for
engaging in interpersonal relationships and creating an institutional
heirarchy, itself regarded as a form of Objective Spirit by Hegel, but
the manifestations of him in the general scheme of things, in the
universal system of reason. This notion of the nature of man, which
is clearly related of course to other, more fundamental notions evoked
many of the most profound nineteenth century responses to Hegel,
principally those of Schopenhauer, Marx, Kierkegaard, and Nietzsche.

Hegel was further convinced that Absolute Spirit itself assumes a
number of forms; namely, art, religion, and philosophy, each of which
demands a progressively higher expression of its content, as Copleston
indicates:

> The infinite divine Being is, as it were, the content or subject-matter of
> all three spiritual activities. But though the content is the same, the
> form is different. That is to say, the Absolute is apprehended in different
> ways in these activities. (6:p. 273).

That is, each attains and conveys a consciousness of Absolute Spirit
in different ways—philosophy in the most satisfactorily complete way;
or, as Friedrich suggests of Hegel's notion as to the nature of philosophy: "Philosophy's task is concerned neither with what has been nor
with what will be, but with what is and is eternally so." (10:p.LIV).

For Hegel, Spirit develops by the interaction of consciousness and
the objects of consciousness. His account of the arts is particularly
revealing in terms of its offering an explanation of this interaction,
both with respect to a direct enhancement of our undertanding of an
idealistic aesthetic, as well as to a potential enhancement of our understanding of the nature and significance of sport and athletics.

THE GENERAL AESTHETIC VIEW OF HEGEL

Hegel expressly wished to construct his aesthetic view from a description of the historical development of art; that is, to work out of traditional concepts of art thereby offering a causative account of it, and not from his metaphysics by which a normative explanation would have been forthcoming. He was in one sense successful in this regard, and, in another sense not so. His aesthetic view is very largely composed of a subtly interspun synthesis of both historical and non-temporal accounts. Though it is generally quite difficult to separate these two directions in Hegel's work (something that should not be at all surprising given the aforementioned character of his metaphysics which allows that the historical process is inherent in its products, and that the scheme of these products is likewise inherent in the processes which produce them), we must make the attempt in the interest of clarity. This so-termed double principle of classification, or the development of an aesthetic view from a permanent-analytic (logical) schema in one direction and from an historical schema in another, allows Hegel to treat the arts generally in the case of the former interest, and individually in the case of the latter. The three forms of art (symbolic, classical, and romantic), as construed by Hegel, taken together compose the major outline of the general historical evolution of the arts (the Ideal). Taken separately, the co-existing modes of expression, or individual arts, repeat themselves in each of these three forms, and are further distinguished only in virtue of the discrete sensuous vehicles (media) they respectively employ. Hegel's general view of art, and the manner of its affiliation with his metaphics and philosophy of history, is well summarized in a passage from his *Lectures on Aesthetics*:

> And, therefore, what the particular arts realize in individual works of art, are according to their abstract conception simply the universal types which constitute the self-unfolding Idea of beauty. It is as the external realization of this Idea that the wide Pantheon of art is being erected, whose architect and builder is the spirit of beauty as it awakens to self-knowledge, and to complete which the history of the world will need its evolution of ages. (10:p. 395).

Hegel's view concerning the relation of the sensuous to the Absolute, though tacitly in evidence from previous discussions, is particularly crucial to an understanding of his general aesthetic posture, and so ought to be made explicit here. Copleston indicates of Hegel's view in this regard that:

> Dialectically or logically speaking, the Absolute is manifested first of all in the form of immediacy, under the guise, that is to say, of objects of sense. As such, it is apprehended as beauty, which is 'the sensuous semblance of the Idea'. And this sensuous appearance of the Idea, this shining of the Absolute through the veils of sense, is called the Ideal . . . Hence the Idea as beauty is termed the Ideal. (6:p. 275).

Accordingly, a work of art is not to be regarded as a natural product, but one clearly superior to one of Nature; that is, one more thoroughly invested with Spirit, one constructed via the rational intent of the artist, as suggested by Copleston:

> While not denying that there can be such a thing as beauty in Nature, Hegel insists that beauty in art is far superior. For artistic beauty is the immediate creation of Spirit; it is Spirit's manifestation of itself to itself. And Spirit and its products are superior to Nature and its phenomena. Hegel confines his attention, therefore, to beauty in art. (6:p. 275).

In accord with his general philosophic view, then, and as revealed in his *Lectures on Aesthetics,* Hegel regards art as effecting a certain measure of unity between the sensuous and the spiritual:

> Inasmuch, however, as it is the function of art to represent the Idea to immediate vision in sensuous shape and not in the form of thought and pure spirituality in the strict sense, and inasmuch as the value and intrinsic worth of this presentment consists in the correspondence and unity of the two aspects, that is the Idea and its sensuous shape, the supreme level and excellence of art and the reality, which is truly consonant with its notion, will depend upon the degree of intimacy and union with which idea and configuration appear together in elaborated fusion. (13:p. 98).

Art imbues sensuous form with spiritual significance. It reveals the truth (spiritual) in concrete shape (sensuous): ". . . the sensuous is spiritualized in art, or, in other words, the life of spirit comes to dwell in it under sensuous guise." (13:p.53). In art, Idea (spirituality) and material (sensuality) coalesce; are reconciled in a synthesis as a form of Absolute Spirit: ". . . it is art's function to reveal truth under the mode of art's sensuous or material configuration, to display the reconciled antithesis . . ." (13:p.77). As Copleston further observes:

The Idea is the unity of subjectivity and objectivity. And in the beautiful work of art this unity is expressed or represented in the union of spiritual content with external or material embodiment. Spirit and matter, subjectivity and objectivity, are fused together in a harmonious unity or synthesis. (6:pp. 275-276).

It is additionally profitable, however, to reinforce the observation that the controlling (primary) impulse in art is rational, and not sensuous, as Friedrich suggests:

Thus its development is not accomplished by virtue of an external activity, but by the specific force inherent in the idea itself; so that the Idea, which develops itself in a totality of particular forms, is what the world of art presents us. (10:p. 333).

"Hence, imperfection of the artistic form betrays itself also as imperfection of the idea." (10:p.334). Art, therefore, is ultimately the mind intuitively perceiving its inner essence in a certain fashion, as several passages from the *Lectures on Aesthetics* indicate:

A work of art is only truly such in so far as originating in the human spirit, it continues to belong to the soil from which it sprang, has received, in short, the baptism of the mind and soul of man, and only presents that which is fashioned in consonance with such a sacrament . . . And for this reason the work of art is of higher rank than any product of Nature whatever, which has not submitted to this passage through the mind . . . Everything which partakes of spirit is better than anything begotten of mere Nature. (13:p. 39).

. . . the sensuous aspect of a work of art has a right to determinate existence only in so far as it exists for the human mind, not, however, in so far as itself, as a material object, exists for itself independently . . . The lowest in grade and that least compatible with relation to intelligence is purely sensuous sensation. (13:p. 48).

Art, consequently, for Hegel, proceeds at a level of consciousness considerably above that enjoyed by the relationship of concrete particular object to concrete particular object, above that of the relationship of such objects to animate entities, above that of the relationship of animate entities to subjective consciousness, even above that of the relationship among subjective consciousnesses; though below that proper to religion and philosophy in which the rational impulse is less sullied by sensuous influence. Since the artistic consciousness operates on a level above the purely particular, art objects (products) are not to be regarded as literal representations (duplications or imitations) of particular objects, but as Hegel termed them 'semblances' of such objects. These 'semblances' occupy a position in the schema intermediate to that held by the purely sensuous and that held by the purely rational. They are objects that combine the concreteness of the material and the abstractness of the spiritual. They are objects which reflect the quality of artistic contemplation from which their forms emerge.

As direct participants in the consciousness of the Abstolute, then, they are significant alone in virtue of their being the unique sorts of objects that they are, in terms of their being what they are in and for themselves, as also in the case of both religion and philosophy. They are disinterested in any particular sense. The significance of the arts is at one with their nature. They care not to look beyond themselves for a discovery of their significance. The so-termed applied arts are, in fact, then, misnomers, and not actually arts at all. The arts proper are to be understood, not employed in the service of that which is other than artistic, as revealed in the *Lectures on Aesthetics*:

> The theoretic contemplation of objects has no interest in consuming the same in their particularity and satisfying or maintaining itself through the sense by their means; its object is to attain a knowledge of them in their universality, to seek out their ideal nature and principle, to comprehend them according to their notional idea. (13:p. 50).

We must be careful to observe at this juncture, however, that Hegel does not deny that art performs functions beyond its merely being understood. He simply rejects the notion, as he must given his prior commitments to the nature of Absolute Spirit, that these mere consequences of artistic activity are essential to it. This view, then, allows him to admit that art may very well convey something of the aesthetic possibilities of man, that it may mollify and/or heighten the forces of emotion, produce delight, offer a palliative to strife and anguish, and that it may be capable of performing a social, moral, and/or didactic function; while at the very same moment denying that such accidental effects, common to many human enterprises, are necessary to art, qua art. The arts, consequently, remain primarily spiritual entities for Hegel despite our utilitarian, instrumental, and imitative treatments of them, as well as our cathartic, communicative, experiential, moral, palliative, pedagogical, and pleasurable responses to them.

From these observations an additional number of notable consequences show themselves. For one, the impulse to art cannot be essentially motivated by the preservation of self, or by the immediate indulgence, or satisfaction, of one's simple pleasures, one's capricious inclinations. That is, this impulse must be of an entirely disinterested variety, as in Kant's *Analytic of the Beautiful*: "Everyone must admit that a judgment on beauty in which the slightest interest mingles is highly partisan and not a pure judgment of taste." (17:p.5). For in the arts the poetic aspiration to, and knowledge of the Absolute is venerated in and for itself; in which case, such a use of it constitutes its employ as a means to the realization of something non-artistic by Hegelian standards. And for another, this intrinsic valuation of the arts (as inherent in the nature of Absolute Spirit), together with the nature of its historicity (also inherent in the nature of Absolute Spirit), commits Hegel to regarding the arts as permanent, universal, enduring, in a sense in which things of a lower order of consciousness are not. For there is nothing contingent in them by which they might change, as suggested in the *Lectures on Aesthetics*:

> . . . all that the mind borrows from its own ideal content it is able, even in the direction of external existence, to endow with permanence. The individual living thing on the contrary is transitory; it vanishes and is unstable in its external aspect. The work of art persists. (13:p. 39).

and as presented in Schiller's *On the Aesthetic Education of Man*: "Beauty gives no individual result whatever . . . But precisely by this means something infinite is attained." (29:p.101).

Art, then, is regarded by Hegel as a free, self-conscious activity of Spirit, a seeking after truth, after a form, albeit an imperfect form, of Absolute Spirit. Man engages himself in artistic activity from a rational impulse to self-knowledge which assumes the form of his offering an external embodiment of himself, as indicated in the *Lectures on Aesthetics*:

> This universal demand for artistic expression is based on the rational impulse in man's nature to exalt both the world of his soul experience and that of Nature for himself into the conscious embrace of mind as an object in which he rediscovers himself. He satisfies the demand of this spiritual freedom by making explicit to his inner life all that exists, no less than from the further point of view giving a realized external embodiment to the self made thus explicit. (13:pp. 42-43).

The production of such a so-termed self-image goes as an expression of something universal as to the fundamental character of reality, however, and not merely as a conveyance of autobiographical information.

Having established the nature of Hegel's general aesthetic position, we now pass to a discussion of his views of art in historical perspective. Of principal interest here is the relation of these views to those of a non-temporal character before treated. In suggesting the tripartite distinction that he does with respect to this issue, Hegel speaks of the artistic embodiment of ideas peculiar to particular epochs, as observed by Friedrich: "The idea of each epoch always finds its appropriate and adequate form; and these are what we designate as the special forms of art." (10:p.334). These three special forms of art (symbolic, classical, and romantic) therefore represent the three specific relations of the Idea to its artistic embodiment. That is, each represents a progressively more satisfactory embodiment of Spirit. In his exposition concerning Hegel's work in aesthetics, Copleston alludes to the greater adequacy of some forms than others in achieving this embodiment, and to the resultant distinction between symbolic, classical, and romantic art:

> In the perfect work of art, therefore, there is complete harmony between ideal content and its sensuous form or embodiment. The two elements interpenetrate and are fused into one. But this artistic ideal is not always attained. And the different possible types of relation between the two elements give us the fundamental types of art. (6:p. 276).

The symbolic form of art grasps Spirit in only a very crude manner according to Hegel. As such, it is overendowed with its material aspect, and consequently more remote from God than either classical or romantic forms. In it the sensuous dominates the spiritual. The Absolute is, in large measure, hidden; that is, not too evidently displayed, mysterious, or enigmatic. In it, the spiritual has not mastered its medium, but is instead overpowered (or dominated) by it, as Friedrich suggests:

> The first is the Symbolic Form. Here the idea seeks its true expression in art without finding it; because, being still abstract and indefinite, it cannot create an external manifestation which conforms to its real essence. (10:p. 334).

Architecture, and its ornamentation, is the art least fitted to expressing the dynamic life of Spirit, and is, resultantly, for Hegel, the typical symbolic form. Not unsurprisingly, then, symbolic art was best suited to the earliest stages of human history—to the ancient Egyptian, Hebrew, Hindu, Indian, and Persian cultures.

In classical art, unlike the symbolic form, spiritual content is actually expressed, and not merely cited or symbolized: the spiritual and the sensuous are harmoniously unified in this form, as Friedrich contends: "This unity, this perfect harmony between the idea and its external manifestation, constitutes the second form of art—the Classic Form." (10:p.334). In classical art, the rational and the material are entirely adequate to one another; that is, they present a tranquility with respect to one another. This marvelous harmony of the spiritual and the sensuous characterizes the classical form as that possessing the greatest beauty according to Hegel. With respect to this harmony, then, no art form exceeds it, though in terms of its quest for the Absolute it is less adequate than romantic art, and religion and philosophy as well for that matter; all of which are less thoroughly endowed with the sensuous. For Hegel, then, sculpture is regarded as the typical classical form of art, and the ancient Graeco-Roman cultures are considered the best suited to its development.

Unlike the case with respect to either symbolic or classical art, no sensuous embodiment is adequate to the spiritual content of romantic art, as Copleston observes: ". . . romantic art, in which Spirit [is] felt as infinite, tends to overflow, as it were, its sensuous embodiment and to abandon the veils of sense." (6:p.278). Romantic art, therefore, is much less concerned with the material, or purely representative form, than with awakening a consciousness of Reality, Spirit, the Infinite. In point of fact, when the Idea of beauty, or the Ideal, becomes aware of itself as Spirit, it, in like manner and moment, discovers itself as no longer realized in material form, but only in the internal world of consciousness—only as unconditionally free, self-conscious, inward intelligence, as in the pure judgment of taste in Kant's *Analytic of the Beautiful*: "A pure judgment of taste is one upon which sensuous and emotional appeals have no influence . . ." (17:p.28). In these terms, then, romantic art transcends itself; that is, overpowers and overflows any finite, sensuous embodiment and becomes a genuine conveyance of Spirit, as from the *Lectures on Aesthetics*: ". . . romantic art must be regarded as art transcending itself, albeit within the boundary of its own province, and in the form of art itself." (13: p.108).

Romantic art, like symbolic forms and unlike classical forms of art, produces a separation of the sensuous and the spiritual, and not a harmonization of them. Somewhat as symbolic forms entail a material excess, however, romantic forms exhibit one of a spiritual disposition. The excess of Spirit apparent in romantic art establishes it as the highest, though not the most beautiful, of the art forms, as from the *Lectures on Aesthetics*:

> As an escape from such a condition the romantic form of art in its turn dissolves the inseparable unity of the classical phase, because it has won a significance which goes beyond the classical form of art and its mode of apprehension. (10:p. 380).

It leads art to a higher form of expression: it approaches a passage into religious consciousness. According to Hegel, music, painting, literature, and poetry are the typical romantic art forms. He regards poetry as the greatest of the arts, and the genius of Christendom as the major historical vehicle for the development of the romantic form. It is important to note as well that, for Hegel, the specifically different arts typically associated with one of these three forms (symbolic, classical, romantic) are not of necessity confined to any one of them, though they generally appear in the manner here outlined.

The precise distinctions between each of the specific arts are not explicitly developed in Hegel. As a result, an understanding of these distinctions is not so readily accessible as is an understanding of many other aspects of the Hegelian aesthetic. The arts are, of course, distinguishable in virtue of their different forms generally aspiring to different orders of consciousness, according to Hegel. That is, some (most particularly poetry for Hegel) more nearly approach a full realization of the Absolute than do others. The proportion of the sensuous and the spiritual indigenous to each differs; such that, a specific art form may be distinguished from any other by reference to this proportion. The individual arts differ in this regard in terms of their being expressible in media quite characteristically different from one another. These media are regarded, then, as adequate embodiments for the spiritual reflections which create the work of art. That is, these media accurately manifest the notions which form what are commonly known as art products, or art objects, and serve to offer a readily available distinction among the arts. By this view, then, that order of consciousness appropriate to, let us say, music is not likewise proper or available to sculpture, and the like.

One very major remaining distinction to be made, independently of the Hegelian view, with respect to these media is that between the arts of spatial and those of temporal media. Those possessing spatial media (architecture, sculpture, painting, literature, drama, poetry) do not require that a performance intermediate between their products, and an observance of those products, qua art forms. For, in accord with the demands of these arts, the product is itself directly observable as that art form. In the case of those possessing temporal media (theater, opera, cinema, dance, music), a performance extracted rather directly from the art product is necessary to an observance (even to the existence) of the art form in question. That is, film script, choreographic score, or musical notation, for example, are art objects only in a derivative sense—not themselves actually cinema, dance, nor music—unlike the case with respect to the arts of spatial media. In point of fact, the temporal arts presuppose the development of a notative form so as to preserve and transmit them. In the case of sport and athletics this form is very poorly developed, though the use of film and systems of not altogether superior choreographic notation have been somewhat helpful. We raise the distinction here as it allows us to presage the alignment of sport and athletics with the arts of temporal media, thereby distinguishing them from those of a spatial sort. It is additionally instructive to note with respect to the media of sport and athletics that, with those of the dance, they are less plastic (less materially encumbered) than the typical symbolic and classical arts, and so possess a metaphysical inherency appropriate to the arts of romantic proportion.

With this foundational knowledge now in hand, we must turn our attention to the central concern of the essay. We must now suggest what it is that the Hegelian conception of reality (to include the arts, most importantly for our interests) allows us to imply of the nature and significance of sport and athletics. More precisely, we must indicate in what terms such a system allows us to construe sport and athletics and of what significant consequence such an interpretation is.

AN HEGELIAN INTERPRETATION OF ART, SPORT, AND ATHLETICS

As Santayana observes, the nature and significance of sport and athletics has been commonly overlooked: "And it seems to me that . . . in this phenomenon of athletics there is an underlying force, a power of human nature that commonly escapes us." (27:p.181). The remainder of the essay will be devoted to an examination of this force, which attracts and guides our involvement in sport and athletics.

Prior to considering the major consequences of Hegelianism for regarding sport and athletics as an art form, it is perhaps wise to develop a brief treatment of their specific natures, by which they are distinguished from other entities with which they are commonly confused; namely, movement, play, work, recreation, dance, exercise, games, and physical education. As in the case of the aforementioned arts, their distinguishing characters are defined in terms of the material embodiment appropriate to their respective spiritual limits, in terms of the nature of the activity as determined by its spiritual source. Since a treatment of these issues is not directly available in Hegel himself, we will need proceed here somewhat independently of the substance of his system, though yet guided in large measure by its spirit.

Movement, it seems, refers to a state of motion, which is inherent in the life of Spirit. This state assumes either an inertial form or a form in which inertial forms are in modification. It gives rise to no conceptual or phenomenal opposite, but is apparently fundamental to a satisfactory account of the dynamic character of reality, as in Metheny's *Movement and Meaning*: ". . . movement is the functional link between the subjective and objective components of human understanding." (24:p.22). It may be best understood in Hegelian terms, then, by regarding it as the principle of spiritual self-generation—the principle by which the Idea activates itself. When manifest in the human body as gross and fine psychomotor movement of a certain sort, it becomes potentially, at any rate, the general medium of the so-termed movement arts (dance, and, so we wish to argue, sport and athletics).

Play appears to be of an entirely different order. If we follow the view of Huizinga in this matter, and regard play as;

> . . . a free activity standing quite consciously outside 'ordinary' life as being 'not serious', but at the same time absorbing the player intensely and utterly, . . . [as] an activity connected with no material interest, and no profit can be gained by it, . . . [and as an activity which] proceeds within its own proper boundaries of time and space according to fixed rules and in an orderly manner. (15:p. 13).

we commit ourselves to the notion that play is best understood, in Hegelian terms, as the spirit of Absolute Spirit. That is, it is regarded as a quality of activity, the primary objective of which is to be understood (given Hegel's thoroughly rational, idealistic allegiances), and, as a result, to be valued in and for itself. It is, then, the spirit of activity necessary to Absolute Spirit, which allows that art, religion, and philosophy be voluntarily and intrinsically approached and discharged. Unlike the case with respect to movement, play does indeed give rise to an antithesis; namely, work. Work, then, it seemingly follows, is to be regarded as the spirit of activity which allows that the activities of which it is an axiologic guide, are extrinsically valued and involuntarily engaged. It is, consequently, in varying degree, the quality of activity necessary to Subjective Spirit and Objective Spirit; that is, necessary to the sustenance of one's biological and psychological integrity, as well as of one's intersubjective involvements with other selves and the socio-political order. By this view, then, play is clearly of a higher order than work, as it is more thoroughly invested with Spirit than is work.

Recreation, it is argued, is best construed as a collective referral to activities conducted at play; that is, to art, religion, and philosophy. By this view, play and recreation are not regarded as the frivolous, capricious, and uncompelling forms or qualities of activity occasionally withheld for them; but, as the respective form and content of Absolute Spirit itself. This position also coheres well with the popular notion that the great triumphs of culture rest upon, or presuppose, the establishment of a leisure-producing social fabric.

In accord with the view expressed by Metheny in her *Movement and Meaning*, exercise is perhaps best regarded as:

> . . . an organization of movements . . . devised for the purpose of producing certain effects on the being of the performer . . . These effects

may be described in anatomical, physiological, or psychological terms; but here we may include all these terms in the general conception of improving the functional capacity of the person in some way. (24:p. 84).

As such, it is clearly of Subjective Spirit, that is, primarily concerned with the use of gross and fine psychomotor movement for the express purpose of enhancing one's individual biology and/or psychology. In exercise, then, the interest in the activity at hand is one of an instrumental sort. It is, in effect, an interest in the bio-psychological effects of the movement, and not in the movement itself as in the case of play activities (recreation). Exercise, then, is conducted in the spirit of work, and possesses the intended content of improving one's bio-psychological constitution.

For the purpose of clarity in the forthcoming discussion, the temporal media characteristic of the movement arts must be further distinguished in terms of those of dance and those of the game arts (athletics, sport, and others). Games, then, are to be regarded as a collective category of activities, containing sport and athletics most importantly, which is distinguishable from the other arts in virtue of its different spiritual/sensuous form, as displayed in its different media. The game arts differ from the dance, then, only in virtue of their occurring in marginally different contexts (media) with marginally different rules and regulations (mosaic of specific, defining conditions). It is a difference in degree and not one of kind. These media of the game arts, which provide a vehicle for expression and a context for definition, are perhaps best explained by setting them out; that is, by suggesting the nature of sport, athletic, and other game arts, which together exhaust the category of games.

The distinction here proposed between athletic, sport, and other games is one based principally upon our interpretation of the Hegelian relation of the spiritual and sensuous content in each. In the case of athletics, its performance is entirely independent of direct, active, external influence in the form of the performance of a teammate, opponent, animate non-human, or inanimate self-propelled object or mechanical contrivance. By this view, then, only individual game activities qualify as authentically athletic; namely, track and field athletics, cross country, swimming and diving, gymnastics, figure skating, speed skating, weight lifting, singles sculling, cycling, skiing (alpine and cross country), ski jumping, mountain climbing, golf, bowling, curling, archery, and shooting. In athletics, consequently, the height of the athlete's performance is determined by the resolve of his own effort to achieve perfection, to achieve an understanding of Absolute Spirit.

In the case of sport, conversely, its performance is in some measure dependent upon the performance of a direct, active, external influence in the form of the performance of a teammate, opponent, animate non-human, or inanimate self-propelled object or mechanical contrivance. As a result, the sportsman is in some respects passive to the performance of which he is a part, unlike the case of the athlete. His resolve (constraint to the spiritual) is more diminished than that of the athlete. The focus of his performance is in this regard more heavily endowed with the sensuous than that of the athlete, and is therefore of a marginally lower order. The sport performance is not entirely synonymous, then, with the performance of the sportsman, unlike the case with respect to athletics. Included in the hierarchical order of sport are the combative dual sports (boxing, wrestling, and fencing), the court dual sports (tennis, badminton, squash, jai jala, and handball), team sports (yachting, rowing, soccer, baseball, basketball, football, ice hockey, field hockey, hurling, water polo, and lacrosse), sports involving an animate non-human (equestrian, polo, and horse racing), and sports involving inanimate self-propelled mechanisms (auto racing, hydroplane racing, and airplane racing).

Other games requiring attention here include board and card games which employ the media of bodily movement only incidentally (there is no significant sensuous embodiment here), games in which man confronts animate non-human (bull fighting, hunting, and fishing) which are destructive of Spirit, and games in which animate non-human confronts animate non-human (cock fighting and dog racing) which are entirely dominated by the sensuous. These games, then, which resemble sport and athletics in some respects, are little related to them in any essential regard. That is, just as aberrant forms of music, let us say, fall short of achieving an artistic order of consciousness and must thereby be regarded as examples of bad art, and therefore not art proper at all, similar episodes in the game arts are likewise explainable. Particularly in the case of the latter two categories, then, the commitment to Spirit is so marginal that they qualify more so as mere spectacles, amusements, divertissements, entertainments, examples of magic, or crafts, than arts. That is, our experience of them is much more akin to the inordinate display of the circus, than to the resolutely austere devotion and seriousness characteristic of an artistic constraint to Absolute Spirit.

In accord with our views, subsequently expressed, of the use and abuse of recreation and the arts generally, and of sport and athletics more specifically, it is clear that when acting principally out of natural, biological, psychological, social, or economic motives (intents) in these activities, we are not engaging in them at their best, and as a result, not engaging in their proper forms, and, consequently, not engaging in *them* at all. Though the arts, to include sport and athletics, are commonly practiced in this spirit of the mundane, and are indeed vulnerable to such practice; we must resist allowing such destructive treatment to be regarded as appropriate to them. For this treatment is destructive of the very spirit (that of intrinsicality) of which sport and athletics are composed. Such practice is, therefore, self-destructive, and no activity rightly disposed can be said to actively favor its own demise, as per Kant's and Hegel's views of the nature of man, duty, and self-legislated law.

It must also be observed that each of the specific sport and athletic forms here mentioned possesses a certain historicity; that is, each has been practiced and recorded for considerable periods throughout the recent, embodied development of Spirit. This is not to suggest, of course, that others might not yet develop, or now be developing, such a substantial place in the life of Spirit (something that cannot be foreseen according to Hegel). We must also observe here that, as in the arts, each of these forms are specifically distinguished one from the others, substantially in virtue of the rules and regulations (to include the equipment and facility) appropriate to the spiritual source of each; which merely goes as a further refinement of medium, and not as an utter distinction in kind.

Yet to be distinguished in this discussion is the nature of physical education, which might best be construed as the game arts in pedagogical trappings. That is, it is apparently either an employment of the media of the game arts so as to improve one's bio-psychology (in which case it is synonymous with exercise as a manifestation of Subjective Spirit), an employment of the media of the game arts so as to improve one's involvement in, or to prepare one's entry into the social substance (in which case it is a mere extension of the exercise motif into the consciousness of Objective Spirit), or a coming to understand the essentially rational nature and significance of the game arts themselves (in which case it is a self-apprehension of those arts as a manifestation of Absolute Spirit). Since all are frequently argued and experienced objectives or outcomes of so-termed physical education, and the latter explanation is able to draw the former two into a higher unity with it (by regarding them as secondary to itself) and account for the phenomena to which they refer in a fashion that they themselves cannot, according to our interpretation of the Hegelian system; this latter explanation appears superior to the other two, and renders physical education synonymous with the game arts.

Having suggested the distinctions we have between movement, play, work, recreation, dance, exercise, games, athletics, sport, and physical education, by no means commits us to the view that athletes and sportsmen, let us say, cannot also engage themselves in exercise; or that those who involve themselves in work cannot also involve themselves in play, and the like. We have, quite obviously, laid claim to the notion, however, that one cannot at the very same moment and in the very same sense both work and play, exercise and be engaged in either sport, athletics, or dance, as these activities mutually exclude one another. One cannot, then, be engaged in exercise qua athlete, sportsman, or dancer, though it is clearly the case that athletes, sportsmen, and dancers employ exercise in their preparation (training) for athletics, sport, and dance. It is even clear that an involvement in athletics, sport, and dance produces many of the effects sought by an involvement in exercise, though incidentally so.

Not unsurprisingly, given the title and expressed intent of the present inquiry, much of that which has been previously claimed for reality generally and the arts more specifically must now be claimed for sport and athletics as well. Hegel's claim as to the universal applicability of his system, commits our interpretation of his view to the thesis that his thought is as central to an understanding of sport and athletics as it is to an understanding of anything else. Our adopting the Hegelian scheme, commits us to its adoption with respect to the whole of reality, to include sport and athletics. Our task, then, is to suggest how it is that sport and athletics are to be further construed given the Hegelian view; more precisely, to suggest what might be made of sport and atheltics as an art form given this view.

Now available to us is a basis for suggesting the fundamentally spiritual disposition of sport and athletics. Sport and athletics are hereafter construed, therefore, in spiritual terms. Though not a popularly embraced notion of sport and athletics, neither is it entirely unknown among sport and athletic theorists. Charles Kennedy's experience of sport and athletics revealed to him that:

> The ideals of sport are intangible. They exist in the hearts of men. They are like the city of 'Camelot,' a city built to music, and therefore never built at all, and therefore built forever. (22:p. 36).

The strength of such a view has been defended in large measure in the course of previous discussion. Most importantly, it allows for the non-fragmentation (unity) of man, art, sport, and athletics, while accounting for the differences among them. As such, it effects a measure of unity between the sensuous and the spiritual: it explains both the involvement of the sensuous and the ennoblement of the spiritual and reconciles them, as for Bannister, the first of the four minute milers: "Sport changed from being a jumbled striving of individual athletes and teams to a new unity with a beauty that is evident in man's highest endeavour." (1:p.81).

The predominance of the spiritual in Hegelianism allows our interpretation of this view to hold that sport and athletic performance is guided primarily by a rational, self-conscious, intellectual intent to embody itself in a particular fashion in a particular medium; and not by a mere sensuous, or material, impulse. This account permits us to regard sport and athletics, not as a mindless sort of activity many have made it out to be, but as a manifestation of artistic intent to employ natural (material) objects in a unique representation of the Ideal. As such, the nature of sport and athletics is interpreted in accord with our best experiences of them, and the body does not assume the problematic status that most alternative views assign it. Consequently, the sorts of problems apparent in suggesting the implications of such dualistic notions of the body as those of Plato and Descartes, let us say, for a coherent philosophic view of sport and athletics, are eliminated. And the attractions of such a notion for pedagogical sport and athletics are also conspicuous, as its primary metaphysical commitment is to the sort of activity traditionally revered most by the academy.

The metaphysical status of the Hegelian arts commits our interpretation of Hegel's view for regarding sport and athletics as an art form, to the notion that sport and athletics are, in the same sense as the arts, permanent, enduring, universal, infinite, as for Cozens and Stumf:

> Sports . . . belong with the arts of humanity. Such activities have formed a basic part of all cultures, including all racial groups and all historical ages, because they are as fundamental a form of human expression as music, poetry, and painting. (7:p. 1).

It likewise commits our interpretation of his view to the notion that sport and athletics are genuinely discrete, as for Bannister: "It brings a joy, freedom and challenge which cannot be found elsewhere." (1:p. 13). The very demanding constraint to the Absolute inherent in them encourages us to consider them (at their best, in their pure and proper forms) as splendid demonstrations of excellence (greatness), ". . . with a beauty that is evident in man's highest endeavour." (1:p.81).

What is being argued here, then, are not the more popular and frequently developed themes suggesting the use of sport and athletic subjects in art, art subjects in sport and athletics; or even art as sport and athletics; but, that sport and athletics themselves properly aspire to artistic orders of consciousness so as to become one with them. Both particular and general discussions of sport and athletics in the literature reveal some inchoate sympathy for this notion, as in the case of Jokl's treatment: "The esthetic value of human movements engendered in sport is synonymous with that which emanates from art at its best." (16:p.29).

> Sport is one of the avenues of mankind's never ceasing strife for excellence. Its uniqueness lies in the . . . general recognizability of the . . . aesthetic values which sport engenders. Sport evokes experiences which are exclusively human and independent of the changing forms, patterns and customs of a civilization. (16:p. 34).

Equally as apparent, however, is that this realization has not been sufficiently well cultivated, as for Santayana:

> But besides the meaning which athletic games may have as physical

dramas, they are capable, like other tragedies, of a great aesthetic development . . . Our own games, in which no attention is paid to the aesthetic side, are themselves full of unconscious effects, which a practiced eye watches with delight. The public, however, is not sufficiently trained, nor the sports sufficiently developed, for this merit to be conspicuous. (27:p. 188).

Consequently, much of what we commonly regard, even yet today, as sport and athletics must be more properly considered spurious forms of them, and therefore not actual forms of them at all.

The intrinsic, and thereby disinterested character of the arts is also crucial to Hegel's view of them, as well, resultantly, as to ours of sport and athletics. As implied by previous discussion of Hegel's arts, then, the significance of sport and athletics is bound unrelentingly to their respective natures. They perform no essential function beyond their being what they are, beyond their being self-understood. They serve no purpose greater than themselves, as there is none other by which they are determined or judged. As in the case of all play activities, they are freely chosen. They resist being in terms other than their own. In sport and athletics we ought have sport and athletics as our interest, and sport and athletics only. They are to be understood alone, and not employed in the service of the other-than-sport or the other-than-athletic. They are not to be consumed by another, as Slusher contends: "It must be sport itself and not its instrumental attempt, that makes it worthy of human involvement . . . If sport is of value . . . it is because of sport . . ." (30:p.7).

Throughout virtually their entire history, however, they have been exploited so as to satisfy ends not their own. They have been specifically utilized as a form of challenge for goods, favors, or privileges, as divertissements in the theater, as amusements for the crowds at religious festivals, in commemoration of military success, in defense of political prestige, in adoration of the body, as a solvent of social ills, as a cultural whim or gadget, and as an instrument of personal or institutional wealth, among many others. More generally, sport and athletics may be said to have been employed as a chauvinistic, cultural, economic, historical, military, natural scientific, pedagogical, political, psychological, and social instrument. Without need of further argument, then, it would appear appropriate to claim that the uses and abuses of sport and athletics have been, and yet continue to be, many.

This observation apparently, however, only indicates that sport and athletics are vulnerable to burlesque (though no more so, let us say, than the other arts, religion, philosophy, and history). Such that, it says more of the disposition of some men to exploit them, than it does of sport and athletics themselves, as Slusher argues:

> It is true that because of emotional and materialistic factors man has frequently exploited the sport situation. This is not, in itself, an indictment against sport as much as a concern for what man [improperly] does with sport. (30:p. 138).

Buber, in his *I and Thou*, notes well the debilitating effects of such instrumental treatment, of such extrinsic regard:

> One cannot treat either an individual or a social organism as a means to an end absolutely, without robbing it of its life substance . . . One cannot in the nature of things expect a little tree that has been turned into a club to put forth leaves. (2:p. 17).

Those engaging in such treatment have made of sport and athletics something fundamentally inimical to them—made them something they are not. They have removed sport and athletics to the role of means and permitted, even encouraged, them to be used in the self-destructive service of something other than themselves, as Horkheimer observes:

> It has often been said that sport should not become an aim, but should remain an instrument . . . As long as it is only an instrument, and consciously recognized as such, it may be used in the service of profit, politics, egotism or just as a pastime. Whether it serves health is, in my view problematic. But all these ends, whether good or problematic, will destroy sport if they are allowed to dominate it totally, will prevent its being an expression of freedom. In this respect sport is like art, literature and philosophy, and all the springs of the productive imagination. (14.pp. 184-185).

Sport and athletics in terms of themselves must therefore become our critical point of departure.

These observations have particularly interesting implications, it would appear, for resolving the amateur-professional controversy in sport and athletics. The most common general characterization of the professional disposition establishes it as appropriate to the work spirit, and thereby at odds with that of play. This characterization leads us to regard the professional sportsman-athlete as one who engages in sport and athletics primarily for the purpose of achieving personal or social gain; or, one who engages in these activities primarily for the purpose of achieving any end other than that of self-understanding the essentially rational character of the activities themselves. This, then, commits our interpretation to the view that professionalism is fundamentally incompatible with sport and athletics, as well as with the whole of Absolute Spirit. It is instead appropriate to the manifestations of Subjective Spirit and Objective Spirit. Conversely, the amateur disposition, as that which establishes the amateur sportsman-athlete as one who engages in sport and athletics primarily for the purpose of understanding them in and for themselves (in the proper Hegelian sense), is tautologically appropriate to the manifestations of Absolute Spirit, sport and athletics among them. All of this is not to suggest, of course, that one who is paid for his sport or athletic perpormance, or in some measure construes that performance in instrumental terms, is necessarily of professional inclination. It does suggest, however, that one who would not engage in these activities, or not wish to engage in them, in the absence of certain instrumental consequences or benefits he realizes as a result of his participation, is indeed of a professional cast of mind. That is, the principal question here is one of primary intent, admitting that secondary purposes are frequently present. The amateur sportsman-athlete, then, is one who participates, or wishes to participate, in sport and atheltics regardless of the instrumental consequences accidental to, and in all important respects incidental to, that engagement.

The professional is also popularly conceived as the more expert performer in the amateur-professional dichotomy. In terms of which he is so regarded (providing that expert here is interpreted as referring to those satisfactorily achieving the embodiment of spiritual form proper to sport and athletics), and the amateur conversely conceived; he is tautologically the superior of the two and productive of performance proper to sport and athletics; and the amateur the inferior of the two and productive of bogus sport and athletic performance (bad sport and athletics).

As in the case of the arts, so the proposal here presented dictates, the standard competitive, or agonistic motif in sport and athletics must be construced as incidental to them. That is, we are well able to conceive of one fulfilling all of the conditions necessary to sport and athletics as here regarded, and yet not necessarily being involved in a standard competitive condition. The involvement of the sportsman-athlete in training sessions is perhaps the most salient instance of such a case, wherein he is not primarily exercising or educating (in either a subjective or objective sense) himself, but seeking (process) and achieving (product) the sort of understanding proper to sport and athletics, and, as a result, necessarily partaking of their media. In this condition we wish to regard the involvement of the sportsman-athlete as an involvement in sport and athletics proper; and yet are very much aware that this involvement is not associated with a standard competitive configuration.

In sport and athletics, then, as in the arts generally (where numerous applications of the standard competitive condition are also apparent), the agonistic element is to be understood in a rather unorthodox fashion. That is, it is to be conceived in terms of the constraint necessarily present to one seeking and achieving the most excellent (rationally perfect, or coherent) of performances. This excellence is not to be achieved at the expense of other men (a spiritually self-destructive activity), but in spiritual community with oneself, as in Mitchell's 'racing;' "Fundamentally racing is in no way a struggle against one's opponents, but rather against oneself." (25:p.249) and with other's, as in Metheny's conception of 'the good strife:'

> In 'the good strife' men treat each other as partners in a common enterprise; in 'the bad strife' they treat each other as animals or things . . . The concept of 'the good strife' is implicit in the word competition, as derived from cum and petere—literally, to strive with rather than against. The word contest has similar implications, being derived from con and testare—to testify with another rather than against him. The concept of 'the bad strife' is implicit in the idea of 'beating the opponent' as distinguished from 'winning the contest.' (23:pp. 41-42).

It is therefore not against, but with others that one properly competes as artist, sportsman, and athlete. There ought to be no attempt, then, to conquer, defeat, dethrone, or vanquish others, so as to plunder or in some sense be destructive of them in forms of competition appropriate to military and commercial sorts of affairs, let us say; but to liberate or free others so as to be constructive of them. We hold to all of this, then, despite the fact, indigenous to all human endeavor, that some will emerge victorious, and others not; some will be champions, others not; some will perform more excellently than others; indeed, some will achieve Absolute consciousness more adequately than will others.

As with reference to the arts, then, we regard the exellence displayed in the sport-athletic performance (the technical, material, or sensuous aspect) as derivative of, and as a result, attributable to (determined by), the quality of the spiritual (expressive aspect) source from which it sprang. The objective standards of judgment (times, distances, heights, scores) common to sport and athletics, and not common to other art forms, are properly conceived merely as more precise standards of technical measure available to the media of sport and athletics, and not available in the same degree to the other arts. Records, then, come simply to one instance of these standards. This distinction is to be regarded as one of degree and not of kind, however. It is, at any rate, not the source of a substantial difference between sport-athletics and the other arts.

It is not, then, the extrinsic effect of the competition which is here considered the primary focus of the agonistic element in sport and athletics, but the sense in which the competitive strife heightens the constraint to the Absolute which is important; somewhat as an Hegelian interpretation of Clark's (double victor in the inaugural Games of the modern Olympic era) view reveals:

> There was much that I aimed to acquire, yet it was not to excel others that I practised and trained. A certain standard of accomplishment was always before me; and to know in my heart, that I had attained it—that was my desire. (4:p. 2).

We conclude, consequently, that sport and athletics are best regarded, in this Hegelian interpretation of them, as of intrinsic value, and as a result of disinterested inclination, despite their association with agonistic dispositions, which might lead one, upon first inspection, to regard them differently.

CONCLUSION

Also of signal interest to an essay treating of the aesthetics of sport and athletics are such considerations as the precise character of aesthetic experience, the role of the teacher-coach, and the role of the audience in sport and athletics. It would also have been advisable to have developed more thoroughly issues that were little more than raised here. Quite unfortunately, however, the scope of the present effort has been such that these concerns will need be left for future reflection. As a result, this essay must be regarded as little more than an introduction to, or outline of, a considerably more exhaustive tract concerning the philosophy of movement, play, work, recreation, dance, exercise, games, physical education, sport, and athletics.

It has been the major specific purpose of the treatise to suggest what might be made of the nature and significance of sport and athletics given the philosophic foundations of Hegelianism, and to further propose what might be made of the relation of sport and athletics to the fine arts given these foundations. The present inquiry represents the first speculative attempt in the literature to deal at some length with an explicit, general idealistic interpretation of sport and athletics themselves, as well as with their relation to the arts; and is the first exposition of its kind to give sufficient attention to the genius of Hegel. In achieving the announced intent of the essay it has been necessary to discuss the general form of idealism and the fundamental nature of the Hegelian enterprise, the general aesthetic view of Hegel, and an Hegelian interpretation of art, sport, and athletics.

If we construe sport and athletics in the fashion here suggested, it both coheres with our best and most profound experiences of them, and allows us to regard them more highly and to treat them with greater and more productive sensitivity than they are commonly regarded and treated. Such regard and treatment may well be necessary to their preservation.

REFERENCES

1. Bannister, Roger: *The Four Minute Mile*. New York, Dodd, 1958.
2. Buber, Martin: *I and Thou*. Edinburgh, T. and T. Clark, 1953.
3. Butler, J. Donald: *Four Philosophies and Their Practice in Education and Religion*. Third edition. New York, Harper and Row, 1968.
4. Clark, Ellery H.: *Reminiscences of an Athlete: Twenty Years on Track and Field*. Boston, Houghton Mifflin, 1911.
5. Collingwood, Robin G.: *The Principles of Art*. New York, Oxford University Press, 1958.
6. Copleston, Frederick: *A History of Philosophy: Modern Philosophy: Fichte to Hegel, Volume VII, Part I*. Garden City, Doubleday, 1965.

7. Cozens, Frederick W. and Stumpf, Florence S.: *Sports in American Life.* Chicago, The University of Chicago Press, 1953.
8. Croce, Benedetto: *My Philosophy.* E. F. Carritt (trans.). New York, Collier Books, 1962.
9. Doherty, J. Kenneth: "Why Men Run," *Quest,* No. 2, 60-66 (April, 1964).
10. Friedrich, Carl J. (ed.): *The Philosophy of Hegel.* Second edition. New York, Random House, 1954.
11. Friedrich, Carl J .(ed.): *The Philosophy of Kant: Immanuel Kant's Moral and Political Writings.* New York, Random House, 1949.
12. Hegel, G. W. F.: *The Phenomenology of Mind.* J. B. Baillie (trans.). New York, Harper and Row, 1967.
13. Hegel, G. W. F.: *The Philosophy of Fine Art, Volume I.* F. P. B. Osmaston (trans.). London, G. Bell and Sons, 1920.
14. Horkheimer, Max: "New Patterns in Social Relations," *International Research in Sport and Physical Education,* E. Jokl and E. Simon (eds.). Thomas, Springfield, 1964.
15. Huizinga, Johan: *Homo Ludens: A Study of the Play-Element in Culture.* Boston, The Beacon Press, 1950.
16. Jokl, Ernst: *Medical Sociology and Cultural Anthropology of Sport and Physical Education.* Springfield, Thomas, 1964.
17. Kant, Immanuel: *Analytic of the the Beautiful.* Walter Cerf (trans.) Indianapolis, Bobbs-Merrill, 1963.
18. Kant, Immanuel: *Foundations of the Metaphysics of Morals.* Lewis White Beck (trans.) Indianapolis, Bobbs-Merrill, 1959.
19. Kaufmann, Walter: *Hegel: A Reinterpretation.* Garden City, Doubleday, 1965.
20. Kaufmann, Walter (ed.): *Hegel: Texts and Commentary.* Garden City, Doubleday, 1966.
21. Keating, James W.: "Sportsmanship as a Moral Category," *Ethics,* Vol. 85, No. 1, 25-35 (October, 1964).
22. Kennedy, Charles W.: *Sport and Sportsmanship.* Princeton, Princeton University Press, 1931.
23. Metheny, Eleanor: *Connotations of Movement in Sport and Dance.* Dubuque, Brown, 1965.
24. Metheny, Eleanor: *Movement and Meaning.* New York, McGraw-Hill, 1968.
25. Mitchell, Brian: "Character and Running," *Run, Run, Run,* Fred Wilt (ed.). Los Altos, Track and Field News Press, 1964.
26. Runes, Dagobert D. (ed.): *Dictionary of Philosophy.* Fifteenth edition. Paterson, Littlefield, 1960.
27. Santayana, George: "Philosophy on the Bleachers," *Harvard Monthly, Vol.* 18, No. 5, 181-190 (July, 1894).
28. Schacht, Richard L.: *Alienation.* Garden City, Doubleday, 1970.
29. Schiller, Friedrich: *On the Aesthetic Education of Man.* Reginald Snell (trans.). New York, Frederick Ungar, 1965.

30. Slusher, Howard S.: *Man, Sport and Existence*: *A Critical Analysis*. Philadelphia, Lea and Febiger, 1967.
31. Smith, William (trans.). *The Popular Works of Johann Gottlieb Fichte, Vol. II*. Fourth edition. London, Trubner, 1889.
32. Thilly, Frank and Wood, Ledger: *A History of Philosophy*. Third edition. New York, Holt, Rinehart and Winston, 1957.
33. Watson, John: *Schelling's Transcendental Idealism*: *A Critical Exposition*. Chicago, Griggs, 1882.
34. Weiss, Paul: *Sport*: *A Philosophic Inquiry*. Carbondale, Southern Illinois University Press, 1969.
35. Zeigler, Earle F.: *Philosophical Foundations for Physical, Health, and Recreation Education*. Englewood Cliffs, Prentice-Hall, 1964.